TRAVELS
IN WEST AFRICA

Travels
in West Africa

*

Mary Kingsley

WITH AN INTRODUCTION BY ANTHONY BRANDT

Adventure Classics

National Geographic
WASHINGTON, D.C.

Cover and interior design by Cinda Rose

Library of Congress Cataloging-in-Publication Data

Kingsley, Mary Henrietta, 1862-1900
    Travels in West Africa/ by Mary Kingsley
       p.cm
    Originally published: London; New York: Macmillan, 1897.
    ISBN 0-7922-6638-2
    I. Africa, West—Description and travel. 2. Kingsley, Mary Henrietta, 1862-1900—
    Journeys—Africa, West. I. Title

DT472 .K53 2002

      916.604'312—dc21   2002025524

One of the world's largest nonprofit scientific and educational organizations, the
National Geographic Society was founded in 1888 "for the increase and diffusion of
geographic knowledge." Fulfilling this mission, the Society educates and inspires
millions every day through its magazines, books, television programs, videos, maps
and atlases, research grants, the National Geographic Bee, teacher workshops, and
innovative classroom materials. The Society is supported through membership dues,
charitable gifts, and income from the sale of its educational products. This support is
vital to National Geographic's mission to increase global understanding and promote
conservation of our planet through exploration, research, and education.

For more information, please call 1-800-NGS LINE (647-5463) or write to the
following address:

NATIONAL GEOGRAPHIC SOCIETY
1145 17th Street N.W.
Washington, D.C. 20036-4688 U.S.A.

Visit the Society's Web site at www.nationalgeographic.com.

Printed and bound by Phoenix Color, Hagerstown, MD

Contents

A Note on the Author

Mary Kingsley's father was a doctor who traveled widely to remote areas as a medical attendant to wealthy aristocrats, but she herself never went anywhere; she stayed home caring for her invalid mother. Her only travels were in books; she read extensively in the literature of Africa and knew a great deal about it, although she had never been there. Then when she was 30 both her parents died. She sailed for Africa 18 months later.

Travels in West Africa grew out of her second trip, in 1894 and 1895, in which she traveled as a trader, going into remote areas where the tribes were reputed to be ferocious and cannibalistic. She got on well with them, however, as she seemed to get on well with everyone. In 1900, on a third trip, this time to South Africa, she volunteered as a nurse during the Boer War and was assigned to a hospital where enteric fever was raging. Within two months she herself died from it. The British buried her at sea with full military honors. *Travels in West Africa* was a huge success, of course, and it has never been out of print. We are reprinting the abridged version that Mary Kingsley prepared herself just before she left for her third trip.

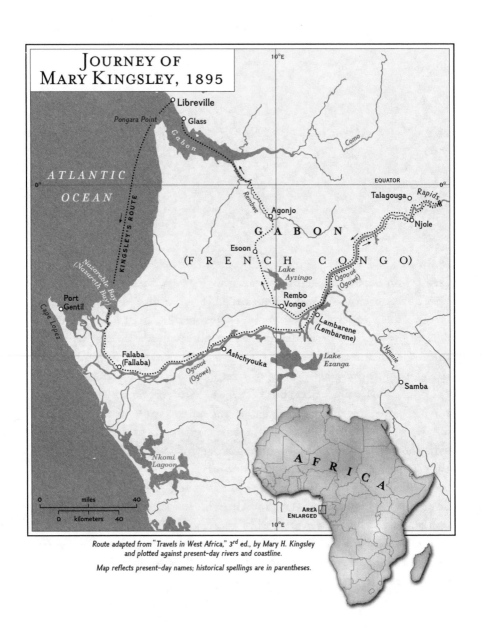

JOURNEY OF MARY KINGSLEY, 1895

10°E

Libreville

Glass

Pongara Point

Gabon

Como

ATLANTIC

OCEAN

EQUATOR

0°

Talagouga

Rapids

Rembwe

Agonjo

Njole

G A B O N

Esoon

(F R E N C H   C O N G O)

Lake Ayzingo

Ogooué (Ogowé)

Rembo Vongo

Port Gentil

Nazareth Bay (Nazareth Bay)

KINGSLEY'S ROUTE

Lambarene (Lembarene)

Cape Lopez

Ngunie

Falaba (Fallaba)

Ashchyouka

Lake Ezanga

Ogooué (Ogowé)

Samba

Nkomi Lagoon

A F R I C A

miles   40

kilometers   40

AREA ENLARGED

10°E

Route adapted from "Travels in West Africa," 3rd ed., by Mary H. Kingsley and plotted against present-day rivers and coastline.

Map reflects present-day names; historical spellings are in parentheses.

Introduction

by Anthony Brandt

Toward the end of this book, her extraordinary account of her second trip to Africa in 1895, Mary Kingsley devotes a few pages to her encounters with leopards.

There was the one she almost tripped over during an especially severe thunderstorm in the forest, the wind roaring through the treetops, the trees crashing to the ground around her. She was scrambling up an embankment and there it was, a yard away, at eye level at the top of the embankment, not aware in the chaos of the storm of her presence. She could only wait there ("My feelings tell me he remained there twelve months, but my calmer judgment puts the time down at 20 minutes"), just out of its sight, until it left.

Another leopard attacked a dog one night outside a hut where she was sleeping. "I, being roused by the uproar, rushed out into the feeble moonlight, thinking she was having one of her habitual turns-up with other dogs, and I saw a whirling mass of animal matter within a yard of me." She hurled two mushroom-shaped native stools "into the brown of it, and the meeting broke up into a leopard and a dog." The leopard crouched, staring at her, ready to spring. She grabbed a water jug and hurled it at the leopard's eyes. "It was a noble shot; it burst on the leopard's head like a shell." The leopard ran away, back into the bush. Kingsley then tended to the dog.

Mary Kingsley, clearly, was no ordinary traveler. When a crocodile tried to climb into her dugout canoe, she slammed it over the head with her paddle. She climbed 13,760-foot Mt. Cameroon during the rainy season, becoming the 28th person to reach the top, and the first woman. She waded through swamps up to her chin in water, and emerged with a necklace of leeches. She fell into an animal trap lined with sharp wooden spikes and climbed out thanking her good judgment for not having followed the advice of friends in England who told her to wear men's clothing in Africa. Her full-length, late-Victorian skirt, with its layers of underskirts, had saved her.

And against all advice, with only none-too-reliable native guides as her companions, she walked on a trading expedition from the Ogowé River in what is now Gabon north some 60 or 70 miles through dense jungle, the territory of a tribe of cannibals known as the Fang (she called them the Fan), to the Rembwe River. Trade was her ticket through the jungle, not her object in being there; what she was really after were "fetish," native belief systems, which fascinated her. She was walking through territory that had never before been visited by a white person. She took trade goods with her because she knew that, however startling the appearance of a white woman would be to tribal peoples who had never seen a white person of any sex before, trade would open the gates to their villages. Every human being, she reasoned, is disposed to trade.

It was perhaps her crowning adventure, yet Kingsley was not in Africa seeking thrills. There were women explorers of that sort, though they were rare; one notable example was Alexine Tinné, a wealthy Dutch heiress who traveled extensively in Africa. In 1869, crossing the Sahara with a large retinue, her guides cut off her hands, stole everything she had, and left her to die.

Mary Kingsley was a much more serious person than Alexine Tinné, and, though a member of a well-known family, she was not wealthy. Her father, George Kingsley, was a doctor whose two brothers, Henry and Charles, were both novelists. Charles was the more famous of the two, the author of *Westward Ho!* and *Water Babies*, books extremely popular in late-Victorian England, as well as the private chaplain to Queen Victoria. George, who had none of his brother's piety, did not distinguish himself in this fashion. He spent much of his life out of England, traveling to exotic and sometimes dangerous locales as a physician-in-waiting and companion to various wealthy aristocrats: the Marquis of Aylesbury, the Duke of Norfolk, the Duke of Sutherland, and two successive Earls of Pembroke. At a particularly careless moment in his life he impregnated a servant, the family cook, Mary Bailey, who was probably illiterate and definitely neurasthenic. He married her just before she delivered their first child: Mary. Her father promptly left on another of his adventures abroad. He was gone once for three years.

George Kingsley left an extensive library at home—full of books of exploration and travel. Mary, who received no formal education of any kind, grew up reading them (when she was not taking care of her mother, who spent much of her life in bed). She taught herself all that she knew, and she came to know a great deal. She once carried on a conversation in Latin with two Portuguese acquaintances, she learned German to help her father with his sporadic research on biology, and she was fully capable of fixing the plumbing in the family house, and did so when it was necessary. The sciences interested her most, that and the travel books, especially the books about West Africa, which she did not merely read, but studied. She pored over Sir Richard Burton's *Two Trips to Gorilla Land,* based on his explorations in what is now Gabon; Burton, incidentally, was the first European to climb Mt. Cameroon. She knew David Livingstone's works as well. But her favorites were the French explorer Paul Belloni du Chaillu, who was the first white man to see a gorilla, and Pierre Savorgnan de Brazza, an Italian nobleman who became a French citizen and explored the Ogowé, the largest river in West Africa between the Niger and the Congo, to its source and did much to claim the area for France. It was thanks largely to Brazza's writings that Kingsley became so interested in that river and the tribes who lived along it.

It was an interest she could indulge only by study, however. Her mother required constant care, her father used her as a secretary and household manager, and she was not free to travel anywhere until they died. That happened in 1892. Within three months, indeed, they were both dead. Mary Kingsley was almost 30 years old. Less than one year later she made her first trip to West Africa, a reconnoitering journey along the coast, up the Congo on the newly built Belgian railroad, then spending two months in the bush in Gabon.

When she returned to Africa in 1895 it was with the determination to spend as much time in the bush as she could. Although she had no formal scientific training, she returned as an amateur scientist interested both in new species of freshwater fish, which the expert on the subject at the British Museum taught her how to collect, and in anthropology. Though three new species of fish would eventually be named after her, it was anthropology that she loved most. She had read extensively on the subject, had made contacts with European anthropologists when back home, and was determined to find out in the field how West Africans thought, what they believed, what their customs were. She had an innate sympathy, it turned out, for what we might call the African mind; once exposed to the context in which it worked, she could see, for example, that polygamy made perfect sense, that the liquor trade was relatively harmless, and that missionaries, whatever the good intentions behind them, destroyed African culture and belief systems and gave very little back in return. She was more like her father in this respect than her uncle Charles; she had no patience at all for self-righteous piety or the condescending attitudes of Europeans toward native cultures.

She left England for West Africa early in January 1895 and spent nearly ten months there, returning to Liverpool at the end of November. The first part of the journey she spent with friends and government officials, visiting Accra and Calabar, then Fernando Po, the island off the Bight of Biafra that is now known as Bioko. But the Ogowé was her goal and she went there alone, knowing only traders. She traveled up past the rapids in dugout canoes, collecting fish and getting to know native people, finally setting off into the jungle in search of the Fang. She carried no firearms, only trade goods. She waded through swamps, walked through torrential downpours, crawled through underbrush to catch a glimpse of a group of gorillas, ate native food, slept in huts where parts of human bodies hung from the rafters in bags, endured insect attacks, fought off leopards and skirted elephants, treated diseases and applied medicine to native wounds (for she was an accomplished nurse), palavered with chiefs and medicine men, and traded for specimens of fish. Imagine her walking into a Fang village, her more or less naked guides trailing along, wearing her white blouse and her long, heavy skirt and a pair of leather boots, speaking straight and thinking fast, offering to trade fishhooks for fish, medical care for information. She loved Africa and it must have shown. They respected her forthrightness, her honesty, and her courage. She loved the place itself, despite the heat and disease, the aura of death that glowed from every inch of it. "Why did I come to Africa?" she asked herself at the end of her ten months there. "Why! who would not come to its twin brother Hell itself for all the beauty and the charm of it!"

Mary Kingsley returned to England in November 1895 to find herself already something of a celebrity. Newspapers had published articles about her travels and a reporter met her at the boat. She gave interviews and more articles appeared. So did social invitations; the lionizing process had begun. When she published *Travels in West Africa* in January 1897, in two long volumes, it sold out almost at once, going rapidly into second and third printings. She began to give lectures and became very good at it, so good that she drew crowds of up to 2,000 people. She used her celebrity well; she had definite views about colonial policy and made them known. Her most recent biographer, Katherine Frank, believes that "her major contribution as an ethnographer was her political role in colonial affairs: her overriding insistence that African culture be protected from the 'smash' of British colonial policy." Kingsley did not think Africans needed to be "reformed" along Christian or Westernized lines.

It is her book, not her political views, however, for which she will be remembered. *Travels in West Africa* sparkles with incident and tells a compelling story. Kingsley herself was one of the most appealing explorers ever to write a book. It was her personal style to be amused at herself and ironic at her own expense while remaining utterly fearless about expressing her strongly held opinions. She could hold her own with native chiefs and French traders as well as government ministers and the *Times* of London. She had no patience with cant or hypocrisy, yet she was modest about her own considerable achievements. It is impossible to read the book and not fall in love with her; indeed, she inspires a level of respect hardly short of adoration. In England she remains to this day a national hero.

It is perhaps fitting that Mary Kingsley died heroically, too. She had planned to return to West Africa as soon as possible after her book was done, but circumstances prevented her. She was constantly being called upon to take care of sick relatives, and her feckless and parasitical younger brother was a drain on her time and attention. She had also committed herself to publishing her father's unpublished papers. But in October 1899 the Boer War broke out in South Africa. She was active in the Colonial Nursing Association and she volunteered to go to the Cape as a nurse. In February 1900 her application was accepted and by April she was in Africa once more, assigned to care for Boer prisoners of war. The conditions were awful, and disease raged through the camps. By the middle of May Mary Kingsley had typhoid. She kept at her work until she could hardly stand. On June 2, weakening fast, she asked to be buried at sea. On June 3 she died. She was 37 years old.

On June 4, the British buried her at sea with full military honors.

A NOTE ON THE TEXT

Shortly after the first edition of *Travels in West Africa* appeared in early 1897, Mary Kingsley began to abridge the book to bring the price down and make it accessible to a wider public. That abridged edition appeared late in 1897 and was reprinted a number of times. We have used that abridged edition as our text, eliminating only the final two chapters of the book and a brief appendix. With the exception of those two chapters, the book here represents the author's own idea of what was important to keep and what could be discarded. Kingsley wrote fluently and she was admittedly verbose. What she cut from the original two-volume edition was largely fetish material, although enough of that remains in the book to give a clear idea of the kinds of anthropological information she was collecting. What we have cut, the two final chapters, discuss issues such as working conditions in West Africa, colonial policy, and the roles of traders and missionaries. They add nothing to the narrative of this book and are now out of date and of little interest. Kingsley bases her arguments in these two chapters, furthermore, on anthropological assumptions about racial differences that have been discredited for generations. They are no loss to this otherwise magnificent account of her journeys.

Introduction

*Relateth the Various Causes Which Impelled the Author
to Embark Upon the Voyage*

IT WAS IN 1893 THAT, for the first time in my life, I found myself in possession of five or six months which were not heavily forestalled, and feeling like a boy with a new half-crown, I lay about in my mind, as Mr. Bunyan would say, as to what to do with them. "Go and learn your tropics," said Science. Where on earth am I to go? I wondered, for tropics are tropics wherever found, so I got down an atlas and saw that either South America or West Africa must be my destination, for the Malayan region was too far off and too expensive. Then I got Wallace's *Geographical Distribution* and after reading that master's article on the Ethiopian region I hardened my heart and closed with West Africa. I did this the more readily because while I knew nothing of the practical condition of it, I knew a good deal both by tradition and report of South East America, and remembered that Yellow Jack was endemic, and that a certain naturalist, my superior physically and mentally, had come very near getting starved to death in the depressing society of an expedition slowly perishing of want and miscellaneous fevers up the Panama.

My ignorance regarding West Africa was soon removed. And although the vast cavity in my mind that it occupied is not even yet half filled up, there is a great deal of very curious information in its place. I use the word curious advisedly, for I think many seemed to translate my request for practical hints and advice into an advertisement that "Rubbish may be shot here." This same information is in a state of great confusion still, although I have made heroic efforts to codify it. I find, however, that it can almost all be got in under the following different headings, namely and to wit:—

The dangers of West Africa.
The disagreeables of West Africa.
The diseases of West Africa.
The things you must take to West Africa.
The things you find most handy in West Africa.
The worst possible things you can do in West Africa.

I inquired of all my friends as a beginning what they knew of West Africa. The majority knew nothing. A percentage said, "Oh, you can't possibly go there; that's where Sierra Leone is, the white man's grave, you know." If these were pressed further, one occasionally found that they had had relations who had gone out there after having been "sad trials," but, on consideration of their having left not only West Africa, but this world, were now forgiven and forgotten.

I next turned my attention to cross-examining the doctors. "Deadliest spot on earth," they said cheerfully, and showed me maps of the geographical distribution of disease. Now I do not say that a country looks inviting when it is coloured in Scheele's green or a bilious yellow, but these colours may arise from lack of artistic gift in the cartographer. There is no mistaking what he means by black, however, and black you'll find they colour West Africa from above Sierra Leone to below the Congo. "I wouldn't go there if I were you," said my medical friends, "you'll catch something; but if you must go, and you're as obstinate as a mule, just bring me—" and then followed a list of commissions from here to New York, any one of which—but I only found that out afterwards.

All my informants referred me to the missionaries. "There were," they said, in an airy way, "lots of them down there, and had been for many years." So to missionary literature I addressed myself with great ardour; alas! only to find that these good people wrote their reports not to tell you how the country they resided in was, but how it was getting on towards being what it ought to be, and how necessary it was that their readers should subscribe more freely, and not get any foolishness into their heads about obtaining an inadequate supply of souls for their money. I also found fearful confirmation of my medical friends' statements about its unhealthiness, and various details of the distribution of cotton shirts over which I did not linger.

From the missionaries it was, however, that I got my first idea about the social condition of West Africa. I gathered that there existed there, firstly the native human beings—the raw material, as it were—and that these were led either to good or bad respectively by the missionary and the trader. There were also the Government representatives, whose chief business it was to strengthen and consolidate the missionary's work, a function they carried on but indifferently well. But as for those traders! Well, I put them down under the dangers of West Africa at once. Subsequently I came across the good old Coast yarn of how, when a trader from that region went thence, it goes without saying where, the Fallen Angel without a moment's hesitation vacated the infernal throne (Milton) in his favour. This, I beg to note, is the marine form of the legend. When it occurs terrestrially the trader becomes a Liverpool mate. But of course no one need believe it either way—it is not a missionary's story.

Naturally, while my higher intelligence was taken up with attending to these statements, my mind got set on going, and I had to go. Fortunately I could number among my acquaintances one individual who had lived on the Coast for seven years. Not, it is true, on that part of it which I was bound for. Still his advice was pre-eminently worth attention, because, in spite of his long residence in the deadliest spot of the region, he was still in fair going order. I told him I intended going to West Africa, and he said, "When you have made up your mind to go to West Africa the very best thing you can do is to get it unmade again and go to Scotland instead; but if your intelligence is not strong enough to do so, abstain from exposing yourself to the direct rays of the sun, take 4 grains of quinine every day for a fortnight before you reach the Rivers, and get some introductions to the Wesleyans; they are the only people on the Coast who have got a hearse with feathers."

My attention was next turned to getting ready things to take with me. Having opened upon myself the sluice gates of advice, I rapidly became distracted. My friends and their friends alike seemed to labour under the delusion that I intended to charter a steamer and was a person of wealth beyond the dreams of avarice. This not being the case, the only thing to do was to gratefully listen and let things drift.

Not only do the things you have got to take, but the things you have got to take them in, present a fine series of problems to the young traveller. Crowds of witnesses testified to the forms of baggage holders they had found invaluable, and these, it is unnecessary to say, were all different in form and material.

With all this *embarras de choix* I was too distracted to buy anything new in the way of baggage except a long waterproof sack neatly closed at the top with a bar and handle. Into this I put blankets, boots, books, in fact anything that would not go into my portmanteau or black bag. From the first I was haunted by a conviction that its bottom would come out, but it never did, and in spite of the fact that it had ideas of its own about the arrangement of its contents, it served me well throughout my voyage.

It was the beginning of August '93 when I first left England for "the Coast." Preparations of quinine with postage partially paid arrived up to the last moment, and a friend hastily sent two newspaper clippings, one entitled "A Week in a Palm-oil Tub," which was supposed to describe the sort of accommodation, companions, and fauna likely to be met with on a steamer going to West Africa, and on which I was to spend seven to *The Graphic* contributor's one; the other from *The Daily Telegraph*, reviewing a French book of "Phrases in common use" in Dahomey. The opening sentence in the latter was, "Help, I am drowning." Then came the inquiry, "If a man is not a thief?" and then another cry, "The boat is upset." "Get up, you lazy scamps," is the next exclamation, followed almost immediately by the question, "Why has not this man been buried?" "It is fetish that has killed him, and he must lie here exposed with nothing on him until only the bones remain," is the cheerful answer. This sounded discouraging to a person whose occupation would necessitate going about considerably in boats, and whose fixed desire was to study fetish. So with a feeling of foreboding gloom I left London for Liverpool—none the more cheerful for the matter-of-fact manner in which the steamboat agents had informed me that they did not issue return tickets by the West African lines of steamers. I will not go into the details of that voyage here, much as I am given to discursiveness. They are more amusing than instructive, for on my first voyage out I did not know the Coast, and the Coast did not know me, and we mutually ter-rified each other. I fully expected to get killed by the local nobility and gentry; they thought I was connected with the World's Women's

Temperance Association, and collecting shocking details for subsequent magic-lantern lectures on the liquor traffic; so fearful misunderstandings arose, but we gradually educated each other, and I had the best of the affair; for all I had got to teach them was that I was only a beetle and fetish hunter, and so forth, while they had to teach me a new world, and a very fascinating course of study I found it. And whatever the Coast may have to say against me—for my continual desire for hair-pins, and other pins, my intolerable habit of getting into water, the abominations full of ants, that I brought into their houses, or things emitting at unexpectedly short notice vivid and awful stenches—they cannot but say that I was a diligent pupil, who honestly tried to learn the lessons they taught me so kindly, though some of those lessons were hard to a person who had never previously been even in a tame bit of tropics, and whose life for many years had been an entirely domestic one in a University town.

One by one I took my old ideas derived from books and thoughts based on imperfect knowledge and weighed them against the real life around me, and found them either worthless or wanting. The greatest recantation I had to make I made humbly before I had been three months on the Coast in 1893. It was of my idea of the traders. What I had expected to find them was a very different thing to what I did find them; and of their kindness to me I can never sufficiently speak, for on that voyage I was utterly out of touch with the governmental circles, and utterly dependent on the traders, and the most useful lesson of all the lessons I learnt on the West Coast in 1893 was that I could trust them. Had I not learnt this very thoroughly I could never have gone out again and carried out the voyage I give you a sketch of in this book.

Thanks to "the Agent," I have visited places I could never otherwise have seen; and to the respect and affection in which he is held by the native, I owe it that I have done so in safety. When I have arrived off his factory in a steamer or canoe unexpected, unintroduced, or turned up equally unheralded out of the bush in a dilapidated state, he has always received me with that gracious hospitality which must have given him, under Coast conditions, very real trouble and inconvenience—things he could have so readily found logical excuses against entailing upon himself for the sake of an individual whom he had never seen before—whom he most likely would never see again—and whom it was no earthly profit to him to see then. He has bestowed himself—Allah only knows where—on his small trading vessels so that I might have his one cabin. He has fished me out of sea and fresh water with boat-hooks; he has continually given me good advice, which if I had only followed would have enabled me to keep out of water and any other sort of affliction; and although he holds the meanest opinion of my intellect for going to such a place as West Africa for beetles, fishes, and fetish, he has given me the greatest assistance in my work. The value of that work I pray you withhold judgment on, until I lay it before you in some ten volumes or so mostly in Latin. All I know that is true regarding West African facts, I owe to the traders; the errors are my own.

To Dr. Günther, of the British Museum, I am deeply grateful for the kindness and interest he has always shown regarding all the specimens of natural history that I have been able to lay before him; the majority of which must have had very old tales to tell him. Yet his courtesy and attention gave me the thing a worker in any work most wants—the sense that the work was worth doing—and sent me back to work again with the knowledge that if these things interested a man like him, it was a more than sufficient reason for me to go on collecting them. To Mr. W. H. F. Kirby I am much indebted for his working out my small collection of certain Orders of insects; and to Mr. Thomas S. Forshaw, for the great help he has afforded me in revising my notes.

It is impossible for me even to catalogue my debts of gratitude still outstanding to the West Coast. Chiefly am I indebted to Mr. C. G. Hudson, whose kindness and influence enabled me to go up the Ogowé and to see as much of Congo Français as I have seen, and his efforts to take care of me were most ably seconded by Mr. Fildes. The French officials in "Congo Français" never hindered me, and always treated me with the greatest kindness. You may say there was no reason why they should not, for there is nothing in this fine colony of France that they need be ashamed of any one seeing; but I find it is customary for travellers to say the French officials throw obstacles in the way of any one visiting their possessions, so I merely beg to state this was decidedly not my experience; although my deplorable ignorance of French prevented me from explaining my humble intentions to them.

The Rev. Dr. Nassau and Mr. R. E. Dennett have enabled me, by placing at my disposal the rich funds of their knowledge of native life and idea, to amplify any deductions from my own observation. Mr. Dennett's work I have not dealt with in this work because it refers to tribes I was not amongst on this journey, but to a tribe I made the acquaintance with in my '93 voyage—the Fjort. Dr. Nassau's observations I have referred to. Herr von Lucke, Vice-governor of Cameroon, I am indebted to for not only allowing me, but for assisting me by every means in his power, to go up Cameroons Peak, and to the Governor of Cameroon, Herr von Puttkamer, for his constant help and kindness. Indeed so great has been the willingness to help me of all these gentlemen, that it is a wonder to me, when I think of it, that their efforts did not project me right across the continent and out at Zanzibar. That this brilliant affair did not come off is owing to my own lack of enterprise; for I did not want to go across the continent, and I do not hanker after Zanzibar, but only to go puddling about obscure districts in West Africa after raw fetish and fresh-water fishes.

I owe my ability to have profited by the kindness of these gentlemen on land, to a gentleman of the sea—Captain Murray. He was captain of the vessel I went out on in 1893, and he saw then that my mind was full of errors that must be eradicated if I was going to deal with the Coast successfully; and so he eradicated those errors and replaced them with sound knowledge from his own stores collected during an acquaintance with the West Coast of over thirty years. The education he has given me has been of the greatest value to me, and I sincerely hope to make many more voyages under him, for I well know he has still much to teach and I to learn.

Last, but not least, I must chronicle my debts to the ladies. First to those two courteous Portuguese ladies, Donna Anna de Sousa Coutinho e Chichorro and her sister Donna Maria de Sousa Coutinho, who did so much for me in Kacongo in 1893, and have remained, I am proud to say, my firm friends ever since. Lady MacDonald and Miss Mary Slessor I speak of in this book, but only faintly sketch the pleasure and help they have afforded me; nor have I fully expressed my gratitude for the kindness of Madame Jacot of Lembarene, or Madame Forget of Talagouga. Then there are a whole list of nuns belonging to the Roman Catholic Missions on the South West Coast, ever cheery and charming companions; and Frau Plehn, whom it was a continual pleasure to see in Cameroons, and discourse with once again on things that seemed so far off then—art, science, and literature; and Mrs. H. Duggan, of Cameroons too, who used, whenever I came into that port to rescue me from fearful states of starvation for toilet necessaries, and lend a sympathetic and intelligent ear to the "awful sufferings" I had gone through, until Cameroons became to me a thing to look forward to.

When in the Canaries in 1892, I used to smile, I regretfully own, at the conversation of a gentleman from the Gold Coast who was up there recruiting after a bad fever. His conversation consisted largely of anecdotes of friends of his, and nine times in ten he used to say, "He's dead now." Alas! my own conversation may be smiled at now for the same cause. Many of my friends mentioned even in this very recent account of the Coast "are dead now." Most of those I learnt to know in 1893; chief among these is my old friend Captain Boler, of Bonny, from whom I first learnt a certain power of comprehending the African and his form of thought.

I have great reason to be grateful to the Africans themselves—to cultured men and women among them like Charles Owoo, Mbo, Sanga Glass, Jane Harrington and her sister at Gaboon, and to the bush natives; but of my experience with them I give further details, so I need not dwell on them here.

I apologise to the general reader for giving so much detail on matters that really only affect myself, and I know that the indebtedness which all African travellers have to the white residents in Africa is a matter usually very lightly touched on. No doubt my voyage would seem a grander thing if I omitted mention of the help I received, but—well, there was a German gentleman once who evolved a camel out of his inner consciousness. It was a wonderful thing; still, you know, it was not a good camel, only a thing which people personally unacquainted with camels could believe in. Now I am ambitious to make a picture, if I make one at all, that people who do know the original can believe in—even if they criticise its points—and so I give you details a more showy artist would omit.

CHAPTER 1

LIVERPOOL TO SIERRA LEONE
AND THE GOLD COAST

*Setting forth how the voyager departs from England in a stout vessel and
in good company, and reaches in due course the Island of the Grand Canary,
and then the Port of Sierra Leone: to which is added some account of this latter place
and the comeliness of its women. Wherein also some descriptions of Cape Coast and
Accra is given, to which are added divers observations on supplies to be obtained there.*

THE WEST COAST OF AFRICA is like the Arctic regions in one particular,
and that is that when you have once visited it you want to go back there
again; and, now I come to think of it, there is another particular in
which it is like them, and that is that the chances you have of returning
from it at all are small, for it is a *Belle Dame sans merci.*

I succumbed to the charm of the Coast as soon as I left Sierra
Leone on my first voyage out, and I saw more than enough during that
voyage to make me recognise that there was any amount of work for me
worth doing down there. So I warned the Coast I was coming back again
and the Coast did not believe me; and on my return to it a second time
displayed a genuine surprise, and formed an even higher opinion of
my folly than it had formed on our first acquaintance, which is saying
a good deal.

During this voyage in 1893, I had been to Old Calabar, and its

Governor, Sir Claude MacDonald, had heard me expatiating on the absorbing interest of the Antarctic drift, and the importance of the collection of fresh-water fishes and so on. So when Lady MacDonald heroically decided to go out to him in Calabar, they most kindly asked me if I would join her, and make my time fit hers for starting on my second journey. This I most willingly did. But I fear that very sweet and gracious lady suffered a great deal of apprehension at the prospect of spending a month on board ship with a person so devoted to science as to go down the West Coast in its pursuit. During the earlier days of our voyage she would attract my attention to all sorts of marine objects overboard, so as to amuse me. I used to look at them, and think it would be the death of me if I had to work like this, explaining meanwhile aloud that "they were very interesting, but Haeckel had done them, and I was out after fresh-water fishes from a river north of the Congo this time," fearing all the while that she felt me unenthusiastic for not flying over into the ocean to secure the specimens.

However, my scientific qualities, whatever they may amount to, did not blind this lady long to the fact of my being after all a very ordinary individual, and she told me so—not in these crude words, indeed, but nicely and kindly—whereupon, in a burst of gratitude to her for understanding me, I appointed myself her honorary aide-de-camp on the spot, and her sincere admirer I shall remain for ever, fully recognising that her courage in going to the Coast was far greater than my own, for she had more to lose had fever claimed her, and she was in those days by no means under the spell of Africa. But this is anticipating.

It was on the 23rd of December, 1894, that we left Liverpool in the *Batanga*, commanded by my old friend Captain Murray, under whose care I had made my first voyage. On the 30th we sighted the Peak of Teneriffe early in the afternoon. It displayed itself, as usual, as an entirely celestial phenomenon. A great many people miss seeing it. Suffering under the delusion that El Pico is a terrestrial affair, they look in vain somewhere about the level of their own eyes, which are striving to penetrate the dense masses of mist that usually enshroud its slopes by day, and then a friend comes along, and gaily points out to the newcomer the glittering white triangle somewhere near the zenith. On some days the Peak stands out clear from ocean to summit, looking every inch and more of its 12,080 ft.; and this is said by the Canary fishermen to be a certain sign of rain, or fine weather, or a gale of wind; but whenever and however it may be seen, soft and dream-like in the sunshine, or melodramatic and bizarre in the moonlight, it is one of the most beautiful things the eye of man may see.

Soon after sighting Teneriffe, Lançarote showed, and then the Grand Canary. Teneriffe is perhaps the most beautiful, but it is hard to judge between it and Grand Canary as seen from the sea. The superb cone this afternoon stood out a deep purple against a serpent-green sky, separated from the brilliant blue ocean by a girdle of pink and gold cumulus, while Grand Canary and Lançarote looked as if they were formed from fantastic-shaped sunset cloud-banks that by some spell had been solidified. The general colour of the mountains of Grand Canary, which rise peak after peak until they culminate in the Pico de las Nieves, some 6,000 feet high, is a yellowish red, and the air which lies among their rocky crevices and swathes their softer sides is a lovely lustrous blue.

Just before the sudden dark came down, and when the sun was taking a curve out of the horizon of sea, all the clouds gathered round the three islands, leaving the sky a pure amethyst pink, and as a good-night to them the sun outlined them with rims of shining gold, and made the snow-clad Peak of Teneriffe blaze with star-white light. In a few minutes came the dusk, and as we neared Grand Canary, out of its cloud-bank gleamed the red flash of the lighthouse on the Isleta, and in a few more minutes, along the sea level, sparkled the five miles of irregularly distributed lights of Puerto de la Luz and the city of Las Palmas.

We reached Sierra Leone at 9 a.m. on the 7th of January, and as the place is hardly so much in touch with the general public as the Canaries are I may perhaps venture to go more into details regarding it. The harbour is formed by the long low strip of land to the north called the Bullam shore, and to the south by the peninsula terminating in Cape Sierra Leone, a sandy promontory at the end of which is situated a lighthouse of irregular habits. Low hills covered with tropical forest growth rise from the sandy shores of the Cape, and along its face are three creeks or bays, deep inlets showing through their narrow entrances smooth beaches of yellow sand, fenced inland by the forest of cottonwoods and palms, with here and there an elephantine baobab.

The first of these bays is called Pirate Bay, the next English Bay, and the third Kru Bay. The wooded hills of the Cape rise after passing Kru Bay, and become spurs of the mountain, 2,500 feet in height, which is the Sierra Leone itself. There are, however, several mountains here besides the Sierra Leone, the most conspicuous of them being the peak known as Sugar Loaf, and when seen from the sea they are very lovely, for their form is noble, and a wealth of tropical vegetation covers them, which, unbroken in its continuity, but endless in its variety, seems to sweep over their sides down to the shore like a sea, breaking here and there into a surf of flowers.

It is the general opinion, indeed, of those who ought to know that Sierra Leone appears at its best when seen from the sea, particularly when you are leaving the harbour homeward bound; and that here its charms, artistic, moral, and residential, end. But, from the experience I have gained of it, I have no hesitation in saying that it is one of the best places for getting luncheon in that I have ever happened on, and that a more pleasant and varied way of spending an afternoon than going about its capital, Free Town, with a certain Irish purser, who is as well known as he is respected among the leviathan old negro ladies, it would be hard to find. Still it must be admitted it is rather hot.

Free Town its capital is situated on the northern base of the mountain, and extends along the sea-front with most business-like wharves, quays, and warehouses. Viewed from the harbour, "The Liverpool of West Africa," as it is called, looks as if it were built of gray stone, which it is not. When you get ashore, you will find that most of the stores and houses—the majority of which, it may be remarked, are in a state of acute dilapidation—are of painted wood, with corrugated iron roofs. Here and there, though, you will see a thatched house, its thatch covered with creeping plants, and inhabited by colonies of creeping insects.

Some of the stores and churches are, it is true, built of stone, but this does not look like stone at a distance, being red in colour—unhewn blocks of the red stone of the locality. In the crannies of these buildings trailing plants covered with pretty mauve or yellow flowers take root, and everywhere, along the tops of the walls, and in the cracks of the houses, are ferns and flowering plants. They must get a good deal of their nourishment from the rich, thick air, which seems composed of 85 per cent of warm water, and the remainder of the odours of Frangipani, orange flowers, magnolias, oleanders, and roses, combined with others that demonstrate that the inhabitants do not regard sanitary matters with the smallest degree of interest.

There is one central street, and the others are neatly planned out at right angles to it. None of them are in any way paved or metalled.

They are covered in much prettier fashion, and in a way more suitable for naked feet, by green Bahama grass, save and except those which are so nearly perpendicular that they have got every bit of earth and grass cleared off them down to the red bed-rock, by the heavy rain of the wet season.

In every direction natives are walking at a brisk pace, their naked feet making no sound on the springy turf of the streets, carrying on their heads huge burdens which are usually crowned by the hat of the bearer, a large limpet-shaped affair made of palm leaves. While some carry these enormous bundles, others bear logs or planks of wood, blocks of building stone, vessels containing palm-oil, baskets of vegetables, or tin tea-trays on which are folded shawls. As the great majority of the native inhabitants of Sierra Leone pay no attention whatever to where they are going, either in this world or the next, the confusion and noise are out of all proportion to the size of the town; and when, as frequently happens, a section of actively perambulating burden-bearers charge recklessly into a sedentary section, the members of which have dismounted their loads and squatted themselves down beside them, right in the middle of the fair way, to have a friendly yell with some acquaintances, the row becomes terrific.

In among these crowds of country people walk stately Mohammedans, Mandingoes, Akers, and Fulahs of the Arabised tribes of the Western Soudan. These are lithe, well-made men, and walk with a peculiarly fine, elastic carriage. Their graceful garb consists of a long white loose-sleeved shirt, over which they wear either a long black mohair or silk gown, or a deep bright blue affair, not altogether unlike a University gown, only with more stuff in it and more folds. They are undoubtedly the gentlemen of the Sierra Leone native population, and they are becoming an increasing faction in the town, by no means to the pleasure of the Christians.

But to the casual visitor at Sierra Leone the Mohammedan is a mere passing sensation. You neither feel a burning desire to laugh with, or at him, as in the case of the country folks, nor do you wish to punch his head, and split his coat up his back—things you yearn to do to that perfect flower of Sierra Leone culture, who yells your bald name across the street at you, condescendingly informs you that you can go and get letters that are waiting for you, while he smokes his cigar and lolls in the shade, or in some similar way displays his second-hand rubbishy white culture—a culture far lower and less dignified than that of either the stately Mandingo or the bush chief. I do not think that the Sierra Leone dandy really means half as much insolence as he shows; but the truth is he feels too insecure of his own real position, in spite of all the "side" he puts on, and so he dare not be courteous like the Mandingo or the bush Fan.

It is the costume of the people in Free Town and its harbour that will first attract the attention of the newcomer, notwithstanding the fact that the noise, the smell, and the heat are simultaneously making desperate bids for that favour. The ordinary man in the street wears anything he may have been able to acquire, anyhow, and he does not fasten it on securely. I fancy it must be capillary attraction, or some other partially-understood force, that takes part in the matter. It is certainly neither braces nor buttons. There are, of course, some articles which from their very structure are fairly secure, such as an umbrella with the stick and ribs removed, or a shirt. This last-mentioned treasure, which usually becomes the property of the ordinary man from a female relative or admirer taking in white men's washing, is always worn flowing free, and has such a charm in itself that the happy possessor cares little what he continues his costume with—trousers, loin cloth, red flannel petticoat, or rice-bag drawers, being, as he would put it, "all same for one" to him.

The ladies are divided into three classes; the young girl you address as "tee-tee"; the young person as "seester"; the more mature charmer as "mammy"; but I do not advise you to employ these terms when you are on your first visit, because you might get misunderstood. For, you see, by addressing a mammy as seester, she might think either that you were unconscious of her dignity as a married lady—a matter she would soon put you right on—or that you were flirting, which of course was totally foreign to your intention, and would make you uncomfortable. My advice is that you rigidly stick to missus or mammy. I have seen this done most successfully.

The ladies are almost as varied in their costume as the gentlemen, but always neater and cleaner; and mighty picturesque they are too, and occasionally very pretty. A market-woman with her jolly brown face and laughing brown eyes—eyes all the softer for a touch of antimony—her ample form clothed in a lively print overall, made with a yoke at the shoulders, and a full long flounce which is gathered on to the yoke under the arms and falls fully to the feet; with her head done up in a yellow or red handkerchief, and her snowy white teeth gleaming through her vast smiles, is a mighty pleasant thing to see, and to talk to. But, Allah! the circumference of them!

The stone-built, white-washed market buildings of Free Town have a creditably clean and tidy appearance considering the climate, and the quantity and variety of things exposed for sale—things one wants the pen of a Rabelais to catalogue. Here are all manner of fruits, some which are familiar to you in England; others that soon become so to you in Africa. You take them as a matter of course if you are outward bound, but on your call homeward (if you make it) you will look on them as a blessing and a curiosity. For lower down, particularly in "the Rivers," these things are rarely to be had, and never in such perfection as here; and to see again lettuces, yellow oranges, and tomatoes bigger than marbles is a sensation and a joy.

One of the chief features of Free Town are the jack crows. Some writers say they are peculiar to Sierra Leone, others that they are not, but both unite in calling them *Picathartes gymnocephalus*. To the white people who live in daily contact with them they are turkey-buzzards; to the natives, Yubu. Anyhow they are evil-looking fowl, and no ornament to the roof-ridges they choose to sit on. The native Christians ought to put a row of spikes along the top of their cathedral to keep them off; the beauty of that edifice is very far from great, and it cannot carry off the effect produced by the row of these noisome birds as they sit along its summit, with their wings arranged at all manner of different angles in an "all gone" way. One bird perhaps will have one straight out in front, and the other casually disposed at right-angles, another both straight out in front, and others again with both hanging hopelessly down, but none with them neatly and tidily folded up, as decent birds' wings should be. They all give the impression of having been extremely drunk the previous evening, and of having subsequently fallen into some sticky abomination—into blood for choice. Being the scavengers of Free Town, however, they are respected by the local authorities and preserved; and the natives tell me you never see either a young or a dead one. The latter is a thing you would not expect, for half of them look as if they could not live through the afternoon. They also told me that when you got close to them, they had a "'trong, 'trong 'niff; 'niff too much." I did not try, but I am quite willing to believe this statement.

The other animals most in evidence in the streets are, first and foremost, goats and sheep. I have to lump them together, for it is exceedingly difficult to tell one from the other. All along the Coast the empirical rule is that sheep carry their tails down, and goats carry their tails up; fortunately you need not worry much anyway, for they both "taste rather like the nothing that the world was made of," as Frau Buchholtz says, and own in addition a fibrous texture, and a certain twang. Small cinnamon-coloured cattle are to be got here, but horses there are practically none. Now and again some one who does not see why a horse should not live here as well as at Accra or Lagos imports one, but it always shortly dies. Some say it is because the natives who get their living by hammock-carrying poison them, others say the *tsetse* fly finishes them off; and others, and these I believe are right, say that entozoa are the cause. Small, lean, lank, yellow dogs with very erect ears lead an awful existence, afflicted by many things, but beyond all others by the goats, who, rearing their families in the grassy streets, choose to think the dogs intend attacking them. Last, but not least, there is the pig—a rich source of practice to the local lawyer.

Cape Coast Castle and then Accra were the next places of general interest at which we stopped. The former looks well from the roadstead, and as if it had very recently been white-washed. It is surrounded by low, heavily-forested hills, which rise almost from the seashore, and the fine mass of its old castle does not display its dilapidation at a distance. Moreover, the three stone forts of Victoria, William, and Macarthy, situated on separate hills commanding the town, add to the general appearance of permanent substantialness so different from the usual ramshackledom of West Coast settlements. Even when you go ashore and have had time to recover your senses, scattered by the surf experience, you find this substantialness a true one, not a mere visual delusion produced by painted wood as the seeming substantialness of Sierra Leone turns out to be when you get to close quarters with it. It causes one some mental effort to grasp the fact that Cape Coast has been in European hands for centuries, but it requires a most unmodern power of credence to realise this of any other settlement on the whole western seaboard until you have the pleasure of seeing the beautiful city of San Paul de Loanda, far away down south, past the Congo.

My experience of Cape Coast on this occasion was one of the hottest, but one of the pleasantest I have ever been through on the Gold

Coast. The former attribute was due to the climate, the latter to my kind friends, Mr. Batty, and Mr. and Mrs. Dennis Kemp. I was taken round the grand stone-built houses with their high stone-walled yards and sculpture-decorated gateways, built by the merchants of the last century and of the century before, and through the great rambling stone castle with its water-tanks cut in the solid rock beneath it, and its commodious accommodation for slaves awaiting shipment, now almost as obsolete as the guns it mounts, but not quite so, for these cool and roomy chambers serve to house the native constabulary and their extensive families.

This being done, I was taken up an unmitigated hill, on whose summit stands Fort William, a pepper-pot-like structure now used as a lighthouse. The view from the top was exceedingly lovely and extensive. Beneath, and between us and the sea, lay the town in the blazing sun. In among its solid stone buildings patches of native mud-built huts huddled together as though they had been shaken down out of a sack into the town to serve as dunnage. Then came the snow-white surf wall, and across it the blue sea with our steamer rolling to and fro on the long, regular swell, impatiently waiting until Sunday should be over and she could work cargo. Round us on all the other sides were wooded hills and valleys, and away in the distance to the west showed the white town and castle of Elmina and the nine-mile road thither, skirting the surf-bound seashore, only broken on its level way by the mouth of the Sweet River. Over all was the brooding silence of the noonday heat, broken only by the dulled thunder of the surf.

After seeing these things we started down stairs, and on reaching ground descended yet lower into a sort of stone-walled dry moat, out of which opened clean, cool, cellar-like chambers tunnelled into the earth. These, I was informed, had also been constructed to keep slaves in when they were the staple export of the Gold Coast. They were so refreshingly cool that I lingered looking at them and their massive doors, ere being marched up to ground level again, and down the hill through some singularly awful stenches, mostly arising from rubber, into the big Wesleyan church in the middle of the town. It is a building in the terrible Africo-Gothic style, but it compares most favourably with the cathedral at Sierra Leone, particularly internally, wherein, indeed, it far surpasses that structure. And then we returned to the Mission House and spent a very pleasant evening, save for the knowledge (which amounted in me to remorse) that, had it not been for my edification, not one of my friends would have spent the day toiling about the town they know only too well. The Wesleyan Mission on the Gold Coast, of which Mr. Dennis Kemp was at that time chairman, is the largest and most influential Protestant mission on the West Coast of Africa, and it is now, I am glad to say, adding a technical department to its scholastic and religious one. The Basel Mission has done a great deal of good work in giving technical instruction to the natives, and practically started this most important branch of their education. There is still an almost infinite amount of this work to be done, the African being so strangely deficient in mechanical culture; infinitely more so, indeed, in this than in any other particular.

After leaving Cape Coast our next port was Accra which is one of the five West Coast towns that look well from the sea. The others don't look well from anywhere. First in order of beauty comes San Paul de Loanda; then Cape Coast with its satellite Elmina, then Gaboon, then Accra with its satellite Christiansborg, and lastly, Sierra Leone.

What there is of beauty in Accra is oriental in type. Seen from the sea, Fort St. James on the left and Christiansborg Castle on the right, both almost on shore level, give, with an outcrop of sandy dwarf cliffs, a certain air of balance and strength to the town, though but for these and the two old castles, Accra would be but a poor place and a flimsy, for the rest of it is a mass of rubbishy mud and palm-leaf huts, and corrugated iron dwellings for the Europeans.

Corrugated iron is my abomination. I quite understand it has points, and I do not attack from an aesthetic standpoint. It really looks well enough when it is painted white. There is, close to Christiansborg Castle, a patch of bungalows and offices for officialdom and wife that from a distance in the hard bright sunshine looks like an encampment of snow-white tents among the coco palms, and pretty enough withal. I am also aware that the corrugated-iron roof is an advantage in enabling you to collect and store rain-water, which is the safest kind of water you can get on the Coast, always supposing you have not painted the aforesaid roof with red oxide an hour or two before so collecting, as a friend of mine did once. But the heat inside those iron houses is far greater than inside mud-walled, brick, or wooden ones, and the alternations of temperature more sudden: mornings and evenings they are cold and clammy; draughty they are always, thereby giving you chill which means fever, and fever in West Africa means more than it does in most places.

Going on shore at Accra with Lady MacDonald gave me opportunities and advantages I should not otherwise have enjoyed, such as the hospitality of the Governor, luxurious transport from the landing place to Christiansborg Castle, a thorough inspection of the cathedral in course of erection, and the strange and highly interesting function of going to a tea-party at a police station to meet a king,—a real reigning king,—who kindly attended with his suite and displayed an intelligent interest in photographs. Tackie (that is His Majesty's name) is an old, spare man, with a subdued manner. His sovereign rights are acknowledged by the Government so far as to hold him more or less responsible for any iniquity committed by his people; and as the Government do not allow him to execute or flagellate the said people, earthly pomp is rather a hollow thing to Tackie.

On landing I was taken in charge by an Assistant Inspector of Police, and after a scrimmage for my chief's baggage and my own, which reminded me of a long ago landing on the distant island of Guernsey, the inspector and I got into a 'rickshaw, locally called a go-cart. It was pulled in front by two government negroes and pushed behind by another pair, all neatly attired in white jackets and knee breeches, and crimson cummerbunds yards long, bound round their middles. Now it is an ingrained characteristic of the uneducated negro, that he cannot keep on a neat and complete garment of any kind. It does not matter what that garment may be; so long as it is whole, off it comes. But as soon as that garment becomes a series of holes, held together by filaments of rag, he keeps it upon him in a manner that is marvellous, and you need have no further anxiety on its behalf. Therefore it was but natural that the governmental cummerbunds, being new, should come off their wearers several times in the course of our two mile trip, and as they wound riskily round the legs of their running wearers, we had to make halts while one end of the cummerbund was affixed to a tree-trunk and the other end to the man, who rapidly wound himself up in it again with a skill that spoke of constant practice.

The road to Christiansborg from Accra, which runs parallel to the sea and is broad and well-kept, is in places pleasantly shaded with pepper trees, eucalyptus, and palms. The first part of it, which forms the main street of Accra, is remarkable. The untidy, poverty-stricken native houses or huts are no credit to their owners, and a constant source of anxiety to a conscientious sanitary inspector. Almost every one of them is a shop, but this does not give rise to the animated commercial life one might imagine, owing, I presume, to the fact that every native inhabitant of Accra who has any money to get rid of is able recklessly to spend it in his own emporium. For these shops are of the store nature, each after his kind, and seem homogeneously stocked with tin pans, loud-patterned basins, iron pots, a few rolls of cloth and bottles of American rum. After passing these there are the Haussa lines, a few European houses, and the cathedral; and when nearly into Christiansborg, a cemetery on either side of the road. That to the right is the old cemetery, now closed, and when I was there, in a disgracefully neglected state: a mere jungle of grass infested with snakes. Opposite to it is the cemetery now in use, and I remember well my first visit to it under the guidance of a gloomy Government official, who said he always walked there every afternoon, "so as to get used to the place before staying permanently in it,"—a rank waste of time and energy, by the way, as subsequent events proved, for he is now safe off the Gold Coast for good and all.

He took me across the well-kept grass to two newly dug graves, each covered with wooden hoods in a most business-like way. Evidently those hoods were regular parts of the cemetery's outfit. He said nothing, but waved his hand with a "take-your-choice,-they-are-both-quite-ready" style. "Why?" I queried laconically. "Oh! we always keep two graves ready dug for Europeans. We have to bury very quickly here, you know," he answered. I turned at bay. I had had already a very heavy dose of details of this sort that afternoon and was disinclined to believe another thing. So I said, "It's exceedingly wrong to do a thing like that, you only frighten people to death. You can't want new-dug graves daily. There are not enough white men in the whole place to keep the institution up." "We do," he replied, "at any rate at this season. Why, the other day we had two white men to bury before twelve o'clock, and at four, another dropped in on a steamer."

"At 4.30," said a companion, an exceedingly accurate member of the staff. "How you fellows *do* exaggerate!" Subsequent knowledge of the Gold Coast has convinced me fully that the extra funeral being placed half-an-hour sooner than it occurred is the usual percentage of exaggeration you will be able to find in stories relating to the local mortality. And at Accra, after I left it, and all along the Gold Coast, came one of those dreadful epidemic outbursts sweeping away more than half the white population in a few weeks.

But to return to our state journey along the Christiansborg road. We soon reached the castle, an exceedingly roomy and solid edifice built by the Danes, and far better fitted for the climate than our modern dwellings, in spite of our supposed advance in tropical hygiene. We entered by the sentry-guarded great gate into the courtyard; on the right hand were the rest of the guard; most of them asleep on their mats, but a few busy saying Dhikr, etc., towards Mecca, like the good Mohammedans these Haussas are, others winding themselves into their cummerbunds. On the left hand was Sir Brandford Griffiths' hobby—a choice and select little garden, of lovely eucharis lilies mostly in tubs, and rare and beautiful flowers brought by him from his Barbadian home; while shading it and the courtyard was a fine specimen of that superb thing of beauty—a flamboyant tree—glorious with its delicate-green acacia-like leaves and vermilion and yellow flowers, and astonishing with its vast beans. A flight of stone stairs leads from the courtyard to the upper part of the castle where the living rooms are, over the extensive series of cool tunnel-like slave barracoons, now used as store chambers. The upper rooms are high and large, and full of a soft pleasant light and the thunder of the everlasting surf breaking on the rocky spit on which the castle is built.

From the day the castle was built, now more than a hundred years ago, the surf spray has been swept by the on-shore evening breeze into every chink and cranny of the whole building, and hence the place is mouldy—mouldy to an extent I, with all my experience in that paradise for mould, West Africa, have never elsewhere seen. The matting on the floors took an impression of your foot as a light snowfall would. Beneath articles of furniture the cryptograms attained a size more in keeping with the coal period than with the nineteenth century.

The Gold Coast is one of the few places in West Africa that I have never felt it my solemn duty to go and fish in. I really cannot say why. Seen from the sea it is a pleasant looking land. The long lines of yellow, sandy beach backed by an almost continuous line of blue hills, which in some places come close to the beach, in other places show in the dim distance. It is hard to think that it is so unhealthy as it is, from just see-ing it as you pass by. It has high land and has not those great masses of mangrove-swamp one usually, at first, associates with a bad fever district, but which prove on acquaintance to be at any rate no worse than this well-elevated open-forested Gold Coast land. There are many things to be had here and in Lagos which tend to make life more tolerable, that you cannot have elsewhere until you are south of the Congo. Horses, for example, do fairly well at Accra, though some twelve miles or so behind the town there is a belt of tsetse fly, specimens of which I have procured and had identified at the British Museum, and it is certain death to a horse, I am told, to take it to Aburi.

The food-supply, although bad and dear, is superior to that you get down south. Goats and sheep are fairly plentiful. In addition to fresh meat and tinned you are able to get a quantity of good sea fish, for the great West African Bank, which fringes the coast in the Bight of Benin, abounds in fish, although the native cook very rarely knows how to cook them. Then, too, you can get more fruit and vegetables on the Gold Coast than at most places lower down: the plantain, not least among them and very good when allowed to become ripe, and then cut into longitudinal strips, and properly fried; the banana, which surpasses it when served in the same manner, or beaten up and mixed with rice, butter, and eggs, and baked. Eggs, by the way, according to the great mass of native testimony, are laid in this country in a state that makes them more fit for electioneering than culinary purposes, and I shall never forget one tribe I was once among, who, whenever I sat down on one of their benches, used to smash eggs round me for ju-ju. They meant well. But I will nobly resist the temptation to tell egg stories and industriously catalogue the sour-sop, guava, grenadilla, aubergine or garden-egg, yam, and sweet potato.

The sweet potato should be boiled, and then buttered and browned in an oven, or fried. When cooked in either way I am devoted to them, but in the way I most frequently come across them I abominate them, for they jeopardise my existence both in this world and the next. It is this way: you are coming home from a long and dangerous beetle-hunt in the forest; you have battled with mighty beetles the size of pie dishes, they have flown at your head, got into your hair and then nipped you smartly. You have been also considerably stung and bitten by flies, ants, &c., and are most like-ly sopping wet with rain, or with the wading of streams, and you are tired and your feet go low along the ground, and it is getting, or has got, dark with that ever-deluding tropical rapidity, and then you for your sins get into a piece of ground which last year was a native's farm, and, placing one foot under the tough vine of a surviving sweet potato, concealed by rank herbage, you plant your other foot on another portion of the same vine. Your head you then deposit promptly in some prickly ground crop, or against a tree stump, and then, if there is human blood in you, you say d—n!

Then there are also alligator-pears, limes, and oranges. There is something about those oranges I should like to have explained. They are usually green and sweetish in taste, nor have they much white pith, but now and again you get a big bright yellow one from those trees that have been imported, and these are very pithy and in full possession of the flavour of verjuice. They have also got the papaw on the Coast, the *Carica papaya* of botanists. It is an insipid fruit. To the newcomer it is a dreadful nuisance, for no sooner does an old coaster set eyes on it than he straightaway says, "Paw-paws are awfully good for the digestion, and even if you just hang a tough fowl or a bit of goat in the tree among the leaves, it gets tender in no time, for there is an awful lot of pepsine in a paw-paw,"—which there is not, papaine being its active principle. After hearing this hymn of praise to the papaw some hundreds of times, it palls, and you usually arrive at this tired feeling about the thing by the time you reach the Gold Coast, for it is a most common object, and the same man will say the same thing about it a dozen times a day if he gets the chance. I got heartily sick of it on my first voyage out, and rashly determined to check the old coaster in this habit of his, preparatory to stamping the practice out. It was one of my many failures. I soon met an old coaster with a papaw fruit in sight, and before he had time to start, I boldly got away with—"The paw-paw is awfully good for the digestion," hoping that this display of knowledge would impress him and exempt me from hearing the rest of the formula. But no. "Right you are," said he solemnly. "It's a powerful thing is the paw-paw. Why, the other day we had a sad case along here. You know what a nuisance young assistants are, bothering about their chop, and scorpions in their beds and boots, and what not and a half, and then, when you have pulled them through these, and often enough before, pegging out with fever, or going on the fly in the native town. Did you know poor B—? Well! he's dead now, had fever and went off like a babe in eight hours though he'd been out fourteen years for A— and D—. They sent him out a new book-keeper, a tender young thing with a dairymaid complexion and the notion that he'd got the indigestion. He fidgeted about it something awful. One night there was a big paw-paw on the table for evening chop, and so B—, who was an awfully good chap, told him about how good it was for the digestion. The book-keeper said his trouble always came on two hours after eating, and asked if he might take a bit of the thing to his room. 'Certainly,' says B—, and as the paw-paw wasn't cut at that meal the book-keeper quietly took it off whole with him.

"In the morning time he did not turn up. B—, just before break-fast, went to his room and he wasn't there, but he noticed the paw-paw was on the bed and that was all, so he thought the book-keeper must have gone for a walk, being, as it were, a bit too tender to have gone on the fly as yet. So he just told the store clerk to tell the people to return him to the firm when they found him straying around lost, and thought no more about it, being, as it was, mail-day, and him busy.

"Well! Fortunately the steward boy put that paw-paw on the table again for twelve o'clock chop. If it hadn't been for that, not a living soul would have known the going of the book-keeper. For when B— cut it open, there, right inside it, were nine steel trouser-buttons, a Waterbury watch, and the poor young fellow's keys. For you see, instead of his digesting his dinner with that paw-paw, the paw-paw took charge and digested him, dinner and all, and when B. interrupted it, it was just getting a grip on the steel things. There's an awful lot of pepsine in a paw-paw, and if you hang, &c., &c."

I collapsed, feebly murmuring that it was very interesting, but sad for the poor young fellow's friends.

"Not necessarily," said the old coaster. So he had the last word, and never again will I attempt to alter the ways of the genuine old coaster. What you have got to do with him is to be very thankful you have had the honour of knowing him.

Still I think we do over-estimate the value of the papaw, although I certainly did once myself hang the leg of a goat no mortal man could have got tooth into, on to a papaw tree with a bit of string for the night. In the morning it was clean gone, string and all; but whether it was the pepsine, the papaine, or a purloining pagan that was the cause of its departure there was no evidence to show. Yet I am myself, as Hans Breitmann says, "still skebdigal" as to the papaw, and I dare say you are too.

But I must forthwith stop writing about the Gold Coast, or I shall go on telling you stories and wasting your time, not to mention the

danger of letting out those which would damage the nerves of the cultured of temperate climes, such as those relating to the youth who
taught himself French from a six months' method book; of the man
who wore brass buttons; the moving story of three leeches and two gentlemen; the doctor up a creek; and the reason why you should not eat
pork along here because all the natives have either got the guinea-
worm, or kraw-kraw or ulcers; and then the pigs go and—dear me! it
was a near thing that time. I'll leave off at once.

CHAPTER 2

FERNANDO PO AND THE BUBIS

*Giving some account of the occupation of this island by the whites
and the manners and customs of the blacks peculiar to it.*

OUR OUTWARD VOYAGE REALLY TERMINATED AT CALABAR, and it terminated gorgeously in fireworks and what not, in honour of the coming of Lady MacDonald, the whole settlement, white and black, turning out to do her honour to the best of its ability; and its ability in this direction was far greater than, from my previous knowledge of Coast conditions, I could have imagined possible. Before Sir Claude MacDonald settled down again to local work, he and Lady MacDonald crossed to Fernando Po, still in the *Batanga*. I accompanied them, thus getting an opportunity of seeing something of Spanish official circles.

I had heard sundry noble legends of Fernando Po, and seen the coast and a good deal of the island before, but although I had heard much of the Governor, I had never met him until I went up to his residence with Lady MacDonald and the Consul-General. He was a delightful person, who, as a Spanish naval officer, some time resident in Cuba, had picked up a lot of English, with a strong American accent clinging to it. He gave a most moving account of how, as soon as his appointment as Governor was announced, all his friends and acquaintances carefully explained to him that this appointment was equivalent to execution, only more uncomfortable in the way it worked out. During the outward voyage this was daily confirmed by the stories told by the sailors and merchants personally acquainted with the place, who were able to support their information with dates and details of the decease of the victims to the climate.

Still he kept up a good heart, but when he arrived at the island he found his predecessor had died of fever; and he himself, the day after landing, went down with a bad attack and he was placed in a bed—the same bed, he was mournfully informed, in which the last Governor had expired. Then he did believe, all in one awful lump, all the stories he had been told, and added to their horrors a few original conceptions of death and purgatory, and a lot of transparent semi-forged images of his own delirium. Fortunately both prophecy and personal conviction alike miscarried, and the Governor returned from the jaws of death. But without a moment's delay he withdrew from the Port of Clarence and went up the mountain to Basile, which is in the neighborhood of the highest native village, where he built himself a house, and around it a little village of homes for the most unfortunate set of human beings I have ever laid eye on. They are the remnant of a set of Spanish colonists, who had been located at some spot in the Spanish possessions in Morocco, and finding that place unfit to support human life, petitioned the Government to remove them and let them try colonising elsewhere.

The Spanish Government just then had one of its occasional fits of interest in Fernando Po, and so shipped them here, and the Governor, a most kindly and generous man, who would have been a credit to any country, established them and their families around him at Basile, to share with him the advantages of the superior elevation; advantages he profoundly believed in, and which he has always placed at the disposal of any sick white man on the island, of whatsoever nationality or religion. Undoubtedly the fever is not so severe at Basile as in the lowlands, but there are here the usual drawbacks to West African high land, namely an over supply of rain, and equally saturating mists, to say nothing of sudden and extreme alternations of temperature, and so the colonists still fall off, and their children die continuously from the various entozoa which abound upon the island.

When the Governor first settled upon the mountain he was very difficult to get at for business purposes, and a telephone was therefore run up to him from Clarence through the forest, and Spain at large felt proud at this dashing bit of enterprise in modern appliance. Alas! the primæval forests of Fernando Po were also charmed with the new toy, and they talked to each other on it with their leaves and branches to such an extent that a human being could not get a word in edgeways. So the Governor had to order the construction of a road along the course of the wire to keep the trees off it, but unfortunately the telephone is still an uncertain means of communication, because another interruption in its usefulness still afflicts it, namely the indigenous natives' habit of stealing bits out of its wire, for they are fully persuaded that they cannot be found out in their depredations provided they take sufficient care that they are not caught in the act. The Governor is thus liable to be cut off at any moment in the middle of a conversation with Clarence, and the amount of "Hellos" "Are you theres?" and "Speak louder, pleases" in Spanish that must at such times be poured out and wasted in the lonely forests before the break is realised and an unfortunate man sent off as a messenger, is terrible to think of.

But nothing would persuade the Governor to come a mile down towards Clarence until the day he should go there to join the vessel that was to take him home, and I am bound to say he looked as if the method was a sound one, for he was an exceedingly healthy, cheery-looking man.

Fernando Po is said to be a comparatively modern island, and not so very long ago to have been connected with the mainland, the strait between them being only nineteen miles across, and not having any deep soundings. I fail to see what grounds there are for these ideas, for though Fernando Po's volcanoes are not yet extinct, but merely have their fires banked, yet, on the other hand, the island has been in existence sufficiently long to get itself several peculiar species of animals and plants, and that is a thing which takes time. I myself do not believe that this island was ever connected with the continent, but arose from the ocean as the result of a terrific upheaval in the chain of volcanic activity which runs across the Atlantic from the Cameroon Mountains in a SSW. direction to Anno Bom island, and possibly even to the Tristan da Cunha group midway between the Cape and South America.

These volcanic islands are all of extreme beauty and fertility. They consist of Fernando Po (10,190 ft.); Principe (3,000 ft.); San Thomé (6,913 ft.); and Anno Bom (1,350 ft.). San Thomé and Principe are Portuguese possessions, Fernando Po and Anno Bom Spanish, and they are all exceedingly unhealthy. San Thomé is still called "The Dutchman's Church-yard," on account of the devastation its climate wrought among the Hollanders when they once occupied it; as they seem, at one time or another, to have occupied all Portuguese possessions out here, during the long war these two powers waged with each other for supremacy in the Bights, a supremacy that neither of them attained to. Principe is said to be the most unhealthy, and the reason of the difference in this particular between Principe and Anno Bom is said to arise from the fact that the former is on the Guinea Current—a hot current—and Anno Bom on the Equatorial, which averages 10° cooler than its neighbour.

The shores of San Thomé are washed by both currents, and the currents round Fernando Po are in a mixed and uncertain state. It is difficult, unless you have haunted these seas, to realise the interest we take down there in currents; particularly when you are navigating small sailing boats, a pursuit I indulge in necessarily from my fishing practices. Their effect on the climate too is very marked. If we could only arrange for some terrific affair to take place in the bed of the Atlantic, that would send that precious Guinea current to the place it evidently comes from, and get the cool Equatorial alongside the mainland shore, West Africa would be quite another place.

Fernando Po is the most important island as regards size on the West African coast, and at the same time one of the most beautiful in the world. It is a great volcanic mass with many craters, and culminates in the magnificent cone, Clarence Peak, called by the Spaniards, Pico de Santa Isabel, by the natives of the island O Wassa. Seen from the sea or from the continent it looks like an immense single mountain that has floated out to sea. It is visible during clear weather (and particularly sharply visible in the strange clearness you get after a tornado) from a hundred miles to seawards, and anything more perfect than Fernando Po when you sight it, as you occasionally do from far-away Bonny Bar, in the sunset, floating like a fairy island made of gold or of amethyst, I cannot conceive. It is almost equally lovely at close quarters, namely from the mainland at Victoria, nineteen miles distant. Its moods of beauty are infinite; for the most part gentle and gorgeous, but I have seen it silhouetted hard against tornado-clouds, and grandly grim from the upper regions of its great brother Mungo. And as for Fernando Po in full moonlight—well there! you had better go and see it yourself.

The whole island is, or rather I should say was, heavily forested almost to its peak, with a grand and varied type of forest, very rich in oil palms and tree-ferns, and having an undergrowth containing an immense variety and quantity of ferns and mosses. Sugar-cane also grows wild here, an uncommon thing in West Africa. The last botanical collection of any importance made from these forests was that of Herr Mann, and its examination showed that Abyssinian genera and species predominated, and that many species similar to those found in the mountains of Mauritius, the Isle de Bourbon, and Madagascar, were present. The number of European plants (forty-three genera, twenty-seven species) is strikingly large, most of the British forms being represented chiefly at the higher elevations. What was more striking was that it showed that South African forms were extremely rare, and not one of the characteristic types of St. Helena occurred.

Cocoa, coffee, and cinchona, alas! flourish in Fernando Po, as the coffee suffers but little from the disease that harasses it on the mainland at Victoria, and this is the cause of the great destruction of the forest that is at present taking place. San Thomé, a few years ago, was discovered by its surprised neighbours to be amassing great wealth by growing coffee, and so Fernando Po and Principe immediately started to amass great wealth too, and are now hard at work with gangs of miscellaneous natives got from all parts of the Coast save the Kru. For to the Kruboy, "Panier," as he calls "Spaniard," is a name of horror worse even than Portugee, although he holds "God made white man and God made black man, but dem debil make Portugee," and he also remembers an unfortunate affair that occurred some years ago now, in connection with coffee-growing.

A number of Krumen engaged themselves for a two years' term of labour on the Island of San Thomé, and when they arrived there, were set to work on coffee plantations by the Portuguese. Now agricultural work is "woman's palaver," but nevertheless the Krumen made shift to get through with it, vowing the while no doubt, as they hopefully notched away the moons on their tally-sticks, that they would never let the girls at home know that they had been hoeing. But when their moons were all complete, instead of being sent home with their pay to "We country," they were put off from time to time; and month after month went by and they were still on San Thomé, and still hoeing. At last the home-sick men, in despair of ever getting free, started off secretly in ones and twos to try and get to "We country" across hundreds of miles of the storm-haunted Atlantic in small canoes, and with next to no provisions. The result was a tragedy, but it might easily have been worse; for a few, a very few, were picked up alive by English vessels and taken back to their beloved "We country" to tell the tale. But many a canoe was found with a dead Kruboy or so in it; and many a one which, floating bottom upwards, graphically spoke of madness caused by hunger, thirst, and despair having driven its occupants overboard to the sharks.

My Portuguese friends assure me that there was never a thought of permanently detaining the boys, and that they were only just keeping them until other labourers arrived to take their place on the plantations. I quite believe them, for I have seen too much of the Portuguese in Africa to believe that they would, in a wholesale way, be cruel to natives. But I am not in the least surprised that the poor Krumen took the Portuguese *logo* and *amanhã* for Eternity itself, for I have frequently done so.

The greatest length of the island lies N.E. and S.W., and amounts to thirty-three miles; the mean breadth is seventeen miles. The port, Clarence Cove, now called Santa Isabel by the Spaniards—who have been giving Spanish names to all the English-named places without any one taking much notice of them—is a very remarkable place, and except perhaps Gaboon the finest harbour on the West Coast. The point that brings Gaboon anchorage up in line with Clarence Cove is its superior healthiness; for Clarence is a section of a circle, and its shores are steep rocky cliffs from 100 to 200 feet high, and the place, to put it very mildly, exceedingly hot and stuffy. The cove is evidently a partly submerged crater, the submerged rim of the crater is almost a perfect semi-circle seawards—having on it 4, 5, 7, 8, and 10 fathoms of water save almost in the centre of the arc where there is a passage with 12 to 14 fathoms. Inside, in the crater, there is deeper water, running in places from 30 to 45 fathoms, and outside the submerged rim there is deeper water again, but rocky shoals abound. On the top of the shore cliffs stands the dilapidated little town of Clarence, on a plateau that falls away slightly towards the mountain for about a mile, when the ground commences to rise into the slopes of the Cordillera. On the narrow beach, tucked close against the cliffs, are a few stores belonging to the merchants, where goods are placed on landing, and there is a little pier too, but as it is usually having something done to its head, or else is closed by the authorities because they intend doing something by and by, the chances are against its being available for use. Hence it usually comes about that you have to land on the beach, and when you have done this you make your way up a very steep path, cut in the cliff-side, to the town. When you get there you find yourself in the very dullest town I know on the Coast. I remember when I first landed in Clarence I found its society in a flutter of expectation and alarm not untinged with horror. Clarence, nay, the whole of Fernando Po, was about to become so rackety and dissipated as to put Paris and Monte Carlo to the blush. Clarence was going to have a café; and what was going to go on in that café I shrink from reciting.

I have little hesitation now in saying this alarm was a false one. When I next arrived in Clarence it was just as sound asleep and its streets as weed-grown as ever, although the café was open. My idea is that the sleepiness of the place infected the café and took all the go out of it. But again it may have been that the inhabitants were too well guarded against its evil influence, for there are on the island fifty-two white laymen, and fifty-four priests to take charge of them—he extra two being, I presume, to look after the Governor's conduct, although this worthy man made a most spirited protest against this view when I suggested it to him; and in addition to the priests there are several missionaries of the Methodist mission, and also a white gentleman who has invented a new religion. Anyhow, the café smoulders like a damp squib.

When you spend the day on shore and when, having exhausted the charms of the town,—a thing that usually takes from between ten min-utes to a quarter of an hour,—you apply to an inhabitant for advice as to the disposal of the rest of your shore leave, you are told to "go and see the coals." You say you have not come to tropical islands to see a coal heap, and applying elsewhere for advice you probably get the same. So, as you were told to "go and see the coals" when you left your ship, you do as you are bid. These coals, the remnant of the store that was kept here for the English men-of-war, were left here when the naval station was removed. The Spaniards at first thought of using them, and ran a tram-way from Clarence to them. But when the tramway was finished, their activity had run out too, and to this day there the coals remain. Now and again some one has the idea that they are quite good, and can be used for a steamer, and some people who have tried them say they are all right, and others say they are all wrong. And so the end of it will be that some few thousand years hence there will be a serious quarrel among geologists on the strange pocket of coal on Fernando Po, and they will run up continents, and raise and lower oceans to explain them, and they will doubtless get more excitement and pleasure out of them than you can get nowadays.

The history of the English occupation of Fernando Po seems often misunderstood, and now and then one hears our Government reviled for handing it over to the Spaniards. But this was unavoidable, for we had it as a loan from Spain in 1827 as a naval station for our ships, at that time energetically commencing to suppress the slave trade in the Bights; the idea being that this island would afford a more healthy and convenient spot for a naval depot than any port on the coast itself.

More convenient Fernando Po certainly was, but not more healthy, and ever since 1827 it has been accumulating for itself an evil reputation for unhealthiness which is only languishing just at present because there is an interval between its epidemics—fever in Fernando Po, even more than on the mainland, having periodic outbursts of a more serious type than the normal intermittent and remittent of the Coast. Moreover, Fernando Po shares with Senegal the undoubted yet doubtful honour of having had regular yellow fever. In 1862 and 1866 this disease was imported by a ship that had come from Havana. Since then it has not appeared in the definite South American form, and therefore does not seem to have obtained the foothold it has in Senegal, where a few years ago all the money voted for the keeping of the *Fête Nationale* was in one district devoted by public consent to the purchase of coffins, required by an overwhelming outbreak of Yellow Jack.

In 1858 the Spanish Government thinking, presumably, that the slave trade was suppressed enough, or at any rate to a sufficiently incon-venient extent, re-claimed Fernando Po, to the horror of the Baptist missionaries who had settled in Clarence apparently under the erro-neous idea that the island had been definitely taken over by the English. This mission had received from the West African Company a large grant of land, and had collected round it a gathering of Sierra Leonians and other artisan and trading Africans who were attracted to Clarence by the work made by the naval station; and these people, with the English traders who also settled here for a like reason, were the founders of Clarence Town. The declaration of the Spanish Government stating that only Roman Catholic missions would be countenanced caused the Baptists to abandon their possessions and withdraw to the mainland in Ambas Bay, where they have since remained, and nowadays Protestantism is represented by a Methodist Mission which has a sub-branch on the mainland on the Akwayafe River and one on the Qua Ibo.

The Spaniards, on resuming possession of the island, had one of their attacks of activity regarding it, and sent out with Don Carlos Chacon, who was to take over the command, four Jesuit priests, a secretary, a commissariat officer, a custom-house clerk, and a transport, the *Santa Maria*, with a number of emigrant families. This attempt to colonise Fernando Po should have at least done the good of preventing such experiments ever being tried again with women and children, for of these unfortunate creatures—for whom, in spite of its being the wet season, no houses had been provided—more than 20 per cent died in the space of five months. Mr. Hutchinson, who was English Consul at the time, tells us that "In a very short time gaunt figures of men, women, and children might be seen crawling through the streets, with scarcely an evidence of life in their faces, save the expression of a sort of torpid carelessness as to how soon it might be their turn to drop off and die. The *Portino*, a steamer, carried back fifty of them to Cadiz, who looked when they embarked more like living skeletons of skin and bone than animated human beings." I quote this not to cast reproach on the Spanish Government, but merely to give a fact, a case in point, of the deadly failure of endeavours to colonise on the West Coast, a thing which is even now occasionally attempted, always with the same sad results, though in most cases these attempts are now made by religious but misinformed people under Bishop Taylor's mission.

The Spaniards did not entirely confine their attention to planting colonists in a ready-made state on the island. As soon as they had settled themselves and built their barracks and Government House, they set to work and cleared away the bush for an area of from four to six miles round the town. The ground soon became overgrown again, but this clearing is still perceptible in the different type of forest on it, and has enabled the gardens and little plantations round Clarence to be made more easily. My Spanish friends assure me that the Portuguese, who discovered the island in 1471, and who exchanged it and Anno Bom in 1778 to the Spaniards for the little island of Catalina and the colony of Sacramento in South America, did not do anything to develop it. When they, the Spaniards, first entered into possession they at once set to work to colonise and clear. Then the colonisation scheme went to the bad, the natives poisoned the wells, it is said, and the attention of the Spaniards was in those days turned, for some inscrutable reason, to the eastern shores of the island—a district now quite abandoned by whites, on account of its unhealthiness—and they lost in addition to the colonists a terrible quantity of their sailors, in Concepcion Bay. A lull then followed, and the Spaniards willingly lent the place to the English as aforesaid. They say we did nothing except establish Clarence as a head-quarters, which they consider to have been a most excellent enterprise, and import the Baptist Mission, which they hold as a less estimable undertaking; but there! that's nothing to what the Baptist Mission hold regarding the Spaniards. For my own part, I wish the Spaniards better luck this time in their activity, for in directing it to plantations they are on a truer and safer road to wealth than they have been with their previous importations of Cuban political prisoners and ready-made families of colonists, and I hope they will send home those unfortunate wretches they have there now, and commence, in their expected two years, to reap the profits of the coffee and cocoa. Certainly the chances are that they may, for the soil of Fernando Po is of exceeding fertility; Mr. Hutchinson says he has known Indian corn planted here on a Monday evening make its appearance four inches above ground on the following Wednesday morning, within a period, he carefully says, of thirty-six hours. I have seen this sort of thing over in Victoria, but I like to get a grown, strong man, and a Consul of Her Britannic Majesty, to say it for me.

Having discoursed at large on the various incomers to Fernando Po we may next turn to the natives, properly so-called, the Bubis. These people, although presenting a series of interesting problems to the ethnologist, both from their insular position, and their differen-tiation from any of the mainland peoples, are still but little known. To a great extent this has arisen from their exclusiveness, and their total lack of enthusiasm in trade matters, a thing that differentiates them more than any other characteristic from the mainlanders, who, young and old, men and women, regard trade as the great affair of life, take to it as soon as they can toddle, and don't even leave it off at death, according to their own accounts of the way the spirits of distinguished traders still dabble and interfere in market matters. But it is otherwise with the Bubi. A little rum, a few beads, and finish—then he will turn the rest of his attention to catching porcupines, or the beautiful little gazelles, gray on the back, and white underneath, with which the island abounds. And what time he may have on hand after this, he spends in building houses and making himself hats. It is only his utterly spare moments that he employs in making just sufficient palm oil from the rich supply of nuts at his command to get that rum and those beads of his. Cloth he does not want; he utterly fails to see what good the stuff is, for he abhors clothes. The Spanish authorities insist that the natives who come into the town should have something on, and so they array themselves in a bit of cotton cloth, which before they are out of sight of the town on their homeward way, they strip off and stuff into their baskets, showing in this, as well as in all other particulars, how uninfluencible by white culture they are. For the Spaniards, like the Portuguese, are great sticklers for clothes, and insist on their natives wearing them—usually with only too much success. I shall never forget the yards and yards of cotton the ladies of Loanda wore; and not content with making cocoons of their bodies, they wore over their heads, as a mantilla, some dozen yards or so of black cloth into the bargain. Moreover this insistence on drapery for the figure is not merely for towns; a German officer told me the other day that when, a week or so before, his ship had called at Anno Bom, they were simply besieged for "clo', clo', clo';" the Anno Bomians explaining that they were all anxious to go across to Principe and get employment on coffee plantations, but that the Portuguese planters would not engage them in an unclothed state.

You must not, however, imagine that the Bubi is neglectful of his personal appearance. In his way he is quite a dandy. But his idea of decoration goes in the direction of a plaster of "tola" pomatum over his body, and above all a hat. This hat may be an antique European one, or a bound-round handkerchief, but it is more frequently a confection of native manufacture, and great taste and variety are displayed in its make. They are of plaited palm leaf—that's all you can safely generalise regarding them—for sometimes they have broad brims, sometimes narrow, sometimes no brims at all. So, too, with the crown. Sometimes it is thick and domed, sometimes non-existent, the wearer's hair aglow with red-tail parrots' feathers sticking up where the crown should be. As a general rule these hats are much adorned with oddments of birds' plumes, and one chief I knew had quite a Regent-street Dolly Varden creation which he used to affix to his wool in a most intelligent way with bonnet-pins made of wood. These hats are also a peculiarity of the Bubi, for none of the mainlanders care a row of pins for hats, except "for dandy," to wear occasionally, whereas the Bubi wears his perpetually, although he has by no means the same amount of sun to guard against owing to the glorious forests of his island.

For earrings the Bubi wears pieces of wood stuck through the lobe of the ear, and although this is not a decorative habit still it is less undecorative than that of certain mainland friends of mine in this region, who wear large and necessarily dripping lumps of fat in their ears and in their hair. His neck is hung round with jujus on strings—bits of the backbones of pythons, teeth, feathers, and antelope horns, and occasionally a bit of fat in a bag. Round his upper arm are bracelets, preferably made of ivory got from the mainland, for celluloid bracelets carefully imported for his benefit he refuses to look at. Often these bracelets are made of beads, or a circlet of leaves, and when on the war-path an armlet of twisted grass is always worn by the men. Men and women alike wear armlets, and in the case of the women they seem to be put on when young, for you see puffs of flesh growing out from between them. They are not entirely for decoration, serving also as pockets, for under them men stick a knife, and women a tobacco pipe, a well-coloured clay. Leglets of similar construction are worn just under the knee on the right leg, while around the body you see belts of *tshibbu*, small pieces cut from Achatectonia shells, which form the native currency of the island. These shells are also made into veils worn by the women at their wedding.

This native coinage-equivalent is very interesting, for such things are exceedingly rare in West Africa. The only other instance I personally know of a tribe in this part of the world using a native-made coin is that of the Fans, who use little bundles of imitation axe-heads. Dr. Oscar Baumann, who knows more than any one else about these Bubis, thinks, I believe, that these bits of Achatectonia shells may have been introduced by the runaway Angola slaves in the old days, who used to fly from their Portuguese owners on San Thomé to the Spaniards on Fernando Po. The villages of the Bubis are in the forest in the interior of the island, and they are fairly wide apart. They are not a sea-beach folk, although each village has its beach, which merely means the place to which it brings its trade, these beaches being usually the dwelling places of the so-called Portos, negroes, who act as middle-men between the Bubis and the whites.

You will often be told that the Bubis are singularly bad house-builders, indeed that they make no definite houses at all, but only rough shelters of branches. This is, however, a mistake. Shelters of this kind that you come across are merely the rough huts put up by hunters, not true houses. The village is usually fairly well built, and surrounded with a living hedge of stakes. The houses inside this are four-cornered, the walls made of logs of wood stuck in edgeways, and surmounted by a roof of thatch pitched at an extremely stiff angle, and the whole is usually surrounded with a dug-out drain to carry off surface water. These houses, as usual on the West Coast, are divisible into two classes—houses of assembly, and private living houses. The first are much the larger. The latter are very low, and sometimes ridiculously small, but still they are houses and better than those awful Loango grass affairs you get on the Congo.

Herr Baumann says that the houses high up on the mountain have double walls between which there is a free space; an arrangement which may serve to minimise the extreme draughtiness of an ordinary Bubi house—a very necessary thing in these relatively chilly upper regions. I may remark on my own account that the Bubi villages do not often lie right on the path, but, like those you have to deal with up the Calabar, some little way off it. This is no doubt for the purpose of concealing their whereabouts from strangers, and it does it successfully too, for many a merry hour have I spent dodging up and down a path trying to make out at what particular point it was advisable to dive into the forest thicket to reach a village. But this cultivates habits of observation, and a short course of this work makes you recognise which tree is which along miles of a bush path as easily as you would shops in your own street at home.

The main interest of the Bubi's life lies in hunting, for he is more of a sportsman than the majority of mainlanders. He has not any big game to deal with, unless we except pythons—which attain a great size on the island—and crocodiles. Elephants, though plentiful on the adjacent mainland, are quite absent from Fernando Po, as are also hippos and the great anthropoid apes; but of the little gazelles, small monkeys, porcupines, and squirrels he has a large supply, and in the rivers a very pretty otter (*Lutra poensis*) with yellow brown fur often quite golden underneath; a creature which is, I believe, identical with the Angola otter.

The Bubis use in their hunting flint-lock guns, but chiefly traps and nets, and, I am told, slings. The advantage of these latter methods are, I expect, the same as on the mainland, where a distinguished sportsman once told me: "You go shoot thing with gun. Berrah well—but you no get him thing for sure. No, sah. Dem gun make nize. Berrah well. You fren hear dem nize and come look him, and you hab to go share what you done kill. Or bad man hear him nize, and he come look him, and you no fit to get share—you fit to get kill yusself. Chii! chii! traps be best." I urged that the traps might also be robbed. "No, sah," says he, "them bian (charm) he look after them traps, he fit to make man who go tief swell up and bust."

The Bubis also fish, mostly by basket traps, but they are not experts either in this or in canoe management. Their chief sea-shore sport is hunting for the eggs of the turtles who lay in the sand from August to October. These eggs—about 200 in each nest—are about the size of a billiard-ball, with a leathery envelope, and are much valued for food, as are also the grubs of certain beetles got from the stems of the palm-trees, and the honey of the wild bees which abound here.

Their domestic animals are the usual African list; cats, dogs, sheep, goats, and poultry. Pigs there are too, very domestic in Clarence and in a wild state in the forest. These pigs are the descendants of those imported by the Spaniards and not long ago became such an awful nuisance in Clarence that the Government issued instructions that all pigs without rings in their noses—i.e. all in a condition to grub up back gardens—should be forthwith shot if found abroad. This proclamation was issued by the governmental bellman thus:—"I say—I say—I say—I say. Suppose pig walk—iron no live for him nose! Gun shoot. Kill him one time. Hear re! hear re!"

However a good many pigs with no iron living in their noses got adrift and escaped into the interior, and have flourished like the green bay-tree, destroying the Bubi's plantation and eating his yams, while the Bubi retaliating kills and eats them. So it's a drawn battle, for the Bubi enjoys the pig and the pig enjoys the yams, which are of singular excellence in this island and celebrated throughout the Bight. Now, I am told, the Government are firmly discouraging the export of these yams, which used to be quite a little branch of Fernando Po trade, in the hope that this will induce the native to turn his attention to working in the coffee and cacao plantations. Hope springs eternal in the human breast, for the Bubi has shown continually since the 16th century that he takes no interest in these things whatsoever. Now and again a man or woman will come voluntarily and take service in Clarence, submit to clothes, and rapidly pick up the ways of a house or store. And just when their owner thinks he owns a treasure, and begins to boast that he has got an exception to all Bubidom, or else that he knows how to manage them better than other men, then a hole in that man's domestic arrangements suddenly appears. The Bubi has gone, without giving a moment's warning, and without stealing his master's property, but just softly and silently vanished away. And if hunted up the treasure will be found in his or her particular village—clothesless, comfortable, utterly unconcerned, and unaware that he or she has lost anything by leaving Clarence and Civilisation. It is this conduct that gains for the Bubi the reputation of being a bigger idiot than he really is.

For West Africans their agriculture is of a fairly high description—the noteworthy point about it, however, is the absence of manioc. Manioc is grown on Fernando Po, but only by the Portos. The Bubi cultivated plants are yams (*Dioscorea alata*), koko (*Colocasia esculenta*—the taro of the South Seas) and plantains. Their farms are well kept, particularly those in the grass districts by San Carlos Bay. The yams of the Cordillera districts are the best flavoured, but those of the east coast the largest. Palm-oil is used for domestic purposes in the usual ways, and palm wine both fresh and fermented is the ordinary native drink. Rum is held in high esteem, but used in a general way in moderation as a cordial and a treat, for the Bubi is, like the rest of the West African natives, by no means an habitual drunkard. Gin he dislikes.

And I may remark you will find the same opinion in regard to the Dualla in Cameroons river—on the undeniable authority of Dr. Buchner, and my own extensive experience of the West Coast bears it out.

Physically the Bubis are a fairly well-formed race of medium height; they are decidedly inferior to the Benga or the Krus, but quite on a level with the Effiks. The women indeed are very comely: their colour is bronze and their skin the skin of the Bantu. Beards are not uncommon among the men, and these give their faces possibly more than anything else, a different look to the faces of the Effiks or the Duallas. Indeed the people physically most like the Bubis that I have ever seen, are undoubtedly the Bakwiri of Cameroons Mountain, who are also liable to be bearded, or possibly I should say more liable to wear beards, for a good deal of the African hairlessness you hear commented on—in the West African at any rate—arises from his deliberately pulling his hair out—his beard, moustache, whiskers, and, occasionally, as among the Fans, his eyebrows.

Dr. Baumann, the great authority on the Bubi language says it is a Bantu stock. I know nothing of it myself save that it is harsh in sound. Their method of counting is usually by fives but they are notably weak in arithmetical ability, differing in this particular from the mainlanders, and especially from their Negro neighbours, who are very good at figures, surpassing the Bantu in this, as indeed they do in most branches of intellectual activity.

But the most remarkable instance of inferiority the Bubis display is their ignorance regarding methods of working iron. I do not know that iron in a native state is found on Fernando Po, but scrap-iron they have been in touch with for some hundreds of years. The mainlanders are all cognisant of native methods of working iron, although many tribes of them now depend entirely on European trade for their supply of knives, &c., and this difference between them and the Bubis would seem to indicate that the migration of the latter to the island must have taken place at a fairly remote period, a period before the iron-working tribes came down to the coast. Of course, if you take the Bubi's usual explanation of his origin, namely that he came out of the crater on the top of Clarence Peak, this argument falls through; but he has also another legend, one moreover which is likewise to be found upon the mainland, which says he was driven from the district north of the Gaboon estuary by the coming of the M'pongwe to the coast, and as this legend is the more likely of the two I think we may accept it as true, or nearly so. But what adds another difficulty to the matter is that the Bubi is not only unlearned in iron lore, but he was learned in stone, and up to the time of the youth of many Porto-negroes on Fernando Po, he was making and using stone implements, and none of the tribes within the memory of man have done this on the mainland. It is true that up the Niger and about Benin and Axim you get polished stone celts, but these are regarded as weird affairs,—thunderbolts—and suitable only for grinding up and making into medicine; there is no trace in the traditions of these places, as far as I have been able to find, of any time at which stone implements were in common use, and certainly the M'pongwe have not been a very long time on the coast, for their coming is still remembered in their traditions. The Bubi stone implements I have seen twice, but on neither occasion could I secure one, and although I have been long promised specimens from Fernando Po, I have not yet received them. They are difficult to procure, because none of the present towns are on really old sites, the Bubi, like most Bantus, moving pretty frequently, either because the ground is witched, demonstrated by outbreaks of sickness, or because another village-full of his fellow creatures, or a horrid white man plantation-making, has come too close to him. A Roman Catholic priest in Ka Congo once told me a legend he laughed much over, of how a fellow priest had enterprisingly settled himself one night in the middle of a Bubi village with intent to devote the remainder of his life to quietly but thoroughly converting it. Next morning, when he rose up, he found himself alone, the people having taken all their portable possessions and vanished to build another village elsewhere. The worthy Father spent some time chivying his flock about the forest, but in vain, and he returned home disgusted, deciding that the Creator, for some wise purpose, had dedicated the Bubis to the Devil.

The spears used by this interesting people are even to this day made entirely of wood, and have such a Polynesian look about them that I intend some time or other to bring some home and experiment on that learned Polynesian-culture-expert, Baron von Hügel, with them:— intellectually experiment, not physically, pray understand.

The pottery has a very early-man look about it, but in this it does not differ much from that of the mainland, which is quite as poor, and similarly made without a wheel, and sun-baked. Those pots of the Bubis I have seen have, however, not had the pattern (any sort of pattern does, and it need not be carefully done) that runs round mainland pots to "keep their souls in"—*i.e.* to prevent their breaking up on their own account.

The basket-work of the Bubis is of a superior order: the baskets they make to hold the palm oil are excellent, and will hold water like a basin, but I am in doubt whether this art is original, or imported by the Portuguese runaway slaves, for they put me very much in mind of those made by my old friends the Kabinders, from whom a good many of those slaves were recruited. I think there is little doubt that several of the musical instruments own this origin, particularly their best beloved one, the elibo. This may be described as a wooden bell having inside it for clappers several (usually five) pieces of stick threaded on a bit of wood jammed into the dome of the bell and striking the rim, beyond which the clappers just protrude. These bells are very like those you meet with in Angola, but I have not seen on the island, nor does Dr. Baumann cite having seen, the peculiar double bell of Angola—the engongui. The Bubi bell is made out of one piece of wood and worked—or played—with both hands. Dr. Baumann says it is customary on bright moonlight nights for two lines of men to sit facing each other and to clap—one can hardly call it ring—these bells vigorously, but in good time, accompanying this performance with a monotonous song, while the delighted women and children dance round. The learned doctor evidently sees the picturesqueness of this practice, but notes that the words of the songs are not "tiefsinnige" (profound), as he has heard men for hours singing "The shark bites the Bubi's hand," only that over and over again and nothing more. This agrees with my own observations of all Bantu native songs. I have always found that the words of these songs were either the repetition of some such phrase as this, or a set of words referring to the recent adventures or experiences of the singer or the present company's little peculiarities; with a very frequent chorus, old and conventional.

The native tunes used with these songs are far superior, and I expect many of them are very old. They are often full of variety and beauty, particularly those of the M'pongwe and Igalwa, of which I will speak later.

The dances I have no personal knowledge of, but there is nothing in Baumann's description to make one think they are distinct in themselves from the mainland dances. I once saw a dance at Fernando Po, but that was among Portos, and it was my old friend the Batuco in all its beauty. But there is a distinct peculiarity about the places the dances are held on, every village having a kept piece of ground outside it which is the dancing place for the village—the ball-room as it were; and exceedingly picturesque these dances must be, for they are mostly held during the nights of full moon. These kept grounds remind one very much of the similar looking patches of kept grass one sees in villages in Ka Congo, but there is no similarity in their use, for the Ka Congo lawns are of fetish, not frivolous, import.

The Bubis have an instrument I have never seen in an identical form on the mainland. It is made like a bow, with a tense string of fibre. One end of the bow is placed against the mouth, and the string is then struck by the right hand with a small round stick, while with the left it is scraped with a piece of shell or a knife-blade. This excruciating instrument, I warn any one who may think of living among the Bubis, is very popular. The drums used are both the Dualla form—all wood—and the ordinary skin-covered drum, and I think if I catalogue fifes made of wood, I shall have nearly finished the Bubi orchestra. I have doubts on this point because I rather question whether I may be allowed to refer to a very old bullock hide—unmounted—as a musical instrument without bringing down the wrath of musicians on my head. These stiff, dry pelts are much thought of, and played by the artistes by being shaken as accompaniments to other instruments—they make a noise, and that is after all the soul of most African instrumental music. These instruments are all that is left of certain bullocks which many years ago the Spaniards introduced, hoping to improve the food supply. They seemed as if they would have flourished well on the island, on the stretches of grass land in the Cordillera and the East, but the Bubis, being great sportsmen, killed them all off.

The festivities of the Bubis—dances, weddings, feasts, &c.,—at which this miscellaneous collection of instruments are used in concert, usually take place in November, the dry season; but the Bubi is liable to pour forth his soul in the bosom of his family at any time of the day or night, from June to January, and when he pours it forth on that bow affair it makes the lonely European long for home.

Divisions of time the Bubi can hardly be said to have, but this is a point upon which all West Africans are rather weak, particularly the Bantu. He has, however, a definite name for November, December, and January—the dry season months—calling them Lobos.

The Fetish of these people, although agreeing on broad lines with the Bantu Fetish, has many interesting points, as even my small knowledge of it showed me, and it is a subject that would repay further investigation; and as by fetish I always mean the governing but underlying ideas of a man's life, we will commence with the child. Nothing, as far as I have been able to make out, happens to him, for fetish reasons, when he first appears on the scene. He receives at birth, as is usual, a name which is changed for another on his initiation into the secret society, this secret society having also, as usual, a secret language. About the age of three or five years the boy is decorated, under the auspices of the witch doctor, with certain scars on the face. These scars run from the root of the nose across the cheeks, and are sometimes carried up in a curve on to the forehead.

Tattooing, in the true sense of the word, they do not use much, but they paint themselves, as the mainlanders do, with a red paint made by burning some herb and mixing the ash with clay or oil, and they occasionally—whether for ju-ju reasons or for mere decoration I do not know—paint a band of yellow clay round the chest; but of the Bubi secret society I know little, nor have I been able to find any one who knows much more. Hutchinson, in his exceedingly amusing description of a wedding he was once present at among these people, would lead one to think the period of seclusion of the women's society was twelve months.

The chief god or spirit, O Wassa, resides in the crater of the highest peak, and by his name the peak is known to the native. Another very important spirit, to whom goats and sheep are offered, is Lobe, resident in a crater lake on the northern slope of the Cordilleras, and the grass you sometimes see a Bubi wearing is said to come from this lake and be a ju-ju of Lobe's. Dr. Baumann says that the lake at Riabba from which the spirit Uapa rises is more holy, and that he is small, and resides in a chasm in a rock whose declivity can only be passed by means of bush ropes, and in the wet season he is not get-at-able at all. He will, if given suitable offerings, reveal the future to Bubis, but Bubis only. His priest is the King of all the Bubis, upon whom it is never permitted to a white man, or a Porto, to gaze. Baumann also gives the residence of another important spirit as being the grotto at Banni. This is a sea-cave, only accessible at low water in calm weather. I have heard many legends of this cave, but have never had an opportunity of seeing it, or any one who has seen it first hand.

The charms used by these people are similar in form to those of the mainland Bantu, but the methods of treating paths and gateways are somewhat peculiar. The gateways to the towns are sometimes covered by freshly cut banana leaves, and during the religious feast in November, the paths to the villages are barred across with a hedge of grass which no stranger must pass through.

The government is a peculiar one for West Africa. Every village has its chief, but the whole tribe obey one great chief or king who lives in the crater-ravine at Riabba. This individual is called Moka, but whether he is now the same man referred to by Rogoszinsky, Mr. Holland, and the Rev. Hugh Brown, who attempted to interview him in the seventies, I do not feel sure, for the Bubis are just the sort of people to keep a big king going with a variety of individuals. Even the indefatigable Dr. Baumann failed to see Moka, though he evidently found out a great deal about the methods of his administration and formed a very high opinion of his ability, for he says that to this one chief the people owe their present unity and orderliness; that before his time the whole island was in a state of internecine war: murder was frequent, and property unsafe. Now their social condition, according to the Doctor's account, is a model to Europe, let alone Africa. Civil wars have been abolished, disputes between villages being referred to arbitration, and murder is swiftly and surely punished. If the criminal has bolted into the forest and cannot be found, his village is made responsible, and has to pay a fine in goats, sheep and tobacco to the value of £16. Theft is extremely rare and offences against the moral code also, the Bubis having an extremely high standard in this matter, even the little children having each a separate sleeping hut. In old days adultery was punished by cutting off the offender's hand. I have myself seen women in Fernando Po who have had a hand cut off at the wrist, but I believe those were slave women who had suffered for theft. Slaves the Bubis do have, but their condition is the mild, poor relation or retainer form of slavery you find in Calabar, and differs from the Dualla form, for the slaves live in the same villages as their masters, while among the Duallas, as among most Bantu slave-holding tribes, the slaves are excluded from the master's village and have separate villages of their own. For marriage ceremonies I refer you to Mr. Hutchinson. Burial customs are exceedingly quaint in the southern and eastern districts, where the bodies are buried in the forest with their heads just sticking out of the ground. In other districts the body is also buried in the forest, but is completely covered and an erection of stones put up to mark the place.

Little is known of all West African fetish, still less of that of these strange people. Dr. Oscar Baumann brought to bear on them his careful unemotional German methods of observation, thereby giving us more valuable information about them and their island than we otherwise should possess. Mr. Hutchinson resided many years on Fernando Po, in the capacity of H. B. M.'s Consul, with his hands full of the affairs of the Oil Rivers and in touch with the Portos of Clarence, but he nevertheless made very interesting observations on the natives and their customs. The Polish exile and his courageous wife who ascended Clarence Peak, Mr. Rogoszinsky, and another Polish exile, Mr. Janikowski, about complete our series of authorities on the island. Dr. Baumann thinks they got their information from Porto sources—sources the learned Doctor evidently regards as more full of imagination than solid fact, but, as you know, all African travellers are occasionally in the habit of pooh-poohing each other, and I own that I myself have been chiefly in touch with Portos, and that my knowledge of the Bubi language runs to the conventional greeting form:—"Ipori?" "Porto." "Ke Soko?" "Hatsi soko":—"Who are you?"—"Porto." "What's the news?" "No news."

Although these Portos are less interesting to the ethnologist than the philanthropist, they being by-products of his efforts, I must not leave Fernando Po without mentioning them, for on them the trade of the island depends. They are the middlemen between the Bubi and the white trader. The former regards them with little, if any, more trust than he regards the white men, and his view of the position of the Spanish Governor is that he is chief over the Portos. That he has any headship over Bubis or over the Bubi land—Itschulla as he calls Fernando Po—he does not imagine possible. Baumann says he was once told by a Bubi: "White men are fish, not men. They are able to stay a little while on land, but at last they mount their ships again and vanish over the horizon into the ocean. How can a fish possess land?" If the coffee and cacao thrive on Fernando Po to the same extent that they have already thriven on San Thomé there is but little doubt that the Bubis will become extinct; for work on plantations, either for other people, or themselves, they will not, and then the Portos will become the most important class, for they will go in for plantations. Their little factories are studded all round the shores of the coast in suitable coves and bays, and here in fairly neat houses they live, collecting palm-oil from the Bubis, and making themselves little cacao plantations, and bringing these products into Clarence every now and then to the white trader's factory. Then, after spending some time and most of their money in the giddy whirl of that capital, they return to their homes and recover. There is a class of them permanently resident in Clarence, the city men of Fernando Po, and these are very like the Sierra Leonians of Free Town, but preferable. Their origin is practically the same as that of the Free Towners. They are the descendants of liberated slaves set free during the time of our occupation of the island as a naval depot for suppressing the slave trade, and of Sierra Leonians and Accras who have arrived and settled since then. They have some of the same "Black gennellum, Sar" style about them, but not developed to the same ridiculous extent as in the Sierra Leonians, for they have not been under our institutions. The "Nanny Po" ladies are celebrated for their beauty all along the West Coast, and very justly. They are not however, as they themselves think, the most beautiful women in this part of the world. Not at least to my way of thinking. I prefer an Elmina, or an Igalwa, or a M'pongwe, or—but I had better stop and own that my affections have got very scattered among the black ladies on the West Coast, and I no sooner remember one lovely creature whose soft eyes, perfect form and winning, pretty ways have captivated me than I think of another. The Nanny Po ladies have often a certain amount of Spanish blood in them, which gives a decidedly greater delicacy to their features:—delicate little nostrils, mouths not too heavily lipped, a certain gloss on the hair, and a light in the eye. But it does not improve their colour, and I am assured that it has an awful effect on their tempers, so I think I will remain, for the present, the faithful admirer of my sable Ingramina, the Igalwa, with the little red blossoms stuck in her night-black hair, and a sweet soft look and word for every one, but particularly for her ugly husband Isaac the "Jack Wash."

CHAPTER 3

Voyage Down Coast

Wherein the voyager before leaving the Rivers discourses on dangers,
to which is added some account of Mangrove swamps
and the creatures that abide therein.

I LEFT CALABAR IN MAY and joined the *Benguela* off Lagos Bar. My voyage down coast in her was a very pleasant one and full of instruction, for Mr. Fothergill, who was her purser, had in former years resided in Congo Français as a merchant, and to Congo Français I was bound with an empty hold as regards local knowledge of the district. He was one of that class of men, of which you most frequently find representatives among the merchants, who do not possess the power so many men along here do possess (a power that always amazes me), of living here for a considerable time in a district without taking any interest in it, keeping their whole attention concentrated on the point of how long it will be before their time comes to get out of it. Mr. Fothergill evidently had much knowledge and experience of the Fernan Vaz district and its natives. He had, I should say, overdone his experiences with the natives, as far as personal comfort and pleasure at the time went, having been nearly killed and considerably chivied by them. Now I do not wish a man, however much I may deplore his total lack of local knowledge, to go so far as this. Mr. Fothergill gave his accounts of these incidents calmly, and in an undecorated way that gave them a power and convincingness verging on being unpleasant, although useful, to a person who was going into the district where they had occurred, for one felt there was no mortal reason why one should not personally get involved in similar affairs. And I must here acknowledge the great subsequent service Mr. Fothergill's wonderfully accurate descriptions of the peculiar character-istics of the Ogowé forests were to me when I subsequently came to deal with these forests on my own account, as ever district of forest has pecu-liar characteristics of its own which you require to know. I should like here to speak of West Coast dangers because I fear you may think that I am careless of, or do not believe in them, neither of which is the case. The more you know of the West Coast of Africa, the more you realise its dangers. For example, on your first voyage out you hardly believe the stories of fever told by the old Coasters. That is because you do not then understand the type of man who is telling them, a man who goes to his death with a joke in his teeth. But a short experience of your own, par-ticularly if you happen on a place having one of its periodic epidemics, soon demonstrates that the underlying horror of the thing is there, a rotting corpse which the old Coaster has dusted over with jokes to cover it so that it hardly shows at a distance, but which, when you come your-self to live alongside, you soon become cognisant of. Many men, when they have got ashore and settled, realise this, and let the horror get a grip on them; a state briefly and locally described as funk, and a state that usually ends fatally; and you can hardly blame them. Why, I know of a case myself. A young man who had never been outside an English coun-try town before in his life, from family reverses had to take a situation as book-keeper down in the Bights. The factory he was going to was in an isolated out-of-the-way place and not in a settlement, and when the ship called off it, he was put ashore in one of the ship's boats with his belongings, and a case or so of goods. There were only the firm's beach-boys down at the surf, and as the steamer was in a hurry the officer from the ship did not go up to the factory with him, but said good-bye and left him alone with a set of naked savages as he thought, but really of good kindly Kru boys on the beach. He could not understand what they said, nor they what he said, and so he walked up to the house and on to the verandah and tried to find the Agent he had come out to serve under. He looked into the open-ended dining-room and shyly round the verandah, and then sat down and waited for some one to turn up. Sundry natives turned up, and said a good deal, but no one white or comprehensible, so in desperation he made another and a bolder tour completely round the verandah and noticed a most peculiar noise in one of the rooms and an infinity of flies going into the venetian shuttered window. Plucking up courage he went in and found what was left of the white Agent, a considerable quantity of rats, and most of the flies in West Africa. He then presumably had fever, and he was taken off, a fortnight afterwards, by a French boat, to whom the natives signalled, and he is not coming down the Coast again. Some men would have died right out from a shock like this.

But most of the new-comers do not get a shock of this order. They either die themselves or get more gradually accustomed to this sort of thing, when they come to regard death and fever as soldiers, who on a battle-field sit down, and laugh and talk round a camp fire after a day's hard battle, in which they have seen their friends and companions falling round them; all the time knowing that to-morrow the battle comes again and that to-morrow night they themselves may never see.

It is not hard-hearted callousness, it is only their way. Michael Scott put this well in *Tom Cringle's Log*, in his account of the yellow fever during the war in the West Indies. Fever, though the chief danger, particularly to people who go out to settlements, is not the only one; but as the other dangers, except perhaps domestic poisoning, are incidental to pottering about in the forests, or on the rivers, among the unsophisticated tribes, I will not dwell on them. They can all be avoided by any one with common sense, by keeping well out of the districts in which they occur; and so I warn the general reader that if he goes out to West Africa, it is not because I said the place was safe, or its dangers overrated. The cemeteries of the West Coast are full of the victims of those people who have said that Coast fever is "Cork fever," and a man's own fault, which it is not; and that natives will never attack you unless you attack them: which they will—on occasions.

My main aim in going to Congo Français was to get up above the tide line of the Ogowé River and there collect fishes; for my object on this voyage was to collect fish from a river north of the Congo. I had hoped this river would have been the Niger, for Sir George Goldie had placed at my disposal great facilities for carrying on work there in comfort; but for certain private reasons I was disinclined to go from the Royal Niger Protectorate into the Royal Niger Company's territory; and the Calabar, where Sir Claude MacDonald did everything he possibly could to assist me, I did not find a good river for me to collect fishes in. These two rivers failing me, from no fault of either of their own presiding genii, my only hope of doing anything now lay on the South West Coast river, the Ogowé, and everything there depended on Mr. Hudson's attitude towards scientific research in the domain of ichthyology. Fortunately for me that gentleman elected to take a favourable view of this affair, and in every way in his power assisted me during my entire stay in Congo Français. But before I enter into a detailed description of this wonderful bit of West Africa, I must give you a brief notice of the manners, habits and customs of West Coast rivers in general, to make the thing more intelligible.

There is an uniformity in the habits of West Coast rivers, from the Volta to the Coanza, which is, when you get used to it, very taking. Excepting the Congo, the really great river comes out to sea with as much mystery as possible; lounging lazily along among its mangrove swamps in a what's-it-matter-when-one-comes-out and where's-the-hurry style, through quantities of channels inter-communicating with each other. Each channel, at first sight as like the other as peas in a pod, is bordered on either side by green-black walls of mangroves, which Captain Lugard graphically described as seeming "as if they had lost all count of the vegetable proprieties, and were standing on stilts with their branches tucked up out of the wet, leaving their gaunt roots exposed in mid-air." High-tide or low-tide, there is little difference in the water; the river, be it broad or narrow, deep or shallow, looks like a pathway of polished metal; for it is as heavy weighted with stinking mud as water e'er can be, ebb or flow, year out and year in. But the difference in the banks, though an unending alternation between two appearances, is weird.

At high-water you do not see the mangroves displaying their ankles in the way that shocked Captain Lugard. They look most respectable, their foliage rising densely in a wall irregularly striped here and there by the white line of an aërial root, coming straight down into the water from some upper branch as straight as a plummet, in the strange, knowing way an aërial root of a mangrove does, keeping the hard straight line until it gets some two feet above water-level, and then spreading out into blunt fingers with which to dip into the water and grasp the mud. Banks indeed at high water can hardly be said to exist, the water stretching away into the mangrove swamps for miles and miles, and you can then go, in a suitable small canoe, away among these swamps as far as you please.

This is a fascinating pursuit. But it is a pleasure to be indulged in with caution; for one thing, you are certain to come across crocodiles. Now a crocodile drifting down in deep water, or lying asleep with its jaws open on a sand-bank in the sun, is a picturesque adornment to the landscape when you are on the deck of a steamer, and you can write home about it and frighten your relations on your behalf; but when you are away among the swamps in a small dug-out canoe, and that croco- dile and his relations are awake—a thing he makes a point of being at flood tide because of fish coming along—and when he has got his foot upon his native heath—that is to say, his tail within holding reach of his native mud—he is highly interesting, and you may not be able to write home about him—and you get frightened on your own behalf; for croc- odiles can, and often do, in such places, grab at people in small canoes. I have known of several natives losing their lives in this way; some native villages are approachable from the main river by a short cut, as it were, through the mangrove swamps, and the inhabitants of such villages will now and then go across this way with small canoes instead of by the con- stant channel to the village, which is almost always winding. In addition to this unpleasantness you are liable—until you realise the danger from experience, or have native advice on the point—to get tide-trapped away in the swamps, the water falling round you when you are away in some deep pool or lagoon, and you find you cannot get back to the main river. Of course if you really want a truly safe investment in Fame, and really care about Posterity, and Posterity's Science, you will jump over into the black batter-like, stinking slime, cheered by the thought of the terrific sensation you will produce 20,000 years hence, and the care you will be taken of then by your fellow-creatures, in a museum. But if you are a mere ordinary person of a retiring nature, like me, you stop in your lagoon until the tide rises again; most of your attention is directed to dealing with an "at home" to crocodiles and mangrove flies, and with the fearful stench of the slime round you. What little time you have over you will employ in wondering why you came to West Africa, and why, after having reached this point of folly, you need have gone and painted the lily and adorned the rose, by being such a colossal ass as to come fool- ing about in mangrove swamps.

Still, even if your own peculiar tastes and avocations do not take you in small dug-out canoes into the heart of the swamps, you can observe the difference in the local scenery made by the flowing of the tide when you are on a vessel stuck on a sand-bank, in the Rio del Rey for example. Moreover, as you will have little else to attend to, save mosquitoes and mangrove flies, when in such a situation, you may as well pursue the study. At the ebb gradually the foliage of the lower branches of the mangrove grows wet and muddy, until there is a great black band about three feet deep above the surface of the water in all directions; gradually a network of gray-white roots rises up, and below this again, gradually, a slope of smooth and lead-grey slime. The effect is not in the least as if the water had fallen, but as if the mangroves had, with one accord, risen up out of it, and into it again they seem silently to sink when the flood comes. But by this more safe, if still unpleasant, method of observing mangrove-swamps, you miss seeing in full the make of them, for away in their fastnesses the mangroves raise their branches far above the reach of tide line, and the great gray roots of the older trees are always sticking up in mid-air. But, fringing the rivers, there is always a hedge of younger mangroves whose lower branches get immersed.

At corners here and there from the river face you can see the land being made from the waters. A mud-bank forms off it, a mangrove seed lights on it, and the thing's done. Well! not done, perhaps, but begun; for if the bank is high enough to get exposed at low water, this pioneer mangrove grows. He has a wretched existence though. You have only got to look at his dwarfed attenuated form to see this. He gets joined by a few more bold spirits and they struggle on together, their network of roots stopping abundance of mud, and by good chance now and then a consignment of miscellaneous *débris* of palm leaves, or a floating tree-trunk, but they always die before they attain any considerable height. Still even in death they collect. Their bare white stems remaining like a net gripped in the mud, so that these pioneer mangrove heroes may be said to have laid down their lives to make that mud-bank fit for colonisation, for the time gradually comes when other mangroves can and do colonise on it, and flourish, extending their territory steadily; and the mud-bank joins up with, and becomes a part of, Africa.

Right away on the inland fringe of the swamp—you may go some hundreds of miles before you get there—you can see the rest of the process. The mangroves there have risen up, and dried the mud to an extent that is more than good for themselves, have over civilised that mud in fact, and so the brackish waters of the tide—which, although their enemy when too deep or too strong in salt, is essential to their existence—cannot get to their roots. They have done this gradually, as a mangrove does all things, but they have done it, and down on to that mud come a whole set of palms from the old mainland, who in their early colonisation days go through similarly trying experiences. First the screw-pines come and live among them; then the wine-palm and various creepers, and then the oil-palm; and the *débris* of these plants being greater and making better soil than dead mangroves, they work quicker and the mangrove is doomed. Soon the salt waters are shut right out, the mangrove dies, and that bit of Africa is made. It is very interesting to get into these regions; you see along the river-bank a rich, thick, lovely wall of soft-wooded plants, and behind this you find great stretches of death;—miles and miles sometimes of gaunt white mangrove skeletons standing on gray stuff that is not yet earth and is no longer slime, and through the crust of which you can sink into rotting putrefaction. Yet, long after you are dead, buried, and forgotten, this will become a forest of soft-wooded plants and palms; and finally of hard-wooded trees. Districts of this description you will find in great sweeps of Kama country for example, and in the rich low regions up to the base of the Sierra del Cristal and the Rumby range.

You often hear the utter lifelessness of mangrove-swamps commented on; why I do not know, for they are fairly heavily stocked with fauna, though the species are comparatively few. There are the crocodiles, more of them than any one wants; there are quantities of flies, particularly the big silent mangrove-fly which lays an egg in you under the skin; the eggs becomes a maggot and stays there until it feels fit to enter into external life. Then there are "slimy things that crawl with legs upon a slimy sea," and any quantity of hopping mud-fish, and crabs, and a certain mollusc, and in the water various kinds of cat-fish. Birdless they are save for the flocks of gray parrots that pass over them at evening, hoarsely squarking; and save for this squarking of the parrots the swamps are silent all the day, at least during the dry season; in the wet season there is no silence night or day in West Africa, but that roar of the descending deluge of rain that is more monotonous and more gloomy than any silence can be. In the morning you do not hear the long, low, mellow whistle of the plantain-eaters calling up the dawn, nor in the evening the clock-bird nor the Handel-Festival-sized choruses of frogs, or the crickets, that carry on their vesper controversy of "she did"—"she didn't" so fiercely on hard land.

But the mangrove-swamp follows the general rule for West Africa, and night in it is noisier than the day. After dark it is full of noises; grunts from I know not what, splashes from jumping fish, the peculiar whirr of rushing crabs, and quaint creaking and groaning sounds from the trees; and—above all in eeriness—the strange whine and sighing cough of crocodiles.

Great regions of mangrove-swamps are a characteristic feature of the West African Coast. The first of these lies north of Sierra Leone; then they occur, but of smaller dimensions—just fringes of river-out-falls—until you get to Lagos, when you strike the greatest of them all:— the swamps of the Niger outfalls (about twenty-three rivers in all) and of the Sombreiro, New Calabar, Bonny, San Antonio, Opobo (false and true), Kwoibo, Old Calabar (with the Cross Akwayafe Qwa Rivers) and Rio del Rey Rivers. The whole of this great stretch of coast is a mangrove-swamp, each river silently rolling down its great mass of mud-laden waters and constituting each in itself a very pretty problem to the navigator by its network of intercommunicating creeks, and the sand and mud bar which it forms off its entrance by dropping its heaviest mud; its lighter mud is carried out beyond its bar and makes the nasty-smelling brown soup of the South Atlantic Ocean, with froth floating in lines and patches on it, for miles to seaward.

In this great region of swamps every mile appears like every other mile until you get well used to it, and are able to distinguish the little local peculiarities at the entrance of the rivers and in the winding of the creeks, a thing difficult even for the most experienced navigator to do during those thick wool-like mists called smokes, which hang about the whole Bight from November till May (the dry season), sometimes lasting all day, sometimes clearing off three hours after sunrise.

The upper or north-westerly part of the swamp is round the mouths of the Niger, and it successfully concealed this fact from geographers down to 1830, when the series of heroic journeys made by Mungo Park, Clapperton, and the two Landers finally solved the problem—a problem that was as great and which cost more men's lives than even the discovery of the sources of the Nile.

That this should have been so may seem very strange to us who now have been told the answer to the riddle; for the upper waters of this great river were known of before Christ and spoken of by Herodotus, Pliny and Ptolemy, and its mouths navigated continuously along by the seaboard by trading vessels since the fifteenth century, but they were not recognised as belonging to the Niger. Some geographers held that the Senegal or the Gambia was its outfall; others that it was the Zaire (Congo); others that it did not come out on the West Coast at all, but got mixed up with the Nile in the middle of the continent, and so on. Yet when you come to know the swamps this is not so strange. You find on going up what looks like a big river—say Forcados, two and a half miles wide at the entrance and a real bit of the Niger. Before you are up it far great, broad, business-like-looking river entrances open on either side, showing wide rivers mangrove-walled, but two-thirds of them are utter frauds which will ground you within half an hour of your entering them. Some few of them do communicate with other main channels to the great upper river, and others are main channels themselves; but most of them intercommunicate with each other and lead nowhere in particular, and you can't even get there because of their shallowness. It is small wonder that the earlier navigators did not get far up them in sailing ships, and that the problem had to be solved by men descending the main stream of the Niger before it commences to what we in Devonshire should call "squander itself about" in all these channels." And in addition it must be remembered that the natives with whom these trading vessels dealt, first for slaves, afterwards for palm-oil, were not, and are not now, members of the Lo family of savages. Far from it: they do not go in for "gentle smiles," but for murdering any unprotected boat's crew they happen to come across, not only for a love of sport but to keep white traders from penetrating to the trade-producing interior, and spoiling prices. And the region is practically foodless.

The rivers of the great mangrove-swamp from the Sombreiro to the Rio del Rey are now known pretty surely not to be branches of the Niger, but the upper regions of this part of the Bight are much neglected by English explorers. I believe the great swamp region of the Bight of Biafra is the greatest in the world, and that in its immensity and gloom it has a grandeur equal to that of the Himalayas.

Take any man, educated or not, and place him on Bonny or Forcados River in the wet season on a Sunday—Bonny for choice. Forcados is good. You'll keep Forcados scenery "indelibly limned on the tablets of your mind when a yesterday has faded from its page," after you have spent even a week waiting for the Lagos branch-boat on its inky waters. But Bonny! Well, come inside the bar and anchor off the factories: seaward there is the foam of the bar gleaming and wicked white against a leaden sky and what there is left of Breaker Island. In every other direction you will see the apparently endless walls of mangrove, unvarying in colour, unvarying in form, unvarying in height, save from perspective. Beneath and between you and them lie the rotting mud waters of Bonny River, and away up and down river, miles of rotting mud waters fringed with walls of rotting mud mangrove-swamp. The only break in them—one can hardly call it a relief to the scenery—are the gaunt black ribs of the old hulks, once used as trading stations, which lie exposed at low water near the shore, protruding like the skeletons of great unclean beasts who have died because Bonny water was too strong even for them.

Raised on piles from the mud shore you will see the white-painted factories and their great store-houses for oil; each factory likely enough with its flag at half-mast, which does not enliven the scenery either, for you know it is because somebody is "dead again." Throughout and over all is the torrential downpour of the wet-season rain, coming down night and day with its dull roar. I have known it to rain six mortal weeks in Bonny River, just for all the world as if it were done by machinery, and the interval that came then was only a few wet days, where-after it settled itself down to work again in the good West Coast waterspout pour for more weeks.

While your eyes are drinking in the characteristics of Bonny scenery you notice a peculiar smell—an intensification of that smell you noticed when nearing Bonny, in the evening, out at sea. That's the breath of the malarial mud, laden with fever, and the chances are you will be down to-morrow. If it is near evening time now, you can watch it becoming incarnate, creeping and crawling and gliding out from the side creeks and between the mangrove-roots, laying itself upon the river, stretching and rolling in a kind of grim play, and finally crawling up the side of the ship to come on board and leave its cloak of moisture that grows green mildew in a few hours over all. Noise you will not be much troubled with: there is only that rain, a sound I have known make men who are sick with fever well-nigh mad, and now and again the depressing cry of the curlews which abound here. This combination is such that after six or eight hours of it you will be thankful to hear your shipmates start to work the winch. I take it you are hard up when you relish a winch. And you will say—let your previous experience of the world be what it may—Good Heavens, what a place!

Five times have I been now in Bonny River and I like it. You always do get to like it if you live long enough to allow the strange fascination of the place to get a hold on you; but when I first entered it, on a ship commanded by Captain Murray in '93, in the wet season, i.e. in August, in spite of the confidence I had by this time acquired in his skill and knowledge of the West Coast, a sense of horror seized on me as I gazed upon the scene, and I said to the old Coaster who then had charge of my education, "Good Heavens! what an awful accident. We've gone and picked up the Styx." He was evidently hurt and said, "Bonny was a nice place when you got used to it," and went on to discourse on the last epidemic here, when nine men out of the resident eleven died in about ten days from yellow fever. Next to the scenery of "a River," commend me for cheerfulness to the local conversation of its mangrove-swamp region; and every truly important West African river has its mangrove-swamp belt, which extends inland as far as the tide waters make it brackish, and which has a depth and extent from the banks depending on the configuration of the country. Above this belt comes uniformly a region of high forest, having towards the river frontage clay cliffs, sometimes high, as in the case of the Old Calabar at Adiabo, more frequently dwarf cliffs, as in the Forcados up at Warree, and in the Ogowé,—for a long stretch through Kama country. After the clay cliffs region you come to a region of rapids, caused by the river cutting its way through a mountain range; such ranges are the Pallaballa, causing the Livingstone rapids of the Congo; the Sierra del Cristal, those of the Ogowé, and many lesser rivers; the Rumby and Omon ranges, those of the Old Calabar and Cross Rivers.

Naturally in different parts these separate regions vary in size. The mangrove-swamp may be only a fringe at the mouth of the river, or it may cover hundreds of square miles. The clay cliffs may extend for only a mile or so along the bank, or they may, as on the Ogowé, extend for 130. And so it is also with the rapids: in some rivers, for instance the Cameroons, there are only a few miles of them, in others there are many miles; in the Ogowé there are as many as 500; and these rapids may be close to the river mouth, as in most of the Gold Coast rivers, save the Ancobra and the Volta; or they may be far in the interior, as in the Cross River, where they commence at about 200 miles; and on the Ogowé, where they commence at about 208 miles from the sea coast; this depends on the nearness or remoteness from the coast line of the mountain ranges which run down the west side of the continent; ranges (apparently of very different geological formations), which have no end of different names, but about which little is known in detail.

And now we will leave generalisations on West African rivers and go into particulars regarding one little known in England, and called by its owners, the French, the greatest strictly equatorial river in the world— the Ogowé.

CHAPTER 4

THE OGOWÉ

Wherein the voyager gives extracts from the Log of the Mové and of the Éclaiveur, and an account of the voyager's first meeting with "those fearful Fans," also an awful warning to all young persons who neglect the study of the French language.

ON THE 20TH OF MAY I reached Gaboon, now called Libreville—the capital of Congo Français, and, thanks to the kindness of Mr. Hudson, I was allowed a passage on a small steamer then running from Gaboon to the Ogowé River, and up it when necessary as far as navigation by steamer is possible—this steamer is, I deeply regret to say, now no more. As experiences of this kind contain such miscellaneous masses of facts, I am forced to commit the literary crime of giving you my Ogowé set of experiences in the form of diary.

June 5th, 1895.—Off on *Mové* at 9.30. Passengers, Mr. Hudson, Mr. Woods, Mr. Huyghens, Père Steinitz, and I. There are black deck-passengers galore; I do not know their honourable names, but they are evidently very much married men, for there is quite a gorgeously coloured little crowd of ladies to see them off. They salute me as I pass down the pier, and start inquiries. I say hastily to them: "Farewell, I'm off up river," for I notice Mr. Fildes bearing down on me, and I don't want him to drop in on the subject of society interest. I expect it is set-tled now, or pretty nearly. There is a considerable amount of mild uproar among the black contingent, and the *Mové* firmly clears off before half the good advice and good wishes for the black husbands are aboard. She is a fine little vessel; far finer than I expected. The accommodation I am getting is excellent. A long, narrow cabin, with one bunk in it and pretty nearly everything one can wish for, and a copying press thrown in. Food is excellent, society charming, captain and engineer quite acquisitions. The saloon is square and roomy for the size of the vessel, and most things, from rowlocks to teapots, are kept under the seats in good nautical style. We call at the guard-ship to pass our papers, and then steam ahead out of the Gaboon estuary to the south, round Pongara Point, keeping close into the land. About forty feet from shore there is a good free channel for vessels with a light draught which if you do not take, you have to make a big sweep seaward to avoid a reef. Between four and five miles below Pongara, we pass Point Gombi, which is fitted with a lighthouse, a lively and conspicuous structure by day as well as night. It is perched on a knoll, close to the extremity of the long arm of low, sandy ground, and is painted black and white, in horizontal bands, which, in conjunction with its general figure, give it a pagoda-like appearance.

Alongside it are a white-painted, red-roofed house for the light-house keeper, and a store for its oil. The light is either a flashing or a revolving or a stationary one, when it is alight. One must be accurate about these things, and my knowledge regarding it is from information received, and amounts to the above. I cannot throw in any personal experience, because I have never passed it at night-time, and seen from Glass it seems just steady. Most lighthouses on this Coast give up fancy tricks, like flashing or revolving, pretty soon after they are established. Seventy-five per cent of them are not alight half the time at all. "It's the climate." Gombi, however, you may depend on for being alight at night, and I have no hesitation in saying you can see it, when it is visible, seventeen miles out to sea, and that the knoll on which the lighthouse stands is a grass-covered sand cliff, about forty or fifty feet above sea-level. As we pass round Gombi point, the weather becomes distinctly rough, particularly at lunch-time. The Mové minds it less than her passengers, and stamps steadily along past the wooded shore, behind which shows a distant range of blue hills. Silence falls upon the black passengers, who assume recumbent positions on the deck, and suffer. All the things from under the saloon seats come out and dance together, and play puss-in-the-corner, after the fashion of loose gear when there is any sea on. As the night comes down, the scene becomes more and more picturesque. The moonlit sea, shimmering and breaking on the darkened shore, the black forest and the hills silhouetted against the star-powdered purple sky, and, at my feet, the engine-room stoke-hole, lit with the rose-coloured glow from its furnace, showing by the great wood fire the two nearly naked Krumen stokers, shining like polished bronze in their perspiration, as they throw in on to the fire the billets of red wood that look like freshly-cut chunks of flesh. The white engineer hovers round the mouth of the pit, shouting down directions and ever and anon plunging down the little iron ladder to carry them out himself. At intervals he stands on the rail with his head craned round the edge of the sun deck to listen to the captain, who is up on the little deck above, for there is no telegraph to the engines, and our gallant commander's voice is not strong. While the white engineer is roosting on the rail, the black engineer comes partially up the ladder and gazes hard at me; so I give him a wad of tobacco, and he plainly regards me as inspired, for of course that was what he wanted. Remember that whenever you see a man, black or white, filled with a nameless longing, it is tobacco he requires. Grim despair accompanied by a gusty temper indicates something wrong with his pipe, in which case offer him a straightened-out hairpin. The black engineer having got his tobacco, goes below to the stoke-hole again and smokes a short clay as black and as strong as himself. The captain affects an immense churchwarden. How he gets through life, waving it about as he does, without smashing it every two minutes, I cannot make out.

At last we anchor for the night just inside Nazareth Bay, for Nazareth Bay wants daylight to deal with, being rich in low islands and sand shoals. We crossed the Equator this afternoon.

June 6th.—Off at daybreak into Nazareth Bay. Anxiety displayed by navigators, sounding taken on both sides of the bows with long bamboo poles painted in stripes, and we go "slow ahead" and "hard astern" successfully, until we get round a good-sized island, and there we stick until four o'clock, high water, when we come off all right, and steam triumphantly but cautiously into the Ogowé. The shores of Nazareth Bay are fringed with mangroves, but once in the river the scenery soon changes, and the waters are walled on either side with a forest rich in bamboo, oil and wine palms. These forest cliffs seem to rise right up out of the mirror-like brown water. Many of the highest trees are covered with clusters of brown-pink young shoots that look like flowers, and others are decorated by my old enemy the climbing palm, now bearing clusters of bright crimson berries. Climbing plants of other kinds are wreathing everything, some blossoming with mauve, some with yellow, some with white flowers, and every now and then a soft sweet heavy breath of fragrance comes out to us as we pass by. There is a native village on the north bank, embowered along its plantations with some very tall cocoapalms rising high above them.

The river winds so that it seems to close in behind us, opening out in front fresh vistas of superb forest beauty, with the great brown river stretching away unbroken ahead like a broad road of burnished bronze. Astern, it has a streak of frosted silver let into it by the *Mové's* screw. Just about six o'clock, we run up to the *Fallaba*, the *Mové's* predecessor in working the Ogowé, now a hulk, used as a depot by Hatton and Cookson. She is anchored at the entrance of a creek that runs through to the Fernan Vaz; some say it is six hours' run, others that it is eight hours for a canoe; all agree that there are plenty of mosquitoes.

The *Fallaba* looks grimly picturesque, and about the last spot in which a person of a nervous disposition would care to spend the night. One half of her deck is dedicated to fuel logs, on the other half are plank stores for the goods, and a room for the black sub-trader in charge of them. I know that there must be scorpions which come out of those logs and stroll into the living room, and goodness only knows what one might not fancy would come up the creek or rise out of the floating grass, or the limitless-looking forest. I am told she was a fine steamer in her day, but those who had charge of her did not make allowances for the very rapid rotting action of the Ogowé water, so her hull rusted through before her engines were a quarter worn out; and there was nothing to be done with her then, but put a lot of concrete in, and make her a depot, in which state of life she is very useful, for during the height of the dry season, the *Mové* cannot get through the creek to supply the firm's Fernan Vaz factories.

Subsequently I heard much of the *Fallaba*, which seems to have been a celebrated, or rather notorious, vessel. Every one declared her engines to have been of immense power, but this I believe to have been a mere local superstition; because in the same breath, the man who referred to them, as if it would have been quite unnecessary for new engines to have been made for H.M.S. Victorious if those Fallaba engines could have been sent to Chatham dockyard, would mention that "you could not get any pace up on her"; and all who knew her sadly owned "she wouldn't steer," so naturally she spent the greater part of her time on the Ogowé on a sand-bank, or in the bush. All West African steamers have a mania for bush, and the delusion that they are required to climb trees. The *Fallaba* had the complaint severely, because of her defective steering powers, and the temptation the magnificent forest, and the rapid currents, and the sharp turns of the creek district, offered her; she failed, of course—they all fail—but it is not for want of practice. I have seen many West Coast vessels up trees, but never more than fifteen feet or so.

The trade of this lower part of the Ogowé, from the mouth to Lembarene, a matter of 130 miles, is almost nil. Above Lembarene, you are in touch with the rubber and ivory trade.

This *Fallaba* creek is noted for mosquitoes, and the black passengers made great and showy preparations in the evening time to receive their onslaught, by tying up their strong chintz mosquito bars to the stanchions and the cook-house. Their arrangements being constantly interrupted by the white engineer making alarums and excursions amongst them; because when too many of them get on one side the Mové takes a list and burns her boilers. Conversation and atmosphere are full of mosquitoes. The decision of widely experienced sufferers amongst us is, that next to the lower Ogowé, New Orleans is the worst place for them in this world.

The day closed with a magnificent dramatic beauty. Dead ahead of us, up through a bank of dun-coloured mist rose the moon, a great orb of crimson, spreading down the oil-like, still river, a streak of blood-red reflection. Right astern, the sun sank down into the mist, a vaster orb of crimson, and when he had gone out of view, sent up flushes of amethyst, gold, carmine and serpent-green, before he left the moon in undisputed possession of the black purple sky.

Forest and river were absolutely silent, but there was a pleasant chatter and laughter from the black crew and passengers away forward, that made the *Mové* seem an island of life in a land of death. I retired into my cabin, so as to get under the mosquito curtains to write; and one by one I heard my companions come into the saloon adjacent, and say to the watchman: "You sabe six o'clock? When them long arm catch them place, and them short arm catch them place, you call me in the morning time." Exit from saloon—silence—then: "You sabe five o'clock?

When them long arm catch them place, and them short arm catch them place, you call me in the morning time." Exit—silence—then: "You sabe half-past five o'clock? When them long arm—" Oh, if I were a watch-man! Anyhow, that five o'clocker will have the whole ship's company roused in the morning time.

June 7th.—Every one called in the morning time by the reflex row from the rousing of the five o'clocker. Glorious morning. The scene the reversal of that of last night. The forest to the east shows a deep blue-purple, mounted on a background that changes as you watch it from daffodil and amethyst to rose-pink, as the sun comes up through the night mists. The moon sinks down among them, her pale face flushing crimson as she goes; and the yellow-gold sunshine comes, glorifying the forest and gilding the great sweep of tufted papyrus growing alongside the bank; and the mist vanishes, little white flecks of it lingering among the water reeds and lying in the dark shadows of the forest stems. The air is full of the long, soft, rich notes of the plantain warblers, and the uproar consequent upon the Mové taking on fuel wood, which comes alongside in canoe loads from the *Fallaba*.

Père Steinitz and Mr. Woods are busy preparing their respective canoes for their run to Fernan Vaz through the creek. Their canoes are very fine ones, with a remarkably clean run aft. The Père's is quite the travelling canoe, with a little stage of bamboo aft, covered with a hood of palm thatch, under which you can make yourself quite comfortable, and keep yourself and your possessions dry, unless something desperate comes on in the way of rain.

By 10.25 we have got all our wood aboard, and run off up river full speed. The river seems broader above the *Fallaba*, but this is mainly on account of its being temporarily unencumbered with islands. A good deal of the bank we have passed by since leaving Nazareth Bay on the south side has been island shore, with a channel between the islands and the true south bank.

The day soon grew dull, and looked threatening, after the delusive manner of the dry season. The climbing plants are finer here than I have ever before seen them. They form great veils and curtains between and over the trees, often hanging so straight and flat, in stretches of twenty to forty feet or so wide, and thirty to sixty or seventy feet high, that it seems incredible that no human hand has trained or clipped them into their perfect forms. Sometimes these curtains are decorated with large bell-shaped, bright-coloured flowers, sometimes with delicate sprays of white blossoms. This forest is beyond all my expectations of tropical luxuriance and beauty, and it is a thing of another world to the forest of the Upper Calabar, which, beautiful as it is, is a sad dowdy to this. There you certainly get a great sense of grimness and vastness; here you have an equal grimness and vastness with the addition of superb colour. This forest is a Cleopatra to which Calabar is but a Quaker. Not only does this forest depend on flowers for its illumination, for there are many kinds of trees having their young shoots, crimson, brown-pink, and creamy yellow: added to this there is also the relieving aspect of the prevailing fashion among West African trees, of wearing the trunk white with here and there upon it splashes of pale pink lichen, and vermilion-red fungus, which alone is sufficient to prevent the great mass of vegetation from being a monotony in green.

All day long we steam past ever-varying scenes of loveliness whose component parts are ever the same, yet the effect ever different. Doubtless it is wrong to call it a symphony, yet I know no other word to describe the scenery of the Ogowè. It is as full of life and beauty and passion as any symphony Beethoven ever wrote: the parts changing, interweaving, and returning. There are *leit motifs* here in it, too. See the papyrus ahead; and you know when you get abreast of it you will find the great forest sweeping away in a bay-like curve behind it against the dull gray sky, the splendid columns of its cotton and red woods looking like a façade of some limitless inchoate temple. Then again there is that stretch of sword-grass, looking as if it grew firmly on to the bottom, so steady does it stand; but as the *Mové* goes by, her wash sets it undulating in waves across its broad acres of extent, showing it is only riding at anchor; and you know after a grass patch you will soon see a red dwarf clay cliff, with a village perched on its top, and the inhabitants thereof in their blue and red cloths standing by to shout and wave to the *Mové*, or legging it like lamp-lighters from the back streets and the plantation to the river frontage, to be in time to do so, and through all these changing phases there is always the strain of the vast wild forest, and the swift, deep, silent river.

At almost every village that we pass—and they are frequent after the *Fallaba*—there is an ostentatious display of firewood deposited either on the bank, or on piles driven into the mud in front of it, mutely saying in their uncivilised way, "Try our noted chunks: best value for money"—

(that is to say, tobacco, &c.), to the *Mové* or any other little steamer that may happen to come along hungry for fuel.

We stayed a few minutes this afternoon at Ashchyouka, where there came off to us in a canoe an enterprising young Frenchman who has planted and tended a coffee plantation in this out-of-the-way region, and which is now, I am glad to hear, just coming into bearing. After leaving Ashchyouka, high land showed to the N.E., and at 5.15, without evident cause to the uninitiated, the *Mové* took to whistling like a liner. A few minutes later a factory shows up on the hilly north bank, which is Woermann's; then just beyond and behind it we see the Government Post; then Hatton and Cookson's factory, all in a line. Opposite Hatton and Cookson's there was a pretty little stern-wheel steamer nestling against the steep clay bank of Lembarene Island when we come in sight, but she instantly swept out from it in a perfect curve, which lay behind her marked in frosted silver on the water as she dropt down river. I hear now she was the Éclaireur, the stern-wheeler which runs up and down the Ogowé in connection with the Chargeurs Réunis Company, sub-sidised by the Government, and when the *Mové* whistled, she was just completing taking on 3,000 billets of wood for fuel. She comes up from the Cape (Lopez) stoking half wood and half coal as far as Njole and back to Lembarene; from Lembarene to the sea downwards she does on wood. In a few minutes we have taken her berth close to the bank, and tied up to a tree. The white engineer yells to the black engineer "Tom-Tom: Haul out some of them fire and open them drains one time," and the stokers, with hooks, pull out the glowing logs on to the iron deck in front of the furnace door, and throw water over them, and the *Mové* sends a cloud of oil-laden steam against the bank, coming perilously near scalding some of her black admirers assembled there. I dare say she felt vicious because they had been admiring the Éclaireur.

After a few minutes, I am escorted on to the broad verandah of Hatton and Cookson's factory, and I sit down under a lamp, prepared to contemplate, until dinner time, the wild beauty of the scene. This idea does not get carried out; in the twinkling of an eye I am stung all round the neck, and recognise there are lots too many mosquitoes and sandflies in the scenery to permit of contemplation of any kind. Never have I seen sandflies and mosquitoes in such appalling quantities. With a wild ping of joy the latter made for me, and I retired promptly into a dark corner of the verandah, swearing horribly, but internally, and

fought them. Mr. Hudson, Agent-general, and Mr. Cockshut, Agent
for the Ogowé, walk up and down the beach in front, doubtless talking
cargo, apparently unconscious of mosquitoes; but by and by, while we
are having dinner, they get their share. I behave exquisitely, and am
quite lost in admiration of my own conduct, and busily deciding in my
own mind whether I shall wear one of those plain ring haloes, or a solid
plate one, *à la* Cimabue, when Mr. Hudson says in a voice full of
reproach to Mr. Cockshut, "You have got mosquitoes here, Mr.
Cockshut." Poor Mr. Cockshut doesn't deny it; he has got four on his
forehead and his hands are sprinkled with them, but he says: "There are
none at Njole," which we all feel is an absurdly lame excuse, for Njole is
some ninety miles above Lembarene, where we now are. Mr. Hudson
says this to him, tersely, and feeling he has utterly crushed Mr. Cockshut,
turns on me, and utterly failing to recognise me as a suffering saint, says
point blank and savagely, "You don't seem to feel these things, Miss
Kingsley." Not feel them, indeed! Why, I could cry over them. Well!
that's all the thanks one gets for trying not to be a nuisance in this world.

After dinner I go back on to the *Mové* for the night, for it is too late
to go round to Kangwe and ask Mme. Jacot, of the Mission Evangelique,
if she will take me in. The air is stiff with mosquitoes, and saying a few
suitable words to them, I dash under the mosquito bar and sleep, lulled
by their shrill yells of baffled rage.

June 8th.—In the morning, up at five. Great activity on beach. Mové
synchronously taking on wood fuel and discharging cargo. A very active
young French pastor from the Kangwe mission station is round after the
mission's cargo. Mr. Hudson kindly makes inquiries as to whether I may
go round to Kangwe and stay with Mme. Jacot. He says: "Oh, yes," but
as I find he is not M. Jacot, I do not feel justified in accepting this statement without its having personal confirmation from Mme. Jacot, and
so, leaving my luggage with the *Mové*, I get them to allow me to go round
with him and his cargo to Kangwe, about three-quarters of an hour's
paddle round the upper part of Lembarene Island, and down the broad
channel on the other side of it. Kangwe is beautifully situated on a hill,
as its name denotes, on the mainland and north bank of the river. Mme.
Jacot most kindly says I may come, though I know I shall be a fearful nuisance, for there is no room for me save M. Jacot's beautifully neat,
clean, tidy study. I go back in the canoe and fetch my luggage from the
Mové, and say good-bye to Mr. Hudson, who gave me an immense

amount of valuable advice about things, which was subsequently of great use to me, and a lot of equally good warnings which, if I had attended to, would have enabled me to avoid many, if not all, my misadventures in Congo Français.

I camped out that night in M. Jacot's study, wondering how he would like it when he came home and found me there; for he was now away on one of his usual evangelising tours. Providentially Mme. Jacot let me have the room that the girls belonging to the mission school usually slept in, to my great relief, before M. Jacot came home.

I will not weary you with my diary during my first stay at Kangwe. It is a catalogue of the collection of fish, &c., that I made, and a record of the continuous, never-failing kindness and help that I received from M. and Mme. Jacot, and of my attempts to learn from them the peculiarities of the region, the natives, and their language and customs, which they both know so well and manage so admirably. I daily saw there what it is possible to do, even in the wildest and most remote regions of West Africa, and recognised that there is still one heroic form of human being whose praise has never adequately been sung, namely, the missionary's wife.

Wishing to get higher up the Ogowé, I took the opportunity of the river boat of the Chargeurs RÈunis going up to the Njole on one of her trips, and joined her.

June 22nd.—*Éclaireur*, charming little stern wheel steamer, exquisitely kept. She has an upper and a lower deck. The lower deck for business, the upper deck for white passengers only. On the upper deck there is a fine long deck-house, running almost her whole length. In this are the officers' cabins, the saloon and the passengers' cabins (two), both large and beautifully fitted up. Captain Verdier exceedingly pleasant and constantly saying "N'est-ce pas?" A quiet and singularly clean engineer completes the white staff.

The passengers consist of Mr. Cockshut, going up river to see after the sub-factories; a French official bound for Franceville, which it will take him thirty-six days, go as quick as he can, in a canoe after Njole; a tremendously lively person who has had black water fever four times, while away in the bush with nothing to live on but manioc, a diet it would be far easier to die on under the circumstances. He is excellent company; though I do not know a word he says, he is perpetually giving lively and dramatic descriptions of things which I cannot but recognise. M. S—, with his pince-nez, the Doctor, and, above all, the rapids of the Ogowé, rolling his hands round and round each other and dashing them forward with a descriptive ejaculation of "Whish, flash, bum, bum, bump," and then comes what evidently represents a terrific fight for life against terrific odds. Wish to goodness I knew French, for wishing to see these rapids, I cannot help feeling anxious and worried at not fully understanding this dramatic entertainment regarding them. There is another passenger, said to be the engineer's brother, a quiet, gentlemanly man. Captain argues violently with every one; with Mr. Cockshut on the subject of the wicked waste of money in keeping the *Mové* and not shipping all goods by the *Éclaireur*, "N'est-ce pas?" and with the French official on goodness knows what, but I fancy it will be pistols for two and coffee for one in the morning time. When the captain feels himself being worsted in argument, he shouts for support to the engineer and his brother. "N'est-ce pas?" he says, turning furiously to them. "Oui, oui, certainement," they say dutifully and calmly, and then he, refreshed by their support, dashes back to his controversial fray. He even tries to get up a row with me on the subject of the English merchants at Calabar, whom he asserts have sworn a kind of blood oath to ship by none but British and African Company's steamers. I cannot stand this, for I know my esteemed and honoured friends the Calabar traders would ship by the *Flying Dutchman* or the Devil himself if either of them would take the stuff at 15s. the ton. We have, however, to leave off this row for want of language, to our mutual regret, for it would have been a love of a fight.

Soon after leaving Lembarene Island, we pass the mouth of the chief southern affluent of the Ogowé, the Ngunie; it flows in unostentatiously from the E.S.E., a broad, quiet river here with low banks and two islands (Walker's Islands) showing just off its entrance. Higher up, it flows through a mountainous country, and at Samba, its furthest navigable point, there is a wonderfully beautiful waterfall, the whole river coming down over a low cliff, surrounded by an amphitheatre of mountains. It takes the Éclaireur two days steaming from the mouth of the Ngunie to Samba, when she can get up; but now, in the height of the long dry season neither she nor the *Mové* can go because of the sandbanks; so Samba is cut off until next October. Hatton and Cookson have factories up at Samba, for it is an outlet for the trade of Achango land in rubber and ivory, a trade worked by the Akele tribe, a powerful, savage and difficult lot to deal with, and just in the same condition, as far as I can learn, as they were when Du Chaillu made his wonderful journeys among them. While I was at Lembarene, waiting for the *Éclaireur*, a notorious chief descended on a Ngunie sub-factory, and looted it. The wife of the black trading agent made a gallant resistance, her husband was away on a trading expedition, but the chief had her seized and beaten, and thrown into the river. An appeal was made to the Doctor then Administrator of the Ogowé, a powerful and helpful official, and he soon came up with the little cannonier, taking Mr. Cockshut with him and fully vindicated the honour of the French flag, under which all factories here are.

The banks of the Ogowé just above Lembarene Island are low; with the forest only broken by village clearings and seeming to press in on those, ready to absorb them should the inhabitants cease their war against it. The blue Ntyankâlâ mountains of Achango land show away to the E.S.E. in a range. Behind us, gradually sinking in the distance, is the high land on Lembarene Island.

Soon we run up alongside a big street of a village with four high houses rising a story above the rest, which are strictly ground floor; it has also five or six little low open thatched huts along the street in front. These may be fetish huts, or, as the captain of the *Sparrow* would say, "again they mayn't." For I have seen similar huts in the villages round Librevile, which were store places for roof mats, of which the natives carefully keep a store dry and ready for emergencies in the way of tornadoes, or to sell. We stop abreast of this village. Inhabitants in scores rush out and form an excited row along the vertical bank edge, several of the more excited individuals falling over it into the water.

Yells from our passengers on the lower deck. Yells from inhabitants on shore. Yells of *vite, vite* from the Captain. Dogs bark, horns bray, some exhilarated individual thumps the village drum, canoes fly out from the bank towards us. Fearful scrimmage heard going on all the time on the deck below. As soon as the canoes are alongside, our passengers from the lower deck, with their bundles and their dogs, pour over the side into them. Canoes rock wildly and wobble off rapidly towards the bank, frightening the passengers because they have got their best clothes on, and fear that the *Éclaireur* will start and upset them altogether with her wash.

On reaching the bank, the new arrivals disappear into brown clouds of wives and relations, and the dogs into fighting clusters of resident dogs. Happy, happy day! For those men who have gone ashore have been away on hire to the government and factories for a year, and are safe home in the bosoms of their families again, and not only they themselves, but all the goods they have got in pay. The remaining passengers below still yell to their departed friends; I know not what they say, but I expect it's the Fan equivalent for "Mind you write. Take care of yourself. Yes, I'll come and see you soon," &c. While this is going on, the *Éclaireur* quietly slides down river, with the current, broadside on as if she smelt her stable at Lembarene. This I find is her constant habit whenever the captain, the engineer, and the man at the wheel are all busy in a row along the rail, shouting overside, which occurs whenever we have passengers to land. Her iniquity being detected when the last canoe load has left for the shore, she is spun round and sent up river again at full speed.

We go on up stream; now and again stopping at little villages to land passengers or at little sub-factories to discharge cargo, until evening closes in, when we anchor and tie up at O'Saomokita, where there is a sub-factory of Messrs. Woermann's, in charge of which is a white man, the only white man between Lembarene and Njole. He comes on board and looks only a boy, but is really aged twenty. He is a Frenchman, and was at Hatton and Cookson's first, then he joined Woermann's, who have put him in charge of this place. The isolation for a white man must be terrible; sometimes two months will go by without his seeing another white face but that in his looking-glass, and when he does see another, it is only by a fleeting visit such as we now pay him, and to make the most of this, he stays on board to dinner.

June 23rd.—Start off steaming up river early in the morning time. Land ahead showing mountainous. Rather suddenly the banks grow higher. Here and there in the forest are patches which look like regular handmade plantations, which they are not, but only patches of egombie-gombie trees, showing that at this place was once a native town. Whenever land is cleared along here, this tree springs up all over the ground. It grows very rapidly, and has great leaves something like a sycamore leaf, only much larger. These leaves growing in a cluster at the top of the straight stem give an umbrella-like appearance to the affair; so the natives call them and an umbrella by the same name, but whether they think the umbrella is like the tree or the tree is like the umbrella, I can't make out. I am always getting myself mixed over this kind of thing in my attempts "to contemplate phenomena from a scientific standpoint," as Cambridge ordered me to do. I'll give the habit up.

"You can't do that sort of thing out here—It's the climate," and I will content myself with stating the fact, that when a native comes into a store and wants an umbrella, he asks for an egombie-gombie.

The uniformity of the height of the individual trees in one of these patches is striking, and it arises from their all starting fair. I cannot make out other things about them to my satisfaction, for you very rarely see one of them in the wild bush, and then it does not bear a fruit that the natives collect and use, and then chuck away the stones round their domicile. Anyhow, there they are all one height, and all one colour, and apparently allowing no other vegetation to make any headway among them. But I found when I carefully investigated egombie-gombie patches that there were a few of the great, slower-growing forest trees coming up amongst them, and in time when these attain a sufficient height, their shade kills off the egombie-gombie, and the patch goes back into the great forest from which it came. The frequency of these patches arises from the nomadic habits of the chief tribe in these regions, the Fans. They rarely occupy one village site for any considerable time on account—firstly, of their wasteful method of collecting rubber by cutting down the vine, which soon stamps it out of a district; and secondly, from their quarrelsome ways. So when a village of Fans has cleared all the rubber out of its district, or has made the said district too hot to hold it by rows with other villages, or has got itself very properly shelled out and burnt for some attack on traders or the French flag in any form, its inhabitants clear off into another district, and build another village; for bark and palm thatch are cheap, and house removing just nothing; when you are an unsophisticated cannibal Fan you don't require a pantechnicon van to stow away your one or two mushroom-shaped stools, knives, and cooking-pots, and a calabash or so. If you are rich, maybe you will have a box with clothes in as well, but as a general rule all your clothes are on your back. So your wives just pick up the stools and the knives and the cooking-pots, and the box, and the children toddle off with the calabashes. You have, of course, the gun to carry, for sleeping or waking a Fan never parts with his gun, and so there you are "finish," as M. Pichault would say, and before your new bark house is up, there grows the egombie-gombie, where your house once stood. Now and again, for lack of immediate neighbouring villages to quarrel with, one end of a village will quarrel with the other end. The weaker end then goes off and builds itself another village, keeping an eye lifting for any member of the stronger end who may come conveniently into its neighbourhood to be killed and eaten. Meanwhile, the egombie-gombie grows over the houses of the empty end, pretending it's a plantation belonging to the remaining half. I once heard a new-comer hold forth eloquently as to how those Fans were maligned. "They say," said he, with a fine wave of his arm towards such a patch, "that these people do not till the soil—that they are not industrious—that the few plantations they do make are ill-kept—that they are only a set of wander-ing hunters and cannibals. Look there at those magnificent plantations!" I did look, but I did not alter my opinion of the Fans, for I know my old friend egombie-gombie when I see him.

This morning the French official seems sad and melancholy. I fancy he has got a Monday head (Kipling), but he revives as the day goes on. As we go on, the banks become hills and the broad river, which has been showing sheets of sandbanks in all directions, now narrows and shows only neat little beaches of white sand in shallow places along the bank. The current is terrific. The *Éclaireur* breathes hard, and has all she can do to fight her way up against it. Masses of black weathered rock in great boulders show along the exposed parts of both banks, left dry by the falling waters. Each bank is steep, and quantities of great trees, naked and bare, are hanging down from them, held by their roots and bush-rope entanglement from being swept away with the rushing current, and they make a great white fringe to the banks. The hills become higher and higher, and more and more abrupt, and the river runs between them in a gloomy ravine, winding to and fro; we catch sight of a patch of white sand ahead, which I mistake for a white painted house, but immediate-ly after doubling round a bend we see the houses of the Talagouga Mission Station. The *Éclaireur* forthwith has an hysteric fit on her whis-tle, so as to frighten M. Forget and get him to dash off in his canoe to her at once. Apparently he knows her, and does not hurry, but comes on board quietly. I find there will be no place for me to stay at Njole, so I decide to go on in the *Éclaireur* and use her as an hotel while there, and then return and stay with Mme. Forget if she will have me. I consult M. Forget on this point. He says, "Oh, yes," but seems to have lost some-thing of great value recently, and not to be quite clear where. Only man-ner, I suppose. When M. Forget has got his mails he goes, and the *Éclaireur* goes on; indeed, she has never really stopped, for the water is too deep to anchor in here, and the terrific current would promptly whisk the steamer down out of Talagouga gorge were she to leave off fighting it. We run on up past Talagouga Island, where the river broadens out again a little, but not much, and reach Njole by nightfall, and tie up to a tree by Dumas factory beach. Usual uproar, but as Mr. Cockshut says, no mosquitoes. The mosquito belt ends abruptly at O'Soamokita.

Next morning I go ashore and start on a walk. Lovely road, bright yellow clay, as hard as paving stone. On each side it is most neatly hedged with pine-apples; behind these, carefully tended, acres of coffee bushes planted in long rows. Certainly coffee is one of the most lovely of crops. Its grandly shaped leaves are like those of our medlar tree, only darker and richer green, the berries set close to the stem, those that are ripe, a rich crimson; these trees, I think, are about three years old, and just coming into bearing; for they are covered with full-sized berries, and there has been a flush of bloom on them this morning, and the delicious fragrance of their stephanotis-shaped and scented flowers lingers in the air. The country spreads before me a lovely valley encompassed by purple-blue mountains. Mount Talagouga looks splendid in a soft, infinitely deep blue, although it is quite close, just the other side of the river. The road goes on into the valley, as pleasantly as ever and more so. How pleasant it would be now, if our government along the Coast had the enterprise and public spirit of the French, and made such roads just on the remote chance of stray travellers dropping in on a steamer once in ten years or so and wanting a walk. Observe extremely neatly Igalwa built huts, people sitting on the bright clean ground outside them, making mats and baskets. "Mboloani," say I. "Ai! Mbolo," say they, and knock off work to stare. Observe large wired-in enclosures on left-hand side of road—investigate—find they are tenanted by animals—goats, sheep, chickens, &c. Clearly this is a *jardin d'acclimatation*. No wonder the colony does not pay, if it goes in for this sort of thing, 206 miles inland, with simply no public to pay gate-money. While contemplating these things, hear awful hiss. Serpents! No, geese. Awful fight. Grand things, good, old-fashioned, long skirts are for Africa! Get through geese and advance in good order, but somewhat rapidly down road, turn sharply round corner of native houses. Turkey cock—terrific turn up. Flight on my part forwards down road, which is still going strong, now in a northerly direction, apparently indefinitely. Hope to goodness there will be a turning that I can go down and get back by, without returning through this ferocious farmyard. Intent on picking up such an outlet, I go thirty yards or so down the road. Hear shouts coming from a clump

of bananas on my left. Know they are directed at me, but it does not do
to attend to shouts always. Expect it is only some native with an awful
knowledge of English, anxious to get up my family history—therefore
accelerate pace. More shouts, and louder, of "Madame Gacon! Madame
Gacon!" and out of the banana clump comes a big, plump, pleasant-
looking gentleman, clad in a singlet and a divided skirt. White people
must be attended to, so advance carefully towards him through a plantation of young coffee, apologising humbly for intruding on his domain.
He smiles and bows beautifully, but—horror!—he knows no English, I no
French. Situation *très inexplicable et très interessante,* as I subsequently heard him
remark; and the worst of it is he is evidently bursting to know who I am,
and what I am doing in the middle of his coffee plantation, for his it
clearly is, as appears from his obsequious bodyguard of blacks, highly
interested in me also. We gaze at each other, and smile some more, but
stiffly, and he stands bareheaded in the sun in an awful way. It's murder
I'm committing, hard all! He, as is fitting for his superior sex, displays
intelligence first and says, "Interpreter," waving his hand to the south. I
say "Yes," in my best Fan, an enthusiastic, intelligent grunt which any one
must understand. He leads the way back towards those geese—perhaps, by
the by, that is why he wears those divided skirts—and we enter a beautifully
neatly built bamboo house, and sit down opposite to each other at a table
and wait for the interpreter who is being fetched. The house is low on the
ground and of native construction, but most beautifully kept, and
arranged with an air of artistic feeling quite as unexpected as the rest of
my surroundings. I notice upon the walls sets of pictures of terrific
incidents in Algerian campaigns, and a copy of that superb head of M. de
Brazza in Arab headgear. Soon the black minions who have been sent to
find one of the plantation hands who is supposed to know French and
English, return with the "interpreter." That young man is a fraud. He
does not know English—not even coast English—and all he has got under
his precious wool is an abysmal ignorance darkened by terror; and so,
after one or two futile attempts and some frantic scratching at both those
regions which an African seems to regard as the seats of intellectual
inspiration, he bolts out of the door. *Situation terrible!* My host and I smile
wildly at each other, and both wonder in our respective languages what,
in the words of Mr. Squeers as mentioned in the classics—we "shall do
in this 'ere most awful go." We are both going mad with the strain of the
situation, when in walks the engineer's brother from the *Éclaireur.* He

seems intensely surprised to find me sitting in his friend the planter's parlour after my grim and retiring conduct on the ...claireur on my voyage up. But the planter tells him all, sousing him in torrents of words, full of the violence of an outbreak of pent-up emotion. I do not understand what he says, but I catch "*très inexplicable*" and things like that. The calm brother of the engineer sits down at the table, and I am sure tells the planter something like this: "Calm yourself, my friend, we picked up this curiosity at Lembarene. It seems quite harmless." And then the planter calmed, and mopped a perspiring brow, and so did I, and we smiled more freely, feeling the mental atmosphere had become less tense and cooler. We both simply beamed on our deliverer, and the planter gave him lots of things to drink. I had nothing about me except a head of tobacco in my pocket, which I did not feel was a suitable offering. Now the engineer's brother, although he would not own to it, knew English, so I told him how the beauty of the road had lured me on, and how I was interested in coffee-planting, and how much I admired the magnificence of this plantation, and all the enterprise it represented.

"*Oui, oui, certainement,*" said he, and translated. My friend the planter seemed charmed; it was the first sign of anything approaching reason he had seen in me. He wanted me to have *eau sucrée* more kindly than ever, and when I rose, intending to bow myself off and go, geese or no geese, back to the *Éclaireur*, he would not let me go. I must see the plantation, *toute la plantation*. So presently all three of us go out and thoroughly do the plantation, the most well-ordered, well-cultivated plantation I have ever seen, and a very noble monument to the knowledge and industry of the planter. For two hot hours these two perfect gentlemen showed me over it. I also behaved well, for petticoats, great as they are, do not prevent insects and catawumpuses of sorts walking up one's ankles and feeding on one as one stands on the long grass which has been most wisely cut and laid round the young trees for mulching. This plantation is of great extent on the hill-sides and in the valley bottom, portions of it are just coming into bearing. The whole is kept as perfectly as a garden, amazing as the work of one white man with only a staff of unskilled native labourers—at present only eighty of them. The coffee planted is of three kinds, the Elephant berry, the Arabian, and the San Thomé. During our inspection, we only had one serious misunderstanding, which arose from my seeing for the first time in my life tree-ferns growing in the Ogowé. There were three of them, evidently carefully taken care of, among some coffee plants. It was highly exciting, and I tried to find out about them. It seemed, even in this centre of enterprise, unlikely that they had been brought just "for dandy" from the Australasian region, and I had never yet come across them in my wanderings save on Fernando Po. Unfortunately, my friends thought I wanted them to keep, and shouted for men to bring things and dig them up; so I had a brisk little engagement with the men, driving them from their prey with the point of my umbrella, ejaculating Kor Kor, like an agitated crow. When at last they understood that my interest in the ferns was scientific, not piratical, they called the men off and explained that the ferns had been found among the bush, when it was being cleared for the plantation.

Ultimately, with many bows and most sincere thanks from me, we parted, providentially beyond the geese, and I returned down the road to Njole, where I find Mr. Cockshut waiting outside his factory. He insists on taking me to the Post to see the Administrator, and from there he says I can go on to the *Éclaireur* from the Post beach, as she will be up there from Dumas'. Off we go up the road which skirts the river bank, a dwarf clay cliff, overgrown with vegetation, save where it is cleared for beaches. The road is short, but exceedingly pretty; on the other side from the river is a steep bank on which is growing a plantation of cacao. Lying out in the centre of the river you see Njole Island, a low, sandy one, timbered not only with bush, but with orange and other fruit trees; for formerly the Post and factories used to be situated on the island—now only their trees remain for various reasons, one being that in the wet season it is a good deal under water. Everything is now situated on the mainland north bank, in a straggling but picturesque line; first comes Woermann's factory, then Hatton and Cookson's, and John Holt's, close together with a beach in common in a sweetly amicable style for factories, who as a rule firmly stockade themselves off from their next door neighbours. Then Dumas' beach, a little native village, the cacao patch and the Post at the up river end of things European, an end of things European, I am told, for a matter of 500 miles. Immediately beyond the Post is a little river falling into the Ogowé, and on its further bank a small village belonging to a chief, who, hearing of the glories of the Government, came down like the Queen of Sheba—in intention, I mean, not personal appearance—to see it, and so charmed has he been that here he stays to gaze on it.

Although Mr. Cockshut hunted the Administrator of the Ogowé out of his bath, that gentleman is exceedingly amiable and charming, all the more so to me for speaking good English. Personally, he is big, handsome, exuberant, and energetic. He shows me round with a gracious enthusiasm, all manner of things—big gorilla teeth and heads, native spears and brass-nail-ornamented guns; and explains, while we are in his study, that the little model canoe full of Kola nuts is the supply of Kola to enable him to sit up all night and work. Then he takes us outside to see the new hospital which he, in his capacity as Administrator, during the absence of the professional Administrator on leave in France, has granted to himself in his capacity as Doctor; and he shows us the captive chief and headmen from Samba busily quarrying a clay cliff behind it so as to enlarge the governmental plateau, and the ex-ministers of the ex-King of Dahomey, who are deported to Njole, and apparently comfortable and employed in various non-menial occupations. Then we go down the little avenue of cacao trees in full bearing, and away to the left to where there is now an encampment of Adoomas, who have come down as a convoy from Franceville, and are going back with another under the command of our vivacious fellow passenger, who, I grieve to see, will have a rough time of it in the way of accommodation in those narrow, shallow canoes which are lying with their noses tied to the bank, and no other white man to talk to. What a blessing he will be conversationally to Franceville when he gets in. The Adooma encampment is very picturesque, for they have got their bright-coloured chintz mosquito-bars erected as tents.

Dr. Pélessier then insists on banging down monkey bread-fruit with a stick, to show me their inside. Of course they burst over his beautiful white clothes. I said they would, but men will be men. Then we go and stand under the two lovely odeaka trees that make a triumphal-arch-like gateway to the Post's beach from the river, and the Doctor discourses in a most interesting way on all sorts of subjects. We go on waiting for the *Éclaireur*, who, although it is past four o'clock, is still down at Dumas' beach. I feel nearly frantic at detaining the Doctor, but neither he nor Mr. Cockshut seem in the least hurry. But at last I can stand it no longer. The vision of the Administrator of the Ogowé, worn out, but chewing Kola nut to keep himself awake all night while he finishes his papers to go down on the *Éclaireur* tomorrow morning, is too painful; so I say I will walk back to Dumas' and go on the *Éclaireur* there, and try to liberate the Administrator from his present engagements, so that he may go back and work. No good! He will come down to Dumas' with Mr. Cockshut and me. Off we go, and just exactly as we are getting on to Dumas' beach, off starts the *Éclaireur* with a shriek for the Post beach. So I say good-bye to Mr. Cockshut, and go back to the Post with Dr. Pélessier, and he sees me on board, and to my immense relief he stays on board a good hour and a half, talking to other people, so it is not on my head if he is up all night.

June 25th.—*Éclaireur* has to wait for the Administrator until ten, because he has not done his mails. At ten he comes on board like an amiable tornado, for he himself is going to Cape Lopez. I am grieved to see them carrying on board, too, a French official very ill with fever. He is the engineer of the canoniere and they are taking him down to Cape Lopez, where they hope to get a ship to take him up to Gaboon, and to the hospital on the MinervÈ. I heard subsequently that the poor fellow died about forty hours after leaving Njole at Achyouka in Kama country.

We get away at last, and run rapidly down river, helped by the terrific current. The *Éclaireur* has to call at Talagouga for planks from M. Gacon's sawmill. As soon as we are past the tail of Talagouga Island, the *Éclaireur* ties her whistle string to a stanchion, and goes off into a series of screaming fits, as only she can. What she wants is to get M. Forget or M. Gacon, or better still both, out in their canoes with the wood waiting for her, because "she cannot anchor in the depth," "nor can she turn round," and "backing plays the mischief with any ship's engines," and "she can't hold her own against the current," and—then Captain Verdier says things I won't repeat, and throws his weight passionately on the whistle string, for we are in sight of the narrow gorge of Talagouga, with the Mission Station apparently slumbering in the sun. This puts the *Éclaireur* in an awful temper. She goes down towards it as near as she dare, and then frisks round again, and runs up river a little way and drops down again, in violent hysterics the whole time. Soon M. Gacon comes along among the trees on the bank, and laughs at her. A rope is thrown to him, and the panting *Éclaireur* tied up to a tree close in to the bank, for the water is deep enough here to moor a liner in, only there are a good many rocks. In a few minutes M. Forget and several canoe loads of beautiful red-brown mahogany planks are on board, and things being finished, I say good-bye to the captain, and go off with M. Forget in a canoe, to the shore.

CHAPTER 5

The Rapids of the Ogowé

*The Log of an Adooma canoe during a voyage undertaken to the rapids
of the River Ogowé, with some account of the divers disasters that befell thereon.*

MME. FORGET RECEIVED ME MOST KINDLY, and, thanks to her ever
thoughtful hospitality, I spent a very pleasant time at Talagouga, wandering about the forest and collecting fishes from the native fishermen:
and seeing the strange forms of some of these Talagouga region fishes
and the marked difference between them and those of Lembarene, I set
my heart on going up into the region of the Ogowé rapids. For some
time no one whom I could get hold of regarded it as a feasible scheme,
but, at last, M. Gacon thought it might be managed; I said I would give
a reward of 100 francs to any one who would lend me a canoe and a
crew, and I would pay the working expenses, food, wages, &c. M.
Gacon had a good canoe and could spare me two English-speaking
Igalwas, one of whom had been part of the way with MM. Allégret and
Teisserès, when they made their journey up to Franceville and then
across to Brazzaville and down the Congo two years ago. He also
thought we could get six Fans to complete the crew. I was delighted,
packed my small portmanteau with a few things, got some trade goods,
wound up my watch, ascertained the date of the day of the month, and
borrowed three hairpins from Mme. Forget, then down came disap-
pointment. On my return from the bush that evening, Mme. Forget

said M. Gacon said "it was impossible," the Fans round Talagouga wouldn't go at any price above Njole, because they were certain they would be killed and eaten by the up-river Fans. Internally consigning the entire tribe to regions where they will get a rise in temperature, even on this climate, I went with Mme. Forget to M. Gacon, and we talked it over; finally M. Gacon thought he could let me have two more Igalwas from Hatton and Cookson's beach across the river. Sending across there we found this could be done, so I now felt I was in for it, and screwed my courage to the sticking point—no easy matter after all the information I had got into my mind regarding the rapids of the River Ogowé.

I establish myself on my portmanteau comfortably in the canoe, my back is against the trade box, and behind that is the usual mound of pillows, sleeping mats, and mosquito-bars of the Igalwa crew; the whole surmounted by the French flag flying from an indifferent stick.

M. and Mme. Forget provide me with everything I can possibly require, and say that the blood of half my crew is half alcohol; on the whole it is patent they don't expect to see me again, and I forgive them, because they don't seem cheerful over it; but still it is not reassuring—nothing is about this affair, and it's going to rain. It does, as we go up the river to Njole, where there is another risk of the affair collapsing, by the French authorities declining to allow me to proceed. On we paddled, M'bo the head man standing in the bows of the canoe in front of me, to steer, then I, then the baggage, then the able-bodied seamen, including the cook also standing and paddling; and at the other extremity of the canoe—it grieves me to speak of it in this unseamanlike way, but in these canoes both ends are alike, and chance alone ordains which is bow and which is stern—stands Pierre, the first officer, also steering; the paddles used are all of the long-handled, leaf-shaped Igalwa type. We get up just past Talagouga Island and then tie up against the bank of M. Gazenget's plantation, and make a piratical raid on its bush for poles. A gang of his men come down to us, but only to chat. One of them, I notice, has had something happen severely to one side of his face. I ask M'bo what's the matter, and he answers, with a derisive laugh, "He be fool man, he go for tief plantain and done got shot." M'bo does not make it clear where the sin in this affair is exactly located; I expect it is in being "fool man." Having got our supply of long stout poles we push off and paddle on again. Before we reach Njole I recognise my crew have got the grumbles, and at once inquire into the reason. M'bo sadly informs me that "they no got chop," having been provided only with plantain, and no meat or fish to eat with it. I promise to get them plenty at Njole, and contentment settles on the crew, and they sing. After about three hours we reach Njole, and I proceed to interview the authorities. Dr. Pélessier is away down river, and the two gentlemen in charge don't understand English; but Pierre translates, and the letter which M. Forget has kindly written for me explains things and so the palaver ends satisfactorily, after a long talk. First, the official says he does not like to take the responsibility of allowing me to endanger myself in those rapids. I explain I will not hold any one responsible but myself, and I urge that a lady has been up before, a Mme. Quinee. He says "Yes, that is true, but Madame had with her a husband and many men, whereas I am alone and have only eight Igalwas and not Adoomas, the proper crew for the rapids, and they are away up river now with the convoy." "True, oh King!" I answer, "but Madame Quinee went right up to Lestourville, whereas I only want to go sufficiently high up the rapids to get typical fish. And these Igalwas are great men at canoe work, and can go in a canoe anywhere that any mortal man can go"—this to cheer up my Igalwa interpreter—"and as for the husband, neither the Royal Geographical Society's list, in their 'Hints to Travellers,' nor Messrs. Silver, in their elaborate lists of articles necessary for a traveller in tropical climates, make mention of husbands." However, the official ultimately says Yes, I may go, and parts with me as with one bent on self-destruction. This affair being settled I start off, like an old hen with a brood of chickens to provide for, to get chop for my men, and go first to Hatton and Cookson's factory. I find its white Agent is down river after stores, and John Holt's Agent says he has got no beef nor fish, and is precious short of provisions for himself; so I go back to Dumas', where I find a most amiable French gentleman, who says he will let me have as much fish or beef as I want, and to this supply he adds some delightful bread biscuits. M'bo and the crew beam with satisfaction; mine is clouded by finding, when they have carried off the booty to the canoe, that the Frenchman will not let me pay for it. Therefore taking the opportunity of his back being turned for a few minutes, I buy and pay for, across the store counter, some trade things, knives, cloth, &c. Then I say good-bye to the Agent. "Adieu, Mademoiselle," says he in a for-ever tone of voice. Indeed I am sure I have caught from these kind people a very pretty and becoming mournful manner, and there's not another white station for 500 miles where I can show it off. Away we go, still damp from the rain we have come through, but drying nicely with the day, and cheerful about the chop.

The Ogowé is broad at Njole and its banks not mountainous, as at Talagouga; but as we go on it soon narrows, the current runs more rapidly than ever, and we are soon again surrounded by the mountain range. Great masses of black rock show among the trees on the hillsides, and under the fringe of fallen trees that hang from the steep banks. Two hours after leaving Njole we are facing our first rapid. Great gray-black masses of smoothed rock rise up out of the whirling water in all directions. These rocks have a peculiar appearance which puzzle me at the time, but in subsequently getting used to it I accepted it quietly and admired. When the sun shines on them they have a soft light blue haze round them, like a halo. The effect produced by this, with the forested hillsides and the little beaches of glistening white sand was one of the most perfect things I have ever seen.

We kept along close to the right-hand bank, dodging out of the way of the swiftest current as much as possible. Ever and again we were unable to force our way round projecting parts of the bank, so we then got up just as far as we could to the point in question, yelling and shouting at the tops of our voices. M'bo said "Jump for bank, sar," and I "up and jumped," followed by half the crew. Such banks! sheets, and walls, and rubbish heaps of rock, mixed up with trees fallen and standing. One appalling corner I shall not forget, for I had to jump at a rock wall, and hang on to it in a manner more befitting an insect than an insect-hunter, and then scramble up it into a close-set forest, heavily burdened with boulders of all sizes. I wonder whether the rocks or the trees were there first? there is evidence both ways, for in one place you will see a rock on the top of a tree, the tree creeping out from underneath it, and in another place you will see a tree on the top of a rock, clasping it with a network of roots and getting its nourishment, goodness knows how, for these are by no means tender, digestible sandstones, but uncommon hard gneiss and quartz which has no idea of breaking up into friable small stuff, and which only takes on a high polish when it is vigorously sanded and canvassed by the Ogowé. While I was engaged in climbing across these promontories, the crew would be busy shouting and hauling the canoe round the point by means of the strong chain provided for such emergencies fixed on to the bow. When this was done, in we got again and paddled away until we met our next affliction.

M'bo had advised that we should spend our first night at the same village that M. Allégret did: but when we reached it, a large village on the north bank, we seemed to have a lot of daylight still in hand, and thought it would be better to stay at one a little higher up, so as to make a shorter day's work for to-morrow, when we wanted to reach Kondo Kondo; so we went against the bank just to ask about the situation and character of the up-river villages. The row of low, bark huts was long, and extended its main frontage close to the edge of the river bank. The inhabitants had been watching us as we came, and when they saw we intended calling that afternoon, they charged down to the river-edge hopeful of excitement. They had a great deal to say, and so had we. After compliments, as they say, in excerpts of diplomatic communication, three of their men took charge of the conversation on their side, and M'bo did ours. To M'bo's questions they gave a dramatic entertainment as answer, after the manner of these brisk, excitable Fans. One chief, however, soon settled down to definite details, prefacing his remarks with the silence-commanding "Azuna. Azuna!" and his companions grunted approbation of his observations. He took a piece of plantain leaf and tore it up into five different-sized bits. These he laid along the edge of our canoe at different intervals of space, while he told M'bo things, mainly scandalous, about the characters of the villages these bits of leaf represented, save of course about bit A, which represented his own. The interval between the bits was proportional to the interval between the villages, and the size of the bits was proportional to the size of the village. Village number four was the only one he should recommend our going to. When all was said, I gave our kindly informants some heads of tobacco and many thanks. Then M'bo sang them a hymn, with the assistance of Pierre, half a line behind him in a different key, but every bit as flat. The Fans seemed impressed, but any crowd would be by the hymn-singing of my crew, unless they were inmates of deaf and dumb asylums. Then we took our farewell, and thanked the village elaborately for its kind invitation to spend the night there on our way home, shoved off and paddled away in great style just to show those Fans what Igalwas could do.

We hadn't gone 200 yards before we met a current coming round the end of a rock reef that was too strong for us to hold our own in, let alone progress. On to the bank I was ordered and went; it was a low slip of rugged confused boulders and fragments of rocks, carelessly arranged, and evidently under water in the wet season. I scrambled along, the men yelled and shouted, and hauled the canoe, and the inhabitants of the village, seeing we were becoming amusing again, came, legging it like lamp-lighters, after us, young and old, male and female, to say nothing of the dogs. Some good souls helped the men haul, while I did my best to amuse the others by diving headlong from a large rock on to which I had elaborately climbed, into a thick clump of willow-leaved shrubs. They applauded my performance vociferously, and then assisted my efforts to extricate myself, and during the rest of my scramble they kept close to me, with keen competition for the front row, in hopes that I would do something like it again. But I refused the *encore*, because, bashful as I am, I could not but feel that my last performance was carried out with all the superb reckless *abandon* of a Sarah Bernhardt, and a display of art of this order should satisfy any African village for a year at least. At last I got across the rocks on to a lovely little beach of white sand, and stood there talking, surrounded by my audience, until the canoe got over its difficulties and arrived almost as scratched as I; and then we again said farewell and paddled away, to the great grief of the natives, for they don't get a circus up above Njole every week, poor dears.

Now there is no doubt that that chief's plantain-leaf chart was an ingenious idea and a credit to him. There is also no doubt that the Fan mile is a bit Irish, a matter of nine or so of those of ordinary mortals, but I am bound to say I don't think, even allowing for this, that he put those pieces far enough apart. On we paddled a long way before we picked up village number one, mentioned in that chart. On again, still longer, till we came to village number two. Village number three hove in sight high up on a mountain side soon after, but it was getting dark and the water worse, and the hill-sides growing higher and higher into nobly shaped mountains, forming, with their forest-graced steep sides, a ravine that, in the gathering gloom, looked like an alley-way made of iron, for the foaming Ogowé. Village number four we anxiously looked for; village number four we never saw; for round us came the dark, seeming to come out on to the river from the forests and the side ravines, where for some hours we had seen it sleeping, like a sailor with his clothes on in bad weather. On we paddled, looking for signs of village fires, and seeing them not. The *Erd-geist* knew we wanted something, and seeing how we personally lacked it, thought it was beauty; and being in a kindly mood, gave it us, sending the lovely lingering flushes of his afterglow across the sky, which, dying, left it that divine deep purple velvet which no one has dared to paint. Out in it came the great stars blazing high above us, and the dark round us was be-gemmed with fireflies: but we were not as satisfied with these things as we should have been; what we wanted were fires to cook by and dry ourselves by, and all that sort of thing. The *Erd-geist* did not understand, and so left us when the afterglow had died away, with only enough starlight to see the flying foam of the rapids ahead and around us, and not enough to see the great trees that had fallen from the bank into the water. These, when the rapids were not too noisy, we could listen for, because the black current rushes through their branches with an impatient "lish, swish"; but when there was a rapid roaring close alongside we ran into those trees, and got ourselves mauled, and had ticklish times getting on our course again. Now and again we ran up against great rocks sticking up in the black water—grim, isolated fellows, who seemed to be standing silently watching their fellow rocks noisily fighting in the arena of the white water. Still on we poled and paddled. About 8 p.m. we came to a corner, a bad one; but we were unable to leap on to the bank and haul round, not being able to see either the details or the exact position of the said bank, and we felt, I think naturally, disinclined to spring in the direction of such bits of country as we had had experience of during the afternoon, with nothing but the aid we might have got from a compass hastily viewed by the transitory light of a lucifer match, and even this would not have informed us how many tens of feet of tree fringe lay between us and the land, so we did not attempt it. One must be careful at times, or nasty accidents may follow. We fought our way round that corner, yelling defiance at the water, and dealt with succeeding corners on the *vi et armis* plan, breaking, ever and anon, a pole. About 9.30 we got into a savage rapid. We fought it inch by inch. The canoe jammed herself on some barely sunken rocks in it. We shoved her off over them. She tilted over and chucked us out. The rocks round being just awash, we survived and got her straight again, and got into her and drove her unmercifully; she struck again and bucked like a broncho, and we fell in heaps upon each other, but stayed inside that time—the men by the aid of their intelligent feet, I by clinching my hands into the bush rope lacing which ran round

the rim of the canoe and the meaning of which I did not understand
when I left Talagouga. We sorted ourselves out hastily and sent her at
it again. Smash went a sorely tried pole and a paddle. Round and
round we spun in an exultant whirlpool, which, in a light-hearted,
maliciously joking way, hurled us tail first out of it into the current.
Now the grand point in these canoes of having both ends alike
declared itself; for at this juncture all we had to do was to revolve on
our own axis and commence life anew with what had been the bow for
the stern. Of course we were defeated, we could not go up any further without the aid of our lost poles and paddles, so we had to go
down for shelter somewhere, anywhere, and down at a terrific pace
in the white water we went. While hitched among the rocks the
arrangement of our crew had been altered, Pierre joining M'bo in
the bows; this piece of precaution was frustrated by our getting
turned round; so our position was what you might call precarious,
until we got into another whirlpool, when we persuaded Nature to
start us right end on. This was only a matter of minutes, whirlpools
being plentiful, and then M'bo and Pierre, provided with our surviving poles, stood in the bows to fend us off rocks, as we shot towards
them; while we midship paddles sat, helping to steer, and when occasion arose, which occasion did with lightning rapidity, to whack the
whirlpools with the flat of our paddles, to break their force. Cook
crouched in the stern concentrating his mind on steering only. A
most excellent arrangement in theory and the safest practical one no
doubt, but it did not work out what you might call brilliantly well;
though each department did its best. We dashed full tilt towards high
rocks, things twenty to fifty feet above water. Midship backed and
flapped like fury; M'bo and Pierre received the shock on their poles;
sometimes we glanced successfully aside and flew on; sometimes we
didn't. The shock being too much for M'bo and Pierre they were
driven back on me, who got flattened on to the cargo of bundles
which, being now firmly tied in, couldn't spread the confusion further aft; but the shock of the canoe's nose against the rock did so in
style, and the rest of the crew fell forward on to the bundles, me, and
themselves. So shaken up together were we several times that night,
that it's a wonder to me, considering the hurry, that we sorted ourselves
out correctly with our own particular legs and arms. And although we
in the middle of the canoe did some very spirited flapping,

our whirlpool-breaking was no more successful than M'bo and Pierre's fending off, and many a wild waltz we danced that night with the waters of the River Ogowé.

Unpleasant as going through the rapids was, when circumstances took us into the black current we fared no better. For good all-round inconvenience, give me going full tilt in the dark into the branches of a fallen tree at the pace we were going then—and crash, swish, crackle and there you are, hung up, with a bough pressing against your chest, and your hair being torn out and your clothes ribboned by others, while the wicked river is trying to drag away the canoe from under you. After a good hour and more of these experiences, we went hard on to a large black reef of rocks. So firm was the canoe wedged that we in our rather worn-out state couldn't move her so we wisely decided to "lef 'em" and see what could be done towards getting food and a fire for the remainder of the night. Our eyes, now trained to the darkness, observed pretty close to us a big lump of land, looming up out of the river. This we subsequently found out was Kembe Island. The rocks and foam on either side stretched away into the darkness, and high above us against the star-lit sky stood out clearly the summits of the mountains of the Sierra del Cristal.

The most interesting question to us now was whether this rock reef communicated sufficiently with the island for us to get to it. Abandoning conjecture; tying very firmly our canoe up to the rocks, a thing that seemed, considering she was jammed hard and immovable, a little unnecessary—but you can never be sufficiently careful in this manner with any kind of boat—off we started among the rock boulders. I would climb up on to a rock table, fall off it on the other side on to rocks again, with more or less water on them—then get a patch of singing sand under my feet, then with varying suddenness get into more water, deep or shallow, broad or narrow pools among the rocks; out of that over more rocks, &c., &c., &c.: my companions, from their noises, evidently were going in for the same kind of thing, but we were quite cheerful, because the probability of reaching the land seemed increasing. Most of us arrived into deep channels of water which here and there cut in between this rock reef and the bank, M'bo was the first to find the way into certainty; he was, and I hope still is, a perfect wonder at this sort of work. I kept close to M'bo, and when we got to the shore, the rest of the wanderers being collected, we said "chances are there's a village round

here"; and started to find it. After a gay time in a rock-encumbered forest, growing in a tangled, matted way on a rough hillside, at an angle of
45 degrees, M'bo sighted the gleam of fires through the tree stems away
to the left, and we bore down on it, listening to its drum. Viewed
through the bars of the tree stems the scene was very picturesque. The
village was just a collection of palm mat-built huts, very low and squalid.
In its tiny street, an affair of some sixty feet long and twenty wide, were
a succession of small fires. The villagers themselves, however, were the
striking features in the picture. They were painted vermilion all over
their nearly naked bodies, and were dancing enthusiastically to the good
old rump-a-tump-tump-tump tune, played energetically by an old
gentleman on a long, high-standing, white-and-black painted drum.
They said that as they had been dancing when we arrived they had failed
to hear us. M'bo secured a—well, I don't exactly know what to call it—for
my use. It was, I fancy, the remains of the village club-house. It had a
certain amount of palm-thatch roof and some of its left-hand side left,
the rest of the structure was bare old poles with filaments of palm mat
hanging from them here and there; and really if it hadn't been for the
roof one wouldn't have known whether one was inside or outside it. The
floor was trodden earth and in the middle of it a heap of white ash and
the usual two bush lights, laid down with their burning ends propped up
off the ground with stones, and emitting, as is their wont, a rather
mawkish, but not altogether unpleasant smell, and volumes of smoke
which finds its way out through the thatch, leaving on the inside of it a
rich oily varnish of a bright warm brown colour. They give a very good
light, provided some one keeps an eye on them and knocks the ash off
the end as it burns gray; the bush lights' idea of being snuffed. Against
one of the open-work sides hung a drum covered with raw hide, and a
long hollow bit of tree trunk, which served as a cupboard for a few small
articles. I gathered in all these details as I sat on one of the hard wood
benches, waiting for my dinner, which Isaac was preparing outside in the
street. The atmosphere of the hut, in spite of its remarkable advantages
in the way of ventilation, was oppressive, for the smell of the bush lights,
my wet clothes, and the natives who crowded into the hut to look at me,
made anything but a pleasant combination. The people were evidently
exceedingly poor; clothes they had very little of. The two head men had
on old French military coats in rags; but they were quite satisfied with
their appearance, and evidently felt through them in touch with

European culture, for they lectured to the others on the habits and customs of the white man with great self-confidence and superiority. The
majority of the village had a slight acquaintance already with this interesting animal, being, I found, Adoomas. They had made a settlement
on Kembe Island some two years or so ago. Then the Fans came and
attacked them, and killed and ate several. The Adoomas left and fled to
the French authority at Njole and remained under its guarding shadow
until the French came up and chastised the Fans and burnt their village;
and the Adoomas—when things had quieted down again and the Fans
had gone off to build themselves a new village for their burnt one—came
back to Kembe Island and their plantain patch. They had only done this
a few months before my arrival and had not had time to rebuild, hence
the dilapidated state of the village. They are, I am told, a Congo region
tribe, whose country lies south-west of Franceville, and, as I have already
said, are the tribe used by the French authorities to take convoys up and
down the Ogowé to Franceville, more to keep this route open than for
transport purposes; the rapids rendering it impracticable to take heavy
stores this way, and making it a thirty-six days' journey from Njole with
good luck. The practical route is via, Loango and Brazzaville. The
Adoomas told us the convoy which had gone up with the vivacious
Government official had had trouble with the rapids and had spent five
days on Kondo Kondo, dragging up the canoes empty by means of
ropes and chains, carrying the cargo that was in them along on land
until they had passed the worst rapid and then repacking. They added
the information that the rapids were at their worst just now, and enter-
tained us with reminiscences of a poor young French official who had
been drowned in them last year—indeed they were just as cheering as my
white friends. As soon as my dinner arrived they politely cleared out,
and I heard the devout M'bo holding a service for them, with hymns, in
the street, and this being over they returned to their drum and dance,
keeping things up distinctly late, for it was 11.10 p.m. when we first
entered the village.

While the men were getting their food I mounted guard over our
little possessions, and when they turned up to make things tidy in my
hut, I walked off down to the shore by a path, which we had elaborately
avoided when coming to the village, a very vertically inclined, slippery
little path, but still the one whereby the natives went up and down to
their canoes, which were kept tied up amongst the rocks. The moon was

rising, illuminating the sky, but not yet sending down her light on the foaming, flying Ogowé in its deep ravine. The scene was divinely lovely; on every side out of the formless gloom rose the peaks of the Sierra del Cristal. Lomba-ngawku on the further side of the river surrounded by his companion peaks, looked his grandest, silhouetted hard against the sky. In the higher valleys where the dim light shone faintly, one could see wreaths and clouds of silver-gray mist lying, basking lazily or rolling to and fro. Olangi seemed to stretch right across the river, blocking with his great blunt mass all passage; while away to the N.E. a cone-shaped peak showed conspicuous, which I afterwards knew as Kangwe. In the darkness round me flitted thousands of fire-flies and out beyond this pool of utter night flew by unceasingly the white foam of the rapids; sound there was none save their thunder. The majesty and beauty of the scene fascinated me, and I stood leaning with my back against a rock pin-nacle watching it. Do not imagine it gave rise, in what I am pleased to call my mind, to those complicated, poetical reflections natural beauty seems to bring out in other people's minds. It never works that way with me; I just lose all sense of human individuality, all memory of human life, with its grief and worry and doubt, and become part of the atmosphere. M'bo, I found, had hung up my mosquito-bar over one of the hard wood benches, and going cautiously under it I lit a night-light and read myself asleep with my damp dilapidated old Horace.

Woke at 4 a.m. lying on the ground among the plantain stems, hav-ing by a reckless movement fallen out of the house. Thanks be there are no mosquitoes. I don't know how I escaped the rats which swarm here, running about among the huts and the inhabitants in the evening, with a tameness shocking to see. I turned in again until six o'clock, when we started getting things ready to go up river again, carefully providing our-selves with a new stock of poles, and subsidising a native to come with us and help us to fight the rapids.

The greatest breadth of the river channel we now saw, in the day-light, to be the S.S.W. branch; this was the one we had been swept into, and was almost completely barred by rock. The other one to the N.N.W. was more open, and the river rushed through it, a terrific, swirling mass of water. Had we got caught in this, we should have got past Kembe Island, and gone to Glory. Whenever the shelter of the spits of land or of the reefs was sufficient to allow the water to lay down its sand, strange shaped sandbanks showed, as regular in form as if they had been smoothed by human hands. They rise above the water in a slope, the low end or tail against the current; the down-stream end terminating in an abrupt miniature cliff, sometimes six and seven feet above the water; that they are the same shape when they have not got their heads above water you will find by sticking on them in a canoe, which I did several times, with a sort of automatic devotion to scientific research peculiar to me. Your best way of getting off is to push on in the direction of the current, carefully preparing for the shock of suddenly coming off the cliff end.

We left the landing place rocks of Kembe Island about 8, and no sooner had we got afloat, than, in the twinkling of an eye, we were swept, broadside on, right across the river to the north bank, and then engaged in a heavy fight with a severe rapid. After passing this, the river is fairly uninterrupted by rock for a while, and is silent and swift. When you are ascending such a piece the effect is strange; you see the water flying by the side of your canoe, as you vigorously drive your paddle into it with short rapid strokes, and you forthwith fancy you are travelling at the rate of a North-Western express; but you just raise your eyes, my friend, and look at that bank, which is standing very nearly still, and you will realise that you and your canoe are standing very nearly still too; and that all your exertions are only enabling you to creep on at the pace of a crushed snail, and that it's the water that is going the pace. It's a most quaint and unpleasant disillusionment.

Above the stretch of swift silent water we come to the Isangaladi Islands, and the river here changes its course from N.N.W., S.S.E. to north and south. A bad rapid, called by our ally from Kembe Island "Unfanga," being surmounted, we seem to be in a mountain-walled lake, and keeping along the left bank of this, we get on famously for twenty whole restful minutes, which lulls us all into a false sense of security, and my crew sing M'pongwe songs, descriptive of how they go to their homes to see their wives, and families, and friends, giving chaffing descriptions of their friends' characteristics and of their failings, which cause bursts of laughter from those among us who recognise the allusions, and how they go to their boxes, and take out their clothes, and put them on—a long bragging inventory of these things is given by each man as a solo, and then the chorus, taken heartily up by his companions, signifies their admiration and astonishment at his wealth and importance— and then they sing how, being dissatisfied with that last dollar's worth of goods they got from "Holty's," they have decided to take their next trade to Hatton and Cookson, or *vice versa*; and then comes the chorus, applauding the wisdom of such a decision, and extolling the excellence of Hatton and Cookson's goods or Holty's. These M'pongwe and Igalwa boat songs are all very pretty, and have very elaborate tunes in a minor key. I do not believe there are any old words to them; I have tried hard to find out about them, but I believe the tunes, which are of a limited number and quite distinct from each other, are very old. The words are put in by the singer on the spur of the moment, and only restricted in this sense, that there would always be the domestic catalogue—whatever its component details might be—sung to the one fixed tune, the trade information sung to another, and so on. A good singer, in these parts, means the man who can make up the best song—the most impressive, or the most amusing; I have elsewhere mentioned pretty much the same state of things among the Ga's and Krumen and Bubi, and in all cases the tunes are only voice tunes, not for instrumental performance. The instrumental music consists of that marvellously developed series of drum tunes—the attempt to understand which has taken up much of my time, and led me into queer company—and the many tunes played on the 'mrimba and the orchid-root-stringed harp: they are, I believe, entirely distinct from the song tunes. And these peaceful tunes my men were now singing were, in their florid elaboration very different from the one they fought the rapids to, of—So Sir—So Sur—So Sir—So Sur—Ush. So Sir, &c.

On we go singing elaborately, thinking no evil of nature, when a current, a quiet devil of a thing, comes round from behind a point of the bank and catches the nose of our canoe; wringing it well, it sends us scuttling right across the river in spite of our ferocious swoops at the water, upsetting us among a lot of rocks with the water boiling over them; this lot of rocks being however of the table-top kind, and not those precious, close-set pinnacles rising up sheer out of profound depths, between which you are so likely to get your canoe wedged in and split. We, up to our knees in water that nearly tears our legs off, push and shove the canoe free, and re-embarking return singing "So Sir" across the river, to have it out with that current. We do; and at its head find a rapid, and notice on the mountain-side a village clearing, the first sign of human habitation we have seen to-day.

Above this rapid we get a treat of still water, the main current of the Ogowé flying along by the south bank. On our side there are sandbanks with their graceful sloping backs and sudden ends, and there is a very strange and beautiful effect produced by the flakes and balls of foam thrown off the rushing main current into the quiet water. These whirl among the eddies and rush backwards and forwards as though they were still mad with wild haste, until, finding no current to take them down, they drift away into the landlocked bays, where they come to a standstill as if they were bewildered and lost and were trying to remember where they were going to and whence they had come; the foam of which they are composed is yellowish-white, with a spongy sort of solidity about it. In a little bay we pass we see eight native women, Fans clearly, by their bright brown faces, and their loads of brass bracelets and armlets; likely enough they had anklets too, but we could not see them, as the good ladies were pottering about waist-deep in the foam-flecked water, intent on breaking up a stockaded fish-trap. We pause and chat, and watch them collecting the fish in baskets, and I acquire some specimens; and then, shouting farewells when we are well away, in the proper civil way, resume our course.

The middle of the Ogowé here is simply forested with high rocks, looking, as they stand with their grim forms above the foam, like a regiment of strange strong creatures breasting it, with their straight faces up river, and their more flowing curves down, as though they had on black mantles which were swept backwards. Across on the other bank rose the black-forested spurs of Lomba-njaku. Our channel was free until we had to fight round the upper end of our bay into a long rush of strong current with bad whirlpools curving its face; then the river widens out and quiets down and then suddenly contracts—a rocky forested promontory running out from each bank. There is a little village on the north bank's promontory, and, at the end of each, huge monoliths rise from the water, making what looks like a gateway which had once been barred and through which the Ogowé had burst.

For the first time on this trip I felt discouraged; it seemed so impossible that we, with our small canoe and scanty crew, could force our way up through that gateway, when the whole Ogowé was rushing down through it. But we clung to the bank and rocks with hands, poles, and paddle, and did it; really the worst part was not in the gateway but just before it, for here there is a great whirlpool, its centre hollowed some one or two feet below its rim. It is caused, my Kembe islander says, by a great cave opening beneath the water. Above the gate the river broadens out again and we see the arched opening to a large cave in the south bank; the mountain-side is one mass of rock covered with the unbroken forest; and the entrance to this cave is just on the upper wall of the south bank's promontory; so, being sheltered from the current here, we rest and examine it leisurely. The river runs into it, and you can easily pass in at this season, but in the height of the wet season, when the river level would be some twenty feet or more above its present one, I doubt if you could. They told me this place is called Boko Boko, and that the cave is a very long one, extending on a level some way into the hill, and then ascending and coming out near a mass of white rock that showed as a speck high up on the mountain.

If you paddle into it you go "far far," and then "no more water live," and you get out and go up the tunnel, which is sometimes broad, sometimes narrow, sometimes high, sometimes so low that you have to crawl, and so get out at the other end.

One French gentleman has gone through this performance, and I am told found "plenty plenty" bats, and hedgehogs, and snakes. They could not tell me his name, which I much regretted. As we had no store of bush lights we went no further than the portals; indeed, strictly between ourselves, if I had had every bush light in Congo Français I personally should not have relished going further. I am terrified of caves; it sends a creaming down my back to think of them.

We went across the river to see another cave entrance on the other bank, where there is a narrow stretch of low rock-covered land at the foot of the mountains, probably under water in the wet season. The mouth of this other cave is low, between tumbled blocks of rock. It looked so suspiciously like a short cut to the lower regions, that I had less exploring enthusiasm about it than even about its opposite neighbour; although they told me no man had gone down "them thing." Probably that much-to-be-honoured Frenchman who explored the other cave, allowed like myself, that if one did want to go from the Equator to Hades, there were pleasanter ways to go than this. My Kembe Island man said that just hereabouts were five cave openings, the two that we had seen and another one we had not, on land, and two under the water, one of the sub-fluvial ones being responsible for the whirlpool we met outside the gateway of Boko Boko.

The scenery above Boko Boko was exceedingly lovely, the river shut in between its rim of mountains. As you pass up it opens out in front of you and closes in behind, the closely-set confused mass of mountains altering in form as you view them from different angles, save one, Kangwe—a blunt cone, evidently the record of some great volcanic outburst; and the sandbanks show again wherever the current deflects and leaves slack water, their bright glistening colour giving a relief to the scene.

For a long period we paddle by the south bank, and pass a vertical cleft-like valley, the upper end of which seems blocked by a finely shaped mountain, almost as conical as Kangwe. The name of this mountain is Njoko, and the name of the clear small river, that apparently monopolises the valley floor, is the Ovata. Our peace was not of long duration, and we were soon again in the midst of a bristling forest of rock; still the current running was not dangerously strong, for the river-bed comes up in a ridge, too high for much water to come over at this season of the year; but in the wet season this must be one of the worst places. This ridge of rock runs two-thirds across the Ogowé, leaving a narrow deep channel by the north bank. When we had got our canoe over the ridge, mostly by standing in the water and lifting her, we found the water deep and fairly quiet.

On the north bank we passed by the entrance of the Okana River. Its mouth is narrow, but, the natives told me, always deep, even in the height of the dry season. It is a very considerable river, running inland to the E.N.E. Little is known about it, save that it is narrowed into a ravine course above which it expands again; the banks of it are thickly populated by Fans, who send down a considerable trade, and have an evil reputation. In the main stream of the Ogowé below the Okana's entrance, is a long rocky island called Shandi. When we were getting over our ridge and paddling about the Okana's entrance my ears recognised a new sound. The rush and roar of the Ogowé we knew well enough, and could locate which particular obstacle to his headlong course was making him say things; it was either those immovable rocks, which threw him back in foam, whirling wildly, or it was that fringe of gaunt skeleton trees hanging from the bank playing a "pull devil, pull baker" contest that made him hiss with vexation. But this was an elemental roar. I said to M'bo: "That's a thunderstorm away among the mountains." "No, sir," says he, "that's the Alemba."

We paddled on towards it, hugging the right-hand bank again to avoid the mid-river rocks. For a brief space the mountain wall ceased, and a lovely scene opened before us; we seemed to be looking into the heart of the chain of the Sierra del Cristal, the abruptly shaped mountains encircling a narrow plain or valley before us, each one of them steep in slope, every one of them forest-clad; one, whose name I know not unless it be what is sometimes put down as Mt. Okana on the French maps, had a conical shape which contrasted beautifully with the more irregular curves of its companions. The colour down this gap was superb, and very Japanese in the evening glow. The more distant peaks were soft gray-blues and purples, those nearer, indigo and black. We soon passed this lovely scene and entered the walled-in channel, creeping up what seemed an interminable hill of black water, then through some whirlpools and a rocky channel to the sand and rock shore of our desired island Kondo Kondo, along whose northern side tore in thunder the Alemba. We made our canoe fast in a little cove among the rocks, and landed, pretty stiff and tired and considerably damp. This island, when we were on it, must have been about half a mile or so long, but during the long wet season a good deal of it is covered, and only the higher parts—great heaps of stone, among which grows a long branched willow-like shrub—are above or nearly above water. The Adooma from Kembe Island especially drew my attention to this shrub, telling me his people who worked the rapids always regarded it with an affectionate veneration; for he said it was the only thing that helped a man when his canoe got thrown over in the dreaded Alemba, for its long tough branches swimming in, or close to, the water are veritable life lines, and his best chance; a chance which must have failed some poor fellow, whose knife and leopard-skin belt we found wedged in among the rocks on Kondo Kondo. The main part of the island is sand, with slabs and tables of polished rock sticking up through it; and in between the rocks grew in thousands most beautiful lilies, their white flowers having a very strong scent of vanilla and their bright light-green leaves looking very lovely on the glistening pale sand among the black-gray rock. How they stand the long submersion they must undergo I do not know; the natives tell me they begin to spring up as soon as ever the water falls and leaves the island exposed; that they very soon grow up and flower, and keep on flowering until the Ogowé comes down again and rides roughshod over Kondo Kondo for months. While the men were making their fire I went across the island to see the great Alemba rapid, of which I had heard so much, that lay between it and the north bank. Nobler pens than mine must sing its glory and its grandeur. Its face was like nothing I have seen before. Its voice was like nothing I have heard. Those other rapids are not to be compared to it; they are wild, headstrong, and malignant enough, but the Alemba is not as they. It does not struggle, and writhe, and brawl among the rocks, but comes in a majestic springing dance, a stretch of waltzing foam, triumphant.

The beauty of the night on Kondo Kondo was superb; the sun went down and the afterglow flashed across the sky in crimson, purple, and gold, leaving it a deep violet-purple, with the great stars hanging in it like moons, until the moon herself arose, lighting the sky long before she sent her beams down on us in this valley. As she rose, the mountains hiding her face grew harder and harder in outline, and deeper and deeper black, while those opposite were just enough illumined to let one see the wefts and floating veils of blue-white mist upon them, and when at last, and for a short time only, she shone full down on the savage foam of the Alemba, she turned it into a soft silver mist. Around, on all sides, flickered the fire-flies, who had come to see if our fire was not a big relation of their own, and they were the sole representation, with ourselves, of animal life. When the moon had gone, the sky, still lit by the stars, seeming indeed to be in itself lambent, was very lovely, but it shared none of its light with us, and we sat round our fire surrounded by an utter darkness. Cold, clammy drifts of almost tangible mist encircled us; ever and again came cold faint puffs of wandering wind, weird and grim beyond description.

I will not weary you further with details of our ascent of the Ogowé rapids, for I have done so already sufficiently to make you understand the sort of work going up them entails, and I have no doubt that, could I have given you a more vivid picture of them, you would join me in admiration of the fiery pluck of those few Frenchmen who traverse them on duty bound. I personally deeply regret it was not my good fortune to meet again the French official I had had the pleasure of meeting on the *Éclaireur*. He would have been truly great in his description of his voyage to Franceville. I wonder how he would have "done" his unpacking of canoes and his experiences on Kondo Kondo, where, by the by, we came across many of the ashes of his expedition's attributive fires. Well! he must have been a pleasure to Franceville, and I hope also to the good Fathers at Lestourville, for those places must be just slightly sombre for Parisians.

Going down big rapids is always, everywhere, more dangerous than coming up, because when you are coming up and a whirlpool or eddy does jam you on rocks, the current helps you off—certainly only with a view to dashing your brains out and smashing your canoe on another set of rocks it's got ready below; but for the time being it helps, and when off, you take charge and convert its plan into an imcompleted fragment; whereas in going down the current is against your backing off. M'bo had a series of prophetic visions as to what would happen to us on our way down, founded on reminiscence and tradition. I tried to comfort him by pointing out that, were any one of his prophecies fulfilled, it would spare our friends and relations all funeral expenses; and, unless they went and wasted their money on a memorial window, that ought to be a comfort to our well-regulated minds. M'bo did not see this, but was too good a Christian to be troubled by the disagreeable conviction that was in the minds of other members of my crew, namely, that our souls, unliberated by funeral rites from this world, would have to hover for ever over the Ogowé near the scene of our catastrophe. I own this idea was an unpleasant one—fancy having to pass the day in those caves with the bats, and then come out and wander all night in the cold mists. However, like a good many likely-looking prophecies, those of M'bo did not quite come off, and a miss is as good as a mile. Twice we had a near call, by being shot in between two pinnacle rocks, within half an inch of being fatally close to each other for us; but after some alarming scrunching sounds, and creaks from the canoe, we were shot ignominiously out down river. Several times we got on to partially submerged table rocks, and were unceremoniously bundled off them by the Ogowé, irritated at the hindrance we were occasioning; but we never met the rocks of M'bo's prophetic soul—that lurking, submerged needle, or knife-edge of a pinnacle rock which was to rip our canoe from stem to stern, neat and clean into two pieces.

The course we had to take coming down was different to that we took coming up. Coming up we kept as closely as might be to the most advisable bank, and dodged behind every rock we could, to profit by the shelter it afforded us from the current. Coming down, fallen-tree-fringed banks and rocks were converted from friends to foes; so we kept with all our power in the very centre of the swiftest part of the current in order to avoid them. The grandest part of the whole time was coming down, below the Alemba, where the whole great Ogowé takes a tiger-like spring for about half a mile, I should think, before it strikes a rock reef below. As you come out from among the rocks in the upper rapid it gives you—or I should perhaps confine myself to saying, it gave me—a peculiar internal sensation to see that stretch of black water, shining like a burnished sheet of metal, sloping down before one, at such an angle. All you have got to do is to keep your canoe-head straight—quite straight, you understand—for any failure so to do will land you the other side of the tomb, instead of in a cheerful no-end-of-a-row with the lower rapid's rocks. This lower rapid is one of the worst in the dry season; maybe it is so in the wet too, for the river's channel here turns an elbow-sharp curve which infuriates the Ogowé in a most dangerous manner.

I hope to see the Ogowé next time in the wet season—there must be several more of these great sheets of water then over what are rocky rapids now. Just think what coming down over that ridge above Boko Boko will be like. I do not fancy however it would ever be possible to get up the river, when it is at its height, with so small a crew as we were when we went and played our knock-about farce, before King Death, in his amphitheatre in the Sierra del Cristal.

CHAPTER 6

LEMBARENE

In which is given some account of the episode of the Hippopotame,
and of the voyager's attempts at controlling an Ogowé canoe;
and also of the Igalwa tribe.

I SAY GOOD-BYE TO TALAGOUGA with much regret, and go on board the *Éclaireur*, when she returns from Njole, with all my bottles and belongings. On board I find no other passenger; the Captain's English has widened out considerably; and he is as pleasant, cheery, and spoiling for a fight as ever; but he has a preoccupied manner, and a most peculiar set of new habits, which I find are shared by the Engineer. Both of them make rapid dashes to the rail, and nervously scan the river for a minute and then return to some occupation, only to dash from it to the rail again. During breakfast their conduct is nerve-shaking. Hastily taking a few mouthfuls, the Captain drops his knife and fork and simply hurls his seamanlike form through the nearest door out on to the deck. In another minute he is back again, and with just a shake of his head to the Engineer, continues his meal. The Engineer shortly afterwards flies from his seat, and being far thinner than the Captain, goes through his nearest door with even greater rapidity; returns, and shakes his head at the Captain, and continues his meal. Excitement of this kind is infectious, and I also wonder whether I ought not to show a sympathetic friendliness by flying from my seat and hurling myself on to the deck through my nearest door, too. But although there are plenty of doors, as four enter the saloon from the deck, I do not see my way to doing this performance aimlessly, and what in this world they are both after I cannot think. So I confine myself to woman's true sphere, and assist in a humble way by catching the wine and Vichy water bottles, glasses, and plates of food, which at every performance are jeopardised by the members of the nobler sex starting off with a considerable quantity of the ample tablecloth wrapped round their legs. At last I can stand it no longer, so ask the Captain point-blank what is the matter. "Nothing," says he, bounding out of his chair and flying out of his doorway; but on his return he tells me he has got a bet on of two bottles of champagne with Woermann's Agent for Njole, as to who shall reach Lembarene first, and the German agent has started off some time before the éclaireur in his little steam launch.

During the afternoon we run smoothly along; the free pulsations of the engines telling what a very different thing coming down the Ogowé is to going up against its terrific current. Every now and again we stop to pick up cargo, or discharge over-carried cargo, and the Captain's mind becomes lulled by getting no news of the Woermann's launch having passed down. He communicates this to the Engineer; it is impossible she could have passed the *Éclaireur* since they started, therefore she must be somewhere behind at a subfactory. "*N'est-ce pas?*" "*Oui, oui, certainement,*" says the Engineer. The Engineer is, by these considerations, also lulled, and feels he may do something else but scan the river *à la* sister Ann. What that something is puzzles me; it evidently requires secrecy, and he shrinks from detection. First he looks down one side of the deck, no one there; then he looks down the other, no one there; good so far. I then see he has put his head through one of the saloon portholes; no one there; he hesitates a few seconds until I begin to wonder whether his head will suddenly appear through my port; but he regards this as an unnecessary precaution, and I hear him enter his cabin which abuts on mine and there is silence for some minutes. Writing home to his mother, think I, as I go on putting a new braid round the bottom of a worn skirt. Almost immediately after follows the sound of a little click from the next cabin, and then apparently one of the denizens of the infernal regions has got its tail smashed in a door and the heavy hot afternoon air is reft by an inchoate howl of agony. I drop my needlework and take to the deck; but it is after all only that shy retiring young man practising secretly on his clarionet.

The Captain is drowsily looking down the river. But repose is not long allowed to that active spirit; he sees something in the water—what? "*Hippopotame*," he ejaculates. Now both he and the Engineer frequently do this thing, and then fly off to their guns—bang, bang, finish; but this time he does not dash for his gun, nor does the Engineer, who flies out of his cabin at the sound of the war shout "*Hippopotame*." In vain I look across the broad river with its stretches of yellow sandbanks, where the "*hippopotame*" should be, but I can see nothing but four black stumps sticking up in the water away to the right. Meanwhile the Captain and the Engineer are flying about getting off a crew of blacks into the canoe we are towing alongside. This being done the Captain explains to me that on the voyage up "the Engineer had fired at, and hit a hippopotamus, and without doubt this was its body floating." We are now close enough even for me to recognise the four stumps as the deceased's legs, and soon the canoe is alongside them and makes fast to one, and then starts to paddle back, hippo and all, to the *Éclaireur*. But no such thing; let them paddle and shout as hard as they like, the hippo's weight simply anchors them. The *Éclaireur* by now has dropped down the river past them, and has to sweep round and run back. Recognising promptly what the trouble is, the energetic Captain grabs up a broom, ties a light cord belonging to the leadline to it, and holding the broom by the end of its handle, swings it round his head and hurls it at the canoe. The arm of a merciful Providence being interposed, the broom-tomahawk does not hit the canoe, wherein, if it had, it must infallibly have killed some one, but falls short, and goes tearing off with the current, well out of reach of the canoe. The Captain seeing this gross dereliction of duty by a Chargeur Réunis broom, hauls it in hand over hand and talks to it. Then he ties the other end of its line to the mooring rope, and by a better aimed shot sends the broom into the water, about ten yards above the canoe, and it drifts towards it. Breathless excitement! surely they will get it now. Alas, no! Just when it is within reach of the canoe, a fearful shudder runs through the broom. It throws up its head and sinks beneath the tide. A sensation of stun comes over all of us. The crew of the canoe, ready and eager to grasp the approaching aid, gaze blankly at the circling ripples round where it sank. In a second the Captain knows what has happened. That heavy hawser which has been paid out after it has dragged it down, so he hauls it on board again.

The *Éclaireur* goes now close enough to the hippo-anchored canoe for a rope to be flung to the man in her bows; he catches it and freezes on gallantly. Saved! No! Oh horror! The lower deck hums with fear that after all it will not taste that toothsome hippo chop, for the man who has caught the rope is as nearly as possible jerked flying out of the canoe when the strain of the *Éclaireur* contending with the hippo's inertia flies along it, but his companion behind him grips him by the legs and is in his turn grabbed, and the crew holding on to each other with their hands, and on to their craft with their feet, save the man holding on to the rope and the whole situation; and slowly bobbing towards us comes the hippopotamus, who is shortly hauled on board by the winners in triumph.

My esteemed friends, the Captain and the Engineer, who of course have been below during this hauling, now rush on to the upper deck, each coatless, and carrying an enormous butcher's knife. They dash into the saloon, where a terrific sharpening of these instruments takes place on the steel belonging to the saloon carving-knife, and down stairs again. By looking down the ladder, I can see the pink, pig-like hippo, whose colour has been soaked out by the water, lying on the lower deck and the Captain and Engineer slitting down the skin intent on gralloching operations. Providentially, my prophetic soul induces me to leave the top of the ladder and go forward—"run to win'ard," as Captain Murray would say—for within two minutes the Captain and Engineer are up the ladder as if they had been blown up by the boilers bursting, and go as one man for the brandy bottle; and they wanted it if ever man did; for remember that hippo had been dead and in the warm river-water for more than a week.

The Captain had had enough of it, he said, but the Engineer stuck to the job with a courage I profoundly admire, and he saw it through and then retired to his cabin; sand-and-canvassed himself first, and then soaked and saturated himself in Florida water. The flesh gladdened the hearts of the crew and lower-deck passengers and also of the inhabitants of Lembarene, who got dashes of it on our arrival there. Hippo flesh is not to be despised by black man or white; I have enjoyed it far more than the stringy beef or vapid goat's flesh one gets down here.

I stayed on board the *Éclaireur* all night; for it was dark when we reached Lembarene, too dark to go round to Kangwe; and next morning, after taking a farewell of her—I hope not a final one, for she is a most luxurious little vessel for the Coast, and the feeding on board is excellent and the society varied and charming—I went round to Kangwe.

I remained some time in the Lembarene district and saw and learnt many things; I owe most of what I learnt to M. and Mme. Jacot, who knew a great deal about both the natives and the district, and I owe much of what I saw to having acquired the art of managing by myself a native canoe. This "recklessness" of mine I am sure did not merit the severe criticism it has been subjected to, for my performances gave immense amusement to others (I can hear Lembarene's shrieks of laughter now) and to myself they gave great pleasure.

My first attempt was made at Talagouga one very hot afternoon. M. and Mme. Forget were, I thought, safe having their siestas, Oranie was with Mme. Gacon. I knew where Mme. Gacon was for certain; she was with M. Gacon; and I knew he was up in the sawmill shed, out of sight of the river, because of the soft thump, thump, thump of the big water-wheel. There was therefore no one to keep me out of mischief, and I was too frightened to go into the forest that afternoon, because on the previous afternoon I had been stalked as a wild beast by a cannibal savage, and I am nervous. Besides, and above all, it is quite impossible to see other people, even if they are only black, naked savages, gliding about in canoes, without wishing to go and glide about yourself. So I went down to where the canoes were tied by their noses to the steep bank, and finding a paddle, a broken one, I unloosed the smallest canoe. Unfortunately this was fifteen feet or so long, but I did not know the disadvantage of having, as it were, a long-tailed canoe then—I did shortly afterwards.

The promontories running out into the river on each side of the mission beach give a little stretch of slack water between the bank and the mill-race-like current of the Ogowé, and I wisely decided to keep in the slack water, until I had found out how to steer—most important thing steering. I got into the bow of the canoe, and shoved off from the bank all right; then I knelt down—learn how to paddle standing up by and by—good so far. I rapidly learnt how to steer from the bow, but I could not get up any pace. Intent on acquiring pace, I got to the edge of the slack water; and then displaying more wisdom, I turned round to avoid it, proud as a peacock, you understand, at having found out how to turn round. At this moment, the current of "the greatest equatorial river in the world," grabbed my canoe by its tail. We spun round and round for a few seconds, like a teetotum, I steering the whole time for all I was worth, and then the current dragged the canoe ignominiously down river, tail foremost.

Fortunately a big tree was at that time temporarily hanging against the rock in the river, just below the sawmill beach. Into that tree the canoe shot with a crash, and I hung on, and shipping my paddle, pulled the canoe into the slack water again, by the aid of the branches of the tree, which I was in mortal terror would come off the rock, and insist on accompanying me and the canoe, viâ, Kama country, to the Atlantic Ocean; but it held, and when I had got safe against the side of the pinnacle-rock I wiped a perspiring brow, and searched in my mind for a piece of information regarding Navigation that would be applicable to the management of long-tailed Adooma canoes. I could not think of one for some minutes. Captain Murray has imparted to me at one time and another an enormous mass of hints as to the management of vessels, but those vessels were all presupposed to have steam power. But he having been the first man to take an ocean-going steamer up to Matadi on the Congo, through the terrific currents that whirl and fly in Hell's Cauldron, knew about currents, and I remembered he had said regarding taking vessels through them, "Keep all the headway you can on her." Good! that hint inverted will fit this situation like a glove, and I'll keep all the tailway I can off her. Feeling now as safe as only a human being can feel who is backed up by a sound principle, I was cautiously crawling to the tail-end of the canoe, intent on kneeling in it to look after it, when I heard a dreadful outcry on the bank. Looking there I saw Mme. Forget, Mme. Gacon, M. Gacon, and their attributive crowd of mission children all in a state of frenzy. They said lots of things in chorus. "What?" said I. They said some more and added gesticulations. Seeing I was wasting their time as I could not hear, I drove the canoe from the rock and made my way, mostly by steering, to the bank close by; and then tying the canoe firmly up I walked over the mill stream and divers other things towards my anxious friends. "You'll be drowned," they said. "Gracious goodness!" said I, "I thought that half an hour ago, but it's all right now; I can steer." After much conversation I lulled their fears regarding me, and having received strict orders to keep in the stern of the canoe, because that is the proper place when you are managing a canoe single-handed, I returned to my studies. I had not however lulled my friends' interest regarding me, and they stayed on the bank watching.

I found first, that my education in steering from the bow was of no avail; second, that it was all right if you reversed it. For instance, when you are in the bow, and make an inward stroke with the paddle on the right-hand side, the bow goes to the right; whereas, if you make an inward stroke on the right-hand side, when you are sitting in the stern, the bow then goes to the left. Understand? Having grasped this law, I crept along up river; and, by Allah! before I had gone twenty yards, if that wretch, the current of the greatest, &c., did not grab hold of the nose of my canoe, and we teetotummed round again as merrily as ever. My audience screamed. I knew what they were saying, "You'll be drowned! Come back! Come back!" but I heard them and I heeded not. If you attend to advice in a crisis you're lost; besides, I couldn't "Come back" just then. However, I got into the slack water again, by some very showy, high-class steering. Still steering, fine as it is, is not all you require and hanker after. You want pace as well, and pace, except when in the clutches of the current, I had not so far attained. Perchance, thought I, the pace region in a canoe may be in its centre; so I got along on my knees into the centre to experiment. Bitter failure; the canoe took to sidling down river broadside on, like Mr. Winkle's horse. Shouts of laughter from the bank. Both bow and stern education utterly inapplicable to centre; and so, seeing I was utterly thrown away there, I crept into the bows, and in a few more minutes I steered my canoe, perfectly, in among its fellows by the bank and secured it there. Mme. Forget ran down to meet me and assured me she had not laughed so much since she had been in Africa, although she was frightened at the time lest I should get capsized and drowned. I believe it, for she is a sweet and gracious lady; and I quite see, as she demonstrated, that the sight of me, teetotumming about, steering in an elaborate and showy way all the time, was irresistibly comic. And she gave a most amusing account of how, when she started looking for me to give me tea, a charming habit of hers, she could not see me in among my bottles, and so asked the little black boy where I was. "There," said he, pointing to the tree hanging against the rock out in the river; and she, seeing me hitched with a canoe against the rock, and knowing the danger and depth of the river, got alarmed.

Well, when I got down to Lembarene I naturally went on with my canoeing studies, in pursuit of the attainment of pace. Success crowned my efforts, and I can honestly and truly say that there are only two things I am proud of—one is that Doctor Günther has approved of my fishes, and the other is that I can paddle an Ogowé canoe. Pace, style, steering and all, "All same for one" as if I were an Ogowé African. A strange, incongruous pair of things: but I often wonder what are the things other people are really most proud of; it would be a quaint and repaying subject for investigation.

Mme. Jacot gave me every help in canoeing, for she is a remarkably clear-headed woman, and recognised that, as I was always getting soaked, anyhow, I ran no extra danger in getting soaked in a canoe; and then, it being the dry season, there was an immense stretch of water opposite Andande beach, which was quite shallow. So she saw no need of my getting drowned.

The sandbanks were showing their yellow heads in all directions when I came down from Talagouga, and just opposite Andande there was sticking up out of the water a great, graceful, palm frond. It had been stuck into the head of the pet sandbank, and every day was visited by the boys and girls in canoes to see how much longer they would have to wait for the sandbank's appearance. A few days after my return it showed, and in two days more there it was, acres and acres of it, looking like a great, golden carpet spread on the surface of the centre of the clear water—clear here, down this side of Lembarene Island, because the river runs fairly quietly, and has time to deposit its mud. Dark brown the Ogowé flies past the other side of the island, the main current being deflected that way by a bend, just below the entrance of the Nguni.

There was great rejoicing. Canoe-load after canoe-load of boys and girls went to the sandbank, some doing a little fishing round its rim, other bringing the washing there, all skylarking and singing. Few prettier sights have I ever seen than those on that sandbank—the merry brown forms dancing or lying stretched on it: the gaudy-coloured patchwork quilts and chintz mosquito-bars that have been washed, spread out drying, looking from Kangwe on the hill above, like beds of bright flowers. By night when it was moonlight there would be bands of dancers on it with bush-light torches, gyrating, intermingling and separating till you could think you were looking at a dance of stars.

They commenced affairs very early on that sandbank, and they kept them up very late; and all the time there came from it a soft murmur of laughter and song. Ah me! if the aim of life were happiness and pleasure, Africa should send us missionaries instead of our sending them to her—but, fortunately for the work of the world, happiness is not. One thing I remember which struck me very much regarding the sandbank, and this was that Mme. Jacot found such pleasure in taking her work on to the verandah, where she could see it. I knew she did not care for the songs and the dancing. One day she said to me, "It is such a relief." "A relief?" I said. "Yes, do you not see that until it shows there is nothing but forest, forest, forest, and that still stretch of river? That bank is the only piece of clear ground I see in the year, and that only lasts a few weeks until the wet season comes, and then it goes, and there is nothing but forest, forest, forest, for another year. It is two years now since I came to this place; it may be I know not how many more before we go home again." I grieve to say, for my poor friend's sake, that her life at Kangwe was nearly at its end. Soon after my return to England I heard of the death of her husband from malignant fever. M. Jacot was a fine, powerful, energetic man, in the prime of life. He was a teetotaler and a vegetarian; and although constantly travelling to and fro in his district on his evangelising work, he had no foolish recklessness in him. No one would have thought that he would have been the first to go of us who used to sit round his hospitable table. His delicate wife, his two young children or I would have seemed far more likely. His loss will be a lasting one to the people he risked his life to (what he regarded) save. The natives held him in the greatest affection and respect, and his influence over them was considerable, far more profound than that of any other missionary I have ever seen. His loss is also great to those students of Africa who are working on the culture or on the languages; his knowledge of both was extensive, particularly of the little known languages of the Ogowé district. He was, when I left, busily employed in compiling a dictionary of the Fan tongue, and had many other works on language in contemplation. His work in this sphere would have had a high value, for he was a man with a University education and well grounded in Latin and Greek, and thoroughly acquainted with both English and French literature, for although born a Frenchman, he had been brought up in America. He was also a cultivated musician, and he and Mme. Jacot in the evenings would sing old French songs, Swiss songs, English songs, in their rich full voices; and then if you stole softly out on to the verandah, you would often find it crowded with a silent, black audience, listening intently.

The amount of work M. and Mme. Jacot used to get through was, to me, amazing, and I think the Ogowé Protestant mission sadly short-handed—its missionaries not being content to follow the usual Protestant plan out in West Africa, namely, quietly sitting down and keeping house, with just a few native children indoors to do the house-work, and close by a school and a little church where a service is held on

Sundays. The representatives of the Mission Évangélique go to and fro throughout the district round each station on evangelising work, among some of the most dangerous and uncivilised tribes in Africa, frequently spending a fortnight at a time away from their homes, on the waterways of a wild and dangerous country. In addition to going themselves, they send trained natives as evangelists and Bible-readers, and keep a keen eye on the trained native, which means a considerable amount of worry and strain too. The work on the stations is heavy in Ogowé districts, because when you have got a clearing made and all the buildings up, you have by no means finished with the affair, for you have to fight the Ogowé forest back, as a Dutchman fights the sea. But the main cause of work is the store, which in this exhausting climate is more than enough work for one man alone.

Payments on the Ogowé are made in goods; the natives do not use any coinage-equivalent, save in the strange case of the Fans, which does not touch general trade and which I will speak of later. They have not even the brass bars and cheetems that are in used in Calabar, or cowries as in Lagos. In order to expedite and simplify this goods traffic, a written or printed piece of paper is employed—practically a cheque, which is called a "bon" or "book," and these "bons" are cashed—i.e. gooded, at the store. They are for three amounts. Five fura = a dollar. One fura = a franc. Desu = fifty centimes = half a fura. The value given for these "bons" is the same from Government, Trade, and Mission. Although the Mission Évangélique does not trade—i.e. buy produce and sell it at a profit, its representatives have a great deal of business to attend to through the store, which is practically a bank. All the native evangelists, black teachers, Bible-readers and labourers on the stations are paid off in these bons; and when any representative of the mission is away on a journey, food bought for themselves and their canoe crews is paid for in bons, which are brought in by the natives at their convenience, and changed for goods at the store. Therefore for several hours every week-day the missionary has to devote himself to store work, and store work out here is by no means playing at shop. It is very hard, tiring, exasperating work when you have to deal with it in full, as a trader, when it is necessary for you to purchase produce at a price that will give you a reasonable margin of profit over storing, customs' duties, shipping expenses, &c., &c. But it is quite enough to try the patience of any Saint when you are only keeping store to pay on bons, à la missionary; for each class of article used in trade—and there are some hundreds of them—has a definite and acknowledged value, but where the trouble comes in is that different articles have the same value; for example, six fish hooks and one pocket-handkerchief have the same value, or you can make up that value in lucifer matches, pomatum, a mirror, a hair comb, tobacco, or scent in bottles.

Now, if you are a trader, certain of these articles cost you more than others, although they have an identical value to the native, and so it is to your advantage to pay what we should call, in Cameroons, "a Kru, cheap copper," and you have a lot of worry to effect this. To the missionary this does not so much matter. It makes absolutely no difference to the native, mind you; so he is by no means done by the trader. Take powder for an example. There is no profit on powder for the trader in Congo Français, but the native always wants it because he can get a tremendous profit on it from his black brethren in the bush; hence it pays the trader to give him his bon out in Boma check, &c., better than in gunpowder. This is a fruitful spring of argument and persuasion. However, whether the native is passing in a bundle of rubber or a tooth of ivory, or merely cashing a bon for a week's bush catering, he is in Congo Français incapable of deciding what he will have when it comes to the point. He comes into the shop with a bon in his hand, and we will say, for example, the idea in his head that he wants fish-hooks—"jupes" he calls them—but, confronted with the visible temptation of pomatum, he hesitates, and scratches his head violently. Surrounding him there are ten or twenty other natives with their minds in a similar wavering state, but yet anxious to be served forthwith. In consequence of the stimulating scratch, he remembers that one of his wives said he was to bring some lucifer matches, another wanted cloth for herself, and another knew of some rubber she could buy very cheap, in tobacco, of a Fan woman who had stolen it. This rubber he knows he can take to the trader's store and sell for pocket-handkerchiefs of a superior pattern, or gunpowder, or rum, which he cannot get at the mission store. He finally gets something and takes it home, and likely enough brings it back, in a day or so, somewhat damaged, desirous of changing it for some other article or articles. Remember also that these Bantu, like the Negroes, think externally, in a loud voice; like Mr. Kipling's 'oont, "'e smells most awful vile," and, if he be a Fan, he accompanies his observations with violent dramatic gestures, and let the customer's tribe or sex be what it may, the customer is sadly, sadly liable to pick up any portable object within reach, under the shadow of his companions' uproar, and stow it away in his armpits, between his legs, or, if his cloth be large enough, in that. Picture to yourself the perplexities of a Christian minister, engaged in such an occupation as storekeeping under these circumstances, with, likely enough, a touch of fever on him and jiggers in his feet; and when the store is closed the goods in it requiring constant vigilance to keep them free from mildew and white ants.

Then in addition to the store work, a fruitful source of work and worry are the schools, for both boys and girls. It is regarded as futile to attempt to get any real hold over the children unless they are removed from the influence of the country fashions that surround them in their village homes; therefore the schools are boarding; hence the entire care of the children, including feeding and clothing, falls on the missionary.

The instruction given in the Mission Évangélique Schools does not include teaching the boys trades. The girls fare somewhat better, as they get instruction in sewing and washing and ironing, but I think in this district the young ladies would be all the better for being taught cooking.

It is strange that all the cooks employed by the Europeans should be men, yet all the cooking among the natives themselves is done by women, and done abominably badly in all the Bantu tribes I have ever come across; and the Bantu are in this particular, and indeed in most particulars, far inferior to the true Negro; though I must say this is not the orthodox view. The Negroes cook uniformly very well, and at moments are inspired in the direction of palm-oil chop and fish cooking. Not so the Bantu, whose methods cry aloud for improvement, they having just the very easiest and laziest way possible of dealing with food. The food supply consists of plantain, yam, koko, sweet potatoes, maize, pumpkin, pineapple, and ochres, fish both wet and smoked, and flesh of many kinds—including human in certain districts—snails, snakes, and crayfish, and big maggot-like pupæ of the rhinoceros beetle and the *Rhyncophorus palmatorum*. For sweetmeats the sugar-cane abounds, but it is only used chewed *au naturel*. For seasoning there is that bark that tastes like an onion, an onion distinctly *passé*, but powerful and permanent, particularly if it has been used in one of the native-made, rough earthen pots. These pots have a very cave-man look about them; they are unglazed, unlidded bowls. They stand the fire wonderfully well, and you have got to stand, as well as you can, the taste of the aforesaid bark that clings to them, and that of the smoke which gets into them during cooking operations over an open wood fire, as well as the soot-like colour they impart to even your own white rice. Out of all this varied material the natives of the Congo Français forests produce, dirtily, carelessly and wastefully, a dull, indigestible diet. Yam, sweet potatoes, ochres, and maize are not so much cultivated or used as among the Negroes, and the daily food is practically plantain—picked while green and the rind pulled off, and the tasteless woolly interior baked or boiled and the widely distributed manioc treated in the usual way. The sweet or non-poisonous manioc I have rarely seen cultivated, because it gives a much smaller yield, and is much longer coming to perfection. The poisonous kind is that in general use; its great dahlia-like roots are soaked in water to remove the poisonous principle, and then dried and grated up, or more commonly beaten up into a kind of dough in a wooden trough that looks like a model canoe, with wooden clubs, which I have seen the curiosity hunter happily taking home as war clubs to alarm his family with. The thump, thump, thump of this manioc beating is one of the most familiar sounds in a bush village. The meal, when beaten up, is used for thickening broths, and rolled up into bolsters about a foot long and two inches in diameter, and then wrapped in plantain leaves, and tied round with tie-tie and boiled, or more properly speaking steamed, for a lot of the rolls are arranged in a brass skillet. A small quantity of water is poured over the rolls of plantain, a plantain leaf is tucked in over the top tightly, so as to prevent the steam from escaping, and the whole affair is poised on the three cooking-stones over a wood fire, and left there until the contents are done, or more properly speaking, until the lady in charge of it has delusions on the point, and the bottom rolls are a trifle burnt or the whole insufficiently cooked.

This manioc meal is the staple food, the bread equivalent, all along the coast. As you pass along you are perpetually meeting with a new named food, fou-fou on the Leeward, kank on the Windward, m'vada in Corisco, ogooma in the Ogowé; but acquaintance with it demonstrates that it is all the same—manioc.

It is a good food when it is properly prepared; but when a village has soaked its soil-laden manioc tubers in one and the same pool of water for years, the water in that pool becomes a trifle strong, and both it and the manioc get a smell which once smelt is never to be forgotten; it is something like that resulting from bad paste with a dash of vinegar, but fit to pass all these things, and has qualities of its own that have no civilised equivalent.

I believe that this way of preparing the staple article of diet is largely responsible for that dire and frequent disease "cut him belly," and several other quaint disorders, possibly even for the sleep disease. The natives themselves say that a diet too exclusively maniocan produces dimness of vision, ending in blindness if the food is not varied; the poisonous principle cannot be anything like soaked out in the surcharged water, and the meal when it is made up and cooked has just the same sour, acrid taste you would expect it to have from the smell.

The fish is boiled, or wrapped in leaves and baked. The dried fish, very properly known as stink-fish, is much preferred; this is either eaten as it is, or put into stews as seasoning, as also are the snails. The meat is eaten either fresh or smoked, boiled or baked. By baked I always mean just buried in the ground and a fire lighted on top, or wrapped in leaves and buried in hot embers.

The smoked meat is badly prepared, just hung up in the smoke of the fires, which hardens it, blackening the outside quickly; but when the lumps are taken out of the smoke, in a short time cracks occur in them, and the interior part proceeds to go bad, and needless to say maggoty. If it is kept in the smoke, as it often is to keep it out of the way of dogs and driver ants, it acquires the toothsome taste and texture of a piece of old tarpaulin.

Now I will ask the surviving reader who has waded through this dissertation on cookery if something should not be done to improve the degraded condition of the Bantu cooking culture? Not for his physical delectation only, but because his present methods are bad for his morals, and drive the man to drink, let alone assisting in riveting him in the practice of polygamy, which the missionary party say is an exceedingly bad practice for him to follow. The inter-relationship of these two subjects may not seem on the face of it very clear, but inter-relationships of customs very rarely are; I well remember M. Jacot coming home one day at Kangwe from an evangelising visit to some adjacent Fan towns, and saying he had had given to him that afternoon a new reason for polygamy, which was that it enabled a man to get enough to eat. This sounds sinister from a notoriously cannibal tribe; but the explanation is that the Fans are an exceedingly hungry tribe, and require a great deal of

providing for. It is their custom to eat about ten times a day when in village, and the men spend most of their time in the palaver-houses at each
end of the street, the women bringing them bowls of food of one kind
or another all day long. When the men are away in the forest rubber or
elephant-hunting, and have to cook their own food, they cannot get
quite so much; but when I have come across them on these expeditions,
they halted pretty regularly every two hours and had a substantial snack,
and the gorge they all go in for after a successful elephant hunt is a thing
to see—once.

There are other reasons which lead to the prevalence of this custom,
beside the cooking. One is that it is totally impossible for one woman to
do the whole work of a house—look after the children, prepare and cook
the food, prepare the rubber, carry the same to the markets, fetch the
daily supply of water from the stream, cultivate the plantation, &c., &c.
Perhaps I should say it is impossible for the dilatory African woman, for
I once had an Irish charwoman, who drank, who would have done the
whole week's work of an African village in an afternoon, and then been
quite fresh enough to knock some of the nonsense out of her husband's
head with that of the broom, and throw a kettle of boiling water or a
paraffin lamp at him, if she suspected him of flirting with other ladies.
That woman, who deserves fame in the annals of her country, was
named Harragan. She has attained immortality some years since, by
falling down stairs one Saturday night from excitement arising from
"the Image's" (Mr. Harragan) conduct; but we have no Mrs. Harragan
in Africa. The African lady does not care a travelling whitesmith's exe-
cration if her husband does flirt, so long as he does not go and give to
other women the cloth, &c., that she should have. The more wives the
less work, says the African lady; and I have known men who would rather
have had one wife and spent the rest of the money on themselves, in a
civilised way, driven into polygamy by the women; and of course this
state of affairs is most common in non-slave-holding tribes like the Fan.

Mission work was first opened upon the Ogowé by Dr. Nassau,
the great pioneer and explorer of these regions. He was acting for the
American Presbyterian Society; but when the French Government
demanded education in French in the schools, the stations on the
Ogowé, Lembarene (Kangwe), and Talagouga were handed over to
the Mission Évangélique of Paris, and have been carried on by its representatives with great devotion and energy. I am unsympathetic, in

some particulars, for reasons of my own, with Christian missions, so my admiration for this one does not arise from the usual ground of admiration for missions, namely, that however they may be carried on, they are engaged in a great and holy work; but I regard the Mission Évangélique, judging from the results I have seen, as the perfection of what one may call a purely spiritual mission.

Lembarene is strictly speaking a district which includes Adânlinan lângâ, and the Island, but the name is locally used to denote the great island in the Ogowé, whose native name is Nenge Ezangy; but for the sake of the general reader I will keep to the everyday term of Lembarene Island.

Lembarene Island is the largest of the islands on the Ogowé. It is some fifteen miles long, east and west, and a mile to a mile and a half wide. It is hilly and rocky, uniformly clad with forest, and several little permanent streams run from it on both sides into the Ogowé. It is situated 130 miles from the sea, at the point, just below the entrance of the N'guni, where the Ogowé commences to divide up into that network of channels by which, like all great West African rivers save the Congo, it chooses to enter the Ocean. The island, as we mainlanders at Kangwe used to call it, was a great haunt of mine, particularly after I came down from Talagouga and saw fit to regard myself as competent to control a canoe.

From Andande, the beach of Kangwe, the breadth of the arm of the Ogowé to the nearest village on the island, was about that of the Thames at Blackwall. One half of the way was slack water, the other half was broadside on to a stiff current. Now my pet canoe at Andande was about six feet long, pointed at both ends, flat bottomed, so that it floated on the top of the water; its freeboard was, when nothing was in it, some three inches, and the poor thing had seen trouble in its time, for it had a hole you could put your hand in at one end; so in order to navigate it successfully, you had to squat in the other, which immersed that to the water level but safely elevated the damaged end in the air. Of course you had to stop in your end firmly, because if you went forward the hole went down into the water, and the water went into the hold, and forthwith you foundered with all hands—i.e., you and the paddle and the calabash baler. This craft also had a strong weather helm, owing to a warp in the tree of which it had been made. I learnt all these things one afternoon, paddling round the sandbank; and the next afternoon, feeling confident in the merits of my vessel, I started for the island, and I actually got there, and associated with the natives, but feeling my arms were permanently worn out by paddling against the current, I availed myself of the offer of a gentleman to paddle me back in his canoe. He introduced himself as Samuel, and volunteered the statement that he was "a very good man." We duly settled ourselves in the canoe, he occupying the bow, I sitting in the middle, and a Mrs. Samuel sitting in the stern. Mrs. Samuel was a powerful, pretty lady, and a conscientious and continuous paddler. Mr. S. was none of these things, but an ex-Bible reader, with an amazing knowledge of English, which he spoke in a quaint, falsetto, far-away sort of voice, and that man's besetting sin was curiosity. "You be Christian, ma?" said he. I asked him if he had ever met a white man who was not. "Yes, ma," says Samuel. I said "You must have been associating with people whom you ought not to know." Samuel fortunately not having a repartee for this, paddled on with his long paddle for a few seconds. "Where be your husband, ma?" was the next conversational bomb he hurled at me. "I no got one," I answer. "No got," says Samuel, paralysed with astonishment; and as Mrs. S., who did not know English, gave one of her vigorous drives with her paddle at this moment, Samuel as near as possible got jerked head first into the Ogowé, and we took on board about two bucketfuls of water. He recovered himself, however and returned to his charge. "No got one, ma?" "No," say I furiously. "Do you get much rubber round here?" "I no be trade man," says Samuel, refusing to fall into my trap for changing conversation. "Why you no got one?" The remainder of the conversation is unreportable, but he landed me at Andande all right, and got his dollar.

The next voyage I made, which was on the next day, I decided to go by myself to the factory, which is on the other side of the island, and did so. I got some goods to buy fish with, and heard from Mr. Cockshut that the poor boy-agent at Osoamokita, had committed suicide. It was a grievous thing. He was, as I have said, a bright, intelligent young Frenchman; but living in the isolation, surrounded by savage, tiresome tribes, the strain of his responsibility had been too much for him. He had had a good deal of fever, and the very kindly head agent for Woermann's had sent Dr. Pélessier to see if he had not better be invalided home; but he told the Doctor he was much better, and as he had no one at home to go to he begged him not to send him, and the Doctor, to his subsequent regret, gave in. No one knows, who has not been to West

Africa, how terrible is the life of a white man in one of these out-of-the-way factories, with no white society, and with nothing to look at, day out and day in, but the one set of objects—the forest, the river, and the beach, which in a place like Osoamokita you cannot leave for months at a time, and of which you soon know every plank and stone. I felt utterly wretched as I started home again to come up to the end of the island, and go round it and down to Andande; and paddled on for some little time, before I noticed that I was making absolutely no progress. I redoubled my exertions, and crept slowly up to some rocks projecting above the water; but pass them I could not, as the main current of the Ogowé flew in hollow swirls round them against my canoe. Several passing canoefuls of natives gave me good advice in Igalwa; but facts were facts, and the Ogowé was too strong for me. After about twenty minutes an old Fan gentleman came down river in a canoe and gave me good advice in Fan, and I got him to take me in tow—that is to say, he got into my canoe and I held on to his and we went back down river. I then saw his intention was to take me across to that disreputable village, half Fan, half Bakele, which is situated on the main bank of the river opposite the island; this I disapproved of, because I had heard that some Senegal soldiers who had gone over there, had been stripped of every rag they had on, and maltreated; besides, it was growing very late, and I wanted to get home to dinner. I communicated my feelings to my pilot, who did not seem to understand at first, so I feared I should have to knock them into him with the paddle; but at last he understood I wanted to be landed on the island and duly landed me, when he seemed much surprised at the reward I gave him in pocket-handkerchiefs. Then I got a powerful young Igalwa dandy to paddle me home.

I did not go to the island next day, but down below Fula, watching the fish playing in the clear water, and the lizards and birds on the rocky high banks; but on my next journey round to the factories I got into another and a worse disaster. I went off there early one morning; and thinking the only trouble lay in getting back up the Ogowé, and having developed a theory that this might be minimised by keeping very close to the island bank, I never gave a thought to dangers attributive to going down river; so, having by now acquired pace, my canoe shot out beyond the end rocks of the island into the main stream. It took me a second to realise what had happened, and another to find out I could not get the canoe out of the current without upsetting it, and that I could not force her back up the current, so there was nothing for it but to keep her head straight now she had bolted. A group of native ladies, who had followed my proceedings with much interest, shouted observations which I believe to have been "Come back, come back; you'll be drowned." "Good-bye, Susannah, don't you weep for me," I courteously retorted, and flew past them and the factory beaches and things in general, keenly watching for my chance to run my canoe up a siding, as it were, off the current main line. I got it at last—a projecting spit of land from the island with rocks projecting out of the water in front of it bothered the current, and after a wild turn round or so, and a near call from my terrified canoe trying to climb up a rock, I got into slack water and took a pause in life's pleasures for a few minutes. Knowing I must be near the end of the island, I went on pretty close to the bank, finally got round into the Kangwe branch of the Ogowé by a connecting creek, and after an hour's steady paddling I fell in with three big canoes going up river; they took me home as far as Fula, whence a short paddle landed me at Andande only slightly late for supper, convinced that it was almost as safe and far more amusing to be born lucky than wise.

Now I have described my circumnavigation of the island, I will proceed to describe its inhabitants. The up-river end of Lembarene Island is the most inhabited. A path round the upper part of the island passes through a succession of Igalwa villages and by the Roman Catholic missionary station. The slave villages belonging to these Igalwas are away down the north face of the island, opposite the Fan town of Fula, which I have mentioned. It strikes me as remarkable that the Igalwa, like the Dualla of Cameroons, have their slaves in separate villages; but this is the case, though I do not know the reason of it. These Igalwa slaves cultivate the plantations, and bring up the vegetables and fruit to their owners' villages and do the housework daily.

The interior of the island is composed of high, rocky, heavily forested hills, with here and there a stream, and here and there a swamp; the higher land is towards the up-river end; down river there is a lower strip of land with hillocks. This is, I fancy, formed by deposits of sand, &c., catching in among the rocks, and connecting what were at one time several isolated islands. There are no big game or gorillas on the island, but it has a peculiar and awful house ant, much smaller than the driver ant, but with a venomous, bad bite; its only good point is that its chief food is the white ants, which are therefore kept in abeyance on

Lembarene Island, although flourishing destructively on the mainland banks of the river in this locality. I was never tired of going and watching those Igalwa villagers, nor were, I think, the Igalwa villagers ever tired of observing me. Although the physical conditions of life were practically identical with those of the mainland, the way in which the Igalwas dealt with them, *i.e.* the culture, was distinct from the culture of the mainland Fans.

The Igalwas are a tribe very nearly akin, if not ethnically identical with, the M'pongwe, and the culture of these two tribes is on a level with the highest native African culture. African culture, I may remark, varies just the same as European in this, that there is as much difference in the manners of life between, say, an Igalwa and a Bubi of Fernando Po, as there is between a Londoner and a Laplander.

The Igalwa builds his house, like that of the M'pongwe, of bamboo, and he surrounds himself with European-made articles. The neat houses, fitted with windows, with wooden shutters to close at night, and with a deal door—a carpenter-made door—are in sharp contrast with the ragged ant-hill looking performances of the Akkas, or the bark huts of the Fan, with no windows, and just an extra broad bit of bark to slip across the hole that serves as a door. On going into an Igalwa house you will see a four-legged table, often covered with a bright-coloured table-cloth, on which stands a water bottle, with two clean glasses, and round about you will see chairs—Windsor chairs. These houses have usually three, sometimes more rooms, and a separate closed-in little kitchen, built apart, wherein you may observe European-made saucepans, in addition to the ubiquitous skillet. Outside, all along the clean sandy streets, the inhabitants are seated. The Igalwa is truly great at sitting, the men pursuing a policy of masterly inactivity, broken occasionally by leisurely netting a fishing net, the end of the netting hitched up on to the roof thatch, and not held by a stirrup. The ladies are employed in the manufacture of articles pertaining to a higher culture—I allude, as Mr. Micawber would say, to bed-quilts and pillow-cases—the most gorgeous bed-quilts and pillow-cases—made of patchwork, and now and again you will see a mosquito-bar in course of construction, of course not made of net or muslin because of the awesome strength and ferocity of the Lembarene strain of mosquitoes, but of stout, fair-flowered and besprigged chintzes; and you will observe these things are often being sewn with a sewing machine.

The women who may not be busy sewing are busy doing each other's hair. Hair-dressing is quite an art among the Igalwa and M'pongwe women, and their hair is very beautiful; very crinkly, but fine. It is plaited up, close to the head, partings between the plaits making elaborate parterres. Into the beds of plaited hair are stuck long pins of river ivory (hippo), decorated with black tracery and openwork, and made by their good men. A lady will stick as many of these into her hair as she can get, but the prevailing mode is to have one stuck in behind each ear, showing their broad, long heads above like two horns; they are exceedingly becoming to these black but comely ladies, verily, I think, the comeliest ladies I have ever seen on the Coast. Very black they are, blacker than many of their neighbours, always blacker than the Fans, and although their skin lacks that velvety pile of the true negro, it is not too shiny, but it is fine and usually unblemished, and their figures are charmingly rounded, their hands and feet small, almost as small as a high-class Calabar woman's, and their eyes large, lustrous, soft and brown, and their teeth as white as the sea surf and undisfigured by filing.

The native dress for men and women alike is the cloth or paun. The men wear it by rolling the upper line round the waist, and in addition they frequently wear a singlet or a flannel shirt worn *more Africano*, flowing free. Rich men will mount a European coat and hat, and men connected with the mission or trading stations occasionally wear trousers. The personal appearance of the men does not amount to much when all's done, so we will return to the ladies. They wrap the upper hem of these cloths round under the armpits, a graceful form of drapery, but one which requires continual readjustment. The cloth is about four yards long and two deep, and there is always round the hem a border, or false hem, of turkey red twill, or some other coloured cotton cloth to the main body of the paun. In addition to the cloth there is worn, when possible, a European shawl, either one of those thick cotton cloth ones printed with Chinese-looking patterns in dull red on a dark ground, this sort is wrapped round the upper part of the body: or what is more highly esteemed is a bright, light-coloured, fancy wool shawl, pink or pale blue preferred, which being carefully folded into a roll is placed over one shoulder, and is entirely for dandy. I am thankful to say they do not go in for hats; when they wear anything on their heads it is a handkerchief folded shawl-wise; the base of the triangle is bound round the forehead just above the eyebrows, the ends carried round over the ears and tied behind over the apex of the triangle of the handkerchief, the three ends being then arranged fan-wise at the back. Add to this costume a sober-coloured silk parasol, not one of your green or red young tent-like, brutally masculine, knobby-sticked umbrellas, but a fair, lady-like parasol, which, being carefully rolled up, is carried handle foremost right in the middle of the head, also for dandy. Then a few strings of turquoise-blue beads, or imitation gold ones, worn round the shapely throat; and I will back my Igalwa or M'pongwe belle against any of those South Sea Island young ladies we nowadays hear so much about, thanks to Mr. Stevenson, yea, even though these may be wreathed with fragrant flowers, and the African lady very rarely goes in for flowers. The only time I have seen the African ladies wearing them for ornament has been among these Igalwas, who now and again stud their night-black hair with pretty little round vividly red blossoms in a most fetching way. I wonder the Africans do not wear flowers more frequently, for they are devoted to scent, both men and women.

The Igalwas are a proud race, one of the noble tribes, like the M'pongwe and the Ajumba. The women do not intermarry with lower-class tribes, and in their own tribe they are much restricted, owing to all relations on the mother's side being forbidden to intermarry. This well-known form of accounting relationships only through the mother (*Mutterrecht*) is in a more perfected and elaborated form among the Igalwa than among any other tribe I am personally acquainted with; brothers and cousins on the mother's side being in one class of relationship.

The father's responsibility, as regards authority over his own children, is very slight. The really responsible male relative is the mother's elder brother. From him must leave to marry be obtained for either girl, or boy; to him and the mother must the present be taken which is exacted on the marriage of a girl; and should the mother die, on him and not on the father lies the responsibility of rearing the children; they go to his house, and he treats and regards them as nearer and dearer to himself than his own children, and at his death, after his own brothers by the same mother, they become his heirs.

Marriage among the Igalwa and the M'pongwe is not direct marriage by purchase, but a certain fixed price present is made to the mother and uncle of the girl. Other propitiatory presents (Kueliki) are made, but do not count legally, and have not necessarily to be returned in case of post-nuptial differences arising leading to a divorce—a very frequent catastrophe in the social circle; for the Igalwa ladies are spirited, and devoted to personal adornment, and they are naggers at their husbands. Many times when walking on Lembarene Island, have I seen a lady stand in the street and let her husband, who had taken shelter inside the house, know what she thought of him, in a way that reminded me of some London slum scenes. When the husband loses his temper, as he surely does sooner or later, being a man, he whacks his wife—or wives, if they have been at him in a body. He may whack with impunity so long as he does not draw blood; if he does, be it never so little, his wife is off to her relations, the present he has given for her is returned, the marriage is annulled, and she can re-marry as soon as she is able.

Her relations are only too glad to get her, because, although the present has to be returned, yet the propitiatory offerings remain theirs, and they know more propitiatory offerings as well as another present will accrue with the next set of suitors. This of course is only the case with the younger women; the older women for one thing do not nag so much, and moreover they have usually children willing and able to support them. If they have not, their state is, like that of all old childless women in Africa, a very desolate one.

Infant marriage is now in vogue among the Igalwa, and to my surprise I find it is of quite recent introduction and adoption. Their own account of this retrograde movement in culture is that in the last generation—some of the old people indeed claim to have known him—there was an exceedingly ugly and deformed man who could not get a wife, the women being then, as the men are now, great admirers of physical beauty. So this man, being very cunning, hit on the idea of becoming betrothed to one before she could exercise her own choice in the matter; and knowing a family in which an interesting event was likely to occur, he made heavy presents in the proper quarters and bespoke the coming infant if it should be a girl. A girl it was, and thus, say the Igalwa, arose the custom; and nowadays, although they do not engage their wives so early as did the founder of the custom, they adopt infant marriage as an institution.

I inquired carefully, in the interests of ethnology, as to what methods of courting were in vogue previously. They said people married each other because they loved each other. I hope other ethnologists will follow this inquiry up, for we may here find a real golden age, which in other races of humanity lies away in the mists of the ages behind the

kitchen middens and the Cambrian rocks. My own opinion in this matter is that the earlier courting methods of the Igalwa involved a certain
amount of effort on the man's part, a thing abhorrent to an Igalwa. It
necessitated his dressing himself up, and likely enough fighting that
impudent scoundrel who was engaged in courting her too; and above all
serenading her at night on the native harp, with its strings made from
the tendrils of a certain orchid, or on the marimba, amongst crowds of
mosquitoes. Any institution that involved being out at night amongst
crowds of those Lembarene mosquitoes would have to disappear, let that
institution be what it might.

The Igalwa are one of the dying-out coast tribes. As well as on
Lembarene Island, their villages are scattered along the banks of the
Lower Ogowé, and on the shores and islands of Elivã Z'Onlange. On
the island they are, so far, undisturbed by the Fan invasion, and laze
their lives away like lotus-eaters. Their slaves work their large plantations, and bring up to them magnificent yams, ready prepared ogooma,
sweet-potatoes, papaw, &c., not forgetting that delicacy Odeaka cheese;
this is not an exclusive inspiration of theirs, for the M'pongwe and the
Benga use it as well. It is made from the kernel of the wild mango, a singularly beautiful tree of great size and stately spread of foliage. I can
compare it only in appearance and habit of growth to our Irish, or ever-
green, oak, but it is an idealisation of that fine tree. Its leaves are a softer,
brighter, deeper green, and in due season (August) it is covered—not
ostentatiously like the real mango, with great spikes of bloom, looking
each like a gigantic head of mignonette—but with small yellow-green
flowers tucked away under the leaves, filling the air with a soft sweet
perfume, and then falling on to the bare shaded ground beneath to
make a deep-piled carpet. I do not know whether it is a mango tree at
all, for I am no botanist: but anyhow the fruit is rather like that of the
mango in external appearance, and in internal still more so, for it has a
disproportionately large stone. These stones are cracked, and the kernel
taken out. The kernels are spread a short time in the shade to dry; then
they are beaten up into a pulp with a wooden pestle, and the pulp put
into a basket lined carefully with plantain leaves and placed in the sun,
which melts it up into a stiff mass. The basket is then removed from the
sun and stood aside to cool. When cool, the cheese can be turned out in
shape, and can be kept a long time if it is wrapped round with leaves and
a cloth, and hung up inside the house. Its appearance is that of almond

rock, and it is cut easily with a knife; but at any period of its existence, if it is left in the sun it melts again rapidly into an oily mass.

The natives use it as a seasoning in their cookery, stuffing fish and plantains with it and so on, using it also in the preparation of a sort of sea-pie they make with meat and fish. To make this, a thing well worth doing, particularly with hippo or other coarse meat, reduce the wood fire to embers, and make plantain leaves into a sort of bag, or cup; small pieces of the meat should then be packed in layers with red pepper and odeaka in between. The tops of the leaves are then tied together with fine tie-tie, and the bundle, without any saucepan of any kind, stood on the glowing embers, the cook taking care there is no flame. The meat is done, and a superb gravy formed, before the containing plantain leaves are burnt through—plantain leaves will stand an amazing lot in the way of fire. This dish is really excellent, even when made with python, hippo, or crocodile. It makes the former most palatable; but of course it does not remove the musky taste from crocodile; nothing I know of will.

The great and important difference between the M'pongwe, Igalwa, and Ajumba fetish, and the Fetish of those tribes round them, consists in their conception of a certain spirit called O Mbuiri. They have, as is constant among the Bantu races of South-West Africa, a great god—the creator, a god who has made all things, and who now no longer takes any interest in the things he has created. Their name for this god is Anyambie, which when pronounced sounds to my ears like anlynlae—the l's being very weak,—the derivation of this name, however, is from Anyima a spirit, and Mbia, good. This god, unlike other forms of the creating god in Fetish, has a viceroy or minister who is a god he has created, and to whom he leaves the government of affairs. This god is O Mbuiri or O Mbwiri, and this O Mbwiri is of very high interest to the student of comparative fetish. He has never been, nor can he ever become, a man, *i.e.* be born as a man, but he can transfuse with his own personality that of human beings, and also the souls of all those things we white men regard as inanimate, such as rocks, trees, &c., in a similar manner.

The M'pongwe know that his residence is in the sea, and some of them have seen him as an old white man, not flesh-colour white, but chalk white. There is another important point here, but it wants a volume to itself, so I must pass it. O Mbuiri's appearance in a corporeal form denotes ill luck, not death to the seer, but misfortune of a severe and diffused character. The ruin of a trading enterprise, the destruction of a village or a family, are put down to O Mbuiri's action. Yet he is not regarded as a malevolent god, a devil, but as an avenger, or punisher of sin; and the M'pongwe look on him as the Being to whom they primarily owe the good things and fortunes of this life, and as the Being who alone has power to govern the host of truly malevolent spirits that exist in nature.

The different instruments with which he works in the shaping of human destiny bear his name when in his employ. When acting by means of water, he is O Mbuiri Aningo; when in the weather, O Mbuiri Ngali; when in the forests, O Mbuiri Ibaka; when in the form of a dwarf, O Mbuiri Akoa, and so on.

The great difference between O Mbuiri and the lesser spirits is this:—the lesser spirits cannot incarnate themselves except through extraneous things; O Mbuiri can, he can become visible without anything beyond his own will to do so. The other spirits must be in something to become visible. This is an extremely delicate piece of Fetish which it took me weeks to work out. I think I may say another thing about O Mbuiri, though I say it carefully, and that is, that among the M'pongwe and the tribe who are the parent tribe of the M'pongwe— the now rapidly dying out Ajumba, and their allied tribe the Igalwa—O Mbuiri is a distinct entity, while among the neighbouring tribes he is a class, i.e. there are hundreds of O Mbuiri or Ibwiri, one for every remarkable place of thing, such as rock, tree, or forest thicket, and for every dangerous place in a river. Had I not observed a similar state of affairs regarding Sasabonsum, a totally different kind of spirit on the Windward coast, I should have had even greater trouble than I had, in finding a key to what seemed at first a mass of conflicting details regarding this important spirit O Mbuiri.

There is one other very important point in M'pongwe Fetish; and that is that the souls of men exist before birth as well as after death. This is indeed, as far as I have been able to find out, a doctrine universally held by the West African tribes, but among the M'pongwe there is this modification in it, which agrees strangely well with the idea I found regarding reincarnated diseases, existent among the Okÿon tribes (pure negroes). The malevolent minor spirits are capable of being born with, what we will call, a man's soul, as well as going in with the man's soul during sleep. For example, an Olâgâ, may be born with a man and that man will thereby be born mad; he may at any period of his life, given certain conditions, become possessed by an evil spirit, Onlogho Abambo, Injembe, Nkandada, and become mad, or ill; but if he is born mad, or sickly, one of the evil spirits such as an Olâgâ, or an Obambo, the soul of a man that has not been buried properly, has been born with him.

The rest of the M'pongwe Fetish is on broad lines common to other tribes, so I relegate it to the general collection of notes on Fetish. M'pongwe jurisprudence is founded on the same ideas as those on which West African jurisprudence at large is founded, but it is so elaborated that it would be desecration to sketch it. It requires a massive monograph.

CHAPTER 7

ON THE WAY FROM KANGWE
TO LAKE NCOVI

In which the voyager goes for bush again and wanders into a new lake and a new river.

JULY 22ND, 1895. LEFT KANGWE. The four Ajumba did not turn up early in the morning as had been arranged, but arrived about eight, in pouring rain, so decided to wait until two o'clock, which will give us time to reach their town of Arevooma before nightfall, and may perhaps give us a chance of arriving there dry. At two we start. We go down river on the Kangwe side of Lembarene Island, make a pause in front of the Igalwa slave town, which is on the Island and nearly opposite the Fan town of Fula on the mainland bank, our motive being to get stores of yam and plantain—and magnificent specimens of both we get—and then, when our canoe is laden with them to an extent that would get us into trouble under the Act if it ran here, off we go again. Every canoe we meet shouts us a greeting, and asks where we are going, and we say "Rembwé"—and they say "What! Rembwé!"—and we say "Yes, Rembwé," and paddle on. I lay among the luggage for about an hour, not taking much interest in the Rembwé or anything else, save my own headache; but this soon lifted, and I was able to take notice, just before we reached the Ajumba's town, called Arevooma. The sandbanks stretch across the river here nearly awash, so all our cargo of yams has to be thrown overboard on to the sand, from which they can be collected by being waded out to. The canoe, thus lightened, is able to go on a little further, but we are soon hard and fast again, and the crew have to jump out and shove her off about once every five minutes, and then to look lively about jumping back into her again, as she shoots over the cliffs of the sandbanks.

When we reach Arevooma, I find it is a very prettily situated town, on the left-hand bank of the river—clean and well kept, and composed of houses built on the Igalwa and M'pongwe plan with walls of split bamboo and a palm thatch roof. I own I did not much care for these Ajumbas on starting, but they are evidently going to be kind and pleasant companions. One of them is a gentlemanly-looking man, who wears a gray shirt; another looks like a genial Irishman who has accidentally got black, very black; he is distinguished by wearing a singlet; another is a thin, elderly man, notably silent; and the remaining one is a strapping, big fellow, as black as a wolf's mouth, of gigantic muscular development, and wearing quantities of fetish charms hung about him. The two first mentioned are Christians; the other two pagans, and I will refer to them by their characteristic points, for their honourable names are awfully alike when you do hear them, and, as is usual with Africans, rarely used in conversation.

Gray Shirt places his house at my disposal, and both he and his exceedingly pretty wife do their utmost to make me comfortable. The house lies at the west end of the town. It is one room inside, but has, I believe, a separate cooking shed. In the verandah in front is placed a table, an ivory bundle chair and a gourd of water, and I am also treated to a calico tablecloth, and most thoughtfully screened off from the public gaze with more calico so that I can have my tea in privacy. After this meal, to my surprise Ndaka turns up. Certainly he is one of the very ugliest men—black or white—I have ever seen, and I fancy one of the best. He is now on a holiday from Kangwe, seeing to the settlement of his dead brother's affairs. The dead brother was a great man in Arevooma and a pagan, but Ndaka, the Christian Bible-reader, seems to get on perfectly with the family and is holding tonight a meeting outside his brother's house and comes with a lantern to fetch me to attend it. Of course I have to go, headache or no headache.

Most of the town was there, mainly as spectators. Ndaka and my two Christian boatmen manage the service between them, and what with the hymns and the mosquitoes the experience is slightly awful. We sit in a line in front of the house, which is brilliantly lit up—our own lantern on the ground before us acting as a rival entertainment to the house lamps inside for some of the best insect society in Africa, who after the manner of the insect world, insist on regarding us as responsible for their own idiocy in getting singed, and sting us in revenge, while we slap hard, as we howl hymns in the fearful Igalwa and M'pongwe way. Next to an English picnic, the most uncomfortable thing I know is an open-air service in this part of Africa. Service being over, Ndaka takes me over the house to show its splendours. The great brilliancy of its illumination arises from its being lit by two hanging lamps burning paraffin oil. The most remarkable point about the house is the floor, which is made of split, plaited bamboo. It gives under your feet in an alarming way, being raised some three or four feet above the ground, and I am haunted by the fear that I shall go through it and give pain to myself, and great trouble to others before I could be got out. It is a beautiful piece of workmanship, and Arevooma has every reason to be proud of it. Having admired these things, I go, dead tired and still headachy, down the road with my host who carries the lantern, through an atmosphere that has 45 per cent of solid matter in the shape of mosquitoes; then wishing him good-night, I shut myself in, and illuminate, humbly, with a candle. The furniture of the house consists mainly of boxes, containing the wealth of Gray Shirt, in clothes, mirrors, &c. One corner of the room is taken up by great calabashes full of some sort of liquor, and there is an ivory bundle chair, a hanging mirror, several rusty guns, and a considerable collection of china basins and jugs. Evidently Gray Shirt is rich. The most interesting article to me, however, just now is the bed hung over with a clean, substantial, chintz mosquito bar, and spread with clean calico and adorned with patchwork-covered pillows. So I take off my boots and put on my slippers; for it never does in this country to leave off boots altogether at any time and risk getting bitten by mosquitoes on the feet, when you are on the march; because the rub of your boot on the bite always produces a sore, and a sore when it comes in the Gorilla country, comes to stay.

No sooner have I carefully swished all the mosquitoes from under the bar and turned in, than a cat scratches and mews at the door—turn out and let her in. She is evidently a pet, so I take her on to the bed with me. She is a very nice cat—sandy and fat—and if I held the opinion of Pythagoras concerning wild fowl, I should have no hesitation in saying she had in her the soul of Dame Juliana Berners, such a whole-souled devotion to sport does she display, dashing out through the flaps of the mosquito bar after rats which, amid squeals from the rats and curses from her, she kills amongst the china collection. Then she comes to me, triumphant, expecting congratulations, and accompanied by mosquitoes, and purrs and kneads upon my chest until she hears another rat.

Tuesday, July 23rd.—Am aroused by violent knocking at the door in the early gray dawn—so violent that two large centipedes and a scorpion drop on to the bed. They have evidently been tucked away among the folds of the bar all night. Well "when ignorance is bliss 'tis folly to be wise," particularly along here. I get up without delay, and find myself quite well. The cat has thrown a basin of water neatly over into my bag during her nocturnal hunts; and when my tea comes I am informed a man "done die" in the night, which explains the firing of guns I heard. I inquire what he has died of, and am told "He just truck luck, and then he die." His widows are having their faces painted white by sympathetic lady friends, and are attired in their oldest, dirtiest clothes, and but very few of them; still, they seem to be taking things in a resigned spirit. These Ajumba seem pleasant folk. They play with their pretty brown children in a taking way. Last night I noticed some men and women playing a game new to me, which consisted in throwing a hoop at each other. The point was to get the hoop to fall over your adversary's head. It is a cheerful game. Quantities of the common house-fly about—and, during the early part of the morning, it rains in a gentle kind of way; but soon after we are afloat in our canoe it turns into a soft white mist.

We paddle still westwards down the broad quiet waters of the O'Rembo Vongo. I notice great quantities of birds about here—great hornbills, vividly coloured kingfishers, and for the first time the great vulture I have often heard of, and the skin of which I will take home before I mention even its approximate spread of wing. There are also noble white cranes, and flocks of small black and white birds, new to me, with heavy razor-shaped bills, reminding one of the Devonian puffin. The hornbill is perhaps the most striking in appearance. It is the size of a small, or say a good-sized hen turkey. Gray Shirt says the flocks, which are of eight or ten, always have the same quantity of cocks and hens, and that they live together "white man fashion," *i.e.* each couple keeping together. They certainly do a great deal of courting, the cock filling out his wattles on his neck like a turkey, and spreading out his tail with great pomp and ceremony, but very awkwardly. To see hornbills on a bare sandbank is a solemn sight, but when they are dodging about in the hippo grass they sink ceremony, and roll and waddle, looking—my man said—for snakes and the little sand-fish, which are close in under the bank; and their killing way of dropping their jaws—I should say opening their bills—when they are alarmed is comic. I think this has something to do with their hearing, for I often saw two or three of them in a line on a long branch, standing, stretched up to their full height, their great eyes opened wide, and all with their great beaks open, evidently listening for something. Their cry is most peculiar and can only be mistaken for a native horn; and although there seems little variety in it to my ear, there must be more to theirs, for they will carry on long confabulations with each other across a river, and, I believe, sit up half the night and talk scandal.

There were plenty of plantain-eaters here, but, although their screech was as appalling as I have heard in Angola, they were not regarded, by the Ajumba at any rate, as being birds of evil omen, as they are in Angola. Still, by no means all the birds here only screech and squark. Several of them have very lovely notes. There is one who always gives a series of infinitely beautiful, soft, rich-toned whistles just before the first light of the dawn shows in the sky, and one at least who has a pro- longed and very lovely song. This bird, I was told in Gaboon, is called *Telephonus erythropterus.* I expect an ornithologist would enjoy himself here, but I cannot—and will not—collect birds. I hate to have them killed any how, and particularly in the barbarous way in which these natives kill them.

The broad stretch of water looks like a long lake. In all directions sandbanks are showing their broad yellow backs, and there will be more showing soon, for it is not yet the height of the dry. We are perpetually grounding on those which by next month will be above water. These canoes are built, I believe, more with a view to taking sandbanks com- fortably than anything else; but they are by no means yet sufficiently spe- cialised for getting off them. Their flat bottoms enable them to glide on to the banks, and sit there, without either upsetting or cutting into the sand, as a canoe with a keel would; but the trouble comes in when you are getting off the steep edge of the bank, and the usual form it takes is upsetting. So far my Ajumba friends have only tried to meet this diffi- culty by tying the cargo in.

I try to get up the geography of this region conscientiously. Fortunately I find Gray Shirt, Singlet, and Pagan can speak trade

English. None of them, however, seem to recognise a single blessed name on the chart, which is saying nothing against the chart and its makers, who probably got their names up from M'pongwes and Igalwas instead of Ajumba, as I am trying to. Geographical research in this region is fraught with difficulty, I find, owing to different tribes calling one and the same place by different names; and I am sure the Royal Geographical Society ought to insert among their "Hints" that every traveller in this region should carefully learn every separate native word, or set of words, signifying "I don't know,"—four villages and two rivers I have come across out here solemnly set down with various forms of this statement, for their native name. Really I think the old Portuguese way of naming places after Saints, &c., was wiser in the long run, and it was certainly pleasanter to the ear. My Ajumba, however, know about my Ngambi and the Vinue all right and Elivã z'Ayzingo, so I must try and get cross bearings from these.

We have an addition to our crew this morning—a man who wants to go and get work at John Holt's sub-factory away on the Rembwé. He has been waiting a long while at Arevooma, unable to get across, I am told, "because the road is now stopped between Ayzingo and the Rembwé by "those fearful Fans." "How are we going to get through that way?" says I, with natural feminine alarm. "We are not, sir," says Gray Shirt. This is what Lady MacDonald would term a chatty little incident; and my hair begins to rise as I remember what I have been told about those Fans and the indications I have already seen of its being true when on the Upper Ogowé. Now here we are going to try to get through the heart of their country, far from a French station, and without the French flag. Why did I not obey Mr. Hudson's orders not to go wandering about in a reckless way! Anyhow I am in for it, and Fortune favours the brave. The only question is: Do I individually come under this class? I go into details. It seems Pagan thinks he can depend on the friendship of two Fans he once met and did business with, and who now live on an island in Lake Ncovi—Ncovi is not down on my map and I have never heard of it before—anyhow thither we are bound now.

Each man has brought with him his best gun, loaded to the muzzle, and tied on to the baggage against which I am leaning—the muzzles sticking out each side of my head: the flint locks covered with cases, or sheaths, made of the black-haired skins of gorillas, leopard skin, and a beautiful bright bay skin, which I do not know, which they say is bush cow—but they call half a dozen things bush cow. These guns are not the "gas-pipes" I have seen up north; but decent rifles which have had the rifling filed out and the locks replaced by flint locks and converted into muzzle loaders, and many of them have beautiful barrels. I find the Ajumba name for the beautiful shrub that has long bunches of red, yellow and cream-coloured young leaves at the end of its branches is "obaa." I also learn that in their language ebony and a monkey have one name. The forest on either bank is very lovely. Some enormously high columns of green are formed by a sort of climbing plant having taken possession of lightning-struck trees, and in one place it really looks exactly as if some one had spread a great green coverlet over the forest, so as to keep it dry. No high land showing in any direction. Pagan tells me the extinguisher-shaped juju filled with medicine and made of iron is against drowning—the red juju is "for keep foot in path." Beautiful effect of a gleam of sunshine lighting up a red sandbank till it glows like the Nibelungen gold. Indeed the effects are Turneresque to-day owing to the mist, and the sun playing in and out among it.

The sandbanks now have their cliffs to the N.N.W. and N.W. At 9.30, the broad river in front of us is apparently closed by sandbanks which run out from the banks thus:—

yellow ⎫
S. bank bright-red ⎬ N. bank.
yellow ⎭

Current running strong along south bank. This bank bears testimony of this also being the case in the wet season, for a fringe of torn-down trees hangs from it into the river. Pass Seke, a town on north bank, interchanging the usual observations regarding our destination. The river seems absolutely barred with sand again; but as we paddle down it, the obstructions resolve themselves into spits of sand from the north bank and the largest island in mid-stream, which also has a long tail, or train, of sandbank down river. Here we meet a picturesque series of canoes, fruit and trade laden, being poled up stream, one man with his pole over one side, the other with his pole over the other, making a St. Andrew's cross as you meet them end on.

Most luxurious, charming, and pleasant trip this. The men are standing up swinging in rhythmic motion their long, rich red wood paddles in perfect time to their elaborate melancholy, minor key boat song. Nearly lost with all hands. Sandbank palaver—only when we were going over the end of it, the canoe slips sideways over its edge. River deep, bottom sand and mud. This information may be interesting to the geologist, but I hope I shall not be converted by circumstances into a human sounding apparatus again to-day. Next time she strikes I shall get out and shove behind.

We are now skirting the real north bank, and not the bank of an island or islands as we have been for some time heretofore. Lovely stream falls into this river over cascades. The water is now rough in a small way and the width of the river great, but it soon is crowded again with wooded islands. There are patches and wreaths of a lovely, vermilion-flowering bush rope decorating the forest, and now and again clumps of a plant that shows a yellow and crimson spike of bloom, very strikingly beautiful. We pass a long tunnel in the bush, quite dark as you look down it—evidently the path to some native town. The south bank is covered, where the falling waters have exposed it, with hippo grass. Terrible lot of mangrove flies about, although we are more than one hundred miles above the mangrove belt. River broad again— tending W.S.W., with a broad flattened island with attributive sandbanks in the middle. The fair way is along the south bank of the river. Gray Shirt tells me this river is called the O'Rembo Vongo, or small River, so as to distinguish it from the main stream of the Ogowé which goes down past the south side of Lembarene Island, as well I know after that canoe affair of mine. Ayzingo now bears due north—and native mahogany is called "Okooma." Pass village called Welli on north bank. It looks like some gipsy caravans stuck on poles. I expect that village has known what it means to be swamped by the rising river; it looks as if it had, very hastily in the middle of some night, taken to stilts, which I am sure, from their present rickety condition, will not last through the next wet season, and then some unfortunate spirit will get the blame of the collapse. I also learn that it is the natal spot of my friend Kabinda, the carpenter at Andande. Now if some of these good people I know would only go and distinguish themselves, I might write a sort of county family history of these parts; but they don't, and I fancy won't. For example, the entrance—or should I say the exit?—of a broadish little river is just away on the south bank. If you go up this river—it runs S.E.—you get to a good-sized lake; in this lake there is an island called Adole; then out of the other side of the lake there is another river which falls into the Ogowé main stream—but that is not the point of the story, which is that on that island of Adole, Ngouta, the interpreter, first saw the light. Why he ever did—there or anywhere—Heaven only knows! I know I shall never want to write his biography.

On the western bank end of that river going to Adole, there is an Igalwa town, notable for a large quantity of fine white ducks and a clump of Indian bamboo. My informants say, "No white man ever live for this place," so I suppose the ducks and bamboo have been imported by some black trader whose natal spot this is. The name of this village is Wanderegwoma. Stuck on sandbank—I flew out and shoved behind, leaving Ngouta to do the balancing performances in the stern. This O'Rembo Vongo divides up just below here, I am told, when we have re-embarked, into three streams. One goes into the main Ogowé opposite Ayshouka in Nkami country—Nkami country commences at Ayshouka and goes to the sea—one into the Ngumbi, and one into the Nunghi— all in the Ouroungou country. Ayzingo now lies N.E. according to Gray Shirt's arm. On our river there is here another broad low island with its gold-coloured banks shining out, seemingly barring the entire channel, but there is really a canoe channel along by both banks.

We turn at this point into a river on the north bank that runs north and south—the current is running very swift to the north. We run down into it, and then, it being more than time enough for chop, we push the canoe on to a sandbank in our new river, which I am told is the Karkola. I, after having had my tea, wander off, and find behind our high sand-bank, which like all the other sandbanks above water now, is getting grown over with hippo grass—a fine light green grass, the beloved food of both hippo and manatee—a forest, and entering this I notice a succession of strange mounds or heaps, made up of branches, twigs, and leaves, and dead flowers. Many of these heaps are recent, while others have fallen into decay. Investigation shows they are burial places. Among the *débris* of an old one there are human bones, and out from one of the new ones comes a stench and a hurrying, exceedingly busy line of ants, demonstrating what is going on. I own I thought these mounds were some kind of bird's or animal's nest. They look entirely unhuman in this desolate reach of forest. Leaving these, I go down to the water edge of the sand, and find in it a quantity of pools of varying breadth and expanse, but each surrounded by a rim of dark red-brown deposit, which you can lift off the sand in a skin. On the top of the water is a film of exquisite iridescent colours like those on a soap bubble, only darker and brighter. In the river alongside the sand, there are thousands of those beautiful little fish with a black line each side of their tails. They are perfectly tame, and I feed them with crumbs in my hand. After making every effort to terrify the unknown object containing the food—gallant bulls, quite two inches long, sidling up and snapping at my fingers—they come and feed right in the palm, so that I could have caught them by the handful had I wished. There are also a lot of those weird, semi-transparent, yellow, spotted little sandfish with cup-shaped pectoral fins, which I see they use to enable them to make their astoundingly long leaps. These fish are of a more nervous and distrustful disposition, and hover round my hand but will not come into it. Indeed I do not believe the other cheeky little fellows would allow them to.

The men, having had their rest and their pipes, shout for me, and off we go again. The Karkola soon widens to about 100 feet; it is evidently very deep here; the right bank (the east) is forested, the left, low and shrubbed, one patch looking as if it were being cleared for a plantation, but no village showing. A big rock shows up on the right bank, which is a change from the clay and sand, and soon the whole character of the landscape changes. We come to a sharp turn in the river, from north and south to east and west—the current very swift. The river channel dodges round against a big bank of sword grass, and then widens out to the breadth of the Thames at Putney. I am told that a river runs out of it here to the west to Ouroungou country, and so I imagine this Karkola falls ultimately into the Nazareth. We skirt the eastern banks, which are covered with low grass with a scanty lot of trees along the top. High land shows in the distance to the S.S.W. and S.W., and then we suddenly turn up into a broad river or straith, shaping our course N.N.E. On the opposite bank, on a high dwarf cliff, is a Fan town. "All Fan now," says Singlet in anything but a gratified tone of voice.

It is a strange, wild, lonely bit of the world we are now in, apparently a lake or broad—full of sandbanks, some bare and some in the course of developing into permanent islands by the growth on them of that floating coarse grass, any joint of which being torn off either by the current, a passing canoe, or hippos, floats down and grows wherever it settles. Like most things that float in these parts, it usually settles on a sandbank, and then grows in much the same way as our couch grass grows on land in England, so as to form a network, which catches for its adopted sandbank all sorts of floating *débris*; so the sandbank comes up in the world. The waters of the wet season when they rise drown off the grass; but when they fall, up it comes again from the root, and so gradually the sandbank becomes an island and persuades real trees and shrubs to come and grow on it, and its future is then secured.

We skirt alongside a great young island of this class; the sword grass some ten or fifteen feet high. It has not got any trees on it yet, but by next season or so it doubtless will have. The grass is stabbled down into paths by hippos, and just as I have realised who are the road-makers, they appear in person. One immense fellow, hearing us, stands up and shows himself about six feet from us in the grass, gazes calmly, and then yawns a yawn a yard wide and grunts his news to his companions, some of whom—there is evidently a large herd—get up and stroll towards us with all the flowing grace of Pantechnicon vans in motion. We put our helm paddles hard a starboard and leave that bank.

Our hasty trip across to the bank of the island on the other side being accomplished, we, in search of seclusion and in the hope that out of sight would mean out of mind to hippos, shot down a narrow channel between semi-island sandbanks, and those sandbanks, if you please, are covered with specimens—as fine a set of specimens as you could wish for—of the West African crocodile. These interesting animals are also having their siestas, lying sprawling in all directions on the sand, with their mouths wide open. One immense old lady has a family of lively young crocodiles running over her, evidently playing like a lot of kittens. The heavy musky smell they give off is most repulsive, but we do not rise up and make a row about this, because we feel hopelessly in the wrong in intruding into these family scenes uninvited, and so apologetically pole ourselves along rapidly, not even singing. The pace the canoe goes down that channel would be a wonder to Henley Regatta. When out of earshot I ask Pagan whether there are many gorillas, elephants, or bushcows round here. "Plenty too much," says he; and it occurs to me that the corn-fields are growing golden green away in England; and soon there rises up in my mental vision a picture that fascinated my youth in the *Fliegende Blätter*, representing "Friedrich Gerstaeker auf der Reise." That gallant man is depicted tramping on a serpent, new to M. Boulenger, while he attempts to club, with the butt end of his gun, a most lively savage who, accompanied by a bison, is attaching him in front. A terrific and obviously enthusiastic crocodile is grabbing the tail of the explorer's coat, and the explorer says "Hurrah! das gibt wieder einen prächtigen Artikel für *Die Allgemeine Zeitung.*" I do not know where in the world Gerstaeker was at the time, but I should fancy hereabouts. My vigorous and lively conscience also reminds me that the last words a most distinguished and valued scientific friend had said to me before I left home was, "Always take measurements, Miss Kingsley, and always take them from the adult male." I know I have neglected opportunities of carrying this commission out on both those banks, but I do not feel like going back. Besides, the men would not like it, and I have mislaid my yard measure.

The extent of water, dotted with sandbanks and islands in all directions, here is great, and seems to be fringed uniformly by low swampy land, beyond which, to the north, rounded lumps of hills show blue. On one of the islands is a little white house which I am told was once occupied by a black trader for John Holt. It looks a desolate place for any man to live in, and the way the crocodiles and hippo must have come up on the garden ground in the evening time could not have enhanced its charms to the average cautious man. My men say, "No man live for that place now." The factory, I believe, has been, for some trade reason, abandoned. Behind it is a great clump of dark-coloured trees. The rest of the island is now covered with hippo grass looking like a beautifully kept lawn. We lie up for a short rest at another island, also a weird spot in its way, for it is covered with a grove of only one kind of tree, which has a twisted, contorted, gray-white trunk and dull, lifeless-looking, green, hard foliage.

I learn that these good people, to make topographical confusion worse confounded, call a river by one name when you are going up it, and by another when you are coming down; just as if you called the Thames the London when you were going up, and the Greenwich when you were coming down. The banks all round this lake or broad, seem all light-coloured sand and clay. We pass out of it into a channel. Current flowing north. As we are entering the channel between banks of grass-overgrown sand, a superb white crane is seen standing on the sand edge to the left. Gray Shirt attempts to get a shot at it, but it—alarmed at our unusual appearance—raises itself up with one of those graceful preliminary curtseys, and after one or two preliminary flaps spreads its broad wings and sweeps away, with its long legs trailing behind it like a thing on a Japanese screen.

The river into which we ran zig-zags about, and then takes a course S.S.E. It is studded with islands slightly higher than those we have passed, and thinly clad with forest. The place seems alive with birds; flocks of pelican and crane rise up before us out of the grass, and every now and then a crocodile slides off the bank into the water. Wonderfully like old logs they look, particularly when you see one letting himself roll and float down on the current. In spite of these interests I began to wonder where in this lonely land we were to sleep to-night. In front of us were miles of distant mountains, but in no direction the slightest sign of human habitation. Soon we passed out of our channel into a lovely, strangely melancholy, lonely-looking lake—Lake Ncovi, my friends tell me. It is exceedingly beautiful. The rich golden sunlight of the late afternoon soon followed by the short-lived, glorious flushes of colour of the sunset and the after-glow, play over the scene as we paddle across the lake to the N.N.E.—our canoe leaving a long trail of frosted silver behind her as she glides over the mirror-like water, and each stroke of the paddle sending down air with it to come up again in luminous silver bubbles—not as before in swirls of sand and mud. The lake shore is, in all directions, wreathed with nobly forested hills, indigo and purple in the dying daylight. On the N.N.E. and N.E. these come directly down into the lake; on N.W., N., S.W., and S.E. there is a band of well-forested ground, behind which they rise. In the north and north-eastern part of the lake several exceedingly beautiful wooded islands show, with gray rocky beaches and dwarf cliffs.

Sign of human habitation at first there was none; and in spite of its beauty, there was something which I was almost going to say was repulsive. The men evidently felt the same as I did. Had any one told me that the air that lay on the lake was poison, or that in among its forests lay some path to regions of utter death, I should have said—"It looks like that"; but no one said anything, and we only looked round uneasily, until the comfortable-souled Singlet made the unfortunate observation that he "smelt blood." We all called him an utter fool to relieve our minds, and made our way towards the second island. When we got near enough to it to see details, a large village showed among the trees on its summit, and a steep dwarf cliff, overgrown with trees and creeping plants came down to a small beach covered with large water-washed gray stones. There was evidently some kind of a row going on in that village, that took a lot of shouting too. We made straight for the beach, and drove our canoe among its outlying rocks, and then each of my men stowed his paddle quickly, slung on his ammunition bag, and picked up his ready loaded gun, sliding the skin sheath off the lock. Pagan got out on to the stones alongside the canoe just as the inhabitants became aware of our arrival, and, abandoning what I hope was a mass meeting to remonstrate with the local authorities on the insanitary state of the town, came—a brown mass of naked humanity—down the steep cliff path to attend to us, whom they evidently regarded as an Imperial interest. Things did not look restful, nor these Fans personally pleasant. Every man among them—no women showed—was armed with a gun, and they loosened their shovel-shaped knives in their sheaths as they came, evidently regarding a fight quite as imminent as we did. They drew up about twenty paces from us in silence. Pagan and Gray Shirt, who had joined him, held out their unembarrassed hands, and shouted out the name of the Fan man they had said they were friendly with: "Kiva-Kiva." The Fans stood still and talked angrily among themselves for some minutes, and then, Silence said to me, "It would be bad palaver if Kiva no live for this place," in a tone that conveyed to me the idea he thought this unpleasant contingency almost a certainty. The Passenger exhibited unmistakable symptoms of wishing he had come by another boat. I got up from my seat in the bottom of the canoe and leisurely strolled ashore, saying to the line of angry faces "M'boloani" in an unconcerned way, although I well knew it was etiquette for them to salute first. They grunted, but did not commit themselves further. A minute after they parted to allow a fine-looking, middle-aged man, naked save for a twist of dirty cloth round his loins and a bunch of leopard and wild cat tails hung from his shoulder by a strip of leopard skin, to come forward. Pagan went for him with a rush, as if he were going to clasp him to his ample bosom, but holding his hands just off from touching the Fan's shoulder in the usual way, while he said in Fan, "Don't you know me, my beloved Kiva? Surely you have not forgotten your old friend?" Kiva grunted feelingly, and raised up his hands and held them just off touching Pagan, and we breathed again. Then Gray Shirt made a rush at the crowd and went through great demonstrations of affection with another gentleman whom he recognised as being a Fan friend of his own, and whom he had not expected to meet here. I looked round to see if there was not any Fan from the Upper Ogowé whom I knew to go for, but could not see one that I could on the strength of a previous acquaintance, and on their individual merits I did not feel inclined to do even this fashionable imitation embrace. Indeed I must say that never—even in a picture book—have I seen such a set of wild wicked-looking savages as those we faced this night, and with whom it was touch-and-go for twenty of the longest minutes I have ever lived, whether we fought—for our lives, I was going to say, but it would not have been even for that, but merely for the price of them.

Peace having been proclaimed, conversation became general. Gray Shirt brought his friend up and introduced him to me, and we shook hands and smiled at each other in the conventional way. Pagan's friend, who was next introduced, was more alarming, for he held his hands for half a minute just above my elbows without quite touching me, but he meant well; and then we all disappeared into a brown mass of humanity and a fog of noise. You would have thought, from the violence and vehemence of the shouting and gesticulation, that we were going to be forthwith torn to shreds; but not a single hand really touched me, and as I, Pagan, and Gray Shirt went up to the town in the midst of the throng, the crowd opened in front and closed in behind, evidently half frightened at my appearance. The row when we reached the town redoubled in volume from the fact that the ladies, the children, and the dogs joined in. Every child in the place as soon as it saw my white face let a howl out of it as if it had seen his Satanic Majesty, horns, hoofs, tail and all, and fled into the nearest hut, headlong, and I fear, from the continuance of the screams, had fits. The town was exceedingly filthy— the remains of the crocodile they had been eating the week before last, and piles of fish offal, and remains of an elephant, hippo or manatee— I really can't say which, decomposition was too far advanced—united to form a most impressive stench. The bark huts are, as usual in a Fan town, in unbroken rows; but there are three or four streets here, not one only, as in most cases. The palaver house is in the innermost street, and there we went, and noticed that the village view was not in the direction in which we had come, but across towards the other side of the lake. I told the Ajumba to explain we wanted hospitality for the night, and wished to hire three carriers for to-morrow to go with us to the Rembwé.

For an hour and three-quarters by my watch I stood in the suffocating, smoky, hot atmosphere listening to, but only faintly understanding, the war of words and gesture that raged round us. At last the fact that we were to be received being settled, Gray Shirt's friend led us

out of the guard house—the crowd flinching back as I came through it—
to his own house on the right-hand side of the street of huts. It was a very
different dwelling to Gray Shirt's residence at Arevooma. I was as high
as its roof ridge and had to stoop low to get through the door-hole.
Inside, the hut was fourteen or fifteen feet square, unlit by any window.
The door-hole could be closed by pushing a broad piece of bark across
it under two horizontally fixed bits of stick. The floor was sand like the
street outside, but dirtier. On it in one place was a fire, whose smoke
found its way out through the roof. In one corner of the room was a
rough bench of wood, which from the few filthy cloths on it and a wood
pillow I saw was the bed. There was no other furniture in the hut save
some boxes, which I presume held my host's earthly possessions. From
the bamboo roof hung a long stick with hooks on it, the hooks made by
cutting off branching twigs. This was evidently the hanging wardrobe,
and on it hung some few fetish charms, and a beautiful ornament of wild
cat and leopard tails, tied on to a square piece of leopard skin, in the
centre of which was a little mirror, and round the mirror were sewn
dozens of common shirt buttons. In among the tails hung three little
brass bells and a brass rattle; these bells and rattles are not only "for
dandy," but serve to scare away snakes when the ornament is worn in the
forest. A fine strip of silky-haired, young gorilla skin made the band to
sling the ornament from the shoulder when worn. Gorillas seem well
enough known round here. One old lady in the crowd outside, I saw, had
a necklace made of sixteen gorilla canine teeth slung on a pine-apple
fibre string. Gray Shirt explained to me that this is the best house in the
village, and my host the most renowned elephant hunter in the district.

We then returned to the canoe, whose occupants had been getting
uneasy about the way affairs were going "on top," on account of the
uproar they heard and the time we had been away. We got into the canoe
and took her round the little promontory at the end of the island to the
other beach, which is the main beach. By arriving at the beach when we
did, we took our Fan friends in the rear, and they did not see us coming in the gloaming. This was all for the best, it seems, as they said they
should have fired on us before they had had time to see we were rank
outsiders, on the apprehension that we were coming from one of the Fan
towns we had passed, and with whom they were on bad terms regarding a
lady who bolted there from her lawful lord, taking with her—cautious
soul!—a quantity of rubber. The only white man who had been here

before in the memory of man, was a French officer who paid Kiva six dollars to take him somewhere, I was told—but I could not find out when, or what happened to that Frenchman. It was a long time ago, Kiva said, but these folks have no definite way of expressing duration of time nor, do I believe, any great mental idea of it; although their ideas are, as usual with West Africans, far ahead of their language.

All the goods were brought up to my hut, and while Ngouta gets my tea we started talking the carrier palaver again. The Fans received my offer, starting at two dollars ahead of what M. Jacot said would be enough, with utter scorn, and every dramatic gesture of dissent; one man, pretending to catch Gray Shirt's words in his hands, flings them to the ground and stamps them under his feet. I affected an easy take-it-or-leave-it-manner, and looked on. A woman came out of the crowd to me, and held out a mass of slimy gray abomination on a bit of plantain leaf—smashed snail. I accepted it and gave her fish hooks. She was delighted and her companions excited, so she put the hooks into her mouth for safe keeping. I hurriedly explained in my best Fan that I do not require any more snail; so another lady tried the effect of a pine-apple. There might be no end to this, so I retired into trade and asked what she would sell it for. She did not want to sell it—she wanted to give it me; so I gave her fish hooks. Silence and Singlet interposed, saying the price for pine-apples is one leaf of tobacco, but I explained I was not buying. Ngouta turned up with my tea, so I went inside, and had it on the bed. The door-hole was entirely filled with a mosaic of faces, but no one attempted to come in. All the time the carrier palaver went on without cessation, and I went out and offered to take Gray Shirt's and Pagan's place, knowing they must want their chop, but they refused relief, and also said I must not raise the price; I was offering too big a price now, and if I once rise the Fan will only think I will keep on rising, and so make the palaver longer to talk. "How long does a palaver usually take to talk round here?" I ask. "The last one I talked," says Pagan, "took three weeks, and that was only a small price palaver." "Well," say I, "my price is for a start to-morrow—after then I have no price—after that I go away." Another hour however sees the jam made, and to my surprise I find the three richest men in this town of M'fetta have personally taken up the contract—Kiva my host, Fika a fine young fellow, and Wiki, another noted elephant hunter. These three Fans, the four Ajumba and the Igalwa, Ngouta, I think will be enough. Moreover

I fancy it safer not to have an overpowering percentage of Fans in the party, as I know we shall have considerable stretches of uninhabited forest to traverse; and the Ajumba say that the Fans will kill people, i.e. the black traders who venture into their country, and cut them up into neat pieces, eat what they want at the time, and smoke the rest of the bodies for future use. Now I do not want to arrive at the Rembwé in a smoked condition, even should my fragments be neat, and I am going in a different direction to what I said I was when leaving Kangwe, and there are so many ways of accounting for death about here—leopard, canoe, capsize, elephants, &c.—that even if I were traced—well, nothing could be done then, anyhow—so will only take three Fans. One must diminish dead certainties to the level of sporting chances along here, or one can never get on.

No one, either Ajumba or Fan, knew the exact course we were to take. The Ajumba had never been this way before—the way for black traders across being *via·* Lake Ayzingo, the way Mr. Goode of the American Mission once went, and the Fans said they only knew the way to a big Fan town called Efoua, where no white man or black trader had yet been. There is a path from there to the Rembwé they knew, because the Efoua people take their trade all to the Rembwé. They would, they said, come with me all the way if I would guarantee them safety if they "found war" on the road. This I agreed to do, and arranged to pay off at Hatton and Cookson's subfactory on the Rembwé, and they have "Look my mouth and it be sweet, so palaver done set." Every load then, by the light of the bush lights held by the women, we arranged. I had to unpack my bottles of fishes so as to equalise the weight of the loads. Every load is then made into a sort of cocoon with bush rope.

I was left in peace at about 11.30 P.M., and clearing off the clothes from the bench threw myself down and tried to get some sleep, for we were to start, the Fans said, before dawn. Sleep impossible—mosquitoes! lice!!—so at 12.40 I got up and slid aside my bark door. I found Pagan asleep under his mosquito bar outside, across the doorway, but managed to get past him without rousing him from his dreams of palaver which he was still talking aloud, and reconnoitred the town. The inhabitants seemed to have talked themselves quite out and were sleeping heavily. I went down then to our canoe and found it safe, high up among the Fan canoes on the stones, and then I slid a small Fan canoe off, and taking a paddle from a cluster stuck in the sand, paddled out on to the dark lake.

It was a wonderfully lovely quiet night with no light save that from the stars. One immense planet shone pre-eminent in the purple sky, throwing a golden path down on to the still waters. Quantities of big fish sprung out of the water, their glistening silver-white scales flashing so that they look like slashing swords. Some bird was making a long, low boom-booming sound away on the forest shore. I paddled leisurely across the lake to the shore on the right, and seeing crawling on the ground some large glow-worms, drove the canoe on to the bank among some hippo grass, and got out to get them.

While engaged on this hunt I felt the earth quiver under my feet, and heard a soft big soughing sound, and looking round saw I had dropped in on a hippo banquet. I made out five of the immense brutes round me, so I softly returned to the canoe and shoved off, stealing along the bank, paddling under water, until I deemed it safe to run out across the lake for my island. I reached the other end of it to that on which the village is situated; and finding a miniature rocky bay with a soft patch of sand and no hippo grass, the incidents of the Fan hut suggested the advisability of a bath. Moreover, there was no china collection in that hut, and it would be a long time before I got another chance, so I go ashore again, and, carefully investigating the neighbourhood to make certain there was no human habitation near, I then indulged in a wash in peace. Drying one's self on one's cummerbund is not pure joy, but it can be done when you put your mind to it. While I was finishing my toilet I saw a strange thing happen. Down through the forest on the lake bank opposite came a violet ball the size of a small orange. When it reached the sand beach it hovered along it to and fro close to the ground. In a few minutes another ball of similarly coloured light came towards it from behind one of the islets, and the two waver to and fro over the beach, sometimes circling round each other. I made off towards them in the canoe, thinking—as I still do—they were some brand new kind of luminous insect. When I got on to their beach one of them went off into the bushes and the other away over the water. I followed in the canoe, for the water here is very deep, and, when I almost thought I had got it, it went down into the water and I could see it glowing as it sunk until it vanished in the depths. I made my way back hastily, fearing my absence with the canoe might give rise, if discovered, to trouble, and by 3.30 I was back in the hut safe, but not so comfortable as I had been on the lake. A little before five my men are stirring and I get my tea. I do not state my escapade to them, but ask what those lights were. "Akom," said the Fan, and pointing to the shore of the lake where I had been during the night they said, "they came there, it was an 'Aku'"—or devil bush. More than ever did I regret not having secured one of those sort of two phenomena. What a joy a real devil, appropriately put up in raw alcohol, would have been to my scientific friends!

Wednesday, July 24th.—We get away about 5.30, the Fans coming in a separate canoe. We call at the next island to M'fetta to buy some more aguma. The inhabitants are very much interested in my appearance, running along the stony beach as we paddle away, and standing at the end of it until we are out of sight among the many islands at the N.E. end of Lake Ncovi. The scenery is savage; there are no terrific cliffs nor towering mountains to make it what one usually calls wild or romantic, but there is a distinction about it which is all its own. This N.E. end has beautiful sand beaches on the southern side, in front of the forested bank, lying in smooth ribbons along the level shore, and in scollops round the promontories where the hills come down into the lake. The forest on these hills, or mountains—for they are part of the Sierra del Cristal—is very dark in colour, and the undergrowth seems scant. We presently come to a narrow but deep channel into the lake coming from the eastward, which we go up, winding our course with it into a valley between the hills. After going up it a little way we find it completely fenced across with stout stakes, a space being left open in the middle, broader than the spaces between the other stakes; and over this is poised a spear with a bush rope attached, and weighted at the top of the haft with a great lump of rock. The whole affair is kept in position by a bush rope so arranged just under the level of the water that anything passing through the opening would bring the spear down. This was a trap for hippo or manatee (Ngany 'imanga), and similar in structure to those one sees set in the hippo grass near villages and plantations, which serve the double purpose of defending the vegetable supply, and adding to the meat supply of the inhabitants. We squeeze through between the stakes so as not to let the trap off, and find our little river leads us into another lake, much smaller than Ncovi. It is studded with islands of fantastic shapes, all wooded with high trees of an equal level, and with little or no undergrowth among them, so their pale gray stems look like clusters of columns supporting a dark green ceiling. The forest comes down steep hill sides to the water edge in all directions; and a dark gloomy-looking herb grows up out of black slime and water, in a bank or ribbon in front of it. There is another channel out of this lake, still to the N.E. The Fans say they think it goes into the big lake far far away, *i.e.*, Lake Ayzingo. From the look of the land, I think this river connecting Ayzingo and Lake Ncovi wanders down this valley between the mountain spurs of the Sierra del Cristal, expanding into one gloomy lake after another. We run our canoe into a bank of the dank dark-coloured water herb to the right, and disembark into a fitting introduction to the sort of country we shall have to deal with before we see the Rembwé—namely, up to our knees in black slime.

CHAPTER 8

FROM NCOVI TO ESOON

Concerning the way in which the voyager goes from the island of M'fetta
to no one knows exactly where, in doubtful and bad company,
and of what this led to and giving also some accounts of the Great Forest
and of those people that live therein.

I WILL NOT BORE YOU WITH MY DIARY in detail regarding our land
journey, because the water-washed little volume attributive to this period
is mainly full of reports of law cases, for reasons hereinafter to be stated;
and at night, when passing through this bit of country, I was usually too
tired to do anything more than make an entry such as: "5 S., 4 R. A.,
N.E. Ebony. T. 1—50, &c., &c."—entries that require amplification to
explain their significance, and I will proceed to explain.

Our first day's march was a very long one. Path in the ordinary
acceptance of the term there was none. Hour after hour, mile after
mile, we passed on, in the under-gloom of the great forest. The pace
made by the Fans, who are infinitely the most rapid Africans I have ever
come across, severely tired the Ajumba, who are canoe men, and who
had been as fresh as paint, after their exceedingly long day's paddling
from Arevooma to M'fetta. Ngouta, the Igalwa interpreter, felt
pumped, and said as much, very early in the day. I regretted very much
having brought him; for, from a mixture of nervous exhaustion arising

from our M'fetta experiences, and a touch of chill he had almost entirely lost his voice, and I feared would fall sick. The Fans were evidently quite at home in the forest, and strode on over fallen trees and rocks with an easy, graceful stride. What saved us weaklings was the Fans' appetites; every two hours they sat down, and had a snack of a pound or so of meat and aguma apiece, followed by a pipe of tobacco. We used to come up with them at these halts. Ngouta and the Ajumba used to sit down; and rest with them, and I also, for a few minutes, for a rest and chat, and then I would go on alone, thus getting a good start. I got a good start, in the other meaning of the word, on the afternoon of the first day when descending into a ravine.

I saw in the bottom, wading and rolling in the mud, a herd of five elephants. I remembered, hastily, that your one chance when charged by several elephants is to dodge them round trees, working down wind all the time, until they lose smell and sight of you, then to lie quiet for a time, and go home. It was evident from the utter unconcern of these monsters that I was down wind now, so I had only to attend to dodging, and I promptly dodged round a tree, and lay down. Seeing they still displayed no emotion on my account, and fascinated by the novelty of the scene, I crept forward from one tree to another, until I was close enough to have hit the nearest one with a stone, and spats of mud, which they sent flying with their stamping and wallowing came flap, flap among the bushes covering me.

One big fellow had a nice pair of 40 lb. or so tusks on him, singularly straight, and another had one big curved tusk and one broken one. Some of them lay right down like pigs in the deeper part of the swamp, some drew up trunkfuls of water and syringed themselves and each other, and every one of them indulged in a good rub against a tree. Presently when they had had enough of it they all strolled off up wind, through the bush in Indian file, now and then breaking off a branch, but leaving singularly little dead water for their tonnage and breadth of beam. When they had gone I rose up, turned round to find the men, and trod on Kiva's back then and there, full and fair, and fell sideways down the steep hillside until I fetched up among some roots.

It seems Kiva had come on, after his meal, before the others, and seeing the elephants, and being a born hunter, had crawled like me down to look at them. He had not expected to find me there, he said. I do not believe he gave a thought of any sort to me in the presence of these fascinating creatures, and so he got himself trodden on. I suggested to him we should pile the baggage, and go and have an elephant hunt. He shook his head reluctantly, saying "Kor, kor," like a depressed rook, and explained we were not strong enough; there were only three Fans— the Ajumba, and Ngouta did not count—and moreover that we had not brought sufficient ammunition owing to the baggage having to be carried, and the ammunition that we had must be saved for other game than elephant, for we might meet war before we met the Rembwé River.

We had by now joined the rest of the party, and were all soon squattering about on our own account in the elephant bath. It was shocking bad going—like a ploughed field exaggerated by a terrific nightmare. It pretty nearly pulled all the legs off me, and to this hour I cannot tell you if it is best to put your foot into a footmark—a young pond, I mean— about the size of the bottom of a Madeira work arm-chair, or whether you should poise yourself on the rim of the same, and stride forward to its other bank boldly and hopefully. The footmarks and the places where the elephants had been rolling were by now filled with water, and the mud underneath was in places hard and slippery. In spite of my determination to preserve an awesome and unmoved calm while among these dangerous savages, I had to give way and laugh explosively; to see the portly, powerful Pagan suddenly convert himself into a quadruped, while Gray Shirt poised himself on one heel and waved his other leg in the air to advertise to the assembled nations that he was about to sit down, was irresistible. No one made such palaver about taking a seat as Gray Shirt; I did it repeatedly without any fuss to speak of. That lordly elephant-hunter, the Great Wiki, would, I fancy, have strode over safely and with dignity, but the man who was in front of him spun round on his own axis and flung his arms round the Fan, and they went to earth together; the heavy load on Wiki's back drove them into the mud like a pile-driver. However we got through in time, and after I had got up the other side of the ravine I saw the Fan let the Ajumba go on, and were busy searching themselves for something.

I followed the Ajumba, and before I joined them felt a fearful pricking irritation. Investigation of the affected part showed a tick of terrific size with its head embedded in the flesh; pursuing this interesting subject, I found three more, and had awfully hard work to get them off and painful too for they give one not only a feeling of irritation at their holding-on place, but a streak of rheumatic-feeling pain up from it.

On completing operations I went on and came upon the Ajumba in a state more approved of by Praxiteles than by the general public nowadays. They had found out about elephant ticks, so I went on and got an excellent start for the next stage.

By this time, shortly after noon on the first day, we had struck into a mountainous and rocky country, and also struck a track—a track you had to keep your eye on or you lost it in a minute, but still a guide as to direction.

The forest trees here were mainly ebony and great hard wood trees, with no palms save my old enemy the climbing palm, *calamus*, as usual, going on its long excursions, up one tree and down another, bursting into a plume of fronds, and in the middle of each plume one long spike sticking straight up, which was an unopened frond, whenever it got a gleam of sunshine; running along the ground over anything it meets, rock or fallen timber, all alike, its long, dark-coloured, rope-like stem simply furred with thorns. Immense must be the length of some of these climbing palms. One tree I noticed that day had hanging from its summit, a good one hundred and fifty feet above us, a long straight rope-like palm stem.

The character of the whole forest was very interesting. Sometimes for hours we passed among thousands upon thousands of gray-white columns of uniform height (about 100-150 feet); at the top of these the boughs branched out and interlaced among each other, forming a canopy or ceiling, which dimmed the light even of the equatorial sun to such an extent that no undergrowth could thrive in the gloom. The statement of the struggle for existence was published here in plain figures, but it was not, as in our climate, a struggle against climate mainly, but an internecine war from over population. Now and again we passed among vast stems of buttressed trees, sometimes enormous in girth; and from their far-away summits hung great bush-ropes, some as straight as plumb lines, others coiled round, and intertwined among each other, until one could fancy one was looking on some mighty battle between armies of gigantic serpents, that had been arrested at its height by some magic spell. All these bush-ropes were as bare of foliage as a ship's wire rigging, but a good many had thorns. I was very curious as to how they got up straight, and investigation showed me that many of them were carried up with a growing tree. The only true climbers were the *calamus* and the rubber vine (*Landolphia*), both of which employ hook tackle.

Some stretches of this forest were made up of thin, spindly stemmed trees of great height, and among these stretches I always noticed the ruins of some forest giant, whose death by lightning or by his superior height having given the demoniac tornado wind an extra grip on him, had allowed sunlight to penetrate the lower regions of the forest; and then evidently the seedlings and saplings, who had for years been living a half-starved life for light, shot up. They seemed to know that their one chance lay in getting with the greatest rapidity to the level of the top of the forest. No time to grow fat in the stem. No time to send out side branches, or any of those vanities. Up, up to the light level, and he among them who reached it first won in this game of life or death; for when he gets there he spreads out his crown of upper branches, and shuts off the life-giving sunshine from his competitors, who pale off and die, or remain dragging on an attenuated existence waiting for another chance, and waiting sometimes for centuries. There must be tens of thousands of seeds which perish before they get their chance; but the way the seeds of the hard wood African trees are packed, as it were in cases specially made durable, is very wonderful. Indeed the ways of Providence here are wonderful in their strange dual intention to preserve and to destroy; but on the whole, as Peer Gynt truly observes, "*Ein guter Wirth— nein das ist er nicht.*"

We saw this influence of light on a large scale as soon as we reached the open hills and mountains of the Sierra del Cristal, and had to pass over those fearful avalanche-like timber falls on their steep sides. The worst of these lay between Efoua and Egaja, where we struck a part of the range that was exposed to the south-east. These falls had evidently arisen from the tornados, which from time to time have hurled down the gigantic trees whose hold on the superficial soil over the sheets of hard bed rock was insufficient, in spite of all the anchors they had out in the shape of roots and buttresses, and all their rigging in the shape of bush ropes. Down they had come, crushing and dragging down with them those near them or bound to them by the great tough climbers.

Getting over these falls was perilous, not to say scratchy work. One or another member of our party always went through; and precious uncomfortable going it was, I found, when I tried it in one above Egaja; ten or twelve feet of crashing creaking timber, and then flump on to a lot of rotten, wet *débris*, with more snakes and centipedes among it than you had any immediate use for, even though you were a collector; but there you had to stay, while Wiki, who was a most critical connoisseur, selected from the surrounding forest a bush-rope that he regarded as the correct remedy for the case, and then up you were hauled, through the sticks you had turned the wrong way on your down journey.

The Duke had a bad fall, going twenty feet or so before he found the rubbish heap; while Fika, who went through with a heavy load on his back, took us, on one occasion, half an hour to recover; and when we had just got him to the top, and able to cling on to the upper sticks, Wiki, who had been superintending operations, slipped backwards, and went through on his own account. The bush-rope we had been hauling on was too worn with the load to use again, and we just hauled Wiki out with the first one we could drag down and cut; and Wiki, when he came up, said we were reckless, and knew nothing of bush ropes, which shows how ungrateful an African can be. It makes the perspiration run down my nose whenever I think of it. The sun was out that day; we were neatly situated on the Equator, and the air was semisolid, with the stinking exhalations from the swamps with which the mountain chain is fringed and intersected; and we were hot enough without these things, because of the violent exertion of getting these twelve to thirteen-stone gentlemen up among us again, and the fine varied exercise of getting over the fall on our own account.

When we got into the cool forest beyond it was delightful; particularly if it happened to be one of those lovely stretches of forest, gloomy down below, but giving hints that far away above us was a world of bloom and scent and beauty which we saw as much of as earth-worms in a flower-bed. Here and there the ground was strewn with great cast blossoms, thick, wax-like, glorious cups of orange and crimson and pure white, each one of which was in itself a handful, and which told us that some of the trees around us were showing a glory of colour to heaven alone. Sprinkled among them were bunches of pure stephanotis-like flowers, which said that the gaunt bush-ropes were rubber vines that had burst into flower when they had seen the sun. These flowers we came across in nearly every type of forest all the way, for rubber abounds here.

I will weary you no longer now with the different kinds of forest and only tell you I have let you off several. The natives have separate names for seven different kinds, and these might, I think, be easily run up to nine.

A certain sort of friendship soon arose between the Fans and me. We each recognised that we belonged to that same section of the human race with whom it is better to drink than to fight. We knew we would each have killed the other, if sufficient inducement were offered, and so we took a certain amount of care that the inducement should not arise. Gray Shirt and Pagan also, their trade friends, the Fans treated with an independent sort of courtesy; but Silence, Singlet, the Passenger, and above all Ngouta, they openly did not care a row of pins for, and I have small doubt that had it not been for us other three they would have killed and eaten these very amicable gentlemen with as much compunction as an English sportsman would kill as many rabbits. They on their part hated the Fan, and never lost an opportunity of telling me "these Fan be bad man too much." I must not forget to mention the other member of our party, a Fan gentleman with the manners of a duke and the habits of a dustbin. He came with us, quite uninvited by me, and never asked for any pay; I think he only wanted to see the fun, and drop in for a fight if there was one going on, and to pick up the pieces generally. He was evidently a man of some importance from the way the others treated him; and moreover he had a splendid gun, with a gorilla skin sheath for its lock, and ornamented all over its stock with brass nails. His costume consisted of a small piece of dirty rag round his loins; and whenever we were going through dense undergrowth, or wading a swamp, he wore that filament tucked up scandalously short. Whenever we were sitting down in the forest having one of our nondescript meals, he always sat next to me and appropriated the tin. Then he would fill his pipe, and turning to me with the easy grace of aristocracy, would say what may be translated as "My dear Princess, could you favour me with a lucifer?"

I used to say, "My dear Duke, charmed, I'm sure," and give him one ready lit.

I dared not trust him with the box whole, having a personal conviction that he would have kept it. I asked him what he would do suppose I was not there with a box of lucifers; and he produced a bush-cow's horn with a neat wood lid tied on with tie tie, and from out of it he produced a flint and steel and demonstrated.

The first day in the forest we came across a snake—a beauty with a new red-brown and yellow-patterned velvety skin, about three feet six inches long and as thick as a man's thigh. Ngouta met it, hanging from a bough, and shot backwards like a lobster, Ngouta having among his many weaknesses a rooted horror of snakes. This snake the Ogowé natives all hold in great aversion. For the bite of other sorts of snakes they profess to have remedies, but for this they have none. If, however, a native is stung by one he usually conceals the fact that it was this particular kind, and tries to get any chance the native doctor's medicine may give. The Duke stepped forward and with one blow flattened its head against the tree with his gun butt, and then folded the snake up and got as much of it as possible into his bag, while the rest hung dangling out. Ngouta, not being able to keep ahead of the Duke, his Grace's pace being stiff, went to the extreme rear of the party, so that other people might be killed first if the snake returned to life, as he surmised it would. He fell into other dangers from this caution, but I cannot chronicle Ngouta's afflictions in full without running this book into an old-fashioned folio size. We had the snake for supper, that is to say the Fan and I; the others would not touch it, although a good snake, properly cooked, is one of the best meats one gets out here, far and away better than the African fowl.

The Fans also did their best to educate me in every way: they told me their names for things, while I told them mine. I found several European words already slightly altered in use among them, such as "Amuck"—a mug, "Alas"—a glass, a tumbler. I do not know whether their "Ami"—a person addressed, or spoken of—is French or not. It may come from "Anw"—M'pongwe for "Ye," "You." They use it as a rule in addressing a person after the phrase they always open up conversation with, "Azuna"—Listen, or I am speaking.

They also showed me many things: how to light a fire from the pith of a certain tree, which was useful to me in after life, but they rather over-did this branch of instruction one way and another; for example, Wiki had, as above indicated, a mania for bush-ropes and a marvellous eye and knowledge of them; he would pick out from among the thousands sur-rounding us now one of such peculiar suppleness that you could wind it round anything, like a strip of cloth, and as strong withal as a hawser; or again another which has a certain stiffness, combined with a slight elastic spring, excellent for hauling, with the ease and accuracy of a lady who picks out the particular twisted strand of embroidery silk from a multi-coloured tangled ball. He would go into the bush after them while other people were resting, and particularly after the sort which, when split, is bright yellow, and very supple and excellent to tie round loads.

On one occasion, between Egaja and Esoon, he came back from one of these quests and wanted me to come and see something, very quietly; I went, and we crept down into a rocky ravine, on the other side of which lay one of the outermost Egaja plantations. When we got to the edge of the cleared ground, we lay down, and wormed our way, with elaborate caution, among a patch of Koko; Wiki first, I following in his trail.

After about fifty yards of this, Wiki sank flat, and I saw before me some thirty yards off, busily employed in pulling down plantains, and other depredations, five gorillas: one old male, one young male, and three females. One of these had clinging to her a young fellow, with beautiful wavy black hair with just a kink in it. The big male was crouching on his haunches, with his long arms hanging down on either side, with the backs of his hands on the ground, the palms upwards. The elder lady was tearing to pieces and eating a pine-apple, while the others were at the plantains destroying more than they ate.

They kept up a sort of a whinnying, chattering noise, quite different from the sound I have heard gorillas give when enraged, or from the ones you can hear them giving when they are what the natives call "dancing" at night. I noticed that their reach of arm was immense, and that when they went from one tree to another, they squattered across the open ground in a most inelegant style, dragging their long arms with the knuckles downwards. I should think the big male and female were over six feet each. The others would be from four to five. I put out my hand and laid it on Wiki's gun to prevent him from firing, and he, thinking I was going to fire, gripped my wrist.

I watched the gorillas with great interest for a few seconds, until I heard Wiki make a peculiar small sound, and looking at him saw his face was working in an awful way as he clutched his throat with his hand violently.

Heavens! think I, this gentleman's going to have a fit; it's lost we are entirely this time. He rolled his head to and fro, and then buried his face into a heap of dried rubbish at the foot of a plantain stem, clasped his hands over it, and gave an explosive sneeze. The gorillas let go all, raised themselves up for a second, gave a quaint sound between a bark and a howl, and then the ladies and the young gentleman started home. The old male rose to his full height (it struck me at the time this was a matter of ten feet at least, but for scientific purposes allowance must be made for a lady's emotions) and looked straight towards us, or rather towards where that sound came from. Wiki went off into a paroxysm of falsetto sneezes the like of which I have never heard; nor evidently had the gorilla, who doubtless thinking, as one of his black co-relatives would have thought, that the phenomenon favoured Duppy, went off after his family with a celerity that was amazing the moment he touched the forest, and disappeared as they had, swinging himself along through it from bough to bough, in a way that convinced me that, given the necessity of getting about in tropical forests, man has made a mistake in getting his arms shortened. I have seen many wild animals in their native wilds, but never have I seen anything to equal gorillas going through bush; it is a graceful, powerful, superbly perfect hand-trapeze performance.

After this sporting adventure, we returned, as I usually return from a sporting adventure, without measurements or the body.

Our first day's march, though the longest, was the easiest, though, providentially I did not know this at the time. From my Woermann road walks I judge it was well twenty-five miles. It was easiest, however, from its lying for the greater part of the way through the gloomy type of forest. All day long we never saw the sky once.

The earlier part of the day we were steadily going up hill, here and there making a small descent, and then up again, until we came on to what was apparently a long ridge, for on either side of us we could look down into deep, dark, ravine-like valleys. Twice or thrice we descended into these to cross them, finding at their bottom a small or large swamp with a river running through its midst. Those rivers all went to Lake Ayzingo.

We had to hurry because Kiva, who was the only one among us who had been to Efoua, said that unless we did we should not reach Efoua that night. I said, "Why not stay for bush?" not having contracted any love for a night in a Fan town by the experience of M'fetta; moreover the Fans were not sure that after all the whole party of us might not spend the evening at Efoua, when we did get there, simmering in its cooking-pots.

Ngouta, I may remark, had no doubt on the subject at all, and regretted having left Mrs. N. keenly, and the Andande store sincerely. But these Fans are a fine sporting tribe, and allowed they would risk it; besides, they were almost certain they had friends at Efoua; and, in addition, they showed me trees scratched in a way that was magnification of the condition of my own cat's pet table leg at home, demonstrating leopards in the vicinity. I kept going, as it was my only chance, because I found I stiffened if I sat down, and they always carefully told me the direction to go in when they sat down; with their superior pace they soon caught me up, and then passed me, leaving me and Ngouta and sometimes Singlet and Pagan behind, we, in our turn, overtaking them, with this difference that they were sitting down when we did so.

About five o'clock I was off ahead and noticed a path which I had been told I should meet with, and, when met with, I must follow. The path was slightly indistinct, but by keeping my eye on it I could see it. Presently I came to a place where it went out, but appeared again on the other side of a clump of underbush fairly distinctly. I made a short cut for it and the next news was I was in a heap, on a lot of spikes, some fifteen feet or so below ground level, at the bottom of a bag-shaped game pit.

It is at these times you realise the blessing of a good thick skirt. Had I paid heed to the advice of many people in England, who ought to have known better, and did not do it themselves, and adopted masculine garments, I should have been spiked to the bone, and done for. Whereas, save for a good many bruises, here I was with the fulness of my skirt tucked under me, sitting on nine ebony spikes some twelve inches long, in comparative comfort, howling lustily to be hauled out. The Duke came along first, and looked down at me. I said, "Get a bush-rope, and haul me out." He grunted and sat down on a log. The Passenger came next, and he looked down. "You kill?" says he. "Not much," say I; "get a bush-rope and haul me out." "No fit," says he, and sat down on the log. Presently, however, Kiva and Wiki came up, and Wiki went and selected the one and only bush-rope suitable to haul an English lady, of my exact complexion, age, and size, out of that one particular pit. They seemed rare round there from the time he took; and I was just casting about in my mind as to what method would be best to employ in getting up the smooth, yellow, sandy-clay, incurved walls, when he arrived with it, and I was out in a twinkling, and very much ashamed of myself, until Silence, who was then leading, disappeared through the path before us with a despairing yell. Each man then pulled the skin cover off his gun lock, carefully looked to see if things there were all right and ready loosened his knife in its snake-skin sheath; and then we set about hauling poor Silence out, binding him up where necessary with cool green leaves; for he, not having a skirt, had got a good deal frayed at the edges on those spikes. Then we closed up, for the Fans said these pits were symptomatic of the immediate neighbourhood of Efoua. We sounded our ground, as we went into a thick plantain patch, through which we could see a great clearing in the forest, and the low huts of a big town.

We charged into it, going right through the guard-house gateway, at one end, in single file, as its narrowness obliged us, and into the street-shaped town, and formed ourselves into as imposing a looking party as possible in the centre of the street. The Efouerians regarded us with much amazement, and the women and children cleared off into the huts, and took stock of us through the door-holes. There were but few men in the town, the majority, we subsequently learnt, being away after elephants. But there were quite sufficient left to make a crowd in a ring round us. Fortunately Wiki and Kiva's friends were present, and as a result of the confabulation, one of the chiefs had his house cleared out for me. It consisted of two apartments almost bare of everything save a pile of boxes, and a small fire on the floor, some little bags hanging from the roof poles, and a general supply of insects. The inner room contained nothing save a hard plank, raised on four short pegs from the earth floor.

I shook hands with and thanked the chief, and directed that all the loads should be placed inside the huts. I must admit my good friend was a villainous-looking savage, but he behaved most hospitably and kindly. From what I had heard of the Fan, I deemed it advisable not to make any present to him at once, but to base my claim on him on the right of an amicable stranger to hospitality. When I had seen all the baggage stowed I went outside and sat at the doorway on a rather rickety mushroom-shaped stool in the cool evening air, waiting for my tea which I wanted bitterly. Pagan came up as usual for tobacco to buy chop with; and after giving it to him, I and the two chiefs, with Gray Shirt acting as interpreter, had a long chat. Of course the first question was, Why was I there?

I told them I was on my way to the factory of H. and C. on the Rembwé. They said they had heard of "Ugumu," i.e., Messrs. Hatton and Cookson, but they did not trade direct with them, passing their trade into towns nearer to the Rembwé, which were swindling bad towns, they said; and they got the idea stuck in their heads that I was a trader, a sort of bagman for the firm, and Gray Shirt could not get this idea out, so off one of their majesties went and returned with twenty-five balls of rubber, which I bought to promote good feeling, subsequently dashing them to Wiki, who passed them in at Ndorko when we got there. I also bought some elephant-hair necklaces from one of the chiefs' wives, by exchanging my red silk tie with her for them, and one or two other things. I saw fish-hooks would not be of much value because Efoua was not near a big water of any sort; so I held fish-hooks and traded handkerchiefs and knives.

One old chief was exceedingly keen to do business, and I bought a meat spoon, a plantain spoon, and a gravy spoon off him; and then he brought me a lot of rubbish I did not want, and I said so, and announced I had finished trade for that night. However the old gentleman was not to be put off, and after an unsuccessful attempt to sell me his cooking-pots, which were roughly made out of clay, he made energetic signs to me that if I would wait he had got something that he would dispose of which Gray Shirt said was "good too much." Off he went across the street, and disappeared into his hut, where he evidently had a thorough hunt for the precious article. One box after another was brought out to the light of a bush torch held by one of his wives, and there was a great confabulation between him and his family of the "I'm sure you had it last," "You must have moved it," "Never touched the thing," sort. At last it was found, and he brought it across the street to me most carefully. It was a bundle of bark cloth tied round something most carefully with tie tie. This being removed, disclosed a layer of rag, which was unwound from round a central article. Whatever can this be? thinks I; some rare and valuable object doubtless, let's hope connected with Fetish worship, and I anxiously watched its unpacking; in the end, however, it disclosed, to my disgust and rage, an old shilling razor. The way the old chief held it out, and the amount of dollars he asked for it, was enough to make any one believe that I was in such urgent need of the thing, that I was at his mercy regarding price. I waved it off with a haughty scorn, and then feeling smitten by the expression of agonised bewilderment on his face, I dashed him a belt that delighted him, and went inside and had tea to soothe my outraged feelings.

The chiefs made furious raids on the mob of spectators who pressed round the door, and stood with their eyes glued to every crack in the bark of which the hut was made. The next door neighbours on either side might have amassed a comfortable competence for their old age, by letting out seats for the circus. Every hole in the side walls had a human eye in it, and I heard new holes being bored in all directions; so I deeply fear the chief, my host, must have found his palace sadly draughty. I felt perfectly safe and content, however, although Ngouta suggested the charming idea that "P'r'aps them M'fetta Fan done sell we." As soon as all my men had come in, and established themselves in the inner room for the night, I curled up among the boxes, with my head on the tobacco sack, and dozed.

After about half an hour I heard a row in the street, and looking out,—for I recognised his grace's voice taking a solo part followed by choruses,—I found him in legal difficulties about a murder case. An *alibi* was proved for the time being; that is to say the prosecution could not bring up witnesses because of the elephant hunt; and I went in for another doze, and the town at last grew quiet. Waking up again I noticed the smell in the hut was violent, from being shut up I suppose, and it had an unmistakably organic origin. Knocking the ash end off the smouldering bush-light that lay burning on the floor, I investigated, and tracked it to those bags, so I took down the biggest one, and carefully noted exactly how the tie-tie had been put round its mouth; for these things are important and often mean a lot. I then shook its contents out in my hat, for fear of losing anything of value. They were a human hand, three big toes, four eyes, two ears, and other portions of the human frame. The hand was fresh, the others only so so, and shrivelled.

Replacing them I tied the bag up, and hung it up again. I subsequently learnt that although the Fans will eat their fellow friendly tribesfolk, yet they like to keep a little something belonging to them as a memento. This touching trait in their character I learnt from Wiki; and, though it's to their credit, under the circumstances, still it's an unpleasant practice when they hang the remains in the bedroom you occupy, particularly if the bereavement in your host's family has been recent. I did not venture to prowl round Efoua; but slid the bark door aside and looked out to get a breath of fresh air.

It was a perfect night, and no mosquitoes. The town, walled in on every side by the great cliff of high black forest, looked very wild as it showed in the starlight, its low, savage-built bark huts, in two hard rows, closed at either end by a guard-house. In both guard-houses there was a fire burning, and in their flickering glow showed the forms of sleeping men. Nothing was moving save the goats, which are always brought into the special house for them in the middle of the town, to keep them from the leopards, which roam from dusk to dawn.

Dawn found us stirring, I getting my tea, and the rest of the party their chop, and binding up anew the loads with Wiki's fresh supple bush-ropes. Kiva amused me much; during our march his costume was exceeding scant, but when we reached the towns he took from his bag garments, and attired himself so resplendently that I feared the charm of his appearance would lead me into one of those dreadful wife palavers which experience had taught me of old to dread; and in the morning time he always devoted some time to repacking. I gave a big dash to both chiefs, and they came out with us, most civilly, to the end of their first plantations; and then we took farewell of each other, with many expressions of hope on both sides that we should meet again, and many warnings from them about the dissolute and depraved character of the other towns we should pass through before we reached the Rembwé.

Our second day's march was infinitely worse than the first, for it lay along a series of abruptly shaped hills with deep ravines between them; each ravine had its swamp and each swamp its river. This bit of country must be absolutely impassable for any human being, black or white, except during the dry season. There were representatives of the three chief forms of the West African bog. The large deep swamps were best to deal with, because they make a break in the forest, and the sun can come down on their surface and bake a crust, over which you can go, if you go quickly. From experience in Devonian bogs, I knew pace was our best chance, and I fancy I earned one of my nicknames among the Fans on these. The Fans went across all right with a rapid striding glide, but the other men erred from excess of caution, and while hesitating as to where was the next safe place to plant their feet, the place that they were stand-ing on went in with a glug. Moreover, they would keep together, which was more than the crust would stand. The portly Pagan and the Passenger gave us a fine job in one bog, by sinking in close together. Some of us slashed off boughs of trees and tore off handfuls of hard canna leaves, while others threw them round the sinking victims to form a sort of raft, and then with the aid of bush-rope, of course, they were hauled out.

The worst sort of swamp, and the most frequent hereabouts, is the deep narrow one that has no crust on, because it is too much shaded by the forest. The slopes of the ravines too are usually covered with an undergrowth of shenja, beautiful beyond description, but right bad to go through. I soon learnt to dread seeing the man in front going down hill, or to find myself doing so, for it meant that within the next half hour we should be battling through a patch of shenja. I believe there are few effects that can compare with the beauty of them, with the golden sunlight coming down through the upper forest's branches on to their exquisitely shaped, hard, dark green leaves, making them look as if they were sprinkled with golden sequins. Their long green stalks, which sup-port the leaves and bear little bunches of crimson berries, take every graceful curve imaginable, and the whole affair is free from insects; and when you have said this, you have said all there is to say in favour of shenja, for those long green stalks of theirs are as tough as twisted wire, and the graceful curves go to the making of a net, which rises round you shoulder high, and the hard green leaves when lying on the ground are fearfully slippery. It is not nice going down through them, particularly when Nature is so arranged that the edge of the bank you are descending is a rock-wall ten or twelve feet high with a swamp of unknown depth at its foot; this arrangement was very frequent on the second and third day's marches, and into these swamps the shenja seemed to want to send you head first and get you suffocated. It is still less pleasant, however, going up the other side of the ravine when you have got through your swamp. You have to fight your way upwards among rough rocks, through this hard tough network of stems; and it took it out of all of us except the Fans.

These narrow shaded swamps gave us a world of trouble and took up a good deal of time. Sometimes the leader of the party would make three or four attempts before he found a ford, going on until the black, batter-like ooze came up round his neck, and then turning back and trying in another place; while the rest of the party sat upon the bank until the ford was found, feeling it was unnecessary to throw away human life, and that the more men there were paddling about in that swamp, the more chance there was that a hole in the bottom of it would be found; and when a hole is found, the discoverer is liable to leave his bones in it. If I happened to be in front, the duty of finding the ford fell on me; for none of us after leaving Efoua knew the swamps personally. I was too frightened of the Fan, and too nervous and uncertain of the stuff my other men were made of, to dare show the white feather at anything that turned up. The Fan took my conduct as a matter of course, never having travelled with white men before, or learnt the way some of them require carrying over swamps and rivers and so on. I dare say I might have taken things easier, but I was like the immortal Schmelzle, during that omnibus journey he made on his way to Flætz in the thunder-storm—afraid to be afraid. I am very certain I should have fared very differently had I entered a region occupied by a powerful and ferocious tribe like the Fan, from some districts on the West Coast, where the inhabitants are used to find the white man incapable of personal exertion, requiring to be carried in a hammock, or wheeled in a go-cart or a Bath-chair about the streets of their coast towns, depending for the defence of their settlement on a body of black soldiers. This is not so in Congo Français, and I had behind me the prestige of a set of white men to whom for the native to say, "You shall not do such and such a thing;" "You shall not go to such and such a place," would mean that those things would be done. I soon found the name of Hatton and Cookson's agent-general for this district, Mr. Hudson, was one to conjure with among the trading tribes; and the Ajumba, moreover, although their knowledge of white men had been small, yet those they had been accustomed to see were fine specimens. Mr. Fildes, Mr. Cockshut, M. Jacot, Dr. Pélessier, Père Lejeune, M. Gacon, Mr. Whittaker, and that vivacious French official, were not men any man, black or white, would willingly ruffle; and in addition there was the memory among the black traders of "that white man MacTaggart," whom an enterprising trading tribe near Fernan Vaz had had the hardihood to tackle, shooting him, and then towing him behind a canoe and slashing him all over with their knives the while; yet he survived, and tackled them again in a way that must almost pathetically have astonished those simple savages, after the real good work they had put in to the killing of him. Of course it was hard to live up to these ideals, and I do not pretend to have succeeded, or rather that I should have succeeded had the real strain been put on me.

But to return to that gorilla-land forest. All the rivers we crossed on the first, second, and third day I was told went into one or other of the branches of the Ogowé, showing that the long slope of land between the Ogowé and the Rembwé is towards the Ogowé. The stone of which the mountains were composed was that same hard black rock that I had found on the Sierra del Cristal, by the Ogowé rapids; only hereabouts there was not amongst it those great masses of white quartz, which are so prominent a feature from Talagouga upwards in the Ogowé valley; neither were the mountains anything like so high, but they had the same abruptness of shape. They look like very old parts of the same range worn down to stumps by the disintegrating forces of the torrential rain and sun, and the dense forest growing on them. Frost of course they had not been subject to, but rocks, I noticed, were often being somewhat similarly split by rootlets having got into some tiny crevice, and by gradual growth enlarged it to a crack.

Of our troubles among the timber falls on these mountains I have already spoken; and these were at their worst between Efoua and Egaja. I had suffered a good deal from thirst that day, unboiled water being my ibet and we were all very nearly tired out with the athletic sports since leaving Efoua. One thing only we knew about Egaja for sure, and that was that not one of us had a friend there, and that it was a town of extra evil repute, so we were not feeling very cheerful when towards evening time we struck its outermost plantations, their immediate vicinity being announced to us by Silence treading full and fair on to a sharp ebony spike driven into the narrow path and hurting himself. Fortunately, after we passed this first plantation, we came upon a camp of rubber collectors—four young men; I got one of them to carry Silence's load and show us the way into the town, when on we went into more plantations.

There is nothing more tiresome that finding your path going into a plantation, because it fades out in the cleared ground, or starts playing games with a lot of other little paths that are running about amongst the crops, and no West African path goes straight into a stream or a plantation, and straight out the other side, so you have a nice time picking it up again.

We were spared a good deal of fine varied walking by our new friend the rubber collector; for I noticed he led us out by a path nearly at right angles to the one by which we had entered. He then pitched into a pit which was half full of thorns, and which he observed he did not know was there, demonstrating that an African guide can speak the truth. When he had got out, he handed back Silence's load and got a dash of tobacco for his help; he left us to devote the rest of his evening by his forest fire to unthorning himself, while we proceeded to wade a swift, deepish river that crossed the path he told us led into Egaja, and then went across another bit of forest and down hill again. "Oh, bless those swamps!" thought I, "here's another," but no—not this time. Across the bottom of the steep ravine, from one side to another, lay an enormous tree as a bridge, about fifteen feet above a river, which rushed beneath it, over a boulder-encumbered bed. I took in the situation at a glance, and then and there I would have changed that bridge for any swamp I have ever seen, yea, even for a certain bush-rope bridge in which I once wound myself up like a buzzing fly in a spider's web. I was fearfully tired, and my legs shivered under me after the falls and emotions of the previous part of the day, and my boots were slippery with water soaking.

The Fans went into the river, and half swam, half waded across. All the Ajumba, save Pagan, followed, and Ngouta got across with their assistance. Pagan thought he would try the bridge, and I thought I would watch how the thing worked. He got about three yards along it and then slipped, but caught the tree with his hands as he fell, and hauled himself back to my side again; then he went down the bank and through the water. This was not calculated to improve one's nerve; I knew by now I had got to go by the bridge, for I saw I was not strong enough in my tired state to fight the water. If only the wretched thing had had its bark on it would have been better, but it was bare, bald, and round, and a slip meant death on the rocks below. I rushed it, and reached the other side in safety, whereby poor Pagan got chaffed about his failure by the others, who said they had gone through the water just to wash their feet.

The other side, when we got there, did not seem much worth reaching, being a swampy fringe at the bottom of a steep hillside, and after a few yards the path turned into a stream or backwater of the river. It was hedged with thickly pleached bushes, and covered with liquid water on the top of semi-liquid mud. Now and again for a change you had a foot of water on top of fearfully slippery harder mud, and then we light-heartedly took headers into the bush, sideways, or sat down; and when it was not proceeding on the evil tenor of its way, like this, it had holes in it; in fact, I fancy the bottom of the holes was the true level, for it came near being as full of holes as a fishing-net, and it was very quaint to see the man in front, who had been paddling along knee-deep before, now plop down with the water round his shoulders; and getting out of these slippery pockets, which were sometimes a tight fit, was difficult.

However that is the path you have got to go by, if you're not wise enough to stop at home; the little bay of shrub overgrown swamp fringing the river on one side and on the other running up to the mountain side.

At last we came to a sandy bank, and on that bank stood Egaja, the town with an evil name even among the Fan, but where we had got to stay, fair or foul. We went into it through its palaver house, and soon had the usual row.

I had detected signs of trouble among my men during the whole day; the Ajumba were tired, and dissatisfied with the Fans; the Fans were in high feather, openly insolent to Ngouta, and anxious for me to stay in this delightful locality, and go hunting with them and divers other choice spirits, whom they assured me we could easily get to join us at Efoua. I kept peace as well as I could, explaining to the Fans I had not enough money with me now, because I had not, when starting, expected such magnificent opportunities to be placed at my disposal; and promising to come back next year—a promise I hope to keep—and then we would go and have a grand time of it. This state of a party was a dangerous one in which to enter a strange Fan town, where our security lay in our being united. When the first burst of Egaja conversation began to boil down into something reasonable, I found that a villainous-looking scoundrel, smeared with soot and draped in a fragment of genuine antique cloth, was a head chief in mourning. He placed a house at my disposal, quite a mansion, for it had no less than four apartments. The first one was almost entirely occupied by a bedstead frame that was being made up inside on account of the small size of the door.

This had to be removed before we could get in with the baggage at all. While this removal was being effected with as much damage to the house and the article as if it were a quarter-day affair in England, the other chief arrived. He had been sent for, being away down the river fishing when we arrived. I saw at once he was a very superior man to any of the chiefs I had yet met with. It was not his attire, remarkable though that was for the district, for it consisted of a gentleman's black frock-coat such as is given in the ivory bundle, a bright blue felt sombrero hat, an ample cloth of Boma check; but his face and general bearing was distinctive, and very powerful and intelligent; and I knew that Egaja, for good or bad, owed its name to this man, and not to the mere sensual, brutal-looking one. He was exceedingly courteous, ordering his people to bring me a stool and one for himself, and then a fly-whisk to battle with the evening cloud of sand-flies. I got Pagan to come and act as interpreter while the rest were stowing the baggage, &c. After compliments, "Tell the chief," I said, "that I hear this town of his is thief town."

"Better not, sir," says Pagan.

"Go on," said I, "or I'll tell him myself."

So Pagan did. It was a sad blow to the chief.

"Thief town, this highly respectable town of Egaja! a town whose moral conduct in all matters (Shedule) was an example to all towns, called a thief town! Oh, what a wicked world!"

I said it was; but I would reserve my opinion as to whether Egaja was a part of the wicked world or a star-like exception, until I had experienced it myself. We then discoursed on many matters, and I got a great deal of interesting fetish information out of the chief, which was valuable to me, because the whole of this district had not been in contact with white culture; and altogether I and the chief became great friends.

Just when I was going in to have my much-desired tea, he brought me his mother—an old lady, evidently very bright and able, but, poor woman, with the most disgusting hand and arm I have ever seen. I am ashamed to say I came very near being sympathetically sick in the African manner on the spot. I felt I could not attend to it, and have my tea afterwards, so I directed one of the canoe-shaped little tubs, used for beating up the manioc in, to be brought and filled with hot water, and then putting into it a heavy dose of Condy's fluid, I made her sit down and lay the whole arm in it, and went and had my tea. As soon as I had done I went outside, and getting some of the many surrounding ladies to hold bush-lights, I examined the case. The whole hand was a mass of yellow pus, streaked with sanies, large ulcers were burrowing into the fore-arm, while in the arm-pit was a big abscess. I opened the abscess at once, and then the old lady frightened me nearly out of my wits by gently subsiding, I thought dying, but I soon found out merely going to sleep. I then washed the abscess well out, and having got a lot of baked plantains, I made a big poultice of them, mixed with boiling water and more Condy in the tub, and laid her arm right in this; and propping her up all round and covered her over with cloths I requisitioned from her son, I left her to have her nap while I went into the history of the case, which was that some forty-eight hours ago she had been wading along the bank, catching crawfish, and had been stung by "a fish like a snake"; so I presume the ulcers were an old-standing palaver. The hand had been a good deal torn by the creature, and the pain and swelling had been so great she had not had a minute's sleep since. As soon as the poultice got chilled I took her arm out and cleaned it again, and wound it round with dressing, and had her ladyship carried bodily, still asleep, into her hut, and after rousing her up, giving her a dose of that fine preparation, *pil. crotonis cum hydrargi,* saw her tucked up on her own plank bedstead for the night, sound asleep again. The chief was very anxious to have some pills too; so I gave him some, with firm injunctions only to take one at the first time. I knew that that one would teach him not to take more than one forever after, better than I could do if I talked from June to January. Then all the afflicted of Egaja turned up, and wanted medical advice. There was evidently a good stiff epidemic of the yaws about; lots of cases of dum with the various symptoms; ulcers of course galore; a man with a bit of a broken spear head in an abscess in the thigh; one which I believe a professional enthusiast would call a "lovely case" of filaria, the entire white of one eye being full of the active little worms and a ridge of surplus population migrating across the bridge of the nose into the other eye, under the skin, looking like the bridge of a pair of spectacles. It was past eleven before I had anything like done, and my men had long been sound asleep, but the chief had conscientiously sat up and seen the thing through. He then went and fetched some rolls of bark cloth to put on my plank, and I gave him a handsome cloth I happened to have with me, a couple of knives, and some heads of tobacco and wished him good-night; blockading my bark door, and picking my way over my sleeping Ajumba into an inner apartment which I also blockaded, hoping I had done with Egaja for some hours. No such thing. At 1.45 the whole town was roused by the frantic yells of a woman. I judged there was one of my beauties of Fans mixed up in it, and there was, and after paying damages, got back again by 2.30 a.m., and off to sleep again instantly. At four sharp, whole town of Egaja plunged into emotion, and worse shindy. I suggested to the Ajumba they should go out; but no, they didn't care a row of pins if one of our Fans did get killed, so I went, recognising Kiva's voice in high expostulation. Kiva, it seems, a long time ago had a transaction *in re* a tooth of ivory with a man who, unfortunately, happened to be in this town to-night, and Kiva owed the said man a coat.

Kiva, it seems, has been spending the whole evening demonstrating to his creditor that, had he only known they were to meet, he would have brought the coat with him—a particularly beautiful coat—and the reason he has not paid it before is that he has mislaid the creditor's address. The creditor says he has called repeatedly at Kiva's village, that notorious M'fetta, and Kiva has never been at home; and moreover that Kiva's wife (one of them) stole a yellow dog of great value from his (the creditor's) canoe. Kiva says, women will be women, and he had gone off to sleep thinking the affair had blown over and the bill renewed for the time being. The creditor had not gone to sleep; but sat up thinking the affair over and remembered many cases, all cited in full, of how Kiva had failed to meet his debts; also Kiva's brother on the mother's side and uncle ditto; and so has decided to foreclose forthwith on the debtor's estate, and as the estate is represented by and consists of Kiva's person, to take and seize upon it and eat it.

It is always highly interesting to observe the germ of any of our own institutions existing in the culture of a lower race. Nevertheless it is trying to be hauled out of one's sleep in the middle of the night, and plunged into this study. Evidently this was a trace of an early form of the Bankruptcy Court; the court which clears a man of his debt, being here represented by the knife and the cooking pot; the whitewashing, as I believe it is termed with us, also shows, only it is not the debtor who is whitewashed, but the creditors doing themselves over with white clay to celebrate the removal of their enemy from his sphere of meretricious activity. This inversion may arise from the fact that whitewashing a creditor who was about to be cooked would be unwise, as the stuff would boil off the bits and spoil the gravy. There is always some fragment of sound sense underlying African institutions. Kiva was, when I got out, tied up, talking nineteen to the dozen; and so was every one else; and a lady was working up white clay in a pot.

I dare say I ought to have rushed at him and cut his bonds, and killed people in a general way with a revolver, and then flown with my band to the bush; only my band evidently had no flying in them, being tucked up in the hut pretending to be asleep, and uninterested in the affair; and although I could have abandoned the band without a pang just then, I could not so light-heartedly fly alone with Kiva to the bush and leave my fishes; so I shouted Azuna to the Bankruptcy Court, and got a Fan who spoke trade English to come and interpret for me; and from him I learnt the above stated outline of the proceedings up to the time. Regarding the original iniquity of Kiva, my other Fans held the opinion that the old Scotch lady had regarding certain passages in the history of the early Jews—that it was a long time ago, and aiblins it was no true.

Fortunately for the reader it is impossible for me to give in full detail the proceedings of the Court. I do not think if the whole of Mr. Pitman's school of shorthand had been there to take them down the thing could possibly have been done in word-writing. If the late Richard Wagner, however, had been present he could have scored the performance for a full orchestra; and with all its weird grunts and roars, and pistol-like finger clicks, and its elongated words and thigh slaps, it would have been a masterpiece.

I got my friend the chief on my side; but he explained he had no jurisdiction, as neither of the men belonged to his town; and I explained to him, that as the proceedings were taking place in his town he had a right of jurisdiction *ipso facto*. The Fan could not translate this phrase, so we gave it the chief raw, and he seemed to relish it, and he and I then cut into the affair together, I looking at him with admiration and approval when he was saying his say, and after his "Azuna" had produced a patch of silence he could move his tongue in, and he similarly regarding me during my speech for the defence. We neither, I expect, understood each other, and we had trouble with our client, who would keep pleading "Not guilty," which was absurd. Anyhow we produced our effect, my success arising from my concluding my speech with the announcement that I would give the creditor a book on Hatton and Cookson for the coat, and I would deduct it from Kiva's pay.

But, said the Court: "We look your mouth and it be sweet mouth, but with Hatton and Cookson we can have no trade." This was a blow to me. Hatton and Cookson was my big Ju Ju, and it was to their sub-factory on the Rembwé that I was bound. On inquiry I elicited another cheerful little fact, which was they could not deal with Hatton and Cookson because there was "blood war on the path that way." The Court said they would take a book on Holty, but with Holty *i.e.* Mr. John Holt, I had no deposit of money, and I did not feel justified in issuing cheques on him, knowing also he could not feel amiable towards wandering scientists, after what he had recently gone through with one. Not that I doubt for one minute but that his representatives would have honoured my book; for the generosity and helpfulness of West African traders is unbounded and long-suffering. But I did not like to encroach on it, all the more so from a feeling that I might never get through to refund the money. So at last I paid the equivalent value of the coat out of my own trade-stuff; and the affair was regarded by all parties as satisfactorily closed by the time the gray dawn was coming up over the forest wall. I went in again and slept in snatches until I got my tea about seven, and then turned out to hurry my band out of Egaja. This I did not succeed in doing until past ten. One row succeeded another with my men; but I was determined to get them out of that town as quickly as possible, for I had heard so much from perfectly reliable and experienced people regarding the treacherousness of the Fan. I feared too that more cases still would be brought up against Kiva, from the résumé of his criminal career I had had last night, and I knew it was very doubtful whether my other three Fans were any better than he. There was his grace's little murder affair only languishing for want of evidence owing to the witnesses for the prosecution being out elephant-hunting not very far away; and Wiki was pleading an *alibi*, and a twin brother, in a bad wife palaver in this town. I really hope for the sake of Fan morals at large, that I did engage the three worst villains in M'fetta, and that M'fetta is the worst town in all Fan land, inconvenient as this arrangement was to me personally. Anyhow, I felt sure my Pappenheimers would take a lot of beating for good solid crime, among any tribe anywhere. Moreover, the Ajumba wanted meat, and the Fans, they said, offered them human. I saw no human meat at Egaja, but the Ajumba seem to think the Fans eat nothing else, which is a silly prejudice of theirs, because the Fans do. I think in this case the Ajumba thought a lot of smoked flesh offered was human. It may have been; it was in neat pieces; and again, as the Captain of the late s.s. *Sparrow* would say, "it mayn't." But the Ajumba have a horror of cannibalism, and I honestly believe never practise it, even for fetish affairs, which is a rare thing in a West African tribe where sacrificial and ceremonial cannibalism is nearly universal. Anyhow the Ajumba loudly declared the Fans were "bad men too much," which was impolitic under existing circumstances, and inexcusable, because it by no means arose from a courageous defiance of them; but the West African! Well! "'E's a devil an' a ostrich an' a orphan child in one."

The chief was very anxious for me to stay and rest, but as his mother was doing wonderfully well, and the other women seemed quite to understand my directions regarding her, I did not feel inclined to risk it. The old lady's farewell of me was peculiar: she took my hand in her two, turned it palm upwards, and spat on it. I do not know whether this is a constant form of greeting among the Fan; I fancy not. Dr. Nassau, who explained it to me when I saw him again down at Baraka, said the spitting was merely an accidental by-product of the performance, which consisted in blowing a blessing; and as I happened on this custom twice afterwards, I feel sure from observation he is right.

The two chiefs saw us courteously out of the town as far as where the river crosses the out-going path again, and the blue-hatted one gave me some charms "to keep my foot in path," and the mourning chief lent us his son to see us through the lines of fortification of the plantation. I gave them an equal dash, and in answer to their question as to whether I had found Egaja a thief-town, I said that to call Egaja a thief-town was rank perjury, for I had not lost a thing while in it; and we parted with mutual expression of esteem and hopes for another meeting at an early date.

The defences of the fine series of plantations of Egaja on this side were most intricate, to judge from the zigzag course our guide led us through them. He explained they had to be because of the character of the towns towards the Rembwé. After listening to this young man, I really began to doubt that the Cities of the Plain had really been destroyed, and wondered whether some future revision committee will not put transported for destroyed. This young man certainly hit off the character of Sodom and Gomorrah to the life, in describing the towns towards the Rembwé, though he had never heard Sodom and Gomorrah named. He assured me I should see the difference between them and Egaja the Good, and I thanked him and gave him his dash when we parted; but told him as a friend, I feared some alteration must take place, and some time elapse before he saw a regular rush of pilgrim worshippers of Virtue coming into even Egaja the Good, though it stood just as good a chance and better than most towns I had seen in Africa.

We went on into the gloom of the Great Forest again; that forest that seemed to me without end, wherein, in a lazy, hazy-minded sort of way, I expected to wander through by day and drop in at night to a noisy savage town for the rest of my days.

We climbed up one hill, skirted its summit, went through our athletic sports over sundry timber falls, and struck down into the ravine as usual. But at the bottom of that ravine, which was exceedingly steep, ran a little river free from swamp. As I was wading it I noticed it had a peculiarity that distinguished it from all the other rivers we had come through; and then and there I sat down on a boulder in its midst and hauled out my compass. Yes, by Allah! it's going north-west and bound as we are for Rembwé River. I went out the other side of that river with a lighter heart than I went in, and shouted the news to the boys, and they yelled and sang as we went on our way.

All along this bit of country we had seen quantities of rubber vines, and between Egaja and Esoon we came across quantities of rubber being collected. Evidently there was a big camp of rubber hunters out in the district very busy. Wiki and Kiva did their best to teach me the trade. Along each side of the path we frequently saw a ring of stout bush rope, raised from the earth on pegs about a foot to eighteen inches. On the ground in the middle stood a calabash, into which the ends of the pieces of rubber vine were placed, the other ends being supported by the bush rope ring. Round the outside of some of these rings was a slow fire, which just singes the tops of the bits of rubber vine as they project over the collar or ring, and causes the milky juice to run out of the lower end into the calabash, giving out as it does so a strong ammoniacal smell. When the fire was alight there would be a group of rubber collectors sitting round it watching the cooking operations, removing those pieces that had run dry and placing others, from a pile at their side, in position. On either side of the path we continually passed pieces of rubber vine cut into lengths of some two feet or so, and on the top one or two leaves plaited together, or a piece of bush rope tied into a knot, which indicated whose property the pile was.

The method of collection employed by the Fan is exceedingly wasteful, because this fool of a vegetable *Landolphia florida (Ovariensis)* does not know how to send up suckers from its root, but insists on starting elaborately from seeds only. I do not, however, see any reasonable hope of getting them to adopt more economical methods. The attempt made by the English houses, when the rubber trade was opened up in 1883 on the Gold Coast, to get the more tractable natives there to collect by incisions only, has failed; for in the early days a man could get a load of rubber almost at his own door on the Gold Coast, and now he has to go fifteen days' journey inland for it. When a Fan town has exhausted the rubber in its vicinity, it migrates, bag and baggage, to a new part of the forest. The young unmarried men are the usual rubber hunters. Parties of them go out into the forest, wandering about in it and camping under shelters of boughs by night, for a month and more at a time, during the dry seasons, until they have got a sufficient quantity together; then they return to their town, and it is manipulated by the women, and finally sold, either to the white trader, in districts where he is within reach, or to the M'pongwe trader who travels round buying it and the collected ivory and ebony, like a Norfolk higgler. In districts like these I was in, remote from the M'pongwe trader, the Fans carry the rubber to the town nearest to them that is in contact with the black trader, and sell it to the inhabitants, who in their turn resell it to their next town, until it reaches him. This passing down of the rubber and ivory gives rise between the various towns to a series of commercial complications which rank with women palaver for the production of rows; it being the sweet habit of the Fans to require a life for a life, and to regard one life as good as another. Also rubber trade and wife palavers sweetly intertwine, for a man on the kill *in re* a wife palaver knows his best chance of getting the life from the village he has a grudge against lies in catching one of that village's men when he may be out alone rubber hunting. So he does this thing, and then the men from the victim's village go and lay for a rubber hunter from the killer's village; and then of course the men from the killer's village go and lay for rubber hunters from victim number one's village, and thus the blood feud rolls down the vaulted chambers of the ages, so that you, dropping in on affairs, cannot see one end or the other of it, and frequently the people concerned have quite forgotten what the killing was started for. Not that this discourages them in the least. Really if Dr. Nassau is right, and these Fans are descendants of Adam and Eve, I expect the Cain and Abel killing palaver is still kept going among them.

Wiki, being great on bush rope, gave me much information regarding rubber, showing me the various other vines besides the true rubber vine, whose juice, mingled with the true sap by the collector when in the forest, adds to the weight; a matter of importance, because rubber is bought by weight. The other adulteration gets done by the ladies in the villages when the collected sap is handed over to them to prepare for the markets.

This preparation consists of boiling it in water slightly, and adding a little salt, which causes the gummy part to separate and go to the bottom of the pot, where it looks like a thick cream. The water is carefully poured off this deposit, which is then taken out and moulded, usually in the hands; but I have seen it run into moulds made of small calabashes with a stick or piece of iron passing through, so that when the rubber is set this can be withdrawn. A hole being thus left the balls can be threaded on to a stick, usually five on one stick, for convenience of transport. It is during the moulding process that most of the adulteration gets in. Down by the side of many of the streams there is a white chalky-looking clay which is brought up into the villages, powdered up, and then hung up over the fire in a basket to attain a uniform smuttiness; it is then worked into the rubber when it is being made up into balls. Then a good chunk of Koko, *Arum esculentum* (Koko is better than yam, I may remark, because it is heavier), also smoked approximately the right colour, is often placed in the centre of the rubber ball. In fact, anything is put there, that is hopefully regarded as likely to deceive the white trader. So great is the adulteration, that most of the traders have to cut each ball open. Even the Kinsembo rubber, which is put up in clusters of bits shaped like little thimbles formed by rolling pinches of rubber between the thumb and finger, and which one would think difficult to put anything inside of, has to be cut, because "the simple children of nature" who collect it and bring it to that "swindling white trader" struck upon the ingenious notion that little pieces of wood shaped like the thimbles and coated by a dip in rubber were excellent additions to a cluster.

The pure rubber, when it is made, looks like putty, and has the same dusky-white colour; but, owing to the balls being kept in the huts in baskets in the smoke, and in wicker-work cages in the muddy pools to soak up as much water as possible before going into the hands of the traders, they get almost inky in colour.

CHAPTER 9

From Esoon to Agonjo

In which the Voyager sets forth the beauties of the way from Esoon to N'dorko,
and gives some account of the local Swamps.

OUR NEXT HALTING PLACE WAS ESOON, which received us with the usual row, but kindly enough; and endeared itself to me by knowing the Rembwé, and not just waving the arm in the air, in any direction, and saying "Far, far plenty bad people live for that side," as the other towns had done. Of course they stuck to the bad people part of the legend; but I was getting quite callous as to the moral character of new acquaintances, feeling sure that for good solid murderous rascality several of my old Fan acquaintances, and even my own party, would take a lot of beating; and yet, one and all, they had behaved well to me. Esoon gave me to understand that of all the Sodoms and Gomorrahs that town of Egaja was an easy first, and it would hardly believe we had come that way. Still Egaja had dealt with us well. However I took less interest—except, of course, as a friend, in some details regarding the criminal career of Chief Blue-hat of Egaja—in the opinion of Esoon regarding the country we had survived, than in the information it had to impart regarding the country we had got to survive on our way to the Big River, which now no longer meant the Ogowé, but the Rembwé. I meant to reach one of Hatton and Cookson's sub-factories there, but—strictly between ourselves—I knew no more at what town that factory was than a

Kindergarten Board School child does. I did not mention this fact;
and a casual observer might have thought that I had spent my youth in
that factory, when I directed my inquiries to the finding out the very
shortest route to it. Esoon shook its head. "Yes, it was close, but it was
impossible to reach Uguma's factory." "Why?" "There was blood war
on the path." I said it was no war of mine. But Esoon said, such was the
appalling depravity of the next town on the road, that its inhabitants lay
in wait at day with loaded guns and shot on sight any one coming up the
Esoon road, and that at night they tied strings with bells on across the
road and shot on hearing them. No one had been killed since the first
party of Esoonians were fired on at long range, because no one had gone
that way; but the next door town had been heard by people who had been
out in the bush at night, blazing down the road when the bells were tin-
kled by wild animals. Clearly that road was not yet really healthy.

The Duke, who as I have said before, was a fine courageous fellow,
ready to engage in any undertaking, suggested I should go up the road—
alone by myself—first—a mile ahead of the party—and the next town,
perhaps, might not shoot at sight, if they happened to notice I was something queer; and I might explain things, and then the rest of the party
would follow. "There's nothing like dash and courage, my dear Duke,"
I said, "even if one display it by deputy, so this plan does you great credit;
but as my knowledge of this charming language of yours is but small, I
fear I might create a wrong impression in that town, and it might think
I had kindly brought them a present of eight edible heathens—you and
the remainder of my followers, you understand." My men saw this was a
real danger, and this was the only way I saw of excusing myself. It is at
such a moment as this that the Giant's robe gets, so to speak, between
your legs and threatens to trip you up. Going up a forbidden road, and
exposing yourself as a pot shot to ambushed natives would be jam and
fritters to Mr. MacTaggart, for example; but I am not up to that form
yet. So I determined to leave that road severely alone, and circumnavi-
gate the next town by a road that leaves Esoon going W.N.W., which
struck the Rembwé by N'dorko, I was told, and then follow up the bank
of the river until I picked up the sub-factory. Subsequent experience did
not make one feel inclined to take out a patent for this plan, but at the
time in Esoon it looked nice enough.

Some few of the more highly cultured inhabitants here could speak
trade English a little, and had been to the Rembwé, and were quite

intelligent about the whole affair. They had seen white men. A village they formerly occupied nearer the Rembwé had been burnt by them, on account of a something that had occurred to a Catholic priest who visited it. They were, of course, none of them personally mixed up in this sad affair, so could give no details of what had befallen the priest. They knew also "the *Mové*," which was a great bond of union between us. "Was I a wife of them *Mové* white man," they inquired—"or them other white man?" I civilly said them *Mové* men were my tribe, and they ought to have known it by the look of me. They discussed my points of resemblance to "the *Mové* white man," and I am ashamed to say I could not forbear from smiling, as I distinctly recognised my friends from the very racy description of their personal appearance and tricks of manner given by a lively Esoonian belle who had certainly met them. So content and happy did I become under these soothing influences, that I actually took off my boots, a thing I had quite got out of the habit of doing, and had them dried. I wanted to have them rubbed with palm oil, but I found, to my surprise, that there was no palm oil to be had, the tree being absent, or scarce in this region, so I had to content myself with having them rubbed with a piece of animal fat instead. I chaperoned my men, while among the ladies of Esoon—a forward set of minxes—with the vigilance of a dragon; and decreed, like the Mikado of Japan, "that whosoever leered or winked, unless connubially linked, should forthwith be beheaded," have their pay chopped, I mean; and as they were beginning to smell their pay, they were careful, and we got through Esoon without one of them going into jail; no mean performance when you remember that every man had a past—to put it mildly.

Esoon is not situated like the other towns, with a swamp and the forest close round it; but it is built on the side of a fairly cleared ravine among its plantain groves. When you are on the southern side of the ravine, you can see Esoon looking as if it were hung on the hillside before you. You then go through a plantation down into the little river, and up into the town—one long, broad, clean-kept street. Leaving Esoon you go on up the hill through another plantation to the summit. Immediately after leaving the town we struck westwards; and when we got to the top of the next hill we had a view that showed us we were dealing with another type of country. The hills to the westward are lower, and the valleys between them broader and less heavily forested, or rather I should say forested with smaller sorts of timber. All our paths took us during the early part of the day up and down hills, through swamps and little rivers, all flowing Rembwé-wards. About the middle of the afternoon, when we had got up to the top of a high hill, after having had a terrible time on a timber fall of the first magnitude, into which four of us had fallen, I of course for one, I saw a sight that made my heart stand still. Stretching away to the west and north, winding in and out among the feet of the now isolated mound-like mountains, was that never to be mistaken black-green forest swamp of mangrove; doubtless the fringe of the River Rembwé, which evidently comes much further inland than the mangrove belt on the Ogowé. This is reasonable and as it should be, though it surprised me at the time; for the great arm of the sea which is called the Gaboon is really a fjord, just like Bonny and Opobo rivers, with several rivers falling into it at its head, and this fjord brings the sea water further inland. In addition to this the two rivers, the 'Como (Nkâmâ,) and Rembwé that fall into this Gaboon, with several smaller rivers, both bring down an inferior quantity of fresh water, and that at nothing like the tearing, tide-beating back pace of the Ogowé. As my brother would say, "It's perfectly simple if you think about it;" but thinking is not my strong point. Anyhow I was glad to see the mangrove-belt; all the gladder because I did not then know how far it was inland from the sea, and also because I was fool enough to think that a long line I could see, running E. and W. to the north of where I stood, was the line of the Rembwé river; which it was not, as we soon found out. Cheered by this pleasing prospect, we marched on forgetful of our scratches, down the side of the hill, and down the foot slope of it, until we struck the edge of the swamp. We skirted this for some mile or so, going N.E. Then we struck into the swamp, to reach what we had regarded as the Rembwé river. We found ourselves at the edge of that open line we had seen from the mountain. Not standing, because you don't so much as try to stand on mangrove roots unless you are a born fool, and then you don't stand long, but clinging, like so many monkeys, to the net of aërial roots which surrounded us, looking blankly at a lake of ink-black slime. It was half a mile across, and some miles long. We could not see either the west or east termination of it, for it lay like a rotten serpent twisted between the mangroves. It never entered into our heads to try to cross it, for when a swamp is too deep for mangroves to grow in it, "No bottom lib for them dam ting," as a Kruboy once said to me, anent a small specimen of this sort of ornament to a landscape. But we just looked round to see which direction we had better take. Then I observed that the roots, aërial and otherwise, were coated in mud, and had no leaves on them, for a foot above our heads. Next I noticed that the surface of the mud before us had a sort of quiver running through it, and here and there it exhibited swellings on its surface, which rose in one place and fell in another. No need for an old coaster like me to look at that sort of thing twice to know what it meant, and feeling it was a situation more suited to Mr. Stanley than myself, I attempted to emulate his methods and addressed my men. "Boys," said I, "this beastly hole is tidal, and the tide is coming in. As it took us two hours to get to this sainted swamp, it's time we started out, one time, and the nearest way. It's to be hoped the practice we have acquired in mangrove roots in coming, will enable us to get up sufficient pace to get out on to dry land before we are all drowned." The boys took the hint. Fortunately one of the Ajumbas had been down in Ogowé, it was Gray Shirt, who "sabed them tide palaver." The rest of them, and the Fans, did not know what tide meant, but Gray Shirt hustled them along and I followed, deeply regretting that my ancestors had parted prematurely with prehensile tails, for four limbs, particularly when two of them are done up in boots and are not sufficient to enable one to get through a mangrove swamp network of slimy roots rising out of the water, and swinging lines of aërial ones coming down to the water *à la* mangrove, with anything approaching safety. Added to these joys were any quantity of mangrove flies, a broiling hot sun, and an atmosphere three-quarters solid stench from the putrefying ooze all round us. For an hour and a half thought I, Why did I come to Africa, or why, having come, did I not know when I was well off and stay in Glass? Before these problems were settled in my mind we were close to the true land again, with the water under us licking lazily among the roots and over our feet.

We did not make any fuss about it, but we meant to stick to dry land for some time, and so now took to the side of a hill that seemed like a great bubble coming out of the swamp, and bore steadily E. until we found a path. This path, according to the nature of paths in this country, promptly took us into another swamp, but of a different kind to our last—a knee-deep affair, full of beautiful palms and strange water plants, the names whereof I know not. There was just one part where that abomination, *pandanus*, had to be got through, but, as swamps go, it was not at all bad. I ought to mention that there were leeches in it, lest I may be thought too enthusiastic over its charms. But the great point was that the mountains we got to on the other side of it, were a good solid ridge, running, it is true, E. and W., while we wanted to go N.; still on we went waiting for developments, and watching the great line of mangrove-swamp spreading along below us to the left hand, seeing many of the lines in its dark face, which betokened more of those awesome slime lagoons that we had seen enough of at close quarters.

About four o'clock we struck some more plantations, and passing through these, came to a path running northeast, down which we went. I must say the forest scenery here was superbly lovely. Along this mountain side cliff to the mangrove-swamp the sun could reach the soil, owing to the steepness and abruptness and the changes of curves of the ground; while the soft steamy air which came up off the swamp swathed everything, and although unpleasantly strong in smell to us, was yet evidently highly agreeable to the vegetation. Lovely wine palms and rafia palms, looking as if they had been grown under glass, so deliciously green and profuse was their feather-like foliage, intermingled with giant red woods, and lovely dark glossy green lianes, blooming in wreaths and festoons of white and mauve flowers, which gave a glorious wealth of beauty and colour to the scene. Even the monotony of the mangrove-belt alongside gave an additional charm to it, like the frame round a picture.

As we passed on, the ridge turned N. and the mangrove line narrowed between the hills. Our path now ran east and more in the middle of the forest, and the cool shade was charming after the heat we had had earlier in the day. We crossed a lovely little stream coming down the hillside in a cascade; and then our path plunged into a beautiful valley. We had glimpses through the trees of an amphitheatre of blue mist-veiled mountains coming down in a crescent before us, and on all sides, save due west where the mangrove-swamp came in. Never shall I forget the exceeding beauty of that valley, the foliage of the trees round us, the delicate wreaths and festoons of climbing plants, the graceful delicate plumes of the palm trees, interlacing among each other, and showing through all a background of soft, pale, purple-blue mountains and forest, not really far away, as the practised eye knew, but only made to look so by the mist, which has this trick of giving suggestion of immense space without destroying the beauty of detail. Those African misty forests have the same marvellous distinctive quality that Turner gives one in his greatest pictures. I am no artist, so I do not know exactly what it is, but

I see it is there. I luxuriated in the exquisite beauty of that valley, little thinking or knowing what there was in it besides beauty, as Allah "in mercy hid the book of fate." On we went among the ferns and flowers until we met a swamp, a different kind of swamp to those we had heretofore met, save the little one last mentioned. This one was much larger, and a gem of beauty; but we had to cross it. It was completely furnished with characteristic flora. Fortunately when we got to its edge we saw a woman crossing before us, but unfortunately she did not take a fancy to our appearance, and instead of staying and having a chat about the state of the roads, and the shortest way to N'dorko, she bolted away across the swamp. I noticed she carefully took a course, not the shortest, although that course immersed her to her armpits. In we went after her, and when things were getting unpleasantly deep, and feeling highly uncertain under foot, we found there was a great log of a tree under the water which, as we had seen the lady's care at this point, we deemed it advisable to walk on. All of us save one, need I say that one was myself? effected this with safety. As for me, when I was at the beginning of the submerged bridge, and busily laying about in my mind for a definite opinion as to whether it was better to walk on a slippy tree trunk bridge you could see, or on one you could not, I was hurled off by that inexorable fate that demands of me a personal acquaintance with fluvial and paludial ground deposits; whereupon I took a header, and am thereby able to inform the world, that there is between fifteen and twenty feet of water each side of that log. I conscientiously went in on one side, and came up on the other. The log, I conjecture, is odum or ebony, and it is some fifty feet long; anyhow it is some sort of wood that won't float. Gray Shirt says it is a bridge across an under-swamp river. Having survived this and reached the opposite bank, we shortly fell in with a party of men and women, who were taking, they said, a parcel of rubber to Holty's. They told us N'dorko was quite close, and that the plantations we saw before us were its outermost ones, but spoke of a swamp, a bad swamp. We knew it, we said, in the foolishness of our hearts thinking they meant the one we had just forded, and leaving them resting, passed on our way; half-a-mile further on we were wiser and sadder, for then we stood on the rim of one of the biggest swamps I have ever seen south of the Rivers. It stretched away in all directions, a great sheet of filthy water, out of which sprang gorgeous marsh plants, in islands, great banks of screw pine, and coppices of wine palm, with their lovely fronds reflected back by the still, mirror-like water, so that the reflection was as vivid as the reality, and above all remarkable was a plant, new and strange to me, whose pale-green stem came up out of the water and then spread out in a flattened surface, thin, and in a peculiarly graceful curve. This flattened surface had growing out from it leaves, the size, shape and colour of lily of the valley leaves; until I saw this thing I had held the wine palm to be the queen of grace in the vegetable kingdom, but this new beauty quite surpassed her.

Our path went straight into this swamp over the black rocks forming its rim, in an imperative, no alternative, "Come-along-this-way" style. Singlet, who was leading, carrying a good load of bottled fish and a gorilla specimen, went at it like a man, and disappeared before the eyes of us close following him, then and there down through the water. He came up, thanks be, but his load is down there now, worse luck. Then I said we must get the rubber carriers who were coming this way to show us the ford; and so we sat down on the bank a tired, disconsolate, dilapidated-looking row, until they arrived. When they came up they did not plunge in forthwith; but leisurely set about making a most nerve-shaking set of preparations, taking off their clothes, and forming them into bundles, which, to my horror, they put on the tops of their heads. The women carried the rubber on their backs still, but rubber is none the worse for being underwater. The men went in first, each holding his gun high above his head. They skirted the bank before they struck out into the swamp, and were followed by the women and by our party, and soon we were all up to our chins.

We were two hours and a quarter passing that swamp. I was one hour and three-quarters; but I made good weather of it, closely following the rubber-carriers, and only going in right over head and all twice. Other members of my band were less fortunate. One and all, we got horribly infested with leeches, having a frill of them round our necks like astrachan collars, and our hands covered with them, when we came out.

We had to pass across the first bit of open country I had seen for a long time—a real patch of grass on the top of a low ridge, which is fringed with swamp on all sides save the one we made our way to, the eastern. Shortly after passing through another plantation, we saw brown huts, and in a few minutes were standing in the middle of a ramshackle village, at the end of which, through a high stockade, with its gateway smeared with blood which hung in gouts, we saw our much longed for

Rembwé River. I made for it, taking small notice of the hubbub our arrival occasioned, and passed through the gateway, setting its guarding bell ringing violently; I stood on the steep, black, mud slime bank, surrounded by a noisy crowd. It is a big river, but nothing to the Ogowé, either in breadth or beauty; what beauty it has is of the Niger delta type—black mud-laden water, with a mangrove swamp fringe to it in all directions. I soon turned back into the village and asked for Ugumu's factory. "This is it," said an exceedingly dirty, good-looking, civil-spoken man in perfect English, though as pure blooded an African as ever walked. "This is it, sir," and he pointed to one of the huts on the right-hand side, indistinguishable in squalor from the rest. "Where's the Agent?" said I. "I'm the Agent," he answered. You could have knocked me down with a feather. "Where's John Holt's factory?" said I. "You have passed it; it is up on the hill." This showed Messrs. Holt's local factory to be no bigger than Ugumu's. At this point a big, scraggy, very black man with an irregularly formed face the size of a tea-tray and looking generally as if he had come out of a pantomime on the *Arabian Nights*, dashed through the crowd, shouting, "I'm for Holty, I'm for Holty." "This is my trade, you go 'way," says Agent number one. Fearing my two Agents would fight and damage each other, so that neither would be any good for me, I firmly said, "Have you got any rum?" Agent number one looked crestfallen, Holty's triumphant. "Rum, fur sure," says he; so I gave him a five-franc piece, which he regarded with great pleasure, and putting it in his mouth, he legged it like a lamplighter away to his store on the hill. "Have you any tobacco?" said I to Agent number one. He brightened, "Plenty tobacco, plenty cloth," said he; so I told him to give me out twenty heads. I gave my men two heads apiece. I told them rum was coming, and ordered them to take the loads on to Hatton and Cookson's Agent's hut and then to go and buy chop and make themselves comfortable. They highly approved of this plan, and grunted assent ecstatically; and just as the loads were stowed Holty's anatomy hove in sight with a bottle of rum under each arm, and one in each hand; while behind him came an acolyte, a fat, small boy, panting and puffing and doing his level best to keep up with his longlegged flying master. I gave my men some and put the rest in with my goods, and explained that I belonged to Hatton and Cookson's (it's the proper thing to belong to somebody), and that therefore I must take up my quarters at their Store; but Holty's energetic agent hung about me like a vulture in hopes of getting more five franc-piece pickings. I sent Ngouta off to get me some tea, and had the hut cleared of an excited audience, and shut myself in with Hatton and Cookson's agent, and asked him seriously and anxiously if there was not a big factory of the firm's on the river, because it was self-evident he had not got anything like enough stuff to pay off my men with, and my agreement was to pay off on the Rembwé, hence my horror at the smallness of the firm's N'dorko store. "Besides," I said, "Mr. Glass (I knew the head Rembwé agent of Hatton and Cookson was a Mr. Glass), you have only got cloth and tobacco, and I have promised the Fans to pay off in whatever they choose, and I know for sure they want powder." "I am not Mr. Glass," said my friend; "he is up at Agonjo, I only do small trade for him here." Joy!!!! but where's Agonjo? To make a long story short I found Agonjo was an hour's paddle up the Rembwé and the place we ought to have come out at. There was a botheration again about sending up a message, because of a war palaver; but I got a pencil note, with my letter of introduction from Mr. Cockshut to Sanga Glass, at last delivered to that gentleman; and down he came, in a state of considerable astonishment, not unmixed with alarm, for no white man of any kind had been across from the Ogowé for years, and none had ever come out at N'dorko. Mr. Glass I found an exceedingly neat, well-educated M'pongwe gentleman in irreproachable English garments, and with irreproachable, but slightly *floreate*, English language. We started talking trade, with my band in the middle of the street; making a patch of uproar in the moonlit surrounding silence. As soon as thought we had got one gentleman's mind settled as to what goods he would take his pay in, and were proceeding to investigate another gentleman's little fancies; gentleman number one's mind came all to pieces again, and he wanted "to room his bundle," *i.e.* change articles in it for other articles of an equivalent value, if it must be, but of a higher, if possible. Oh ye shopkeepers in England who grumble at your lady customers, just you come out here and try to serve, and satisfy a set of Fans! Mr. Glass was evidently an expert at the affair, but it was past II p.m. before we got the orders written out, and getting my baggage into some canoes, that Mr. Glass had brought down from Agonjo, for N'dorko only had a few very wretched ones, I started off up river with him and all the Ajumba, and Kiva, the Fan, who had been promised a safe conduct. He came to see the bundles for his fellow Fans were made up satisfactorily.

The canoes being small there was quite a procession of them. Mr. Glass and I shared one, which was paddled by two small boys; how we ever got up the Rembwé that night I do not know, for although neither of us were fat, the canoe was a one man canoe, and the water lapped over the edge in an alarming way. Had any of us sneezed, or had it been day-light when two or three mangrove flies would have joined the party, we must have foundered; but all went well; and on arriving at Agonjo Mr. Glass most kindly opened his store, and by the light of lamps and lanterns, we picked out the goods from his varied and ample supply, and handed them over to the Ajumba and Kiva, and all, save three of the Ajumba, were satisfied. The three, Gray Shirt, Silence, and Pagan quietly explained to me that they found the Rembwé price so little better than the Lembarene price that they would rather get their pay off Mr. Cockshut, than risk taking it back through the Fan country, so I gave them books on him. I gave all my remaining trade goods, and the rest of the rum to the Fans as a dash, and they were more than satisfied. I must say they never clamoured for dash for top. The Passenger we had brought through with us, who had really made himself very helpful, was quite surprised at getting a bundle of goods from me. My only anxiety was as to whether Fika would get his share all right; but I expect he did, for the Ajumbas are very honest men; and they were going back with my Fan friends. I found out, by the by, the reason of Fika's shyness in coming through to the Rembwé; it was a big wife palaver.

I had a touching farewell with the Fans: and so in peace, good feeling, and prosperity I parted company for the second time with "the terrible M'pangwe," whom I hope to meet with again, for with all their many faults and failings, they are real men. I am faint-hearted enough to hope, that our next journey together, may not be over a country that seems to me to have been laid down as an obstacle race track for Mr. G. F. Watts's Titans, and to have fallen into shocking bad repair.

CHAPTER 10

BUSH TRADE AND FAN CUSTOMS

Wherein the Voyager, having fallen among the black traders,
discourses on these men and their manner of life; and the difficulties and dangers
attending the barter they carry on with the bush savages; and on some of the reasons
that makes this barter so beloved and followed by both the black trader and the savage.
To which is added an account of the manner of life of the Fan tribe;
the strange form of coinage used by these people;
their manner of hunting the elephant, working in iron; and such like things.

I SPENT A FEW, LAZY, PLEASANT DAYS AT AGONJO, Mr. Glass doing all
he could to make me comfortable, though he had a nasty touch of fever
on him just then. His efforts were ably seconded by his good lady, an
exceedingly comely Gaboon woman, with pretty manners, and an excellent gift in cookery. The third member of the staff was the store-keeper,
a clever fellow: I fancy a Loango from his clean-cut features and spare
make, but his tribe I know not for a surety.

One of these black trader factories is an exceedingly interesting
place to stay at, for in these factories you are right down on the bed rock
of the trade. On the Coast, for the greater part, the white traders are
dealing with black traders, middle men, who have procured their trade
stuff from the bush natives, who collect and prepare it. Here, in the
black trader factory, you see the first stage of the export part of the trade:

namely the barter of the collected trade stuff between the collector and the middleman. I will not go into details regarding it. What I saw merely confirmed my opinion that the native is not cheated; no, not even by a fellow African trader; and I will merely here pause to sing a paean to a very unpopular class—the black middleman as he exists on the South-West Coast. It is impossible to realise the gloom of the lives of these men in bush factories, unless you have lived in one. It is no use saying "they know nothing better and so don't feel it," for they do know several things better, being very sociable men, fully appreciative of the joys of a Coast town, and their aim, object and end in life is, in almost every case, to get together a fortune that will enable them to live in one, give a dance twice a week, card parties most nights, and dress themselves up so that their fellow Coast townsmen may hate them and their townswomen love them. From their own accounts of the dreadful state of trade; and the awful and unparalleled series of losses they have had, from the upsetting of canoes, the raids and robberies made on them and their goods by "those awful bush savages"; you would, if you were of a trustful disposition, regard the black trader with an admiring awe as the man who has at last solved the great commercial problem of how to keep a shop and live by the loss. Nay, not only live, but build for himself an equivalent to a palatial residence, and keep up, not only it, but half a dozen wives, with a fine taste for dress every one of them. I am not of a trustful disposition and I accept those "losses" with a heavy discount, and know most of the rest of them have come out of my friend the white trader's pockets. Still I can never feel the righteous indignation that I ought to feel, when I see the black trader "down in a seaport town with his Nancy," &c., as Sir W. H. S. Gilbert classically says, because I remember those bush factories.

Mr. Glass, however, was not a trader who made a fortune by losing those of other people; for he had been many years in the employ of the firm. He had risen certainly to the high post and position of charge of the Rembwé, but he was not down giddy-flying at Gaboon. His accounts of his experiences when he had been many years ago away up the still little known Nguni River, in a factory in touch with the lively Bakele, then in a factory among Fans and Igalwa on the Ogowé, and now among Fans and Skekiani on the Rembwé, were fascinating, and told vividly of the joys of first starting a factory in a wild district. The way in which your customers, for the first month or so, enjoyed themselves by trying to frighten you, the trader, out of your wits and goods, and into giving them fancy prices for things you were trading in, and for things of no earthly use to you, or any one else! The trader's existence during this period is marked by every unpleasantness save dulness; from that he is spared by the presence of a mob of noisy, dangerous, thieving savages all over his place all day; invading his cook-house, to put some nastiness into his food as a trade charm; helping themselves to portable property at large; and making themselves at home to the extent of sitting on his dining-table. At night those customers proceed to sleep all over the premises, with a view to being on hand to start shopping in the morning. Woe betide the trader if he gives in to this, and tolerates the invasion, for there is no chance of that house ever being his own again; and in addition to the local flies, &c., on the table-cloth, he will always have several big black gentlemen to share his meals. If he raises prices, to tide over some extra row, he is a lost man; for the Africans can understand prices going up, but never prices coming down; and time being no object, they will hold back their trade. Then the district is ruined, and the trader along with it, for he cannot raise the price he gets for the things he buys.

What that trader has got to do, is to be a "Devil man." They always kindly said they recognised me as one, which is a great compliment. He must betray no weakness, but a character which I should describe as a compound of the best parts of those of Cardinal Richelieu, Brutus, Julius Caesar, Prince Metternich, and Mezzofanti, the latter to carry on the native language part of the business; and he must cast those customers out, not only from his house; but from his yard; and adhere to the "No admittance except on business" principle. This causes a good deal of unpleasantness, and the trader's nights are now cheered by lively war-dances outside his stockade; the accompanying songs advertising that the customers are coming over the stockade to raid the store, and cut up the trader "into bits like a fish." Sometimes they do come—and then—finish; but usually they don't; and gradually settle down, and respect the trader greatly as "a Devil man"; and do business on sound lines during the day. Over the stockade at night, by ones and twos, stealing, they will come to the end of the chapter.

Moonlight nights are fairly restful for the bush trader, but when it is inky black, or pouring with rain, he has got to be very much out and about, and particularly vigilant has he got to be on tornado nights—a most uncomfortable sort of weather to attend to business in, I assure you.

The factory at Agonjo was typical; the house is a fine specimen of the Igalwa style of architecture; mounted on poles above the ground; the space under the house being used as a store for rubber in barrels, and ebony in billets; thereby enabling the trader to hover over these precious possessions, sleeping and waking, like a sitting hen over her eggs. Near to the house are the sleeping places for the beach hands, and the cook-house. In front, in a position commanded by the eye from the verandah, and well withdrawn from the stockade, are great piles of billets of red bar wood. The whole of the clean, sandy yard containing these things, and divers others, is surrounded by a stout stockade, its main face to the river frontage, the water at high tide lapping its base, and at low tide exposing in front of it a shore of black slime. Although I cite this factory as a typical factory of a black trader, it is a specimen of the highest class, for, being in connection with Messrs. Hatton and Cookson it is well kept up and stocked. Firms differ much in this particular. Messrs. Hatton and Cookson, like Messrs. Miller Brothers in the Bights, take every care that lies in their power of the people who serve them, down to the Kruboys working on their beaches, giving ample and good rations and providing good houses. But this is not so with all firms on the Coast. I have seen factories belonging to the Swedish houses beside which this factory at Agonjo is a palace although those factories are white man factories, and the unfortunate white men in them are expected by these firms to live on native chop—an expectation the Agents by no means realise, for they usually die. Black hands, however, do not suffer much at the hands of such firms, for the Swedish Agents are a quiet, gentlemanly set of men, in the best sense of that much misused term, and they do not employ on their beaches such a staff of black helpers as the English houses, so the two or three Kruboys on a starvation beach can fairly well fend for themselves, for there is always an adjacent village, and in that village there are always chickens, and on the shore crabs, and in the river fish, and for the rest of his diet the Kruboy flirts with the local ladies.

Although, as I have laid down, the bush factory at its best is a place, as Mr. Tracey Tupman would say, more fitted for a wounded heart than for one still able to feast on social joys, it is a luxurious situation for a black trader compared to the other form of trading he deals with—that of travelling among the native villages in the bush. This has one hundred times the danger, and a thousand times the discomfort, and is a thoroughly unhealthy pursuit. The journeys these bush traders make are often remarkable, and they deserve great credit for the courage and enterprise they display. Certainly they run less risk of death from fever than a white man would; but, on the other hand, their colour gives them no protection; and their chance of getting murdered is distinctly greater, the white governmental powers cannot revenge their death, in the way they would the death of a white man, for these murders usually take place away in some forest region, in a district no white man has ever penetrated.

You will naturally ask how it is that so many of these men do survive "to lead a life of sin" as a missionary described to me their Coast town life to be. This question struck me as requiring explanation. The result of my investigations, and the answers I have received from the men themselves, show that there is a reason why the natives do not succumb every time to the temptation to kill the trader, and take his goods, and this is twofold: firstly, all trade in West Africa follows definite routes, even in the wildest parts of it; and so a village far away in the forest, but on the trade route, knows that as a general rule twice a year, a trader will appear to purchase its rubber and ivory. If he does not appear somewhere about the expected time, that village gets uneasy. The ladies are impatient for their new clothes; the gentlemen half wild for want of tobacco; and things coming to a crisis, they make inquiries for the trader down the road, one village to another, and then, if it is found that a village has killed the trader, and stolen all his goods, there is naturally a big palaver, and things are made extremely hot, even for equatorial Africa, for that village by the tobaccoless husbands of the clothesless wives. Herein lies the trader's chief safety, the village not being an atom afraid, or disinclined to kill him, but afraid of their neighbouring villages, and disinclined to be killed by them. But the trader is not yet safe. There is still a hole in his armour, and this is only to be stopped up in one way, namely, by wives; for you see although the village cannot safely kill him, and take all his goods, they can still let him die safely of a disease, and take part of them, passing on sufficient stuff to the other villages to keep them quiet. Now the most prevalent disease in the African bush comes out of the cooking pot, and so to make what goes into the cooking pot— which is the important point, for earthen pots do not in themselves breed poison—safe and wholesome, you have got to have some one who is devoted to your health to attend to the cooking affairs, and who can do this like a wife? So you have a wife—one in each village up the whole of your route. I know myself one gentleman whose wives stretch over 300 miles of country, with a good wife base in a Coast town as well. This system of judiciously conducted alliances, gives the black trader a security nothing else can, because naturally he marries into influential families at each village, and all his wife's relations on the mother's side regard him as one of themselves, and look after him and his interests. That security can lie in women, especially so many women, the so-called civilised man may ironically doubt, but the security is there, and there only, and on a sound basis, for remember the position of a travelling trader's wife in a village is a position that gives the lady prestige, the discreet husband showing little favours to her family and friends, if she asks for them when he is with her; and then she has not got the bother of having a man always about the house, and liable to get all sorts of silly notions into his head if she speaks to another gentleman, and then go and impart these notions to her with a cutlass, or a kassengo, as the more domestic husband, I am assured by black ladies, is prone to.

You may now, I fear, be falling into the other adjacent error—from the wonder why any black trader survives, namely, into the wonder why any black trader gets killed, with all these safeguards, and wives. But there is yet another danger, which no quantity of wives, nor local jealousies avail to guard him through. This danger arises from the nomadic habits of the bush tribes, notably the Fan. For when a village has made up its mind to change its district, either from having made the district too hot to hold it, with quarrels with neighbouring villages; or because it has exhausted the trade stuff, i.e. rubber and ivory in reach of its present situation; or because some other village has raided it, and taken away all the stuff it was saving to sell to the black trader; it resolves to give itself a final treat in the old home, and make a commercial *coup* at one fell swoop. Then when the black trader turns up with his boxes of goods, it kills him, has some for supper, smokes the rest, and takes it and the goods, and departs to found new homes in another district.

The bush trade I have above sketched is the bush trade with the Fans. In those districts on the southern banks of the Ogowé the main features of the trade, and the trader's life are the same, but the details are more intricate, for the Igalwa trader from Lembarene, Fernan Vaz, or Njole, deals with another set of trading tribes, not first hand with the collectors. The Fan villages on the trade routes may, however, be regarded as trade depots, for to them filters the trade stuff of the more remote villages, so the difference is really merely technical, and in all villages alike the same sort of thing occurs.

The Igalwa or M'pongwe trader arrives with the goods he has received from the white trader, and there are great rejoicing and much uproar as his chests and bundles and demijohns are brought up from the canoe. And presently, after a great deal of talk, the goods are opened. The chiefs of the village have their pick, and divide this among the principal men of the village, who pay for it in part with their store of collected rubber or ivory, and take the rest on trust, promising to collect enough rubber to pay the balance on the next visit of the trader. Thereby the trader has a quantity of debts outstanding in each village, liable to be bad debts, and herein lies his chief loss. Each chief takes a certain understood value in goods as a commission for himself—*nyeno*—giving the trader, as a consideration for this, an understood bond to assist him in getting in the trust granted to his village. This *nyeno* he utilises in buying trade stuff from villages not on the trade route. Among the Fans the men who have got the goods stand by with these to trade for rubber with the general public and bachelors of the village, in a way I will presently explain. In tribes like Ajumbas, Adooma, &c., the men having the goods travel off, as traders, among their various bush tribes, similarly paying their *nyeno*, and so by the time the goods reach the final producing men, only a small portion of them is left, but their price has necessarily risen. Still it is quite absurd for a casual white traveller, who may have dropped in on the terminus of a trade route, to cry out regarding the small value the collector (who is often erroneously described as the producer) gets for his stuff, compared to the price it fetches in Europe. For before it even reaches the factory of the Coast Settlement, that stuff has got to keep a whole series of traders. It appears at first bad that this should be the case, but the case it is along the west coast of the continent save in the districts commanded by the Royal Niger company, who, with courage and enterprise, have pushed far inland, and got in touch with the great interior trade routes—a performance which has raised in the breasts of the Coast trader tribes who have been supplanted, a keen animosity, which like most animosity in Africa, is not regardful of truth. The tribes that have had the trade of the Bight of Biafra passing through their hands have been accustomed, according to the German Government who are also pressing inland, to make seventy-five per cent profit on it, and they resent being deprived of this. A good deal is to be said in favour of their views; among other things that the greater part of the seaboard districts of West Africa, I may say every part from Sierra Leone to Cameroon, is structurally incapable of being self-supporting under existing conditions. Below Cameroon, on my beloved South-west coast, which is infinitely richer than the Bight of Benin, rich producing districts come down to the sea in most places until you reach the Congo; but here again the middleman is of great use to the interior tribes, and if they do have to pay him seventy-five per cent, serve them right. They should not go making wife palaver, and blood palaver all over the place to such an extent that the inhabitants of no village, unless they go *en masse*, dare take a ten mile walk, save at the risk of their lives, in any direction, so no palaver live.

We will now enter into the reason that induces the bush man to collect stuff to sell among the Fans, which is the expensiveness of the ladies in the tribe. A bush Fan is bound to marry into his tribe, because over a great part of the territory occupied by them there is no other tribe handy to marry into; and a Fan residing in villages in touch with other tribes, has but little chance of getting a cheaper lady. For there is, in the Congo Français and the country adjacent to the north of it (Batanga), a regular style of aristocracy which may be summarised firstly thus: All the other tribes look down on the Fans, and the Fans look down on all the other tribes. This aristocracy has sub-divisions, the M'pongwe of Gaboon are the upper circle tribe; next come the Benga of Corisco; then the Bapuka; then the Banaka. This system of aristocracy is kept up by the ladies. Thus a M'pongwe lady would not think of marrying into one of the lower tribes, so she is restricted, with many inner restrictions, to her own tribe. A Benga lady would marry a M'pongwe, or a Benga, but not a Banaka, or Bapuka; and so on with the others; but not one of them would marry a Fan. As for the men, well of course they would marry any lady of any tribe, if she had a pretty face, or a good trading connection, if they were allowed to: that's just man's way. To the south-east the Fans are in touch with the Bakele, a tribe that has much in common with the Fan, but who differ from them in getting on in a very friendly way with the little dwarf people, the Matimbas, or Watwa, or Akoa: people the Fans cannot abide. With these Bakele the Fan can intermarry, but there is not much advantage in so doing, as the price is equally high, but still marry he must.

A young Fan man has to fend for himself, and has a scratchy kind of life of it, aided only by his mother until—if he be an enterprising youth—he is able to steal a runaway wife from a neighbouring village, or if he is a quiet and steady young man, until he has amassed sufficient money to buy a wife. This he does by collecting ebony and rubber and selling it to the men who have been allotted goods by the chief of the village, from the consignment brought up by the black trader. He supports himself meanwhile by, if the situation of his village permits, fishing and selling the fish, and hunting and killing game in the forest. He keeps steadily at it in his way, reserving his roysterings until he is settled in life. A truly careful young man does not go and buy a baby girl cheap, as soon as he has got a little money together; but works and saves on until he has got enough to buy a good, tough widow lady, who, although personally unattractive, is deeply versed in the lore of trade, and who knows exactly how much rubbish you can incorporate in a ball of india rubber, without the white trader, or the black bush factory trader, instantly detecting it. When the Fan young man has married his wife, in a legitimate way on the cash system, he takes her round to his relations, and shows her off; and they make little presents to help the pair set up housekeeping. But the young man cannot yet settle down, for his wife will not allow him to. She is not going to slave herself to death doing all the work of the house, &c., and so he goes on collecting, and she preparing, trade stuff, and he grows rich enough to buy other wives— some of them young children, others widows, no longer necessarily old. But it is not until he is well on in life that he gets sufficient wives, six or seven. For it takes a good time to get enough rubber to buy a lady, and he does not get a grip on the ivory trade until he has got a certain position in the village, and plantations of his own which the elephants can be discovered raiding, in which case a percentage of the ivory taken from the herd is allotted to him. Now and again he may come across a dead elephant, but that is of the nature of a windfall; and on rubber and ebony he has to depend during his early days. These he changes with the rich men of his village for a very peculiar and interesting form of coinage—bikei—little iron imitation axe-heads which are tied up in bundles called ntet, ten going to one bundle, for with bikei must the price of a wife be paid. You do not find bikei close down to Libreville, among the Fans who are there in a semi-civilised state, or more properly speaking in a state of disintegrating culture. You must go for bush. I thought I saw in bikei a certain resemblance in underlying idea with the early Greek coins I have seen at Cambridge, made like the fore-parts of cattle; and I have little doubt that the articles of barter among the Fans before the introduction of the rubber, ebony, and ivory trades, which in their districts are comparatively recent, were iron implements. For the Fans are good workers in iron; and it would be in consonance with well-known instances among other savage races in the matter of stone implements, that these things, important of old, should survive, and be employed in the matter of such an old important affair as marriage. They thus become ju-ju; and indeed all West African legitimate marriage, although appearing to the casual observer a mere matter of barter, is never solely such, but always has ju-ju in it.

We may as well here follow out the whole of the domestic life of the Fan, now we have got him married. His difficulty does not only consist in getting enough bikei together but in getting a lady he can marry. No amount of bikei can justify a man in marrying his first cousin, or his aunt; and as relationship among the Fans is recognised with both his father and his mother, not as among the Igalwa with the latter's blood relations only, there are an awful quantity of aunts and cousins about from whom he is debarred. But when he has surmounted his many difficulties, and dodged his relations, and married, he is seemingly a better husband than the man of a more cultured tribe. He will turn a hand to anything, that does not necessitate his putting down his gun outside his village gateway. He will help chop firewood, or goat's chop, or he will carry the baby with pleasure, while his good lady does these things; and in bush villages, he always escorts her so as to be on hand in case of leopards, or other local unpleasantnesses. When inside the village he will lay down his gun, within handy reach, and build the house, tease out fibre to make game nets with, and plait baskets, or make pottery with the ladies, cheerily chatting the while.

Fan pottery, although rough and sunbaked, is artistic in form and ornamented, for the Fan ornaments all his work; the articles made in it consist of cooking pots, palm-wine bottles, water bottles and pipes, but not all water bottles, nor all pipes are made of pottery. I wish they were, particularly the former, for they are occasionally made of beautifully plaited fibre coated with a layer of a certain gum with a vile taste, which it imparts to the water in the vessel. They say it does not do this if the vessel is soaked for two days in water, but it does, and I should think contaminates the stream it was soaked in into the bargain. The pipes are sometimes made of iron very neatly. I should imagine they smoked hot, but of this I have no knowledge. One of my Ajumba friends got himself one of these pipes when we were in Efoua, and that pipe was, on and off, a curse to the party. Its owner soon learnt not to hold it by the bowl, but by the wooden stem, when smoking it; the other lessons it had to teach he learnt more slowly. He tucked it, when he had done smoking, into the fold in his cloth, until he had had three serious conflagrations raging round his middle. And to the end of the chapter, after having his last pipe at night with it, he would lay it on the ground, before it was cool. He learnt to lay it out of reach of his own cloth, but his fellow Ajumbas and he himself persisted in always throwing a leg on to it shortly after, and there was another row.

The Fan basket-work is strongly made, but very inferior to the Fjort basket-work. Their nets are, however, the finest I have ever seen. These are made mainly for catching small game, such as the beautiful little gazelles (*Ncheri*) with dark gray skins on the upper part of the body, white underneath, and satin-like in sleekness all over. Their form is very dainty, the little legs being no thicker than a man's finger, the neck long and the head ornamented with little pointed horns and broad round ears. The nets are tied on to trees in two long lines, which converge to an acute angle, the bottom part of the net lying on the ground. Then a party of men and women accompanied by their trained dogs, which have bells hung round their necks, beat the surrounding bushes, and the frightened small game rush into the nets, and become entangled. The fibre from which these nets are made has a long staple, and is exceedingly strong. I once saw a small bush cow caught in a set of them and unable to break through, and once a leopard; he, however, took his section of the net away with him, and a good deal of vegetation and sticks to boot. In addition to nets, this fibre is made into bags, for carrying things in while in the bush, and into the water bottles already mentioned.

The iron-work of the Fans deserves especial notice for its excellence. The anvil is a big piece of iron which is embedded firmly in the ground. Its upper surface is flat, and pointed at both ends. The hammers are solid cones of iron, the upper part of the cones prolonged so as to give a good grip, and the blows are given directly downwards, like the blows of a pestle. The bellows are of the usual African type, cut out of one piece of solid but soft wood; at the upper end of these bellows there are two chambers hollowed out in the wood and then covered with the skin of some animal, from which the hair has been removed. This is bound firmly round the rim of each chamber with tie-tie, and the bag of it at the top is gathered up, and bound to a small piece of stick, to give a convenient hand hold. The straight cylinder, terminating in the nozzle, has two channels burnt in it which communicate with each of the chambers respectively, and half-way up the cylinder, there are burnt from the outside into the air passages, three series of holes, one series on the upper surface, and a series at each side. This ingenious arrangement gives a constant current of air up from the nozzle when the bellows are worked by a man sitting behind them, and rapidly and alternately pulling up the skin cover over one chamber, while depressing the other. In order to make the affair firm it is lashed to pieces of stick stuck in the ground in a suitable way so as to keep the bellows at an angle with the nozzle directed towards the fire. As wooden bellows like this if stuck into the fire would soon be aflame, the nozzle is put into a cylinder made of clay. This cylinder is made sufficiently large at the end, into which the nozzle of the bellows goes, for the air to have full play round the latter.

The Fan bellows only differ from those of the other iron-working West Coast tribes in having the channels from the two chambers in one piece of wood all the way. His forge is the same as the other forges, a round cavity scooped in the ground; his fuel also is charcoal. His other smith's tool consists of a pointed piece of iron, with which he works out the patterns he puts at the handle-end of his swords, &c.

I must now speak briefly on the most important article with which the Fan deals, namely ivory. His methods of collecting this are several, and many a wild story the handles of your table knives could tell you, if their ivory has passed through Fan hands. For ivory is everywhere an evil thing before which the quest for gold sinks into a parlour game; and when its charms seize such a tribe as the Fans, "conclusions pass their careers." A very common way of collecting a tooth is to kill the person who owns one. Therefore in order to prevent this catastrophe happening to you yourself, when you have one, it is held advisable, unless you are a powerful person in your own village, to bury or sink the said tooth and say nothing about it until the trader comes into your district or you get a chance of smuggling it quietly down to him. Some of these private ivories are kept for years and years before they reach the trader's hands. And quite a third of the ivory you see coming on board a vessel to go to Europe is dark from this keeping: some teeth a lovely brown like a well-coloured meerschaum, others quite black, and gnawed by that strange little creature—much heard of, and abused, yet little known in ivory ports—the ivory rat.

Ivory, however, that is obtained by murder is private ivory. The public ivory trade among the Fans is carried on in a way more in accordance with European ideas of a legitimate trade. The greater part of this ivory is obtained from dead elephants. There are in this region certain places where the elephants are said to go to die. A locality in one district pointed out to me as such a place, was a great swamp in the forest. A swamp that evidently was deep in the middle, for from out its dark waters no swamp plant, or tree grew, and evidently its shores sloped suddenly, for the band of swamp plants round its edge was narrow. It is just possible that during the rainy season when most of the surrounding country would be under water, elephants might stray into this natural trap and get drowned, and on the drying up of the waters be discovered, and the fact being known, be regularly sought for by the natives cognisant of this. I inquired carefully whether these places where the elephants came to die always had water in them, but they said no, and in one district spoke of a valley or round-shaped depression in among the mountains. But natives were naturally disinclined to take a stranger to these ivory mines, and a white person who has caught—as any one who has been in touch must catch—ivory fever, is naturally equally disinclined to give localities.

A certain percentage of ivory collected by the Fans is from live elephants, but I am bound to admit that their method of hunting elephants is disgracefully unsportsmanlike. A herd of elephants is discovered by rubber hunters or by depredations on plantations, and the whole village, men, women, children, babies and dogs turn out into the forest and stalk the monsters into a suitable ravine, taking care not to scare them. When they have gradually edged the elephants on into a suitable place, they fell trees and wreathe them very roughly together with bush ropes, all round an immense enclosure, still taking care not to scare the elephants into a rush. This fence is quite inadequate to stop any elephant in itself, but it is made effective by being smeared with certain things, the smell whereof the elephants detest so much that when they wander up to it, they turn back disgusted. I need hardly remark that this preparation is made by the witch doctors and its constituents a secret of theirs, and I was only able to find out some of them. Then poisoned plantains are placed within the enclosure, and the elephants eat these and grow drowsier and drowsier; if the water supply within the enclosure is a pool it is poisoned, but if it is a running stream this cannot be done. During this time the crowd of men and women spend their days round the enclosure, ready to turn back any elephant who may attempt to break out, going to and fro to the village for their food. Their nights they spend in little bough shelters by the enclosure, watching more vigilantly than by day, as the elephants are more active at night, it being their usual feeding time. During the whole time the witch doctor is hard at work making incantations and charms, with a view to finding out the proper time to attack the elephants. In my opinion, his decision fundamentally depends on his knowledge of the state of poisoning the animals are in, but his version is that he gets his information from the forest spirits. When, however, he has settled the day, the best hunters steal into the enclosure and take up safe positions in trees, and the outer crowd set light to the ready-built fires, and make the greatest uproar possible, and fire upon the staggering, terrified elephants as they attempt to break out. The hunters in the trees fire down on them as they rush past, the fatal point at the back of the skull being well exposed to them.

When the animals are nearly exhausted, those men who do not possess guns dash into the enclosure, and the men who do, reload and join them, and the work is then completed. One elephant hunt I chanced upon at the final stage had taken two months' preparation, and although the plan sounds safe enough, there is really a good deal of danger left in it with all the drugging and ju-ju. There were eight elephants killed that day, but three burst through everything, sending energetic spectators flying, and squashing two men and a baby as flat as botanical specimens.

The subsequent proceedings were impressive. The whole of the people gorged themselves on the meat for days, and great chunks of it were smoked over the fires in all directions. A certain portion of the flesh of the hind leg was taken by the witch doctor for ju-ju, and was supposed to be put away by him, with certain suitable incantations in the recesses of the forest; his idea being apparently either to give rise to more elephants, or to induce the forest spirits to bring more elephants into the district.

Dr. Nassau tells me that the manner in which the ivory gained by one of these hunts is divided is as follows:—"The witch doctor, the chiefs, and the family on whose ground the enclosure is built, and especially the household whose women first discovered the animals, decide in council as to the division of the tusks and the share of the flesh to be given to the crowd of outsiders. The next day the tusks are removed and each family represented in the assemblage cuts up and distributes the flesh." In the hunt I saw finished, the elephants had not been discovered, as in the case Dr. Nassau above speaks of, in a plantation by women, but by a party of rubber hunters in the forest some four or five miles from any village, and the ivory that would have been allotted to the plantation holder in the former case, went in this case to the young rubber hunters.

Such are the pursuits, sports and pastimes of my friends the Fans. I have been considerably chaffed both by whites and blacks about my partiality for this tribe, but as I like Africans in my way—not à la Sierra Leone—and these Africans have more of the qualities I like than any other tribe I have met, it is but natural that I should prefer them. They are brave and so you can respect them, which is an essential element in a friendly feeling. They are on the whole a fine race, particularly those in the mountain districts of the Sierra del Cristal, where one continually sees magnificent specimens of human beings, both male and female. Their colour is light bronze, many of the men have beards, and albinoes are rare among them. The average height in the mountain districts is five feet six to five feet eight, the difference in stature between men and women not being great. Their countenances are very bright and expressive, and if once you have been among them, you can never mistake a Fan. But it is in their mental characteristics that their difference from the lethargic, dying-out coast tribes is most marked. The Fan is full of fire, temper, intelligence and go; very teachable, rather difficult to manage, quick to take offence, and utterly indifferent to human life. I ought to say that other people, who should know him better than I, say he is a treacherous, thievish, murderous cannibal. I never found him treacherous; but then I never trusted him, remembering one of the aphorisms of my great teacher Captain Boler of Bonny, "It's not safe to go among bush tribes, but if you are such a fool as to go, you needn't go and be a bigger fool still, you've done enough." And Captain Boler's other great aphorism was: "Never be afraid of a black man." "What if I can't help it?" said I. "Don't show it," said he. To these precepts I humbly add another: "Never lose your head." My most favourite form of literature, I may remark, is accounts of mountaineering exploits, though I have never seen a glacier or a permanent snow mountain in my life. I do not care a row of pins how badly they may be written, and what form of bumble-puppy grammar and composition is employed, as long as the writer will walk along the edge of a precipice with a sheer fall of thousands of feet on one side and a sheer wall on the other; or better still crawl up an *arête* with a precipice on either. Nothing on earth would persuade me to do either of these things myself, but they remind me of bits of country I have been through where you walk along a narrow line of security with gulfs of murder looming on each side, and where in exactly the same way you are as safe as if you were in your easy chair at home, as long as you get sufficient holding ground: not on rock in the bush village inhabited by murderous cannibals, but on ideas in those men's and women's minds; and these ideas, which I think I may say you will always find, give you safety. It is not advisable to play with them, or to attempt to eradicate them, because you regard them as superstitious; and never, never shoot too soon. I have never had to shoot, and hope never to have to; because in such a situation, one white alone with no troops to back him means a clean finish. But this would not discourage me if I had to start, only it makes me more inclined to walk round the obstacle, than to become a mere blood splotch against it, if this can be done without losing your self-respect, which is the mainspring of your power in West Africa.

As for flourishing about a revolver and threatening to fire, I hold it utter idiocy. I have never tried it, however, so I speak from prejudice which arises from the feeling that there is something cowardly in it. Always have your revolver ready loaded in good order, and have your hand on it when things are getting warm, and in addition have an exceedingly good bowie knife, not a hinge knife, because with a hinge knife you have got to get it open—hard work in a country where all things go rusty in the joints—and hinge knives are liable to close on your own fingers. The best form of knife is the bowie, with a shallow half moon cut out of the back at the point end, and this depression sharpened to a cutting edge. A knife is essential, because after wading neck deep in a swamp your revolver is neither use nor ornament until you have had time to clean it. But the chances are you may go across Africa, or live years in it, and require neither. It is just the case of the gentleman who asked if one required a revolver in Carolina and was answered, "You may be here one year, and you may be here two and never want it; but when you do want it you'll want it very bad."

The cannibalism of the Fans, although a prevalent habit, is no danger, I think, to white people, except as regards the bother it gives one in preventing one's black companions from getting eaten. The Fan is not a cannibal from sacrificial motives like the negro. He does it in his common sense way. Man's flesh, he says, is good to eat, very good, and he wishes you would try it. Oh dear no, he never eats it himself, but the next door town does. He is always very much abused for eating his relations, but he really does not do this. He will eat his next door neighbour's relations and sell his own deceased to his next door neighbour in return; but he does not buy slaves and fatten them up for his table as some of the Middle Congo tribes I know of do. He has no slaves, no prisoners of war, no cemeteries, so you must draw your own conclusion. No, my friend, I will not tell you any cannibal stories. I have heard how good M. du Chaillu fared after telling you some beauties, and now you come away from the Fan village and down the Rembwé river.

CHAPTER 11

DOWN THE REMBWÉ

Setting forth how the Voyager descends the Rembwé River, with divers excursions
and alarms, in the company of a black trader, and returns safely to the Coast.

GETTING AWAY FROM AGONJO seemed as if it would be nearly as difficult as getting to it, but as the quarters were comfortable and the society fairly good, I was not anxious. I own the local scenery was a little too much of the Niger Delta type for perfect beauty, just the long lines of mangrove, and the muddy river lounging almost imperceptibly to sea, and nothing else in sight. Mr. Glass, however, did not take things so philosophically. I was on his commercial conscience, for I had come in from the bush and there was money in me. Therefore I was a trade product—a new trade stuff that ought to be worked up and developed; and he found himself unable to do this, for although he had secured the first parcel, as it were, and got it successfully stored, yet he could not ship it, and he felt this was a reproach to him.

Many were his lamentations that the firm had not provided him with a large sailing canoe and a suitable crew to deal with this new line of trade. I did my best to comfort him, pointing out that the most enterprising firm could not be expected to provide expensive things like these, on the extremely remote chance of ladies arriving per bush at Agonjo—in fact not until the trade in them was well developed. But he refused to see it in this light and harped upon the subject, wrapped up, poor man, in a great coat and a muffler, because his ague was on him.

I next tried to convince Mr. Glass that any canoe would do for me to go down in. "No," he said, "any canoe will not do;" and he explained that when you got down the Rembwé to 'Como Point you were in a rough, nasty bit of water, the Gaboon, which has a fine confused set of currents from the tidal wash and the streams of the Rembwé and 'Como rivers, in which it would be improbable that a river canoe could live any time worth mentioning. Progress below 'Como Point by means of mere paddling he considered impossible. There was nothing for it but a big sailing canoe, and there was no big sailing canoe to be had. I think Mr. Glass got a ray of comfort out of the fact that Messrs. John Holt's sub-agent was, equally with himself, unable to ship me.

At this point in the affair there entered a highly dramatic figure. He came on to the scene suddenly and with much uproar, in a way that would have made his fortune in a transpontine drama. I shall always regret I have not got that man's portrait, for I cannot do him justice with ink. He dashed up on to the verandah, smote the frail form of Mr. Glass between the shoulders, and flung his own massive one into a chair. His name was Obanjo, but he liked it pronounced Captain Johnson, and his profession was a bush and river trader on his own account. Every move-ment of the man was theatrical, and he used to look covertly at you every now and then to see if he had produced his impression, which was evi-dently intended to be that of a reckless, rollicking skipper. There was a Hallo-my-Hearty atmosphere coming off him from the top of his hat to the soles of his feet, like the scent off a flower; but it did not require a genius in judging men to see that behind, and under this was a very dif-ferent sort of man, and if I should ever want to engage in a wild and awful career up a West African river I shall start on it by engaging Captain Johnson. He struck me as being one of those men, of whom I know five, whom I could rely on, that if one of them and I went into the utter bush together, one of us at least would come out alive and have made something substantial by the venture; which is a great deal more than I could say, for example, of Ngouta, who was still with me, as he desired to see the glories of Gaboon and buy a hanging lamp.

Captain Johnson's attire calls for especial comment and admira-tion. However disconnected the two sides of his character might be, his clothes bore the impress of both of his natures to perfection. He wore, when first we met, a huge sombrero hat, a spotless singlet, and a suit of clean, well-got-up dungaree, and an uncommonly picturesque, powerful figure he cut in them, with his finely moulded, well-knit form and good-looking face, full of expression always, but always with the keen small eyes in it watching the effect his genial smiles and hearty laugh produced. The eyes were the eyes of Obanjo, the rest of the face the property of Captain Johnson. I do not mean to say that they were the eyes of a bad bold man, but you had not to look twice at them to see they belonged to a man courageous in the African manner, full of energy and resource, keenly intelligent and self-reliant, and all that sort of thing.

I left him and the refined Mr. Glass together to talk over the palaver of shipping me, and they talked it at great length. Finally the price I was to pay Obanjo was settled and we proceeded to less important details. It seemed Obanjo, when up the river this time, had set about constructing a new and large trading canoe at one of his homes, in which he was just thinking of taking his goods down to Gaboon. Next morning Obanjo with his vessel turned up, and saying farewell to my kind host, Mr. Sanga Glass, I departed.

She had the makings of a fine vessel in her; though roughly hewn out of an immense hard-wood tree: her lines were good, and her type was that of the big sea-canoes of the Bight of Panavia. Very far forward was a pole mast, roughly made, but European in intention, and carrying a long gaff. Shrouds and stays it had not, and my impression was that it would be carried away if we dropped in for half a tornado, until I saw our sail and recognised that that would go to darning cotton instantly if it fell in with even a breeze. It was a bed quilt that had evidently been in the family some years, and although it had been in places carefully patched with pieces of previous sets of the captain's dungarees, in other places, where it had not, it gave "free passage to the airs of Heaven;" which I may remark does not make for speed in the boat mounting such canvas. Partly to this sail, partly to the amount of trading affairs we attended to, do I owe the credit of having made a record trip down the Rembwé, the slowest white man time on record.

Fixed across the stern of the canoe there was the usual staging made of bamboos, flush with the gunwale. Now this sort of staging is an exceedingly good idea when it is fully finished. You can stuff no end of things under it; and over it there is erected a hood of palm-thatch, giving a very comfortable cabin five or six feet long and about three feet high in the centre, and you can curl yourself up in it and, if you please, have a mat hung across the opening. But we had not got so far as that yet on our vessel, only just got the staging fixed in fact; and I assure you a bamboo staging is but a precarious perch when in this stage of formation. I made myself a reclining couch on it in the Roman manner with my various belongings, and was exceeding comfortable until we got nearly out of the Rembwé into the Gaboon. Then came grand times. Our noble craft had by this time got a good list on her from our collected cargo—ill stowed. This made my home, the bamboo staging, about as reposeful a place as the slope of a writing desk would be if well polished; and the rough and choppy sea gave our vessel the most peculiar set of motions imaginable. She rolled, which made it precarious for things on the bamboo staging, but still a legitimate motion, natural and foreseeable. In addition to this, she had a cataclysmic kick in her—that I think the heathenish thing meant to be a pitch—which no mortal being could foresee or provide against, and which projected portable property into the waters of the Gaboon over the stern and on to the conglomerate collection in the bottom of the canoe itself, making Obanjo repeat, with ferocity and feeling, words he had heard years ago, when he was boatswain on a steamboat trading on the Coast. It was fortunate, you will please understand, for my future, that I have usually been on vessels of the British African or the African lines when voyaging about this West African sea-board, as the owners of these vessels prohibit the use of bad language on board, or goodness only knows the words I might not have remembered and used in the Gaboon estuary.

We left Agonjo with as much bustle and shouting and general air of brisk seamanship as Obanjo could impart to the affair, and the hopeful mind might have expected to reach somewhere important by nightfall. I did not expect that; neither, on the other hand, did I expect that after we had gone a mile and only four, as the early ballad would say, that we should pull up and anchor against a small village for the night; but this we did, the captain going ashore to see for cargo, and to get some more crew.

There were grand times ashore that night, and the captain returned on board about 2 a.m. with some rubber and pissava and two new hands whose appearance fitted them to join our vessel; for a more villainous-looking set than our crew I never laid eye on. One enormously powerful fellow looked the incarnation of the horrid negro of buccaneer stories, and I admired Obanjo for the way he kept them in hand. We had now also acquired a small dug-out canoe as tender, and a large fishing-net.

About 4 a.m. in the moonlight we started to drop down river on the tail of the land breeze, and as I observed Obanjo wanted to sleep I offered to steer. After putting me through an examination in practical seamanship, and passing me, he gladly accepted my offer, handed over the tiller which stuck out across my bamboo staging, and went and curled himself up, falling sound asleep among the crew in less time than it takes to write. On the other nights we spent on this voyage I had no need to offer to steer; he handed over charge to me as a matter of course, and as I prefer night to day in Africa, I enjoyed it. Indeed, much as I have enjoyed life in Africa, I do not think I ever enjoyed it to the full as I did on those nights dropping down the Rembwé. The great, black, winding river with a pathway in its midst of frosted silver where the moonlight struck it: on each side the ink-black mangrove walls, and above them the band of star and moonlit heavens that the walls of man-grove allowed one to see. Forward rose the form of our sail, idealised from bed-sheetdom to glory; and the little red glow of our cooking fire gave a single note of warm colour to the cold light of the moon. Three or four times during the second night, while I was steering along by the south bank, I found the mangrove wall thinner, and standing up, looked through the network of their roots and stems on to what seemed like plains, acres upon acres in extent, of polished silver—more specimens of those awful slime lagoons, one of which, before we reached Ndorko, had so very nearly collected me. I watched them, as we leisurely stole past, with a sort of fascination. On the second night, towards the dawn, I had the great joy of seeing Mount Okoneto, away to the S.W., first showing moonlit, and then taking the colours of the dawn before they reached us down below. Ah me! give me a West African river and a canoe for sheer good pleasure. Drawbacks, you say? Well, yes, but where are there not drawbacks? The only drawbacks on those Rembwé nights were the series of horrid frights I got by steering on to tree shadows and thinking they were mud banks, or trees themselves, so black and solid did they seem. I never roused the watch fortunately, but got her off the shadow gallantly single-handed every time, and called myself a fool instead of getting called one. My nautical friends carp at me for getting on shadows, but I beg them to consider before they judge me, whether they have ever steered at night down a river quite unknown to them an unhandy canoe, with a bed-sheet sail, by the light of the moon. And what with my having a theory of my own regarding the proper way to take a vessel round a corner, and what with having to keep the wind in the bed-sheet where the bed-sheet would hold it, it's a wonder to me I did not cast that vessel away, or go and damage Africa.

By daylight the Rembwé scenery was certainly not so lovely, and might be slept through without a pang. It had monotony, without having enough of it to amount to grandeur. Every now and again we came to villages, each of which was situated on a heap of clay and sandy soil, presumably the end of a spit of land running out into the mangrove swamp fringing the river. Every village we saw we went alongside and had a chat with, and tried to look up cargo in the proper way. One village in particular did we have a lively time at. Obanjo had a wife and home there, likewise a large herd of goats, some of which he was desirous of taking down with us to sell at Gaboon. It was a pleasant-looking village, with a clean yellow beach which most of the houses faced. But it had ramifications in the interior. I being very lazy, did not go ashore, but watched the pantomime from the bamboo staging. The whole flock of goats enter at right end of stage, and tear violently across the scene, disappearing at left. Two minutes elapse. Obanjo and his gallant crew enter at right hand of stage, leg it like lamplighters across front, and disappear at left. Fearful pow-wow behind the scenes. Five minutes elapse. Enter goats at right as before, followed by Obanjo and company as before, and so on *da capo*. It was more like a fight I once saw between the armies of Macbeth and Macduff than anything I have seen before or since; only our Rembwé play was better put on, more supers, and noise, and all that sort of thing, you know. It was a spirited performance I assure you and I and the inhabitants of the village, not personally interested in goat-catching, assumed the rôle of audience and cheered it to the echo.

We had another cheerful little incident that afternoon. While we were going along softly, softly as was our wont, in the broiling heat, I wishing I had an umbrella—for sitting on that bamboo stage with no sort of protection from the sun was hot work after the forest shade I had had previously—two small boys in two small canoes shot out from the bank and paddled hard to us and jumped on board. After a few minutes' conversation with Obanjo one of them carefully sank his canoe; the other just turned his adrift and they joined our crew. I saw they were Fans, as indeed nearly all the crew were, but I did not think much of the affair. Our tender, the small canoe, had been sent out as usual with the big black man and another A. B. to fish; it being one of our industries to fish hard all the time with that big net. The fish caught, sometimes a bushel or two at a time, almost all grey mullet, were then brought alongside, split open, and cleaned. We then had all round as many of them for supper as we wanted, the rest we hung on strings over our fire, more or less insufficiently smoking them to prevent decomposition, it being Obanjo's intention to sell them when he made his next trip up the 'Como; for the latter being less rich in fish than the Rembwé they would command a good price there. We always had our eye on things like this, being, I proudly remark, none of your gilded floating hotel of a ferry-boat like those Cunard or White Star liners are, but just a good trader that was not ashamed to pay, and not afraid of work.

Well, just after we had leisurely entered a new reach of the river, round the corner after us, propelled at a phenomenal pace, came our fishing canoe, which we had left behind to haul in the net and then rejoin us. The occupants, particularly the big black A. B., were shouting something in terror stricken accents. "What?" says Obanjo springing to his feet. "The Fan! the Fan!" shouted the canoe men as they shot towards us like agitated chickens making for their hen. In another moment they were alongside and tumbling over our gunwale into the bottom of the vessel still crying "The Fan! The Fan! The Fan!" Obanjo then by means of energetic questioning externally applied, and accompanied by florid language that cast a rose pink glow smelling of sulphur, round us, elicited the information that about 40,000 Fans, armed with knives and guns, were coming down the Rembwé with intent to kill and slay us, and might be expected to arrive within the next half wink. On hearing this, the whole of our gallant crew took up masterly recumbent positions in the bottom of our vessel and turned gray round the lips. But Obanjo rose to the situation like ten lions. "Take the rudder," he shouted to me, "take her into the middle of the stream and keep the sail full." It occurred to me that perhaps a position underneath the bamboo staging might be more healthy than one on the top of it, exposed to every microbe of a bit of old iron and what not and a half that according to native testimony would shortly be frisking through the atmosphere from those Fan guns; and moreover I had not forgotten having been previously shot in a somewhat similar situation, though in better company.

However I did not say anything; neither, between ourselves, did I some-how believe in those Fans. So regardless of danger, I grasped the helm, and sent our gallant craft flying before the breeze down the bosom of the great wild river (that's the proper way to put it, but in the interests of sci-ence it may be translated into crawling towards the middle). Meanwhile Obanjo performed prodigies of valour all over the place. He triced up the mainsail, stirred up his faint-hearted crew, and got out the sweeps, *i.e.* one old oar and four paddles, and with this assistance we solemnly trudged away from danger at a pace that nothing slower than a Thames dumb barge, going against stream, could possibly overhaul. Still we did not feel safe, and I suggested to Ngouta he should rise up and help; but he declined, stating he was a married man. Obanjo cheering the pad-dlers with inspiriting words sprang with the agility of a leopard on to the bamboo staging aft, standing there with his gun ready loaded and cocked to face the coming foe, looking like a statue put up to himself at the public expense. The worst of this was, however, that while Obanjo's face was to the coming foe, his back was to the crew, and they forthwith commenced to re-subside into the bottom of the boat, paddles and all. I, as second in command, on seeing this, said a few blood-stirring words to them, and Obanjo sent a few more of great power at them over his shoulder, and so we kept the paddles going.

Presently from round the corner shot a Fan canoe. It contained a lady in the bows, weeping and wringing her hands, while another lady sympathetically howling, paddled it. Obanjo in lurid language requested to be informed why they were following us. The lady in the bows said, "My son! my son!" and in a second more three other canoes shot round the corner full of men with guns. Now this looked like business, so Obanjo and I looked round to urge our crew to greater exertions and saw, to our disgust, that the gallant band had successfully subsided into the bottom of the boat while we had been eying the foe. I did not follow it, but got the job done, for Obanjo could not take his eye and gun off the leading canoe and the canoes having crept up to within some twenty yards of us, poured out their simple tale of woe.

It seemed that one of those miscreant boys was a runaway from a Fan village. He had been desirous, with the usual enterprise of young Fans, of seeing the great world that he knew lay down at the mouth of the river, *i.e.* Libreville Gaboon. He had pleaded with his parents for leave to go down and engage in work there, but the said parents holding the tenderness of his youth unfitted to combat with Coast Town life and temptation, refused this request, and so the young rascal had run away without leave and with a canoe, and was surmised to have joined the well-known Obanjo. Obanjo owned he had (more armed canoes were coming round the corner), and said if the mother would come and fetch her boy she could have him. He for his part would not have dreamed of taking him if he had known his relations disapproved. Every one seemed much relieved, except the *causa belli*. The Fans did not ask about two boys and providentially we gave the lady the right one. He went reluctantly. I feel pretty nearly sure he foresaw more kassengo than fatted calf for him on his return home. When the Fan canoes were well back round the corner again, we had a fine hunt for the other boy, and finally unearthed him from under the bamboo staging. When we got him out he told the same tale. He also was a runaway who wanted to see the world, and taking the opportunity of the majority of the people of his village being away hunting, he had slipped off one night in a canoe, and dropped down river to the village of the boy who had just been reclaimed. The two boys had fraternised, and come on the rest of their way together, lying waiting, hidden up a creek, for Obanjo, who they knew was coming down river; and having successfully got picked up by him, they thought they were safe. But after this affair boy number two judged there was no more safety yet, and that his family would be down after him very shortly; for he said he was a more valuable and important boy than his late companion, but his family were an uncommon savage set. We felt not the least anxiety to make their acquaintance, so clapped heels on our gallant craft and kept the paddles going, and as no more Fans were in sight our crew kept at work bravely. While Obanjo, now in a boisterous state of mind, and flushed with victory, said things to them about the way they had collapsed when those two women in a canoe came round that corner, that must have blistered their feelings, but they never winced. They laughed at the joke against themselves merrily. The other boy's family we never saw and so took him safely to Gaboon, where Obanjo got him a good place.

Really how much danger there was proportionate to the large amount of fear on our boat I cannot tell you. It never struck me there was any, but on the other hand the crew and Obanjo evidently thought it was a bad place; and my white face would have been no protection, for the Fans would not have suspected a white of being on such a canoe and might have fired on us if they had been unduly irritated and not treated by Obanjo with that fine compound of bully and blarney that he is such a master of.

Whatever may have been the true nature of the affair, however, it had one good effect, it got us out of the Rembwé into the Gaboon, and although at the time this seemed a doubtful blessing, it made for progress. I had by this time mastered the main points of incapability in our craft. *A.* we could not go against the wind. *B.* we could not go against the tide. While we were in the Rembwé there was a state we will designate as *C*—the tide coming one way, the wind another. With this state we could progress, backwards if the wind came up against us too strong, but seawards if it did not, and the tide was running down. If the tide was running up, and the wind was coming down, then we went seaward, softly, softly alongside the mangrove bank, where the rip of the tide stream is least. When, however, we got down off 'Como Point, we met there a state I will designate as *D*—a fine confused set of marine and fluvial phenomena. For away to the north the 'Como and Boqué and two other lesser, but considerable streams, were, with the Rembwé, pouring down their waters in swirling, intermingling, interclashing currents; and up against them, to make confusion worse confounded, came the tide, and the tide up the Gaboon is a swift strong thing, and irregular, and has a rise of eight feet at the springs, two-and-a-half at the neaps. The wind was lulled too, it being evening time. In this country it is customary for the wind to blow from the land from 8 p.m. until 8 a.m., from the south-west to the east. Then comes a lull, either an utter dead hot brooding calm, or light baffling winds and draughts that breathe a few panting hot breaths into your sails and die. Then comes the sea breeze up from the south-south-west or north-west, some days early in the forenoon, some days not till two or three o'clock. This breeze blows till sundown, and then comes another and a hotter calm.

Fortunately for us we arrived off the head of the Gaboon estuary in this calm, for had we had wind to deal with we should have come to an end. There were one or two wandering puffs, about the first one of which sickened our counterpane of its ambitious career as a marine sail, so it came away from its gaff and spread itself over the crew, as much as to say, "Here, I've had enough of this sailing. I'll be a counterpane again." We did a great deal of fine varied, spirited navigation, details of which, however, I will not dwell upon because it was successful. We made one or two circles, taking on water the while and then returned into the south bank backwards. At that bank we wisely stayed for the night, our meeting with the Gaboon so far having resulted in wrecking our sail, making Ngouta sea-sick and me exasperate; for from our noble vessel having during the course of it demonstrated for the first time her cataclysmic kicking power, I had had a time of it with my belongings on the bamboo stage. A basket constructed for catching human souls in, given me as a farewell gift by a valued friend, a witch doctor, and in which I kept the few things in life I really cared for, *i.e.* my brush, comb, tooth brush, and pocket handkerchiefs, went over the stern; while I was recovering this with my fishing line (such was the excellent nature of the thing, I am glad to say it floated) a black bag with my blouses and such essentials went away to leeward, Obanjo recovered that, but meanwhile my little portmanteau containing my papers and trade tobacco slid off to leeward; and as it also contained geological specimens of the Sierra del Cristal, a massive range of mountains, it must have hopelessly sunk had it not been for the big black, who grabbed it. All my bedding, six Equetta cloths, given me by Mr. Hamilton in Opobo River before I came South, did get away successfully, but were picked up by means of the fishing line, wet but safe. After this I did not attempt any more Roman reclining couch luxuries, but stowed all my loose gear under the bamboo staging, and spent the night on the top of the stage, dozing precariously with my head on my knees.

When the morning broke, looking seaward I saw the welcome forms of König (Dambe) and Perroquet (Mbini) Islands away in the distance, looking, as is their wont, like two lumps of cloud that have dropped on to the broad Gaboon, and I felt that I was at last getting near something worth reaching, *i.e.* Glass, which though still out of sight, I knew lay away to the west of those islands on the northern shore of the estuary. And if any one had given me the choice of being in Glass within twenty-four hours from the mouth of the Rembwé, or in Paris or London in a week, I would have chosen Glass without a moment's hesitation. Much as I dislike West Coast towns as a general rule, there are exceptions, and of all exceptions, the one I like most is undoubtedly Glass Gaboon; and its charms loomed large on that dank chilly morning after a night spent on a bamboo staging in an unfinished native canoe.

The Rembwé, like the Como, is said to rise in the Sierra del Cristal. It is navigable to a place called Isango which is above Agonjo; just above Agonjo it receives an affluent on its southern bank and runs through

mountain country, where its course is blocked by rapids for anything but
small canoes. Obanjo did not seem to think this mattered, as there was
not much trade up there, and therefore no particular reason why any
one should want to go higher up. Moreover he said the natives were an
exceedingly bad lot; but Obanjo usually thinks badly of the bush natives
in these regions. Anyhow they are Fans—and Fans are Fans. He was anxious for me, however, to start on a trading voyage with him up another
river, a notorious river in the neighbouring Spanish territory. The idea
was I should buy goods at Glass and we should go together and he would
buy ivory with them in the interior. I anxiously inquired where my profits were to come in. Obanjo who had all the time suspected me of having
trade motives, artfully said, "What for you come across from Ogowé?
You say, see this country. Ah! I say you come with me. I show you plenty
country, plenty men, elephants, leopards, gorillas. Oh! plenty thing.
Then you say where's my trade?" I disclaimed trade motives in a lordly
way. Then says he, "You come with me up there." I said I'd see about it
later on, for the present I had seen enough men, elephants, gorillas and
leopards, and I preferred to go into wild districts under the French flag
to any flag. I am still thinking about taking that voyage, but I'll not
march through Coventry with the crew we had down the Rembwé—that's
flat, as Sir John Falstaff says. Picture to yourselves, my friends, the
charming situation of being up a river surrounded by rapacious savages
with a lot of valuable goods in a canoe and with only a crew to defend
them possessed of such fighting mettle as our crew had demonstrated
themselves to be. Obanjo might be all right, would be I dare say; but
suppose he got shot and you had eighteen stone odd of him thrown on
your hands in addition to your other little worries. There is little doubt
such an excursion would be rich in incident and highly interesting, but
I am sure it would be, from a commercial point of view, a failure.

Trade has a fascination for me, and going transversely across the
nine-mile-broad rough Gaboon estuary in an unfinished canoe with an
inefficient counterpane sail has none; but I return duty bound to this
unpleasant subject. We started very early in the morning. We reached the
other side entangled in the trailing garments of the night. I was thankful
during that broiling hot day of one thing, and that was that if Sister Ann
was looking out across the river, as was Sister Ann's invariable way of
spending spare moments, Sister Ann would never think I was in a canoe
that made such audaciously bad tacks, missed stays, got into irons, and

in general behaved in a way that ought to have lost her captain his certificate. Just as the night came down, however, we reached the northern shore of the Grand Gaboon at Dongila, just off the mouth of the 'Como, still some eleven miles east of König Island, and further still from Glass, but on the same side of the river, which seemed good work. The foreshore here is very rocky, so we could not go close alongside but anchored out among the rocks. At this place there is a considerable village and a station of the Roman Catholic Mission. When we arrived a nun was down on the shore with her school children, who were busy catching shell-fish and generally merry-making. Obanjo went ashore in the tender, and the holy sister kindly asked me, by him, to come ashore and spend the night; but I was dead tired and felt quite unfit for polite society after the long broiling hot day and getting soaked by water that had washed on board.

We lay off Dongila all night, because of the tide. I lay off everything, Dongila, canoe and all, a little after midnight. Obanjo and almost all the crew stayed on shore that night, and I rolled myself up in an Equetta cloth and went sound and happily asleep on the bamboo staging, leaving the canoe pitching slightly. About midnight some change in the tide, or original sin in the canoe, caused her to softly swing round a bit, and the next news was that I was in the water. I had long expected this to happen, so was not surprised, but highly disgusted, and climbed on board, needless to say, streaming. So, in the darkness of the night I got my portmanteau from the hold and thoroughly tidied up. The next morning we were off early, coasting along to Glass, and safely arriving there, I attempted to look as unconcerned as possible, and vaguely hoped Mr. Hudson would be down in Libreville; for I was nervous about meeting him, knowing that since he had carefully deposited me in safe hands with Mme. Jacot, with many injunctions to be careful, that there were many incidents in my career that would not meet with his approval. Vain hope! he was on the pier! He did not approve! He had heard of most of my goings on.

This however in no way detracts from my great obligation to Mr. Hudson, but adds another item to the great debt of gratitude I owe him; for had it not been for him I should never have seen the interior of this beautiful region of the Ogowé. I tried to explain to him how much I had enjoyed myself and how I realised I owed it all to him; but he persisted in his opinion that my intentions and ambitions were suicidal, and took me out the ensuing Sunday, as it were on a string.

CHAPTER 12

FETISH

*In which the Voyager attempts cautiously to approach the subject of Fetish,
and gives a classification of spirits, and some account of the Ibet and Orunda.*

HAVING GIVEN SOME ACCOUNT of my personal experiences among
an African tribe in its original state, i.e. in a state uninfluenced by
European ideas and culture, I will make an attempt to give a rough
sketch of the African form of the thought and the difficulties of
studying it, because the study of this thing is my chief motive for
going to West Africa. Since 1893 I have been collecting information
in its native states regarding Fetish, and I use the usual terms fetish
and juju because they have among us a certain fixed value-a conventional value, but a useful one. Neither "fetish" nor "ju-ju" are native
words. Fetish comes from the word the old Portuguese explorers used
to designate the objects they thought the natives worshipped, and in
which they were wise enough to recognize a certain similarity to their
own little images and relics of Saints, "Feitico." Ju-ju, on the other
hand, is French, and comes from the word for a toy or dollı, so it is
not so applicable as the Portuguese name, for the native image is not
a doll or toy, and has far more affinity to the image of a saint,
inasmuch as it is not venerated for itself, or treasured because of its
prettiness, but only because it is the residence, or the occasional
haunt, of a spirit.

Stalking the wild West African idea is one of the most charming pursuits in the world. Quite apart from the intellectual, it has a high sporting interest; for its pursuit is as beset with difficulty and danger as grizzly bear hunting, yet the climate in which you carry on this pursuit—vile as it is—is warm, which to me is almost an essential of existence. I beg you to understand that I make no pretension to a thorough knowledge of Fetish ideas; I am only on the threshold. "Ich weiss nicht all doch viel ist mir bekannt," as Faust said—and, like him after he had said it, I have got a lot to learn.

I do not intend here to weary you with more than a small portion of even my present knowledge, for I have great collections of facts that I keep only to compare with those of other hunters of the wild idea, and which in their present state are valueless to the cabinet ethnologist. Some of these may be rank lies, some of them mere individual mind—freaks, others have underlying them some idea I am not at present in touch with.

The difficulty of gaining a true conception of the savage's real idea is great and varied. In places on the Coast where there is, or has been, much missionary influence the trouble is greatest, for in the first case the natives carefully conceal things they fear will bring them into derision and contempt, although they still keep them in their innermost hearts; and in the second case, you have a set of traditions which are Christian in origin, though frequently altered almost beyond recognition by being kept for years in the atmosphere of the African mind. For example, there is this beautiful story now extant among the Cabindas. God made at first all men black—He always does in the African story—and then He went across a great river and called men to follow Him, and the wisest and the bravest and the best plunged into the great river and crossed it; and the water washed them white, so they are the ancestors of the white men. But the others were afraid too much, and said, "No, we are comfortable here; we have our dances, and our tom-toms, and plenty to eat—we won' t risk it, we'll stay here"; and they remained in the old place, and from them come the black men. But to this day the white men come to the bank, on the other side of the river, and call to the black men, saying, "Come, it is better over here." I fear there is little doubt that this story is a modified version of some parable preached to the Cabindas at the time the Capuchins had such influence among them, before they were driven out of the lower Congo regions more than a hundred years ago, for political reasons by the Portuguese.

In the bush—where the people have been little, or not at all, in contact with European ideas—in some ways the investigation is easier; yet another set of difficulties confronts you. The difficulty that seems to occur most easily to people is the difficulty of the language. The West African languages are not difficult to pick up; nevertheless, there are an awful quantity of them and they are at the best most imperfect mediums of communication. No one who has been on the Coast can fail to recognize how inferior the native language is to the native's mind behind it—and the prolixity and repetition he has therefore to employ to make his thoughts understood.

The great comfort is the wide diffusion of that peculiar language, "trade English"; it is not only used as a means of intercommunication between whites and blacks, but between natives using two distinct languages. On the south-west Coast you find individuals in villages far from the sea, or a trading station, who know it, and this is because they have picked it up and employ it in their dealings with the Coast tribes and traveling traders. It is by no means an easy language to pick up—it is not a farrago of bad words and broken phrases, but is a definite structure, has a great peculiarity in its verb forms, and employs no genders. There is no grammar of it out yet; and one of the best ways of learning it is to listen to a seasoned second mate regulating the unloading or loading, of cargo, over the hatch of the hold. No, my Coast friends, I have *not* forgotten—but though you did not mean it helpfully, this was one of the best hints you ever gave me.

Another good way is the careful study of examples which display the highest style and the most correct diction; so I append the letter given by Mr. Hutchinson as being about the best bit of trade English I know.

"To Daddy nah Tampin Office,—

Ha Daddy, do, yah, nah beg you tell dem people for me; make dem Sally-own pussin know. Do yah. Berrah well.

Ah lib nah Pademba Road—one bwoy lib dah oberside lakah dem two Docter lib overside you Tampin office. Berrah well.

Dah bwoy head big too much—he say nah Militie Ban—he got one long long ting so so brass, something lib dah go flip flap, dem call am key. Berrah well. Had ! Dah bwoy kin blow!—she ah!—na marin, oh!—nah sun time, oh! Nah evenin, oh!—nah middle night, oh!—all same—

no make pussin sleep. Not ebry bit dat, more lib da! One Boney bwoy lib oberside nah he like blow bugle. When dem two woh-woh bwoy blow dem ting de nize too much too much.

When white man blow dat ting and pussin sleep he kin tap wah make dem bwoy carn do so? Dem bwoy kin blow ebry day eben Sunday dem kin blow. When ah yerry dem blow Sunday ah wish dah bugle kin go down na dem troat or dem kin blow them head-bone inside.

Do nah beg you yah tell all dem people 'bout dah ting wah dem two bwoy dah blow. Till am Amtrang Boboh had febah bad. Till am titty carn sleep nah night. Dah nize go kill me two pickin, oh!

        Plabba done. Good by Daddy.

        Crashey Jane."

Now for the elementary student we will consider this letter. The complaint in Crashey Jane's letter is about two boys who are torturing her morning, noon, and night, Sunday and week day, by blowing some "long long brass ting" as well as a bugle, and the way she dwells on their staying power must bring a sympathetic pang for that black sister into the heart of many a householder in London who lives next to a ladies' school, or a family of musical tastes. "One touch of nature," &c "Daddy" is not a term of low familiarity but one of esteem and respect, and the "Tampin Office" is a respectful appellation for the Office of the "New Era" in which this letter was once published. "Bwoy head big too much," means that the young man is swelled with conceit because he is connected with "Militie ban." "Woh woh" you will find, among all the natives in the Bights, to mean extremely bad. I think it is native, having some connection with the root Wo—meaning power, &c.; but Mr. Hutchinson may be right, and it may mean "a capacity to bring double woe."

"Amtrang Boboh" is not the name of some uncivilised savage, as the uninitiated may think; far from it. It is Bob Armstrong—upside down, and slightly altered, and refers to the Hon. Robert Armstrong, stipendiary magistrate of Sierra Leone, &c.

"Berrah well" is a phrase used whenever the native thinks he has succeeded in putting his statement well. He sort of turns round and looks at it, says "Berrah well," in admiration of his own art, and then proceeds.

"Pickin" are children.

"Boney bwoy" is not a local living skeleton, but a native from Bonny River.

"Sally own" is Sierra Leone.

"Blow them head-bone inside" means, blow the top off their heads.

I have a collection of trade English letters and documents, for it is a language that I regard as exceedingly charming, and it really requires study, as you will see by reading Crashey Jane's epistle without the aid of a dictionary. It is, moreover, a language that will take you unexpectedly far in Africa, and if you do not understand it, land you in some pretty situations. One important point that you must remember is that the African is logically right in his answer to such a question as "You have not cleaned this lamp?"—he says, "Yes, sah"—which means, "yes, I have not cleaned the lamp." It does not mean a denial to your accusation; he always uses this form, and it is liable to confuse you at first, as are many other of the phrases, such as "I look him, I no see him" ; this means "I have been searching for the thing but have not found it"; if he really meant he had looked upon the object but had been unable to get to it, he would say: "I look him, I no catch him," &c.

The difficulty of the language is, however, far less than the whole set of difficulties with your own mind. Unless you can make it pliant enough to follow the African idea step by step, however much care you may take, you will not bag your game. I heard an account the other day of a representative of Her Majesty in Africa who went out for a day's antelope shooting. There were plenty of antelope about, and he stalked them with great care; but always, just before he got within shot of the game, they saw something and bolted. Knowing he and the boy behind him had been making no sound and could not have been seen, he stalked on, but always with the same result; until happening to look round, he saw the boy behind him was supporting the dignity of the Empire at large, and this representative of it in particular, by steadfastly holding aloft the consular flag. Well, if you go hunting the African idea with the flag of your own religion or opinions floating ostentatiously over you, you will similarly get a very poor bag.

A few hints as to your mental outfit when starting on this sport may be useful. Before starting for West Africa, burn all your notions about sun-myths and worship of the elemental forces. My own opinion is you had better also burn the notion, although it is fashionable, that human beings got their first notion of the origin of the soul from dreams.

I went out with my mind full of the deductions of every book on Ethnology, German or English, that I had read during fifteen years—

and being a good Cambridge person, I was particularly confident that from Mr. Frazer's book, *The Golden Bough*, I had got a semi-universal key to the underlying idea of native custom and belief. But I soon found this was very far from being the case. His idea is a true key to a certain quantity of facts, but in West Africa only to a limited quantity.

I do not say, do not read Ethnology—by all means do so; and above all things read, until you know it by heart, *Primitive Culture*, by Dr. E. B. Tylor, regarding which book I may say that I have never found a fact that flew in the face of the carefully made, broad-minded deductions of this greatest of Ethnologists. In addition, you must know your Westermarck on *Human Marriage*, and your Waitz *Anthropologie*, and your Topinard—not that you need expect to go measuring people's skulls and chests as this last named authority expects you to do, for no self-respecting person black or white likes that sort of thing from the hands of an utter stranger, and if you attempt it you'll get yourself disliked in West Africa. Add to this the knowledge of all A. B. Ellis's works; Burton's *Anatomy of Melancholy*; Pliny's *Natural History*; and as much of Aristotle as possible. If you have a good knowledge of the Greek and Latin classics, I think it would be an immense advantage; an advantage I do not possess, for my classical knowledge is scrappy, and in place of it I have a knowledge of Red Indian dogma: a dogma by the way that seems to me much nearer the African in type than Asiatic forms of dogma.

Armed with these instruments of observation, with a little industry and care you should in the mill of your mind be able to make the varied tangled rag-bag of facts that you will soon become possessed of into a paper. And then I advise you to lay the results of your collection before some great thinker and he will write upon it the opinion that his greater and clearer vision makes him more fit to form.

You may say, Why not bring these home their things in the raw state? And bring them home in a raw state you must, for purposes of reference; but in this state they are of little use to a person unacquainted with the conditions which surround them in their native homes. Also very few African stories bear on one subject alone, and they hardly ever stick to a point. Take this Fernando Po legend. Winwood Reade (*Savage Africa*, p. 62) gives it, and he says he heard it twice. I have heard it, in variants, four times—once on Fernando Po, once in Calabar and twice in Gaboon. So it is evidently an old story:—

"The first man called all people to one place. His name was Raychow. 'Hear this, my people' said he, 'I am going to give a name to every place, I am King in this River.' One day he came with his people to the Hole of Wonga Wonga, which is a deep pit in the ground from which fire comes at night. Men spoke to them from the Hole, but they could not see them. Raychow said to his son, 'Go down into the Hole'— and his son went. The son of the King of the Hole came to him and defied him to a contest of throwing the spear. If he lost he should be killed, if he won he should go back in safety. He won—then the son of the King of the Hole said, 'It is strange you should have won, for I am a spirit. Ask whatever you wish,' and the King's son asked for a remedy for every disease he could remember; and the spirit gave him the medicines, and when he had done so, he said, 'There is one sickness you have forgotten—it is the Krawkraw, and of that you shall die.'

"'A tribe named Ndiva was then strong but now none remain (Winwood Reade says four remain). They gave Raychose's son a canoe and forty men, to take him back to his father's town, and when he saw his father he did not speak. His father said, 'My son, if you are hungry eat.' He did not answer, and his father said 'Do you wish me to kill a goat?' He did not answer; his father said, 'Do you wish me to give you new wives?' He did not answer. Then his father said, 'Do you want me to build you a fetish hut?' Then he answered, 'Yes,' and the hut was built, and the medicines he had brought back from the Hole were put into it.

"'Now,' said the son of King Raychow, 'I go to make Moondah enter the Orongo' (Gaboon); so he went and dug a canal and when this was finished all his men were dead. Then he said, 'I will go and kill riverhorse in the Benito.' He killed four, and as he was killing the fifth, the people descended from the mountains against him. So he made fetish on his great war-spear and sang

> My spear, go kill these people,
> Or these people will kill me;

and the spear went and killed the people, except a few who got into canoes and flew to Fernando Po. Then said their King, 'My people shall never wear cloth till we have conquered the M'pongwe,' and to this day the Fernando Poians go naked and hate with a special hatred the M'pongwe.'"

Now this is a noble story—there is a lot of fine confused feeding in it, as the Scotchman said of boiled sheep's head.

You learn from it —A. The name of the first man, and also that he was filled with a desire for topographical nomenclature.

B. You hear of the Hole Wonga Wonga, and this is most interesting because to this day, apart from the story, you are told by the natives of a hole that emits fire, and Dr. Nassau says it is always said to be north of Gaboon; but so far no white man has any knowledge of an active volcano there, although the district is of volcanic origin. The crater of Fernando Po may be referred to in the legend because of the king's son being sent home in a canoe; but I do not think it is, because the Hole is known not to be Fernando Po, and it has got, according to local tradition, a river running from it or close to it.

C. The kraw-kraw is a frightfully prevalent disease; no one has a remedy for it, presumably owing to Raychow's son's forgetfulness.

D. The silence of the son to the questions is remarkable, because you always find people who have been among spirits lose their power of asking for what they want, for a time, and can only answer to the right question.

E. The sudden way in which Raychow's son gets fired with the desire to turn civil engineer just when he has got a magnificent opening in life as a doctor is merely the usual flightiness of young men, who do not see where their true advantages lie—and the conduct of the men in dying, after digging a canal is normal, and modern experiences support it, for men who dig canals down in West Africa die plentifully, be they black, white, or yellow; so you can't help believing in those men, although it is strange a black man should have been so enterprising as to go in for canal digging at all. There is no other case of it extant to my knowledge, and a remarkable fact is, that the Moondah does so nearly connect, by one creek, with the Gaboon estuary that you can drag a boat across the little intervening bit of land.

F. Is a sporting story that turns up a little unexpectedly, certainly; but the Benito is within easy distance north of the Moondah, so the geography is all right.

G. The inhabitants of Fernando Po have still an especial hatred for the M'pongwe, and both they and the M'pongwe have this account of the one tribe driving the other off the mainland. Then the Bubis—as the inhabitants on Fernando Po are called, from a confusion arising in the minds of the sailors calling at Fernando Po, between their stupidity and their word Babi = stranger, which they use as a word of greeting—these Bubis are undoubtedly a very early African race. Their culture, though presenting some remarkable points, is on the whole exceedingly low. They never wear clothes unless compelled to, and their language depends so much on gesture that they cannot talk in it to each other in the dark.

I give this as a sample of African stories. It is far more connected and keeps to the point in a far more business-like way than most of them. They are of great interest when you know the locality and the tribe they come from; but I am sure if you were to bring home a heap of stories like this, and empty them over any distinguished ethnologist's head, without ticketing them with the culture of the tribe they belonged to, the conditions it lives under, and so forth, you would stun him with the seeming inter-contradiction of some, and utter pointlessness of the rest, and he would give up ethnology and hurriedly devote his remaining years to the attempt to collect a million postage stamps, so as to do something definite before he died. Remember, you must always have your original material—carefully noted down at the time of occurrence—with you, so that you may say in answer to his Why? Because of this, and this, and this.

However good may be the outfit for your work that you take with you, you will have, at first, great difficulty in realizing that it is possible for the people you are among really to believe things in the way they do. And you cannot associate with them long before you must recognize that these Africans have often a remarkable mental acuteness and a large share of common sense; that there is nothing really "child-like" in their form of mind at all. Observe them further and you will find they are not a flighty-minded, mystical set of people in the least. They are not dreamers, or poets, and you will observe, and I hope observe closely—for to my mind this is the most important difference between their make of mind and our own—that they are notably deficient in all mechanical arts: they have never made, unless under white direction and instruction, a single fourteenth-rate piece of cloth, pottery, a tool or machine, house, road, bridge, picture or statue; that a written language of their own construction they none of them possess. A careful study of the things a man, black or white, fails to do, whether for good or evil, usually gives you a truer knowledge of the man than the things he succeeds in doing. When you fully realize this acuteness on one hand and this mechanical incapacity on the other which exist in the people you are studying, you can go ahead. Only, I beseech you, go ahead carefully. When you have found the easy key that opens the reason underlying a series of facts, as for example, these: a Benga spits on your hand as a greeting; you see a man who has been marching regardless through the broiling sun all the forenoon, with a heavy load, elaborately steal round in the shelter of the houses, instead of crossing the street; you come across a tribe that cuts its dead up into small pieces and scatters them broadcast, and another tribe that thinks a white man's eye-ball is a most desirable thing to be possessed of—do not, when you have found this key, drop your collecting work, and go home with a shriek of "I know all about Fetish," because you don't, for the key to the above facts will not open the reason why it is regarded advisable to kill a person who is making Ikung; or why you should avoid at night a cotton tree that has red earth at its roots; or why combings of hair and paring of nails should be taken care of; or why a speck of blood that may fall from your flesh should be cut out of wood—if it has fallen on that—and destroyed, and if it has fallen on the ground stamped and rubbed into the soil with great care. This set requires another key entirely.

I must warn you also that your own mind requires protection when you send it stalking the savage idea through the tangled forests, the dark caves, the swamps and the fogs of the Ethiopian intellect. The best protection lies in recognizing the untrustworthiness of human evidence regarding the unseen, and also the seen, when it is viewed by a person who has in his mind an explanation of the phenomenon before it occurs. The truth is, the study of natural phenomena knocks the bottom out of any man's conceit if it is done honestly and not by selecting only those facts that fit in with his preconceived or engrafted notions. And, to my mind, the wisest way is to get into the state of mind of an old marine engineer who oils and sees that every screw and bolt of his engines is clean and well watched, and who loves them as living things, caressing and scolding them himself, defending them, with stormy language, against the aspersions of the silly, uninformed outside world, which persists in regarding them as mere machines, a thing his superior intelligence and experience knows they are not. Even animistic-minded I got awfully sat upon the other day in Cameroon by a superior but kindred spirit, in the form of a First Engineer. I had thoughtlessly repeated some scandalous gossip against the character of a naphtha launch in the river. "Stuff!" said he furiously; "she's all right, and she'd go from June to January if those blithering fools would let her alone." Of course I apologised.

The religious ideas of the Negroes, *i.e.* the West Africans in the district from the Gambia to the Cameroon region, say roughly to the Rio del Rey (for the Bakwiri appear to have more of the Bantu form of idea than the Negro, although physically they seem nearer the latter), differ very considerably from the religious ideas of the Bantu South-West Coast tribes. The Bantu is vague on religious subjects; he gives one accustomed to the Negro the impression that he once had the same set of ideas, but has forgotten half of them, and those that he possesses have not got that hold on him that the corresponding or super-imposed Christian ideas have over the true Negro; although he is quite as keen on the subject of witchcraft, and his witchcraft differs far less from the witchcraft of the Negro than his religious ideas do.

The god, in the sense we use the word, is in essence the same in all of the Bantu tribes I have met with on the Coast: a non-interfering and therefore a negligible quantity. He varies his name: Anzambi, Anyambi, Nyambi, Nzambi, Anzam, Nyam, Ukuku, Suku, and Nzam, but a better investigation shows that Nzam of the Fans is practically identical with Suku south of the Congo in the Bihe country, and so on.

They regard their god as the creator of man, plants, animals, and the earth, and they hold that having made them, he takes no further interest in the affair. But not so the crowd of spirits with which the universe is peopled, they take only too much interest and the Bantu wishes they would not and is perpetually saying so in his prayers, a large percentage whereof amounts to "Go away, we don't want you." "Come not into this house, this village, or its plantations." He knows from experience that the spirits pay little heed to these abjurations, and as they are the people who must be attended to, he develops a cult whereby they may be managed, used, and understood. This cult is what we call witchcraft.

As I am not here writing a complete work on Fetish I will leave Nzam on one side, and turn to the inferior spirits. These are almost all malevolent; sometimes they can be coaxed into having creditable feelings. like generosity and gratitude, but you can never trust them. No, not even if you are yourself a well-established medicine man. Indeed they are particularly dangerous to medicine men, just as lions are to lion tamers, and many a professional gentleman in the full bloom of his practice, gets eaten up by his own particular familiar which he has to keep in his own inside whenever he has not sent it off into other people's.

I am indebted to the Reverend Doctor Nassau for a great quantity of valuable information regarding Bantu religious ideas—information which no one is so competent to give as he, for no one else knows the West Coast Bantu tribes with the same thoroughness and sympathy. He has lived among them since 1851, and is perfectly conversant with their languages and culture, and he brings to bear upon the study of them a singularly clear, powerful, and highly-educated intelligence.

I shall therefore carefully ticket the information I have derived from him, so that it may not be mixed with my own. I may be wrong in my deductions, but Dr. Nassau's are above suspicion.

He says the origin of these spirits is vague—some of them come into existence by the authority of Anzam (by which you will understand, please, the same god I have quoted above as having many names), others are self-existent—many are distinctly the souls of departed human beings, "which in the future which is all around them" retain their human wants and feelings, and the Doctor assures me he has heard dying people with their last breath threatening to return as spirits to revenge themselves upon their living enemies. He could not tell me if there was any duration set upon the existence as spirits of these human souls, but two Congo Français natives, of different tribes, Benga and Igalwa, told me that when a family had quite died out, after a time its spirits died too. Some, but by no means all, of these spirits of human origin, as is the case among the Negro Effiks, undergo reincarnation. The Doctor told me he once knew a man whose plantations were devastated by an elephant. He advised that the beast should be shot, but the man said he dare not because the spirit of his dead father had passed into the elephant.

Their number is infinite and their powers as varied as human imagination can make them; classifying them is therefore a difficult work, but Doctor Nassau thinks this may be done fairly completely into:

1. Human disembodied spirits—*Manu*.

2. Vague begins, well described by our word ghosts: *Abambo*.

3. Beings something like dryads, who resent intrusion into their territory, on to their rock, past their promontory, or tree. When passing the residence of one of these beings, the traveler must go by silently, or

with some cabalistic invocation, with bowed or bared head, and deposit some symbol of an offering or tribute even if it be only a pebble. You occasionally come across great trees that have fallen across a path that have quite little heaps of pebbles, small shells, &c., upon them deposited by previous passers-by. This class is called *Ombwiri.*

4. Beings, who are the agents in causing sickness, and either aid or hinder human plans—*Mionde.*

5. There seems to be, the Doctor says, another class of spirits somewhat akin to the ancient Lares and Penates, who especially belong to the household, and descend by inheritance with the family. In their honor are secretly kept a bundle of finger, or other bones, nail-clippings, eyes, brains, skulls, particularly the lower jaws, called in M'pongwe *oginga,* accumulated from deceased members of successive generations.

Dr. Nassau says "secretly," and he refers to this custom being existent in non-cannibal tribes. I saw bundles of this character among the cannibal Fans, and among the non-cannibal Adooma, openly hanging up in the thatch of the sleeping apartment.

6. He also says there may be a sixth class, which may, however only be a function of any of the other classes—namely, those that enter into any animal body, generally a leopard. Sometimes the spirits of living human beings do this, and the animal is then guided by human intelligence, and will exercise its strength for the purposes of its temporary human possessor. In other cases it is a non-human soul that enters into the animal, as in the case of Ukuku.

Spirits are not easily classified by their functions because those of different class may be employed in identical undertakings. Thus one witch doctor may have, I find, particular influence over one class of spirit and another over another class; yet they will both engage to do identical work. But in spite of this I do not see how you can classify spirits otherwise than by their functions; you cannot weigh and measure them, and it is only a few that show themselves in corporeal form.

There are characteristics that all the authorities seem agreed on, and one is that individual spirits in the same class vary in power: some are strong of their sort, some weak.

They are all to a certain extent limited in the nature of their power; there is no one spirit that can do all things; their efficiency only runs in certain lines of action and all of them are capable of being influenced, and made subservient to human wishes, by proper incantations. This latter characteristic is of course to human advantage, but it has its disadvantages, for you can never really trust a spirit, even if you have paid a considerable sum to a most distinguished medicine man to get a powerful one put up in a ju-ju or monde, as it is called in several tribes. The method of making these charms is much the same among Bantu and Negroes. I have elsewhere described the Gold Coast method, so here confine myself to the Bantu. This similarity of procedure naturally arises from the same underlying idea existing in the two races.

You call in the medicine man, the "oganga," as he is commonly called in Congo Français tribes. After a variety of ceremonies and processes, the spirit is induced to localize itself in some object subject to the will of the possessor. The things most frequently used are antelopes' horns, the large snail-shells, and large nutshells, according to Doctor Nassau. Among the Fan I found the most frequent charm-case was in the shape of a little sausage, made very neatly of pineapple fiber, the contents being the residence of the spirit or power, and the outside coloured red to flatter and please him—for spirits always like red because it is like blood.

The substance put inside charms is all manner of nastiness, usually on the sea coast having a high percentage of fowl dung.

The nature of the substance depends on the spirit it is intended to be attractive to—attractive enough to induce it to leave its present abode and come and reside in the charm.

In addition to this attractive substance I find there are other materials inserted which have relations towards the work the spirit will be wanted to do for its owner. For example, charms made either to influence a person to be well disposed towards the owner, or the still larger class made with intent to work evil on other human beings against whom the owner has a grudge, must have in them some portion of the person to be dealt with—his hair, blood, nail-parings, &c.—or, failing that, his or her most intimate belonging, something that has got his smell in—a piece of his old waist-cloth for example.

This ability to obtain power over people by means of their blood, hair, nails, &c., is universally diffused; you will find it down in Devon, and away in far Cathay, and the Chinese, I am told, have in some parts of their empire little ovens to burn their nail-and hair-clippings in. The fear of these latter belongings falling into the hands of evilly-disposed persons is ever present to the West Africans. The Igalwa and other tribes will allow no one but a trusted friend to do their hair, and bits of nails and hair are carefully burnt or thrown away into a river; and blood, even that from a small cut or a fit of nose-bleeding, is most carefully covered up and stamped out if it has fallen on the earth. The underlying idea regarding blood is of course the old one that the blood is the life.

The life in Africa means a spirit, hence the liberated blood is the liberated spirit, and liberated spirits are always whipping into people who do not want them.

Charms are made for every occupation and desire in life—loving, hating, buying, selling, fishing, planting, travelling, hunting, &c., and although they are usually in the form of things filled with a mixture in which the spirit nestles, yet there are other kinds; for example, a great love charm is made of the water the lover has washed in, and this, mingled with the drink of the loved one, is held to soften the hardest heart.

Some kinds of charms, such as those to prevent your getting drowned, shot, seen by elephants, &c., are worn on a bracelet or necklace. A new-born child starts with a health-knot tied round the wrist, neck, or loins, and throughout the rest of its life its collection of charms goes on increasing. This collection does not, however, attain inconvenient dimensions, owning to the failure of some of the charms to work.

That is the worst of charms and prayers. The thing you wish of them may, and frequently does, happen in a strikingly direct way, but other times it does not. In Africa this is held to arise from the bad character of the spirits; their gross ingratitude and fickleness. You may have taken every care of a spirit for years, given it food and other offerings that you wanted for yourself, wrapped it up in your cloth on chilly nights and gone cold, put it in the only dry spot in the canoe, and so on, and yet after all this, the wretched thing will be capable of being got at by your rival or enemy and lured away, leaving you only the case it once lived in.

Finding, we will say, that you have been upset and half-drowned, and your canoe-load of goods lost three times in a week, that your paddles are always breaking, and the amount of snags in the river and so on is abnormal, you judge that your canoe-charm has stopped. Then you go to the medicine man who supplied you with it and complain. He says it was a perfectly good charm when he sold it to you and he never had any complaints before, but he will investigate the affair; when he has done so, he either says the spirit has been lured away from the home he prepared for it by incantations and presents from other people, or that he finds the spirit is dead; it has been killed by a more powerful spirit of its class, which is in the pay of some enemy of yours. In all cases the little thing you kept the spirit in is no use now, and only fit to sell to a white man as "a big curio!" and the sooner you let him have sufficient money to procure you a fresh and still more powerful spirit—necessarily more expensive—the safer it will be for you, particularly as your misfortunes distinctly point to some one being desirous of your death. You of course grumble, but seeing the thing in his light you pay up, and the medicine man goes busily to work with incantations, dances, looking into mirrors or basins of still water, and concoctions of messes to make you a new protecting charm.

Human eye-balls, particularly of white men, I have already said are a great charm. Dr. Nassau says he has known graves rifled for them. This, I fancy, is to secure the "man that lives in your eyes" for the service of the village, and naturally the white man, being regarded as a superior being, would be of high value if enlisted into its service. A similar idea of the possibility of gaining possession of the spirit of a dead man obtains among the Negroes, and the heads of important chiefs in the Calabar districts are usually cut off from the body on burial and kept secretly for fear the head, and thereby the spirit, of the dead chief, should be stolen from the town. If it were stolen it would be not only a great advantage to its new possessor, but a great danger to the chief's old town, because he would know all the peculiar ju-ju relating to it. For each town has a peculiar one, kept exceedingly secret, in addition to the general ju-jus, and this secret one would then be in the hands of the new owners of the spirit. It is for similar reasons that brave General MacCarthy's head was treasured by the Ashantees, and so on.

Charms are not all worn upon the body, some go to the plantations, and are hung there, ensuring an unhappy and swift end for the thief who comes stealing. Some are hung round the bows of the canoe, others over the doorway of the house, to prevent evil spirits from coming in—a sort of tame watch-dog spirits.

The entrances to the long street-shaped villages are frequently closed with a fence of saplings and this sapling fence you will see hung with fetish charms to prevent evil spirits from entering the village and sometimes in addition to charms you will see the fence wreathed with leaves and flowers. Bells are frequently hung on these fences, but I do not fancy ever for fetish reasons. At Ndorko, on the Rembwé, there were many guards against spirit visitors, but the bell, which was carefully hung so that you could not pass through the gateway without ringing it, was a guard against thieves and human enemies only.

Frequently a sapling is tied horizontally near the ground across the entrance. Dr. Nassau could not tell me why, but says it must never be trodden on. When the smallpox, a dire pestilence in these regions, is raging, or when there is war, these gateways are sprinkled with the blood of sacrifices, and for theses sacrifices and for the payments of heavy blood fines, &c., goats and sheep are kept. They are rarely eaten for ordinary purposes, and these West Coast Africans have all a perfect horror of the idea of drinking milk, holding this custom to be a filthy habit, and saying so in unmitigated language.

The villagers eat the meat of the sacrifice, that having nothing to do with the sacrifice to the spirits, which is the blood, for the blood is the life.

Beside the few spirits that the Bantu regards himself as having got under control in his charms, he has to worship the uncontrolled army of the air. This he does by sacrifice and incantation.

The sacrifice is the usual killing of something valuable as an offering to the spirits. The value of the offering in these S.W. Coast regions has certainly a regular relationship to the value of the favor required of the spirits. Some favours are worth a dish of plantains, some a fowl, some a goat and some a human being, though human sacrifice is very rare in Congo Français, the killing of people being nine times in ten of witchcraft palaver.

Dr. Nassau, however, says that "the intention of the giver ennobles the gift," the spirit being supposed, in some vague way, to be gratified by the recognition of itself, and even sometimes pleased with the homage of the mere simulacrum of a gift. I believe the only class of spirits that have this convenient idea are the Imbwiri; thus the stones heaped by passers-by on the foot of some great tree, or rock, or the leaf cast from a passing canoe towards a promontory on the river, &c., although intrinsically valueless and useless to the Ombwiri nevertheless gratify him. It is a sort of bow or taking off one's hat to him. Some gifts, the Doctor says, are supposed to be actually utilised by the spirit.

In some part of the long single street of most villages there is built a low hut in which charms are hung, and by which grows a consecrated plant, a lily, a euphorbia, or a fig. In some tribes a rudely carved figure, generally female, is set up as an idol before which offerings are laid. I saw at Egaja two figures about 2 feet 6 inches high, in the house placed at my disposal. They were left in it during my occupation, save that the rolls of cloth (their power) which were round their necks, were removed by the owner chief; of the significance of these rolls I will speak elsewhere.

Incantations may be divided into two classes, supplications analogous to our idea of prayers, and certain cabalistic words and phrases. The supplications are addresses to the higher spirits. Some are made even to Anzam himself, but the spirit of the new moon is that most commonly addressed to keep the lower spirits from molesting.

Dr. Nassau gave me many instances out of the wealth of his knowledge. One night when he was stopping at a village, he saw standing out in the open street a venerable chief who addressed the spirits of the air and begged them, "Come ye not into my town;" he then recounted his good deeds, praising himself as good, just, honest, kind to his neighbors, and so on. I must remark that this man had not been in touch with Europeans, so his ideal of goodness was the native one—which you will find everywhere among the most remote West Coast natives. He urged these things as a reason why no evil should befall him, and closed with an impassioned appeal to the spirits to stay away. At another time, in another village, when a man's son had been wounded and a bleeding artery which the Doctor had closed had broken out again and the hæmorrhage seemed likely to prove fatal, the father rushed out into the street wildly gesticulating towards the sky, saying, "Go away, go away, go away, ye spirits, why do you come to kill my son?" In another case a woman rushed into the street, alternately objurgating and pleading with the spirits, who, she said, were vexing her child which had convulsions. "Observe," said the Doctor in his impressive way, "these were distinctly prayers, appeals for mercy, agonizing protests, but there was no praise, no love, no thanks, no confession of sin." I said, considering the underlying idea, I did not see how that could be, thinking of the thing as they did, and the Doctor and I had one of our little disagreements. I shall always feel grateful to him for his great toleration of me, but I am sure this arose from his feeling that I saw there was an underlying idea in the minds of the people he loved well enough to lay down his life for in the hope of benefiting and ennobling them, and that I did not, as many do, set them down as idiotic brutes, glorying in an aimless cruelty that would be a disgrace to a devil.

Regarding the cabalistic words and phrases, things which had long given me great trouble to get any comprehension of, the Doctor gave me great help. He says some of these phrases and words are coined by the person himself, others are archaisms handed down from ancestors and believed to possess an efficacy, though their actual meaning is forgotten. He says they are used at any time as defence from evil, when a person is startled, sneezes, or stumbles. Among these I think I ought to class that peculiar form of friendly farewell or greeting which the Doctor poetically calls a "blown blessing" and the natives Ibata. I thought the three times it was given to me that it was just spitting on the hand. Practically it is so, but the Doctor says the spitting is accidental, a by-product I suppose. The method consists in taking the right hand in both yours, turning it palm upwards, bending your head low over it, and saying with great energy and a violent propulsion of the breath, Ibata.

Idols are comparatively rare in Congo Français, but where they are used the people have the same idea about them as the true Negroes have, namely, that they are things which spirits reside in, or haunt, but not in their corporeal nature adorable. The resident spirit in them and in the charms and plants, which are also regarded as residences of spirits, has to be placated with offerings of food and other sacrifices. You will see in the Fetish huts above mentioned dishes of plantain and fish left till they rot. Dr. Nassau says the life or essence of the food only is eaten by the spirit, the form of the vegetable or flesh being to be removed when its life is gone out.

In cases of emergency a fowl with its blood is laid at the door of the Fetish hut, or when pestilence is expected, or an attack by enemies, or a great man or woman is very ill, goats and sheep are sacrificed and the blood put in the Fetish hut as well as on the gateways of the village. These sacrifices among the Fan are made with a very peculiar-shaped knife, a fine specimen of which I secured by the kindness of Captain Davies; it is shaped like the head of a hornbill and is quite unlike the knives in common use among the tribes, which are either long, leaf-shaped blades sharpened along both edges, or broad, trowel-shaped, almost triangular daggers. All Fan knives are fine weapons, superior to the knives of all the other Coast tribes I have met with, but the sacrifice knife is distinctly peculiar. I found to my great interest the same superstition in Congo Français that I met with first in the Oil Rivers. Its meaning I am unable to fully account for, but I believe it to be a form of sacrifice.

In Calabar each individual has a certain forbidden thing or things. These things are either forms of food, or the method of eating. In Calabar this prohibition is called Ibet, and when, in consequence of the influence of white culture, a man gives up his Ibet, he is regarded by good sound ju-juists as leading an irregular and dissipated life, and even the unintentional breaking of the Ibet is regarded as very dangerous. Special days are set apart by each individual; on these days he eats only the smallest quantity and plainest quality of food. No one must eat with him, nor any dog, fowl, &c., feed off the crumbs, nor any one watch him while eating. I suspect on this day the Ibet is eaten, but I have not verified this, only getting, from an untrustworthy source, a statement that supported it.

Dr. Nassau told me that among Congo Français tribes certain rites are performed for children during infancy or youth, in which a prohibition is laid upon the child as regards the eating of some particular article of food, or the doing of certain acts. "It is difficult," he said, "to get the exact object of the 'Orunda.' Certainly the prohibited article is not in itself evil, for others but the inhibited individual may eat or do with it as they please. Most of the natives blindly follow the custom of their ancestors without being able to give any *raison d' être*, but again, from those best able to give a reason, you learn the prohibited article is a sacrifice ordained for the child by its parents and the magic doctor as a gift to the governing spirit of life. The thing prohibited becomes removed from the child's common use, and is made sacred to the spirit. Any use of it by the child or man would therefore be a sin, which would bring down the spirit's wrath in the form of sickness or other evil, which can be atoned for only by expensive ceremonies or gifts to the magic doctor who intercedes for the offender."

Anything may be an Orunda or Ibet provided only that it is connected with food; I have been able to find no definite ground for the selection of it. The Doctor said, for example, that "once when on a boat journey, and camped in the forest for the noon-day meal, the crew of four had no meat. They needed it. I had a chicken but ate only a portion, and gave the rest to the crew. Three men ate it with their manioc meal, the fourth would not touch it. It was his Orunda." "On another journey," said the Doctor, "instead of all my crew leaving me respectfully alone in the canoe to have my lunch and going ashore to have theirs, one of them stayed behind in the canoe, and I found his Orunda was only to eat over water when on a journey by the water." "At another place, a chief at whose village we once anchored in a small steamer when a glass of rum was given him, had a piece of cloth held up before his mouth that the people might not see him drink, which was his Orunda."

I know some ethnologists will think this last case should be classed under another head, but I think the Doctor is right. He is well aware of the existence of the other class of prohibitions regarding chiefs and I have seen plenty of chiefs myself up the Rembwé who have no objection to take their drinks *coram publico*, and I have no doubt this was only an individual Orunda of this particular Rembwé chief.

Great care is requisite in these matters, because a man may do or abstain from doing one and the same thing for diverse reasons.

CHAPTER 13

Fetish (continued)

In which the Voyager discourses on deaths and witchcraft, and, with no intentional slur on the medical profession, on medical methods and burial customs, concluding with sundry observations on twins.

IT IS EXCEEDINGLY INTERESTING to compare the ideas of the Negroes with those of the Bantu. The mental condition of the lower forms of both races seems very near the other great border-line that separates man from the anthropoid apes, and I believe that if we had the material, or rather if we could understand it, we should find little or no gap existing in mental evolution in this old, undisturbed continent of Africa.

Let, however, these things be as they may, one thing about Negro and Bantu races is very certain, and that is that their lives are dominated by a profound belief in witchcraft and its effects.

Among both alike the rule is that death is regarded as a direct consequence of the witchcraft of some malevolent human being, acting by means of spirits, over which he has, by some means or another, obtained control.

To all rules there are exceptions. Among the Calabar Negroes, who are definite in their opinions, I found two classes of exceptions. The first arises from their belief in a bush-soul. They believe every man has four souls: *a*, the soul that survives death; *b*, the shadow on the path; *c*, the dream-soul; *d*, the bush-soul.

This bush-soul is always in the form of an animal in the forest-never of a plant. Sometimes when a man sickens it is because his bush—soul is angry at being neglected, and a witch-doctor is called in, who, having diagnosed this as being the cause of the complaint, advises the administration of some kind of offering to the offended one. When you wander about in the forests of the Calabar region, you will frequently see little dwarf huts with these offerings in them. You must not confuse these huts with those of similar construction you are continually seeing in plantations, or near roads, which refer to quite other affairs. These offerings, in the little huts in the forest, are placed where your bush-soul was last seen. Unfortunately, you are compelled to call in a doctor, which is an expense, but you cannot see your own bush-soul, unless you are an Ebumtup, a sort of second-sighter.

But to return to the bush-soul of an ordinary person. If the offering in the hut works well on the bush-soul, the patient recovers, but if it does not he dies. Diseases arising from derangements in the temper of the bush-soul however, even when treated by the most eminent practitioners, are very apt to be intractable, because it never realizes that by injuring you it endangers its own existence. For when its human owner dies, the bush-soul can no longer find a good place, and goes mad, rushing to and fro— if it sees a fire it rushes into it; if it sees a lot of people it rushes among them, until it is killed, and when it is killed it is "finish" for it, as M. Pichault would say, for it is not an immortal soul.

The bush-souls of a family are usually the same for a man and for his sons, for a mother and for her daughters. Sometimes, however, I am told all the children take the mother's, sometimes all take the father's. They may be almost any kind of animal, sometimes they are leopards, sometimes fish, or tortoises, and so on.

There is another peculiarity about the bush-soul, and that is that it is on its account that old people are held in such esteem among the Calabar tribes. For, however bad these old people's personal record may have been, the fact of their longevity demonstrates the possession of powerful and astute bush-souls. On the other hand, a man may be a quiet, respectable citizen, devoted to peace and a whole skin, and yet he may have a sadly flighty disreputable bush-soul which will get itself killed or damaged and cause him death or continual ill-health.

There is another way by which a man dies apart from the action of bush-souls or witchcraft; he may have had a bad illness from some cause in his previous life and, when reincarnated, part of this disease may get reincarnated with him and then he will ultimately die of it. There is no medicine of any avail against these reincarnated diseases.

The idea of reincarnation is very strong in the Niger Delta tribes. It exists, as far as I have been able to find out, throughout all Africa, but usually only in scattered cases, as it were; but in the Delta, most—I think I may say all—human souls of the "surviving soul" class are regarded as returning to the earth again, and undergoing a reincarnation shortly after the due burial of the soul.

These two exceptions from the rule of all deaths and sickness being caused by witchcraft are, however, of minor importance, for infinitely the larger proportion of death and sickness is held to arise from witchcraft itself, more particularly among the Bantu.

Witchcraft acts in two ways, namely, witching something out of a man, or witching something into him. The former method is used by both Negro and Bantu, but is decidedly more common among the Negroes, where the witches are continually setting traps to catch the soul that wanders from the body when a man is sleeping; and when they have caught this soul, they tie it up over the canoe fire and its owner sickens as the soul shrivels.

This is merely a regular line of business, and not an affair of individual hate or revenge. The witch does not care whose dream-soul gets into the trap, and will restore it on payment. Also witch-doctors, men of unblemished professional reputation, will keep asylums for lost souls, *i.e.* souls who have been out wandering and found on their return to their body that their place has been filled up by a Sisa, a low class soul I will speak of later. These doctors keep souls and administer them to patients who are short of the article.

But there are other witches, either wicked on their own account, or hired by people who are moved by some hatred to individuals, and then the trap is carefully set and baited for the soul of the particular man they wish to injure, and concealed in the bait at the bottom of the pot are knives and sharp hooks which tear and damage the soul, either killing it outright, or mauling it so that it causes its owner sickness on its return to him. I knew the case of a Kruman who for several nights had smelt in his dreams the savory smell of smoked crawfish seasoned with red peppers. He became anxious, and the headman decided some witch had set a trap baited with this dainty for his dream-soul, with intent to do him grievous bodily harm, and great trouble was taken for the next few nights to prevent this soul of his from straying abroad.

The witching of things into a man is far the most frequent method among the Bantu, hence the prevalence among them of the post-mortem examination,—a practice I never found among the Negroes.

The belief in witchcraft is the cause of more African deaths than anything else. It has killed and still kills more men and women than the slave-trade. Its only rival is perhaps the smallpox, the Grand Kraw-Kraw, as the Krumen graphically call it.

At almost every death a suspicion of witchcraft arises. The witch-doctor is called in, and proceeds to find out the guilty person. Then woe to the unpopular men, the weak women, and the slaves; for on some of them will fall the accusation that means ordeal by poison, or fire, followed, if these point to guilt, as from their nature they usually do, by a terrible death: slow roasting alive—mutilation by degrees before the throat is mercifully cut—tying to stakes at low tide that the high tide may come and drown—and any other death human ingenuity and hate can devise.

The terror in which witchcraft is held is interesting in spite of all its horror. I have seen mild, gentle men and women turned by it, in a moment, to incarnate fiends, ready to rend and destroy those who a second before were nearest and dearest to them. Terrible is the fear that falls like a spell upon a village when a big man, or big woman is just known to be dead. The very men catch their breaths, and grow gray round the lips, and then every one, particularly those belonging to the household of the deceased, goes in for the most demonstrative exhibition of grief. Long, low howls creep up out of the first silence—those blood-curdling, infinitely melancholy, wailing howls—once heard, never to be forgotten.

The men tear off their clothes and wear only the most filthy rags; women, particularly the widows, take off ornaments and almost all dress; their faces are painted white with chalk, their heads are shaven, and they sit crouched on the earth in the house, in the attitude of abasement, the hands resting on the shoulders, palm downwards, not crossed across the breast, unless they are going into the street.

Meanwhile the witch-doctor has been sent for, if he is not already present, and he sets to work in different ways to find out who are the persons guilty of causing the death.

Whether the methods vary with the tribe, or with the individual witch-doctor, I cannot absolutely say, but I think largely with the latter.

Among the Benga I saw a witch-doctor going round a village ringing a small bell which was to stop ringing outside the hut of the guilty. Among the Cabindas (Fjort) I saw, at different times, two witch-doctors trying to find witches, one by means of taking on and off the lid of a small basket while he repeated the names of all the people in the village. When the lid refused to come off at the name of a person, that person was doomed. The other Cabinda doctor first tried throwing nuts upon the ground, also repeating names. That method apparently failed. Then he resorted to another, rubbing the flattened palms of his hands against each other. When the palms refused to meet at a name, and his hands flew wildly, he had got his man.

The accused person, if he denies the guilt, and does not claim the ordeal, is tortured until he not only acknowledges his guilt but names his accomplices in the murder, for remember this witchcraft is murder in the African eyes.

If he claims the ordeal, as he usually does, he usually has to take a poison drink. Among all the Bantu tribes I know this is made from Sass wood (sass = bad; sass water = rough water; sass surf = bad surf, &c.), and is a decoction of the freshly pulled bark of a great hard wood forest tree, which has a tall unbranched stem, terminating in a crown of branches bearing small leaves. Among the Calabar tribes the ordeal drink is of two kinds; one made from the Calabar bean, the other, the great ju-ju drink Mbiam, which is used also in taking oaths.

In both the sass-wood and Calabar bean drink the only chance for the accused lies in squaring the witch-doctor, so that in the case of the sass-wood drink it is allowed to settle before administration, and in the bean that you get a heavy dose, both arrangements tending to produce the immediate emetic effect indicative of innocence. If this effect does not come on quickly you die a miserable death from the effects of the poison interrupted by the means taken to kill you as soon as it is decided from the absence of violent sickness that you are guilty.

The Mbiam is not poisonous, nor is its use confined, as the use of the bean is, entirely to witch palaver; but it is the most respected and dreaded of all oaths, and from its decision there is but one appeal, the appeal open to all condemned persons, but rarely made— the appeal to Long ju-ju. This Long ju-ju means almost certain death, and before it a severe frightening that is worse to a Negro mind than mere physical torture.

The Mbiam oath formula I was able to secure in the upper districts of the Calabar. One form of it runs thus, and it is recited before swallowing the drink made of filth and blood :—

"If I have been guilty of this crime,
"If I have gone and sought the sick one's hurt,
"If I have sent another to seek the sick one's hurt,
"If I have employed any one to make charms or to cook bush,
"Or to put anything in the road,
"Or to touch his cloth,
"Or to touch his yams,
"Or to touch his goats,
"Or to touch his fowl,
"Or to touch his children,
"If I have prayed for his hurt,
"If I have thought to hurt him in my heart,
"If I have any intention to hurt him,
"If I ever, at any time, do any of these things (recite in full),
"Or employ others to do these things (recite in full)
"Then, Mbiam! *Thou* deal with me."

This form I give was for use when a man was sick, and things were generally going badly with him, for it is not customary in cases of disease to wait until death occurs before making an accusation of witchcraft. In the case of Mbiam being administered after a death this long and complicated oath would be worded to meet the case most carefully, the future intention clauses being omitted. In all cases, whenever it is used, the greatest care is taken that the oath be recited in full, oath-takers being sadly prone to kiss their thumb, as it were, particularly ladies who are taking Mbiam for accusations of adultery, in conjunction with the boiling oil ordeal. Indeed, so unreliable is this class of offenders, or let us rather say this class of suspected persons, that some one usually says the oath for them.

From the penalty and inconveniences of these accusations of witchcraft there is but one escape, namely flight to a sanctuary. There are several sanctuaries in Congo Français. The great one in the Calabar district is at Omon. Thither mothers of twins, widows, thieves, and

slaves fly, and if they reach it are safe. But an attempt at flight is a confession of guilt; no one is quite certain the accusation will fall on him,
or her, and hopes for the best until it is generally too late. Moreover,
flying anywhere beyond a day's march, is difficult work in West Africa.
So the killing goes on and it is no uncommon thing for ten or more
people to be destroyed for one man's sickness or death; and thus over
immense tracts of the country the death-rate exceeds the birth-rate.
Indeed some of the smaller tribes have thus been almost wiped out. In
the Calabar district I have heard of an entire village taking the bean voluntarily because another village had accused it *en bloc* of witchcraft. Miss
Slessor has frequently told me how, during a quarrel, one person has
accused another of witchcraft, and the accused has bolted off in a towering rage and swallowed the bean.

The witch-doctor is not always the cause of people being subjected
to the ordeal or torture. In Calabar and the Okÿon districts all the
widows of a dead man are subjected to ordeal.

They have to go the next night after the death, before an assemblage
of chiefs and the general surrounding crowd, to a cleared space where
there is a fire burning. A fowl is tied to the right hand of each widow, and
should that fowl fail to cluck at the sight of the fire the woman is held guilty
of having bewitched her dead husband and is dealt with accordingly.

Among the Bantu, although the killing among the wives from the
accusation of witchcraft is high, some of them being almost certain to
fall victims, yet there is not the wholesale slaughter of women and slaves
sent down with the soul of the dead that there is among the Negroes.

In doubtful cases of death, *i.e.* in all cases not arising from actual
violence, when blood shows in the killing, the Bantu of the S.W. Coast
make post-mortem examinations. Notably common is this practice
among the Cameroons and Batanga region tribes. The body is cut open
to find in the entrails some sign of the path of the injected witch.

I am informed that it is the lung that is most usually eaten by the
spirit. If the deceased is a witch-doctor it is thought, as I have mentioned
before, that his familiar spirit has eaten him internally, and he is opened
with a view of securing and destroying his witch. In 1893 I saw in a village in Kacongo five unpleasant-looking objects stuck on sticks. They
were the livers and lungs, and in fact the plucks, of witch-doctors, and
the inhabitants informed me they were the witches that had been found
in them on post-mortems and had been secured.

Mrs. Grenfell, of the Upper Congo, told me in the same year, when I had the pleasure of travelling with her from Victoria to Matadi, that a similar practice was in vogue among several of the Upper Congo tribes.

Again in 1893 I came across another instance of the post-mortem practice. A woman had dropped down dead on a factory beach at Corisco Bay. The natives could not make it out at all. They were irritated about her conduct: "She no sick, she no complain, she no nothing, and then she go die one time."

The post-mortem showed a burst aneurism. The native verdict was "She done witch herself," *i.e.* she was a witch eaten by her own familiar.

The general opinion held by people living near a river is that the spirit of a witch can take the form of a crocodile to do its work in; those who live away from large rivers or in districts in Congo Français, where crocodiles are not very savage, hold that the witch takes on the form of a leopard. Still the crocodile spirit form is believed in Congo Français, and to a greater extent in Kacongo, because here the crocodiles of the Congo are very ferocious and numerous, taking as heavy a toll in human life as they do in the delta of the Niger and the estuaries of the Sierra Leone and Sherboro' Rivers.

One witch-doctor I know in Kacongo had a strange professional method. When, by means of his hand rubbings, &c., he had got hold of a witch or a bewitched one, he always gave the unfortunate an emetic and always found several lively young crocodiles in the consequence, and the stories of the natives in this region abound in accounts of people who have been carried off by witch crocodiles, and kept in places underground for years. I often wonder whether this idea may not have arisen from the well-known habit of the crocodile of burying its prey on the bank. Sometimes it will take off a limb of its victim at once, but frequently it buries the body whole for a few days before eating it. The body is always buried if it is left to the crocodile.

I have a most profound respect for the whole medical profession, but I am bound to confess that the African representatives of it are a little empirical in their methods of treatment. The African doctor is not always a witch-doctor in the bargain, but he is usually. Lady doctors abound. They are a bit dangerous in pharmacy, but they do not often venture on surgery, so on the whole they are safer, for African surgery is heroic. Dr. Nassau cited the worst case of it I know of. A man had been accidentally shot in the chest by another man with a gun on the Ogowé.

The native doctor who was called in made a perpendicular incision into the man's chest, extending down to the last rib; he then cut diagonally across, and actually lifted the wall of the chest, and groped about among the vitals for the bullet which he successfully extracted. Patient died. No anæsthetic was employed.

I came across a minor operation. A man had broken the ulna of the left arm. The native doctor got a piece—a very nice piece—of bamboo, drove it in through the muscles and integuments from the wrist to the elbow, then encased the limb in plantain leaves, and bound it round, tightly and neatly, needless to say with tie-tie. The arm and hand when I saw it, some six or seven months after the operation, was quite useless, and was withering away.

Many of their methods, however, are better. The Dualla medicos are truly great on poultices for extracting foreign substances, such as bits of iron cooking-pot—a very frequent form of foreign substance in a man out here, owing to their being generally used as bullets. Almost incredible stories are told by black and white of the efficacy of these poultices; one case I heard from a reliable source of a man who had been shot with fragments of iron pot in the thigh. The white doctor extracted several pieces and said he had got all out, but the man still went on suffering, and could not walk, so, at his request, a native doctor was called in, and he applied his poultice. In a few minutes he removed it, and on its face were two pieces of jagged iron pot. Probably they had been in the poultice when it was applied, anyhow the patient recovered rapidly.

Baths accompanied by massage are much esteemed. The baths are sometimes of hot water with a few herbs thrown in, sometimes they are made by digging a hole in the earth and putting into it a quantity of herbs, and bruised cardamoms, and peppers. Boiling water is then plentifully poured over these and the patient is placed in the bath and is covered over with the parboiled green stuff; a coating of clay is then placed over all, leaving just the head sticking out. The patient remains in this bath for a period of a few hours, up to a day and a half, and when taken out is well rubbed and kneaded. This form of bath I saw used by the M'pongwe and Igalwas, and it is undoubtedly good for many diseases, notably for that curse of the Coast, rheumatism, which afflicts black and white alike. Rubbing and kneading and hot baths are, I think, the best native remedies, and the plaster of grains-of-paradise pounded up, and mixed with clay, and applied to the forehead as a remedy for malarial headache, or brow ague, is often very useful, but apart from these, I have never seen, in any of those herbal remedies, any trace of a really valuable drug.

The Calabar natives are notably behindhand in their medical methods, depending more on ju-ju than the Bantus. In a case of rheumatism, for example, instead of ordering the hot bath, the local practitioner will "woka" his patient and extract from the painful part even when it has not been wounded, pieces of iron pot, millipedes, etc., and, in cases of dysentery, bundles of shred-up palm-leaves. These things, he asserts, have been by witchcraft inserted into the patient. His conduct can hardly be regarded as professional; and moreover as he goes on to diagnose who has witched these things into the patient's anatomy, it is highly dangerous to the patient's friends, relations, and neighbors into the bargain.

With no intentional slur on the medical profession after this discussion on their methods I will pass on the question of dying.

Dying in West Africa particularly in the Niger Delta, is made very unpleasant for the native by his friends and relations.

When a person is insensible, violent means are taken to recall the spirit to the body. Pepper is forced up the nose and into the eyes. The mouth is propped open with a stick. The shredded fibers of the outside of the oil-nut are set alight and held under the nose and the whole crowd of friends and relations with whom the stifling hot hut is tightly packed yell the dying man's name at the top of their voices, in a way that makes them hoarse for days, just as if they were calling to a person lost in the bush or to a person struggling and being torn or lured away from them. "Hi, hi, don't you hear? Come back, come back. See here. This is your place," &c.

This custom holds good among both Negroes and Bantus; but the funeral ceremonies vary immensely, in fact with every tribe, and form a subject the details of which I will reserve for a separate work on Fetish.

Among the Okÿon tribes especial care is taken in the case of a woman dying and leaving a child over six months old. The underlying idea is that the spirit of the mother is sure to come back and fetch the child, and in order to pacify her and prevent the child dying, it is brought in and held just in front of the dead body of the mother and then gradually carried away behind her where she cannot see it, and the person holding the child makes it cry out and says, "See, your child is here, you are going to have it with you all right." Then the child is hastily smuggled out of the hut, while a bunch of plantains is put in with the body of the woman and bound up with the funeral binding clothes.

Very young children they do not attempt to keep, but throw them away in the bush alive, as all children are thrown who have not arrived in this world in the way considered orthodox, or who cut their teeth in an improper way. Twins are killed among all the Niger Delta tribes, and in districts out of English control the mother is killed too, except in Omon, where the sanctuary is.

There is always a sense of there being something uncanny regarding twins in West Africa, and in those tribes where they are not killed they are regarded as requiring great care to prevent them from dying on their own account. I remember once among the Tschwi trying to amuse a sickly child with an image which was near it and which I thought was its doll. The child regarded me with its great melancholy eyes pityingly, as much as to say, "A pretty fool *you* are making of yourself," and so I was, for I found out that the image was not a doll at all but an image of the child's dead twin which was being kept near it as a habitation for the deceased twin's soul, so that it might not have to wander about, and, feeling lonely, call its companion after it.

The terror with which twins are regarded in the Niger Delta is exceedingly strange and real. When I had the honor of being with Miss Slessor at Okÿon, the first twins in that district were saved with their mother from immolation owing entirely to Miss Slessor's great influence with the natives and her own unbounded courage and energy. The mother in this case was a slave woman—an Eboe, the most expensive and valuable of slaves. She was the property of a big woman who had always treated her—as indeed most slaves are treated in Calabar—with great kindness and consideration, but when these two children arrived all was changed; immediately she was subjected to torrents of virulent abuse, her things were torn from her, her English china basins, possessions she valued most highly, were smashed, her clothes were torn, and she was driven out as an unclean thing. Had it not been for the fear of incurring Miss Slessor's anger, she would, at this point, have been killed with her children, and the bodies thrown into the bush.

As it was, she was hounded out of the village. The rest of her possessions were jammed into an empty gin-case and cast to her. No one would touch her, as they might not touch to kill. Miss Slessor had heard of the twins' arrival and had started off, barefooted and bare-headed, at that pace she can go down a bush path. By the time she had gone four miles she met the procession, the woman coming to her and all the rest of the village yelling and howling behind her. On the top of her head was the gin-case, into which the children had been stuffed, on the top of them the woman's big brass skillet, and on the top of that her two market calabashes. Needless to say, on arriving Miss Slessor took charge of affairs, relieving the unfortunate, weak, staggering woman from her load and carrying it herself, for no one else would touch it, or anything belonging to those awful twin things, and they started back together to Miss Slessor's house in the forest-clearing, saved by that tact which, coupled with her courage, has given Miss Slessor an influence and a power among the Negroes unmatched in its way by that of any other white.

She did not take the twins and their mother down the village path to her own house, for though had she done so the people of Okẏon would not have prevented her, yet so polluted would the path have been, and so dangerous to pass down, that they would have been compelled to cut another, no light task in that bit of forest, I assure you. So Miss Slessor stood waiting in the broiling sun, in the hot season's height, while a path was being cut to enable her just to get through to her own grounds. The natives worked away hard, knowing that it saved the polluting of a long stretch of market road, and when it was finished Miss Slessor went to her own house by it and attended with all kindness, promptness, and skill, to the woman and children. I arrived in the middle of this affair for my first meeting with Miss Slessor, and things at Okẏon were rather crowded, one way or another that afternoon. All the attention one of the children wanted—the boy, for there was a boy and a girl—was burying, for the people who had crammed them into the box had utterly smashed the child's head. The other child was alive, and is still a member of that household of rescued children all of whom owe their lives to Miss Slessor. There are among them twins from other districts, and delicate children who must have died had they been left in their villages, and a very wonderful young lady, very plump and very pretty, aged about four. Her mother died a few days after her birth, so the child was taken and thrown into the bush, by the side of the road that led to the market. This was done one market-day some distance from the Okẏon town. This particular market is held every ninth day, and on the succeeding market-day some women from the village by the side of Miss Slessor's house happened to pass along the path and heard the child feebly crying: they came into Miss Slessor's yard in the evening, and sat chatting over the day's shopping, &c., and casually mentioned in the way of conversation that they had heard the child crying, and that it was rather remarkable it should still be alive. Needless to say, Miss Slessor was off, and had that waif home. It was truly in an awful state, but just alive. In a marvelous way it had been left by leopards and snakes, with which the bit of forest abounds, and, more marvelous still, the driver ants had not scented it. Other ants had considerably eaten into it one way and another; nose, eyes, &c., were swarming with them and flies; the cartilage of the nose and part of the upper lip had been absolutely eaten into, but in spite of this she is now one of the prettiest black children I have ever seen, which is saying a good deal, for Negro children are very pretty with their round faces, their large mouths not yet coarsened by heavy lips, their beautifully shaped flat little ears, and their immense melancholy deer-like eyes, and above these charms they possess that of being fairly quiet. This child is not an object of terror, like the twin children; it was just thrown away because no one would be bothered to rear it, but when Miss Slessor had had all the trouble of it the natives had no objection to pet and play with it, calling it "the child of wonder," because of its survival.

With the twin baby it was very different. They would not touch it and only approached it after some days, and then only when it was held by Miss Slessor or me. If either of us wanted to do or get something, and we handed over the bundle to one of the house children to hold, there was a stampede of men and women off the verandah, out of the yard, and over the fence, if need be, that was exceedingly comic, but most convincing as to the reality of the terror and horror in which they held the thing. Even its own mother could not be trusted with the child; she would have killed it. She never betrayed the slightest desire to have it with her, and after a few days' nursing and feeding up she was anxious to go back to her mistress, who, being an enlightened woman, was willing to have her if she came without the child.

The main horror is undoubtedly of the child, the mother being killed more as a punishment for having been so intimately mixed up in bringing the curse, danger, and horror into the village than for anything else.

The woman went back by the road that had been cut for her coming, and would have to live for the rest of her life an outcast, and for a long time in a state of isolation, in a hut of her own into which no one would enter, neither would any one eat or drink with her, nor partake of the food or water she had cooked or fetched. She would lead the life of a leper, working in the plantation by day, and going into her lonely hut at night, shunned and cursed. I tried to find out whether there was any set period for this quarantine, and all I could arrive at was that if—and a very considerable if—a man were to marry her and she were subsequently to present to Society an acceptable infant, she would be to a certain extent socially rehabilitated, but she would always be a woman with a past—a thing the African, to his credit be it said, has no taste for.

The woman's own lamentations were pathetic. She would sit for hours singing or rather mourning out a kind of dirge over herself: "Yesterday I was a woman, now I am a horror, a thing all people run from. Yesterday they would eat with me, now they spit on me. Yesterday they would talk to me with a sweet mouth, now they greet me only with curses and execrations. They have smashed my basin, they have torn my clothes," and so on, and so on. These was no complaint against the people for doing these things, only a bitter sense of injury against some superhuman power that had sent this withering curse of twins down on her. She knew not why; she sang "I have not done this, I have not done that"—and highly interesting information regarding the moral standpoint a good deal of it was. I have tried to find out the reason of this widely diffused custom which is the cause of such a pitiful waste of life; for in addition to the mother and children being killed it often leads to other people, totally unconcerned in the affair, being killed by the relatives of the sufferer on the suspicion of having caused the calamity by witchcraft, and until one gets hold of the underlying idea, and can destroy that, the custom will be hard to stamp out in a district like the great Niger Delta. But I have never been able to hunt it down, though I am sure it is there, and a very quaint idea it undoubtedly is. The usual answer is, "It was the custom of our fathers," but that always and only means, "We don't intend to tell."

Funeral customs vary considerably between the Negro and Bantu, and I never yet found among the Bantu those unpleasant death charms which are in vogue in the Niger Delta.

The Calabar people, when the Consular eye is off them, bury under the house. In the case of a great chief the head is cut off and buried with great secrecy somewhere else, for reasons I have already stated.

The body is buried a few days after death, but the really important part of the funeral is the burying of the spirit, and this is the thing that causes all the West Africans, Negro and Bantu alike, great worry, trouble, and expense. For the spirit, no matter what its late owner may have been, is malevolent—all native-made spirits are. The family have to get together a considerable amount of wealth to carry out this burial of the spirit, so between the body-burying and the spirit-burying a considerable time usually elapses; maybe a year, maybe more. The custom of keeping the affair open until the big funeral can be made obtains also in Cabinda and Loango, but there, instead of burying the body in the meantime, it is placed upon a platform of wood, and slow fires keep going underneath to dry it, a mat roof being usually erected over it to keep off rain. When sufficiently dried, it is wrapped in clothes and put into a coffin, until the money to finish the affair is ready. The Duallas are more tied down; their death-dances must be celebrated, I am informed, on the third, seventh, and ninth day after death. On these days the spirit is supposed to be particularly present in its old home. In all the other cases, I should remark, the spirit does not leave the home until its devil is made and if this is delayed too long he naturally becomes fractious.

Among the Congo Français tribes there are many different kinds of burial—as the cannibalistic of the Fan. I may remark, however, that they tell me themselves that it is considered decent to bury a relative, even if you subsequently dig him up and dispose of the body to the neighbours. Then there is the earth-burial of the Igalwas and M'pongwe, and the beating into unrecognizable pulp of the body which, I am told on good native authority, is the method of several Upper Ogowe tribes, including the Adoomas. I had no opportunity of making quiet researches on burial customs when I was above Njoli, because I was so busy trying to avoid qualifying for a burial myself; so I am not quite sure whether this method is the general one among these little-known tribes, as I am told by native traders, who have it among them that it is—or whether it is reserved for the bodies of people believed to have been possessed of dangerous souls.

Destroying the body by beating up, or by cutting up, is a widely diffused custom in West Africa in the case of dangerous souls, and is universally followed with those that have contained wanderer-souls, i.e. those souls which keep turning up in the successive infants of a family. A child dies, then another child comes to the same father or mother, and that dies, after giving the usual trouble and expense. A third arrives and if that dies, the worm—the father, I mean—turns, and if he is still desirous of more children, he just breaks one of the legs of the body before throwing it in the bush.

This he thinks will act as a warning to the wanderer-soul and give it to understand that if it persist in coming into his family, it must settle down there and give up its flighty ways. If a fourth child arrives in the family, "it usually limps," and if it dies, the justly irritated parent cuts its body up carefully into very small pieces, and scatters them, doing away with the soul altogether.

The Kama country people of the lower Ogowé are more superstitious and full of observances than the upper river tribes.

Particularly rich in Fetish are the Ncomi, a Fernan Vaz tribe. I once saw a funeral where they had been called in to do the honors, and M. Jacot told me of an almost precisely similar occurrence that he had met with in one of his many evangelising expeditions from Lembarene. I will give his version because of his very superior knowledge of the language.

He was staying in a Fan town where one of the chiefs had just died. The other chief (there are usually two in a Fan town) decided that his deceased *confrère* should have due honor paid him, and resolved to do the thing handsomely.

The Fans openly own to not understanding thoroughly about death and life and the immortality of the soul, and things of that sort, and so the chief called in the Ncomi, who are specialists in these subjects, to make the funeral customs.

M. Jacot said the chief made a speech to the effect that the Fans did not know about these things, but their neighbours, the Ncomi, were known to be well versed in them and the proper things to do, so he had called them in to pay honour to the dead chief. Then the Ncomi started and carried on their weird, complicated death-dance.

The Fans sat and stood round watching them in a ring for a long time, but to a rational, common-sense, shrewd, unimaginative set of people like the Fans, just standing hour after hour gazing on a dance you do not understand, and which consists of a wriggle and a stamp, a wriggle and a stamp, in a solemn walk, or prance, round and round, to the accompaniment of a monotonous phrase thumped on a tom-tom and a monotonous, melancholy chant, uttered in a minor key interspersed every few minutes with an emphatic howl, produces a feeling of boredom, therefore the Fans softly stole away and went to bed, which disgusted the Ncomi, and there was a row. In the dance I saw the same thing happened, only when the Ncomi saw the audience getting thin they complained and said that they were doing this dance in honour of the Fans' chief, in a neighbourly way, and the very least the Fans could do, as they couldn't dance themselves, was to sit still and admire people who could. The Fan chief in my village quite saw it, and went and had the Fans who had gone home early turned up and made them come and see the performance some more; this they did for a time, and then stole off again, or slept in their seats, and the Ncomi were highly disgusted at those brutes of Fans, whom they regarded, they said in their way, as Philistines of an utterly obtuse and degraded type.

The Ncomi themselves put the body into coffins. A barrel is the usual one, but gun-cases or two trade boxes, the ends knocked out and the cases fitted together, is another frequent form of coffin used by them. These coffins are not buried, but are put into special places in the forest.

Along the bank of the Ogowé you will notice here and there long stretches of swamp forest. If you land on some of these and go in a little way you will find the forest full of mounds—or rather heaps, because they have no mould over them—made of branches of trees and leaves; under-neath each of these heaps there are the remains of a body. One very evil-looking place so used I found when I was on the Karkola river. Dr. Nassau tells me they are the usual burying grounds (*Abe*) of the Ajumbas.

CHAPTER 14

FETISH (CONTINUED)

*In which the Voyager discourses on the legal methods of natives of this country,
the ideas governing forms of burial, of their manner of mourning for their dead,
and the condition of the African soul in the under-world.*

GREAT AS ARE THE INCIDENTAL MISERIES and dangers surrounding
death to all the people in the village in which a death occurs, undoubtedly those who suffer most are the widows of a chief or free man.

The uniform custom among both Negroes and Bantus is that those
who escape execution on the charge of having witched the husband to
death, shall remain in a state of filth and abasement, not even removing
vermin from themselves, until after the soul-burial is complete—the
soul of the dead man being regarded as hanging about them and liable
to be injured. Therefore, also to the end of preventing his soul from
getting damaged, they are confined to their huts; this latter restriction
is not rigidly enforced, but it is held theoretically to be the correct thing.

They maintain the attitude of grief and abasement, sitting on the
ground, eating but little food, and that of a coarse kind. In Calabar their
legal rights over property, such as slaves, are meanwhile considerably in
abeyance, and they are put to great expense during the time the spirit is
awaiting burial. They have to keep watch, two at a time, in the hut, where
the body is buried, keeping lights burning, and they have to pay out of
their separate estate for the entertainment of all the friends of the

deceased who come to pay him compliment; and if he has been an important man, a big man, the whole district will come, not in a squadron, but just when it suits them, exactly as if they were calling on a live friend. Thus it often happens that even a big woman is bankrupt by the expense. I will not go into the legal bearings of the case here, for they are intricate, and, to a great extent, only interesting to a student of Negro law.

The Bantu women occupy a far inferior position in regard to the rights of property to that held by the Negro women.

The disposal of wives after the death of the husband among the M'pongwe and Igalwa is a subject full of interest; but it is, like most of their law, very complicated. The brothers of the deceased are supposed to take them—the younger brother may not marry the elder brother's widows, but the elder brothers may marry those of the younger brother. Should any of the women object to the arrangement, they may "leave the family."

I own that the ground principle of African law practically is "the simple plan that they should take who have the power, and they should keep who can," and this tells particularly against women and children who have not got living, powerful relations of their own. Unless the children of a man are grown up and sufficiently powerful on their own account, they have little chance of sharing in the distribution of his estate; but in spite of this abuse of power there is among Negroes and Bantus a definite and acknowledged Law, to which an appeal can be made by persons of all classes, provided they have the wherewithal to set the machinery of it in motion. The difficulty the children and widows have in sharing in the distribution of the estate of the father and husband arises, I fancy, in the principle of the husband's brothers being the true heir, which has sunk into a fossilized state near the trading stations in the face of white culture. The reason for this inheritance of goods passing from the man to his brother by the same mother has no doubt for one of its origins the recognition of the fact that the brother by the same mother must be a near relation, whereas, in spite of the strict laws against adultery, the relationship to you of the children born of your wives is not so certain. Nevertheless this is one of the obvious and easy explanations for things it is well to exercise great care before accepting, for you must always remember that the African's mind does not run on identical lines with the European—what may be self-evident to you is not so to him, and *vice versa*. I have frequently heard African metaphysicians complain that white men make great jumps in their thought-course, and do not follow an idea step by step. You soon become conscious of the careful way a Negro follows his idea. Certain customs of his you can, by the exercise of great patience, trace back in a perfectly smooth line from their source in some natural phenomenon. Others, of course, you cannot, the traces of the intervening steps of the idea have been lost, owing partly to the veneration in which old customs are held, which causes them to regard the fact that their fathers had this fashion as reason enough for their having it, and above all to the total absence of all but oral tradition. But so great a faith have I in the lack of inventive power in the African, that I feel sure all their customs, had we the material that has slipped down into the great swamp of time, could be traced back either, as I have said, to some natural phenomenon, or to the thing being advisable, for reasons of utility.

The uncertainty in the parentage of offspring may seem to be such a utilitarian underlying principle, but, on the other hand, it does not sufficiently explain the varied forms of the law of inheritance, for in some tribes the eldest or most influential son does succeed to his father's wealth; in other places you have the peculiar custom of the chief slave inheriting. I think, from these things, that the underlying idea in inheritance of property is the desire to keep the wealth of "the house," i.e. estate, together, and if it were allowed to pass into the hands of weak people, like women and young children, this would not be done. Another strong argument against the theory that it arises from the doubtful relationship of the son, is that certain ju-ju always go to the son of the chief wife, if he is old enough, at the time of the father's death, even in those tribes where the wealth goes elsewhere.

Certain tribes acknowledge the right of the women and children to share in the dead man's wealth, given that these are legally married wives, or the children of legally married wives; it is so in Cameroons, for example. An esteemed friend of mine who helps to manage things for the Fatherland down there was trying a palaver the other day with a patience peculiar to him, and that intelligent and elaborate care I should think only a mind trained on the methods of German metaphysicians could impart into that most wearisome of proceedings, wherein every one says the same thing over fourteen different times at least, with a similar voice and gesture, the only variation being in the statements regarding the important points, and the facts of the case, these varying with each individual. This palaver was made by a son claiming to inherit part of his father's property; at last, to the astonishment, and, of course, the horror, of the learned judge, the defendant, the wicked uncle, pleaded through the interpreter, "This man cannot inherit his father's property, because his parents married for love." There is no encouragement to foolishness of this kind in Cameroon, where legal marriage consists in purchase.

In Bonny River and in Opobo the inheritance of "the house" is settled primarily by a vote of the free men of the house; when the chief dies, their choice has to be ratified by the other chiefs of the house; but in Bonny and Opobo the white traders have had immense influence for a long time, so one cannot now find out how far this custom is purely native in idea.

Among the Fans the uncle is, as I have before said, an important person although the father has more rights than among the Igalwa, and here I came across a peculiar custom regarding widows. M. Jacot cited to me a similar case or so, one of which I must remark was in an Ajumba town. The widows were inside the dead husband's hut, as usual; the Fan huts are stoutly built of sheets of flattened bark, firmly secured together with bark rope, and thatched—they never build them in any other way except when they are in the bush rubber-collecting or elephant-hunting, when they make them of the branches of trees. Well, round the bark hut, with the widows inside, there was erected a hut made of branches, and when this was nearly completed, the Fans commenced pulling down the inner bark hut, and finally cleared it right out, thatch and all, and the materials of which it had been made were burnt. I was struck with the performance because the Fans, though surrounded by intensely superstitious tribes, are remarkably free from superstition themselves, taking little or no interest in speculative matters, except to get charms to make them invisible to elephants, to keep their feet in the path, to enable them to see things in the forest, and practical things of that sort, and these charms they frequently gave me to assist and guard me in my wanderings.

The M'pongwe and Igalwa have a peculiar funeral custom, but it is not confined in its operation to widows, all the near relatives sharing in it. The mourning relations are seated on the floor of the house, and some friend—Dr. Nassau told me he was called in in this capacity—comes in and "lifts them up," bringing to them a small present, a factor of which is always a piece of soap. This custom is now getting into the survival form in Libreville and Glass. Nowadays the relatives do not thus sit, unwashed and unkempt, keenly requiring the soap. Among the bush Igalwa, I am told, the soap is much wanted.

It is not only the widows that remain, either theoretically or practically unwashed; all the mourners do. The Ibibios seem to me to wear the deepest crape in the form of accumulated dirt, and all the African tribes I have met have peculiar forms of hair cutting—shaving the entire head, not shaving it at all, shaving half of it, &c.—when in mourning. The period of the duration of wearing mourning is, I believe, in all West Coast tribes that which elapses between the death and the burial of the soul. I believe a more thorough knowledge would show us that there is among the Bantu also a fixed time for the lingering of the soul on earth after death, but we have not got sufficient evidence on the point yet. The only thing we know is that it is not proper for the widow to re-marry while her husband's soul is still in her vicinity.

Among the Calabar tribes the burial of his spirit liberates the woman. Among the Tschwi she requires special ceremonies on her own account. In Togoland, among the Ewe people, I know the period is between five and six weeks, during which time the widow remains in the hut, armed with a good stout stick, as a precaution against the ghost of her husband, so as to ward off attacks should he be ill-tempered. After these six weeks the widow can come out of the hut, but as his ghost has not permanently gone hence, and is apt to revisit the neighbourhood for the next six months, she has to be taken care of during this period. Then, after certain ceremonies, she is free to marry again. So I conclude the period of mourning, in all tribes, it that period during which the soul remains round its old possessions, whether these tribes have a definite soul-burial or devil-making or not.

The ideas connected with the under-world to which the ghost goes are exceedingly interesting. The Negroes and Bantus are at one on these subjects in one particular only, and that is that no marriages take place there. The Tschwis say that this under-world, Srahmandazi, is just the same as this world in all other particulars, save that it is dimmer, a veritable shadow-land where men have not the joys of life, but only the shadow of the joy. Hence, says the Tschwi proverb, "One day in this world is worth a year in Srahmandazi." The Tschwis, with their usual definiteness in this sort of detail, know all about their Srahmandazi. Its entrance is just east of the middle Volta, and the way down is difficult to follow, and when the sun sets on this world it rises on Srahmandazi. The

Bantus are vague on this important and interesting point. The Benga, for example, although holding the absence of marriage there, do not take steps to meet the case as the Tschwis do, and kill a supply of wives to take down with them. This reason for killing wives at a funeral is another instance that, however strange and cruel a custom may be here in West Africa, however much it may at first appear to be the flower of a rootless superstition, you will find on close investigation that it has some root in a religious idea, and a common-sense element. The common-sense element in the killing of wives and slaves among both the Tschwi and the Calabar tribes consists in the fact that it discourages poisoning. A Calabar chief elaborately explained to me that the rigorous putting down of killing at funerals that was being carried on by the Government not only landed a man in the next world as a wretched pauper, but added an additional chance to his going there prematurely, for his wives and slaves, no longer restrained by the prospect of being killed at his death and sent off with him would, on very slight aggravation, put "bush in his chop." It is sad to think of this thorn being added to the rose-leaves of a West Coast chief's life, as there are 99 9/10 per cent of thorns in it already.

I came across a similar case on the Gold Coast, when a chief complained to me of the way the Government were preserving vermin, in the shape of witches, in the districts under its surveillance. You were no longer allowed to destroy them as of old, and therefore the vermin were destroying the game; for, said he, the witches here live almost entirely on the blood they suck from children at night. They used, in old days, to do this furtively, and do so now where native custom is unchecked; but in districts where the Government says that witchcraft is utter nonsense, and killing its proficient utter murder which will be dealt with accordingly, the witch flourishes exceedingly, and blackmails the fathers and mothers of families, threatening that if they are not bought off they will have their child's blood; and if they are not paid, the child dies away gradually—poison again, most likely.

I often think it must be the common-sense element in fetish customs that enables them to survive, in the strange way they do, in the minds of Africans who have been long under European influence and education. In witching, for example, every intelligent native knows there is a lot of poison in the affair, but the explanation he gives you will not usually display this knowledge, and it was not until I found the wide diffusion of the idea of the advisability of administering an emetic to the bewitched person, that I began to suspect my black friends of sound judgment.

The good ju-juist will tell you all things act by means of their life, which means their power, their spirit. Dr. Nassau tells me the efficacy of drugs is held to depend on their benevolent spirits, which, on being put into the body, drive away the malevolent disease-causing spirits—a leucocytes-versus-pathogenic-bacteria sort of influence, I suppose. On this same idea also depends the custom of the appeal to ordeal, the working of which is supposed to be spiritual. Nevertheless, the intelligent native, believing all the time in this factor, squares the common-sense factor by bribing the witch-doctor who makes the ordeal drink.

The feeling regarding the importance of funeral observances is quite Greek in its intensity. Given a duly educated African, I am sure that he would grasp the true inwardness of the Antigone far and away better than any European now living can. A pathetic story which bears on this feeling was told me some time ago by Miss Slessor when she was stationed at Creek Town. An old blind slave woman was found in the bush, and brought into the mission. She was in a deplorable state, utterly neglected and starving, her feet torn by thorns and full of jiggers, and so on. Every care was taken of her and she soon revived and began to crawl about, but her whole mind was set on one thing with a passion that had made her alike indifferent to her past sufferings and to her present advantages. What she wanted was a bit, only a bit, of white cloth. Now, I may remark, white cloth is anathema to the Missions, for it is used for ju-ju offerings, and a rule has to be made against its being given to the unconverted, or the missionary becomes an accessory before the fact to pagan practices, so white cloth the old woman was told she could not have, she had been given plenty of garments for her own use and that was enough. The old woman, however, kept on pleading and saying the spirit of her dead mistress kept coming to her asking and crying for white cloth, and white cloth she must get for her, and so at last, finding it was not to be got at the Mission station, she stole away one day, unobserved, and wandered off into the bush, from which she never again reappeared, doubtless falling a victim to the many leopards that haunted hereabouts.

To provide a proper burial for the dead relation is the great duty of a Negro's life, its only rival in his mind is the desire to avoid having a burial of his own. But, in a good Negro, this passion will go under before the other, and he will risk his very life to do it. He may know, surely and well, that killing slaves and women at a dead brother's grave means hanging for him when their Big Consul knows of it, but in the Delta he will do it. On the Coast, Leeward and Windward, he will spend every penny he possess and, on top, if need be, go and pawn himself, his wives, or his children into slavery to give a deceased relation a proper funeral.

This killing at funerals I used to think would be more easily done away with in the Delta than among the Tschwi tribes, but a little more knowledge of the Delta's idea about the future life showed me I was wrong.

Among the Tschwi the slaves and women killed are to form for the dead a retinue, and riches wherewith to start life in Srahmandazi (Yboniadse of the Oji), where there are markets and towns and all things as on this earth, and so the Tschwi would have little difficulty in replacing human beings at funerals with gold-dust, cloth, and other forms of riches, and this is already done in districts under white influence. But in the Delta there is no under-world to live in, the souls shortly after reaching the under-world being forwarded back to this, in new babies, and the wealth that is sent down with a man serves as an indication as to what class of baby the soul is to be repacked and sent up in. As wealth in the Delta consists of women and slaves I do not believe the under-world gods of the Niger would understand the status of a chief who arrived before them, let us say, with ten puncheons of palm oil, and four hundred yards of crimson figured velvet; they would say, "Oh! Very good as far as it goes, but where is your real estate? The chances are you are only a trade slave boy and have stolen these things"; and in consequence of this, killing at funerals will be a custom exceedingly difficult to stamp out in these regions. Try and imagine yourself how abhorrent it must be to send down a dear and honoured relative to the danger of his being returned to this world shortly as a slave. There is no doubt a certain idea among the Negroes that some souls may get a rise in status on their next incarnation. You often hear a woman saying she will be a man next time, a slave he will be a freeman, and so on, but how or why some souls obtain promotion I have not yet sufficient evidence to show. I think a little more investigation will place this important point in my possession. I once said to a Calabar man, "But surely it would be easy for a man's friends to cheat; they could send down a chief's outfit with a man, though he was only a small man here?"

"No," said he, "the other souls would tell on him, and then he would get sent up as a dog or some beast as a punishment."

My first conception of the prevalence of the incarnation idea was also gained from a Delta Negro. I said, "Why in the world do you throw away in the bush the bodies of your dead slaves? Where I have been they tie a string to the leg of a dead slave and when they bury him bring the string to the top and fix it to a peg, with the owner's name on, and then when the owner dies he has that slave again down below."

"They be fool men," said he, and he went on to explain that the ghost of that slave would be almost immediately back on earth again growing up ready to work for some one else, and would not wait for its last owner's soul down below, and out of the luxuriant jungle of information that followed I gathered that no man's soul dallies below long, and also that a soul returning to a family, a thing ensured by certain ju-jus, was identified. The new babies as they arrive in the family are shown a selection of small articles belonging to deceased members whose souls are still absent; the thing the child catches hold of identifies him. "Why he's Uncle John, see! He knows his own pipe;" or "That's cousin Emma, see! She knows her market calabash," and so on.

I remember discoursing with a very charming French official on the difficulty of eradicating fetish customs.

"Why not take the native in the rear, Mademoiselle," said he, "and convert the native gods?"

I explained that his ingenious plan was not feasible, because you cannot convert gods. Even educating gods is hopeless work. All races of men through countless ages, have been attempting to make their peculiar deities understand how they are wanted to work, and what they are wanted to do, and the result is anything but encouraging.

As I have dwelt on the repellent view of Negro funeral custom, I must in justice to them cite their better view. There is a custom that I missed much on going south of Calabar, for it is a pretty one. Outside the villages in the Calabar districts, by the sides of the most frequented roads, you will see erections of boughs. I do not think these are intended for huts, but for beds, for they are very like the Calabar type of bed, only made in wood instead of clay. Over them a roof of mats is put, to furnish a protection against rain.

These shelters—graves or fetish huts they are wrongly called by Europeans—are made by driving four longish stout poles into the ground while at the height of about three feet or so four more poles are tied so as to make a skeleton platform which is filled in with withies and made flat. Another set of five poles is tied above, and to these the roof is affixed. On the platform, is placed the bedding belonging to the deceased, the under cloth, counterpane, &c., and at the head are laid the pillows, bolster-shaped and stuffed with cotton-tree fluff, or shredded palm-leaves, and covered with some gaily-colored cotton cloth. In every case I have seen—and they amount to hundreds, for you cannot take an hour's walk even from Duke Town without coming upon a dozen or so of these erections—the pillows are placed so that the person lying on the bed would look towards the village.

On the roof and on the bed, and underneath it on the ground, are placed the household utensils that belonged to the deceased; the calabashes, the basins, the spoons cut out of wood, and the boughten iron ones, as we should say in Devon, and on the stakes are hung the other little possessions; there is one I know of made for the ghost of a poor girl who died, on to the stakes of which are hung the dolls and the little pincushions, &c., given her by a kind missionary.

Food is set out at these places and spirit poured over them from time to time, and sometimes, though not often, pieces of new cloth are laid on them. Most of the things are deliberately damaged before they are put on the home for the spirit; I do not think this is to prevent them from being stolen, because all are not damaged sufficiently to make them useless. There was a beautifully made spoon with a burnt-in pattern on one of these places when I left Calabar to go South, and on my return, some six months after, it was still there. On another there was a very handsome pair of market calabashes, also much decorated, that were only just chipped and in better repair than many in use in Calabar markets, and I make no doubt the spoon and they are still lying rotting among the *débris* of the pillows, &c. These places are only attended to during the time the spirit is awaiting burial, as they are regarded merely as a resting-place for it while it is awaiting the ceremony. The body is not buried near them, I may remark.

In spite, however, of the care that is taken to bury spirits, a considerable percentage from various causes—poverty of the relations, the deceased being a stranger in the land, accidental death in some unknown part of the forest or the surf—remain unburied, and hang about to the common danger of the village they may choose to haunt. Many devices are resorted to, to purify the villages from these spirits. One which was in use in Creek Town, Calabar, to within a few years ago, and which I am informed is still customary in some interior villages, was very ingenious, and believed to work well by those who employed it.

In the houses were set up Nbakim, - large, grotesque images carved of wood and hung about with cloth strips and gew-gaws. Every November in Creek Town (I was told by some authorities it was every second November) there was a sort of festival held. Offerings of food and spirits were placed before these images; a band of people accompanied by the rest of the population used to make a thorough round of the town, up and down each street and round every house, dancing, singing, screaming and tom-toming, in fact making all the noise they knew how to—and a Calabar Effik is very gifted in the power of making noise. After this had been done for what was regarded as a sufficient time, the images were taken out of the houses, the crowd still making a terrific row and were then thrown into the river, and the town was regarded as being cleared of spirits.

The rationale of the affair is this. The wandering spirits are attracted by the images, and take shelter among their rags, like earwigs or something of that kind. The *charivari* is to drive any of the spirits who might be away from their shelters back into them. The shouting of the mob is to keep the spirits from venturing out again while they are being carried to the river. The throwing of the images, rags, and all, into the river, is to destroy the spirits or at least send them elsewhere. They did not go and pour boiling water on their earwig-traps, as wicked white men do, but they made and set up new images for fresh spirits who might come into the town, and these were kept and tended as before, until the next N'dok ceremony came round.

It is owing to the spiritual view which the African takes of existence at large that ceremonial observances form the greater part of even his common-law procedure.

There is, both among the Negro and Bantu, a recognized code of law, founded on principles of true but merciless justice. It is not often employed, because of the difficulty and the danger to the individual who appeals to it, should that individual be unbacked by power, but nevertheless the code exists.

The African is particularly hard on theft; he by no means "compounds for sins he is inclined to by damning those he has no mind to," for theft is a thing he revels in.

Persons are tried for theft on circumstantial evidence, direct testimony, and ordeal. Laws relating to mortgage are practically the same among Negroes and Bantu and Europeans. Torts are not recognized; unless the following case from Cameroon points to a vague realization of them. A. let his canoe out to B., in good order, so that B. could go up river, and fetch down some trade. B. did not go himself, but let C., who was not his slave, but another free man who also wanted to go up for trade, have the canoe on the understanding that in payment for the loan of the said canoe C. should bring down B's. trade.

A. was not told about this arrangement at all. B. says A. was, only A. was so blind drunk at the time he did not understand. Well, up river C. goes in the canoe, and fetches up on a floating stump in the river, and staves a hole you could put your head in, in the bow of the said canoe. C. returns it to B. in this condition. B. returns it to A. in this condition. A. sues B. before native chief, saying he lent his canoe to B. on the understanding, always implied in African loans, that it was to be returned in the same state as when lent, fair wear and tear alone excepted. B. tries first to get C. to pay for the canoe, and for the rent of the canoe on top, as a compensation for the delay in bringing down his, B's., trade. C. calls B. the illegitimate offspring of a greenhouse-lizard, and pleads further that the floating log was a *force majeure*—an act of God, and denies liability on all counts. B. then pleads this as his own defence in the case of A. and B. (authorities cited in support of this view); he also pleads he is not liable, because C. is a free man, and not his slave.

The case went on for a week; the judge was drunk for five days in his attempt to get his head clear. The decision finally was that B. was to pay A. full compensation. B. *v.* C. is still pending.

The laws against adultery are, theoretically, exceedingly severe. The punishment is death, and this is sometimes carried out. The other day King Bell in Cameroon flogged one of his wives to death, and the German Government have deposed and deported him, for you cannot do that sort of thing with impunity within a stone's throw of a Government head-quarters. But as a general rule all along the Coast the death penalty for murder or adultery is commuted to a fine, or you can send a substitute to be killed for you, if you are rich. This is frequently done, because it is cheaper, if you have a seedy slave, to give him to be killed in your stead than to pay a fine which is often enormous.

The adultery itself is often only a matter of laying your hand, even in self-defence from a virago, on a woman—or brushing against her in the path. These accusations of adultery are, next to witchcraft, the great social danger to the West Coast native, and they are often made merely from motives of extortion or spite, and without an atom of truth in them.

It is customary for the chief to put his wives frequently to ordeal on this point, and this is almost always done after there has been a big devil-making, or a dance, which his family have been gracing with their presence. The usual method of applying the ordeal is by boiling palm-oil—a pot is nearly filled with the oil, which is brought to the boil over a fire; when it is seething, the woman to be tried is brought out in front of it. She first dips her hand into water, and then has administered to her the M'biam oath saying or having said for her that long elaborate formula, in a form adjusted to meet the case. Then she plunges her hand into the boiling oil for an instant, and shakes the oil off with all possible rapidity, and the next woman comes forward and goes through the same performance, and so on. Next day, the hands of the women are examined, and those found blistered are adjudged guilty, and punished. In order to escape heavy punishment the women will accuse some man of having hustled against her, or sat down on a bench beside her, and so on, and the accused man has to pay up. If he does not, in the Calabar district, Egbo will come and "eat the adultery," and there won't be much of that man's earthly goods left. Sometimes the accusation is volunteered by the woman, and frequently the husband and wife conspire together and cook up a case against a man for the sake of getting the damages. There is nothing that ensures a man an unblemished character in West Africa, save the possession of sufficient power to make it risky work for people to cast slurs on it.

The ownership of children is a great source of palaver. The law among Negroes and Bantus is that the children of a free woman belong to her. In the case of tribes believing in the high importance of uncles considerable powers are vested in that relative, while in other tribes certain powers are vested in the father.

The children of slave wives are the only children the father has absolute power over if he is the legal owner of the slave woman. If, as is frequently the case, a free man marries a slave woman who belongs to another man, all her children are the absolute property of her owner, not her husband; and the owner of the woman can take them and sell them, or do whatsoever he chooses with them, unless the free man father redeems them, as he usually does, although the woman may still remain the absolute property of the owner, recallable by him at any time.

This law is the cause of the most brain-spraining palavers that come before the white authorities. There is naturally no statute of limitations in West Africa, because the African does not care a row of pins about time. The wily A. will let his slave woman live with B. without claiming the redemption fees as they become due—letting them stand over, as it were, at compound interest. All the male as well as the female children of the first generation are A.'s property, and all the female children of these children are his property even unto the second and third generations and away into eternity. A. may die before he puts in his claim, in which case the ownership passes on into the hands of his heir or assignees, who may foreclose at once, on entering into their heritage, or may again let things accumulate for their heirs. Anyhow, sooner or later the foreclosure comes and then there is trouble. X., Y., Z., &c., free men, have married some of the original A.'s slave woman's descendants. They have either bought them right out, or kept on conscientiously redeeming children of theirs as they arrived. Of course A., or his heirs, contend that X., Y., Z., &c. have been wasting time and money by so doing, because the people X., Y., Z. have paid the money to had no legal title to the women. Of course X., Y., Z. contend that their particular woman, or her ancestress, was duly redeemed from the legal owner.

Remember there is no documentary evidence available, and squads of equally reliable and oldest inhabitants are swearing hard-all both ways. Just realise this, and that your Government says that whenever native law is not blood-stained it must be supported, and you may be able to realise the giddy mazes of a native palaver, which if you conscientiously attempt to follow with the determination that justice shall be duly administered, will for certain lay you low with an attack of fever.

The law of ownership is not all in favour of the owner, masters being responsible for damage done by their slaves, and this law falls very heavily and expensively on the owner of a bad slave. Indeed, when one lives out here and sees the surrounding conditions of this state of culture, the conviction grows on you that, morally speaking, the African is far from being the brutal fiend he is often painted, a creature that loves cruelty and blood for their own sake. The African does not; and though his culture does not contain our institutions, lunatic asylums, prisons, workhouses, hospitals, &c., he has to deal with the same classes of people who requires these things. So with them he deals by means of his equivalent institutions, slavery, the lash, and death. You have just as much right, my logical friend, to call the West Coast Chief hard names for his habit of using brass bars, heads of tobacco, and so on, in place of sixpenny pieces, as you have to abuse him for clubbing an inveterate thief. It's deplorably low of him, I own, but by what alternative plan of government his can be replaced I do not quite see, under existing conditions. In religious affairs, the affairs which lead him into the majority of his iniquities, his real sin consists in believing too much. In his witchcraft, the sin is the same. Toleration means indifference, I believe, among all men. The African is not indifferent on the subject of witchcraft, and I do not see how one can expect him to be. Put yourself in his place and imagine you have got hold of a man or woman who has been placing a live crocodile or a catawumpus of some kind into your own or a valued relative's, or fellow-townsman's inside, so that it may eat up valuable viscera, and cause you or your friend suffering and death. How would you feel? A little like lynching your captive, I fancy.

I confess that the more I know of the West Coast Africans the more I like them. I own I think them fools of the first water for their power of believing in things; but I fancy I have analogous feelings towards even my fellow-countrymen when they go and violently believe in something that I cannot quite swallow.

CHAPTER 15

FETISH (CONTINUED)

In which the Voyager complains
of the inconveniences arising from the method of African thought,
and discourses on apparitions and Deities.

HOWEVER MUCH SOME OF THE AFRICAN'S mental attributes get under-rated, I am sure there are others of them for which he gets more credit than he deserves. One of these is his imagination. It strikes the new-comer with awe, and frequently fills him with rage, when he first meets it; but as he matures and gets used to the African, he sees the string. For the African fancy is not the "aërial fancy flying free," mentioned by our poets, but merely the aërial of the theatre suspended by a wire or cord. The wire that supports the African's fancy may be a very thing, small fact indeed, or in some cases merely his incapacity to distinguish between animate and inanimate objects, which give rise to his idea that everything is possessed of a soul. Everything has a soul to him, and to make confusion worse confounded, he usually believes in the existence of matter apart from its soul. But there is little he won't believe in, if it comes to that; and I have a feeling of thankfulness that Buddhism, Theosophy, and above all Atheism, which chases its tail and proves that nothing can be proved, have not yet been given the African to believe in.

The African's want of making it clear in his language whether he is referring to an animate or inanimate thing, has landed me in many a dilemma, and his foolishness in not having a male and female gender in his languages amounts to a nuisance. For example, I am a most ladylike old person and yet get constantly called "Sir." The other day, circumstances having got beyond my control during the afternoon, I arrived in the evening in a saturated condition at a white settlement, and wishing to get accommodation for myself and my men, I made my way to the factory of a firm from whose representatives I have always received great and most courteous help. The agent in charge was not at home, and his steward-boy said, "Massa live for Mr. B.'s house." "Go tell him I live for come from," &c., said I, and "I fit for want place for my men." I had nothing to write on, or with, and I thought the steward-boy could carry this little message to its destination without dropping any of it, as Mr. B.'s house was close by; but I was wrong. Off he went, and soon returned with the note I here give a copy of:—

"Dear Old Man,
"You must be in a deuce of a mess after the tornado. Just help yourself to a set of my dry things. The shirts are in the bottom drawer, the trousers are in the box under the bed, and then come over here to the sing-song. My leg is dickey or I'd come across.—Yours,"&c.

Had there been any smelling salts or sal volatile in this subdivision of the Ethiopian region I should have forthwith fainted on reading this, but I well knew there was not, so I blushed until the steam from my soaking clothes (for I truly was "in a deuce of a mess") went up in a cloud and then, just as I was, I went "across" and appeared before the author of that awful note. When he came round, he said it had taken seven years' growth out of him, and was intensely apologetic. I remarked it had very nearly taken thirty years' growth out of me, and he said the steward boy had merely informed him that "White man live for come from X," a place where he knew there was another factory belonging to his firm, and he naturally thought it was the agent from X who had come across.

You rarely, indeed I believe never, find an African with a gift for picturesque descriptions of scenery. The nearest approach to it I ever got was from my cook when we were on Mungo mah Lobeh. He proudly boasted he had been on a mountain, up Cameroon River, with a German officer, and on that mountain, "If you fall down one side you die, if you fall down other side you die."

Graphic and vivid descriptions of incidents you often get, but it is
not Art. The effect is produced entirely by a bald brutality of statement,
the African having no artistic reticence whatsoever. One fine touch,
however, which does not come in under this class was told me by my
lamented friend Mr. Harris of Calabar. Some years ago he had out a
consignment of Dutch clocks with hanging weights, as is natural to the
Dutch clock. They were immensely popular among the chiefs, and were
soon disposed of save one, which had seen trouble on the voyage out and
lost one of its weights. Mr. Harris, who was a man of great energy and
resource, melted up some metal spoons and made a new weight and
hung it on the clock. The day he finished this a chief came in, anxious
for a Dutch clock, and Mr. Harris forthwith sold him the repaired one.
About a week elapsed, and then the chief turned up at the factory again
with a rueful countenance, followed by a boy carrying something
swathed in a cloth. It was the clock.

"You do me bad too much, Mr. Harris," said the chief. Mr. Harris
denied this on the spot with the vehemence of injured innocence. The
chief shook his head and spat profusely and sorrowfully.

"You no sabe him clock you done sell me?" said he. "When I look him
clock it no be to-day, it be to-morrow." Mr. Harris took the clock back, to
see what was the cause of this strange state of affairs. Of course it arose from
him having been too liberal in the amount of spoon in the weight, and this
being altered, the chief was not hurried onward to his grave at such a
rattling pace; "but," said Mr. Harris, "that clock was a flyer to the last."

But I will not go into the subject of African languages here, but only
remark of them that although they are elaborate enough to produce, for
their users, nearly every shade of erroneous statement, they are not, save
perhaps M'pongwe, elaborate enough to enable a native to state his exact
thought. Some of them are very dependent on gesture. When I was with
the Fans they frequently said, "We will go to the fire so that we can see
what they say," when any question had to be decided after dark, and the
inhabitants of Fernando Po, the Bubis, are quite unable to converse with
each other unless they have sufficient light to see the accompanying gestures of the conversation. In all cases I feel sure the African's intelligence
is far ahead of his language.

The African is usually great at dreams, and has them very noisily;
but he does not seem to me to attach immense importance to them,
certainly not so much as the Red Indian does. I doubt whether there is

much real ground for supposing that from dreams came man's first conception of the spirit world, and I think the origin of man's religious belief lies in man's misfortunes.

There can be little doubt that the very earliest human beings found, as their descendants still find, their plans frustrated, let them plan ever so wisely and carefully; they must have seen their companions overtaken by death and disaster, arising both from things they could see and from things they could not see. The distinction between these two classes of phenomena is not so definitely recognized by savages or animals as it is by the more cultured races of humanity. I doubt whether a savage depends on his five senses alone to teach him what the world is made of, any more than a Fellow of the Royal Society does. From this method of viewing nature I feel sure that the general idea arose—which you find in all early cultures — that death was always the consequence of the action of some malignant spirit, and that there is no accidental or natural death, as we call it; and death is, after all, the most impressive attribute of life.

If a man were knocked on the head with a club, or shot with an arrow, the cause of death is clearly the malignancy of the person using these weapons; and so it is easy to think that a man killed by a fallen tree, or by the upsetting of a canoe in the surf, or in an eddy in the river, is also the victim of some being using these things as weapons.

A man having thus gained a belief that there are more than human actors in life's tragedy, the idea that disease is also a manifestation of some invisible being's wrath and power seems to me natural and easy; and he knows you can get another man for a consideration to kill or harm a third party, and so he thinks that, for a consideration, you can also get one of these superhuman beings, which we call gods or devils, but which the African regards in another light, to do so.

A certain set of men and women then specialise off to study how these spirits can be managed, and so arises a priesthood; and the priests, or medicine men as they are called in their earliest forms, gradually, for their own ends, elaborate and wrap round their profession with ritual and mystery.

The savage is also conscious of another great set of phenomena which, he soon learns, take no interest in human affairs. The sun which rises and sets, the moon which changes, the tides which come and go:—what do they care? Nothing; and what is more, sacrifice to them what you may, you cannot get them to care about you and your affairs, and so the savage turns his attention to those other spirits that do take only too much interest, as is proved by those unexpected catastrophes; and, as their actions show, these spirits are all malignant, so he deals with them just as he would deal with a bad man whom he was desirous of managing. He flatters and fees them, he deprives himself of riches to give to them as sacrifices, believing they will relish it all the more because it gives him pain of some sort to give it to them. He holds that they think it will be advisable for them to encourage him to continue the giving by occasionally doing what he asks them. Naturally he never feels sure of them; he sees that you may sacrifice to a god for years, you may wrap him up—or more properly speaking, the object in which he resides—in your only cloth on chilly nights while you shiver yourself; you and your children, and your mother, and your sister and her children, may go hungry that food may rot upon his shrine; and yet, in some hour of dire necessity, the power will not come and save you—because he has been lured away by some richer gifts than yours.

You white men will say, "Why go on believing in him then?" but that is an idea that does not enter the African mind. I might just as well say "Why do you go on believing in the existence of hansom cabs," because one hansom cab driver malignantly fails to take you where you want to go, or fails to arrive in time to catch a train you wished to catch.

The African fully knows the liability of his fetish to fail, but he equally fully knows its power. One, to me, grandly tragic instance of this I learnt at Opobo. There was a very great Fetish doctor there, universally admired and trusted, who lived out on the land at the mouth of the Great River. One day he himself fell sick, and he made ju-ju against the sickness; but it held on, and he grew worse. He made more ju-ju of greater power, but again in vain, and then he made the greatest ju-ju man can make, and it availed naught, and he knew he was dying; and so, with his remaining strength, he broke up and dishonored and destroyed all the Fetishes in which the spirits lived, and cast them out into the surf and died like a man.

Then horror came upon the people when they knew he had done this, and they burnt his house and all things belonging to him, and cried upon the spirits not to forsake them, not to lay this one man's deadly sin at their doors.

In connection with the gods of West Africa I may remark that in almost all the series of native tradition there, you will find accounts of a time when there was direct intercourse between the gods or spirits that live in the sky, and men. That intercourse is always said to have been cut off by some human error; for example, the Fernando Po people say that once upon a time there was no trouble or serious disturbance upon earth because there was a ladder, made like the one you get palm-nuts with, "only long, long;" and this ladder reached from earth to heaven so the gods could go up and down it and attend personally to mundane affairs. But one day a cripple boy started to go up the ladder, and he had got a long way up when his mother saw him, and went up in pursuit. The gods, horrified at the prospect of having boys and women invading heaven, threw down the ladder, and have since left humanity severely alone. The Timneh people, north-east of Sierra Leone, say that in old times God was very friendly with men, and when He thought a man had lived long enough on earth, He sent a messenger to him telling him to come up into the sky, and stay with Him; but once there was a man who, when the messenger of God came, did not want to leave his wives, his slaves, and his riches, and so the messenger had to go back without him; and God was very cross and sent another messenger for him, who was called Disease, but the man would not come for him either, and so Disease sent back word to God that he must have help to bring the man; and so God sent another messenger whose name was Death; and Disease and Death together got hold of the man, and took him to God; and God said in future He would always send these messengers to fetch men.

The Fernando Po legend may be taken as fairly pure African, but the Timneh, I expect, is a transmogrified Arabic story—though I do not know of anything like it among Arabic stories; but they are infinite in quantity, and there is a certain ring about it I recognize, and these Timnehs are much in contact with the Mohammedan, Mandingoes, &c. In none of the African stories is there given anything like the importance to dreams that there is given to attempts to account for accidents and death; and surely it must have been more impressive and important to a man to have got his leg or arm snapped off by a crocodile in the river, or by a shark in the surf, or to have got half killed, or have seen a friend killed by a falling tree in the forest in the day time, than to have experienced the most wonderful of dreams. He sees that however terrific his dream-experiences may have been, he was not much the worse for them. Not so in the other case, a limb gone or a life gone is more impressive, and more necessary to account for.

No trace of sun-worship have I ever found. The firmament is, I believe, always the great indifferent and neglected god, the Nyan Kupon of the Tschwi, and the Anzambe, Nzam, &c., of the Bantu races. The

African thinks this god has great power if he would only exert it, and when things go very badly with him, when the river rises higher than usual and sweeps away his home and his plantations; when the smallpox stalks through the land, and day and night the corpses float down the river past him, and he finds them jammed among his canoes that are tied to the beach, and choking up his fish traps; and then when at last the death-wail over its victims goes up night and day from his own village, he will rise up and call upon this great god in a terror maddened by despair, that he may hear and restrain the evil workings of these lesser devils; but he evidently finds, as Peer Gynt says, "Nein, er hört nicht. Er ist taub wie gewöhnlich" for there is no organized cult for Anzam.

Accounts of apparitions abound in all the West Coast districts, and although the African holds them all in high horror and terror, he does not see anything super-natural in his "Duppy." It is a horrid thing to happen on, but there is nothing strange about it, and he is ten thousand times more frightened than puzzled over the affair. He does not want to "investigate" to see whether there is anything in it. He wants to get clear away, and make ju-ju against it, "one time."

These apparitions have a great variety of form, for, firstly, there are all the true spirits, nature spirits; secondly, the spirits of human beings—these human spirits are held to exist before as well as during and after bodily life; thirdly, the spirits of things. Probably the most horrid of class one is the Tschwee's Sasabonsum. Whether Sasabonsum is an individual or a class is not quite clear, but I believe he is a class of spirits, each individual of which has the same characteristics, the same manner of showing anger, the same personal appearance, and the same kind of residence. I am a devoted student of his cult and I am always coming across equivalent forms of him in other tribes as well as the Tschwi, and I think he is very early. As the Tschwi have got their religious notions in a most tidy and definite state, we will take their version of Sasabonsum.

He lives in the forest, in or under those great silk-cotton trees around the roots of which the earth is red. This colored earth identifies a silk-cotton tree as being the residence of a Sasabonsum, as its color is held to arise from the blood it whips off him as he goes down to his under-world home after a night's carnage. All silk-cotton trees are suspected because they are held to be the roosts for Duppies. But the red earth ones are feared with a great fear, and no one makes a path by them, or a camp near them at night.

Sasabonsum is a friend of witches. He is of enormous size, and of a red color. He wears his hair straight and he waylays unprotected wayfarers in the forest at night, and in all districts except that of Apollonia he eats them. Round Apollonia he only sucks their blood. Natives of this district after meeting him have crawled home and given an account of his appearance, and then expired.

Ellis says he is believed to be implacable, and when angered can never be mollified or propitiated, but it is certain that human victims are constantly sacrificed to him in districts beyond white control; in districts under it, the equivalent value of a human sacrifice in sheep and goats is offered to him. In Ashantee he has priests, and of course human sacrifice. Away among the Dahomeyan tribes—where he has kept his habits but got another name, and seems to have crystallized from a class into an individual—the usual way in which a god develops—he has priests and priestesses, and they are holy terrors; but among the Tschwi, Sasabonsum is mainly dealt with by witches, and people desirous of possessing the power of becoming witches. They derive their power from him in a remarkable way. I put myself to great personal inconvenience (fever risk, mosquito certainty, high leopard and snake palaver probability, and grave personal alarm and apprehension) to verify Colonel Ellis's account of the methods witches employ in this case, to obtain ehsuhman and I find his account correct.

The chief use of a suhman is the power it gives its owner to procure the death of other people, not necessarily his own enemies, for he will sell charms made by the agency of his suhman to another person whose nerves have not been equal to facing Sasabonsum on his own account. He can also provide by its agency other charms, such as those that protect houses from fire, and things and individuals from accidents on the road, or in canoes, and the home circle from good-looking but unprincipled young men, and so on.

As a rule the person who has a suhman keeps the fact pretty quiet, for the possession of such an article would lead half the catastrophes in his district, from the decease of pigs, fowls, and babies, to fires, &c., to be accredited to him, which would lead to his neighbors making "witch palaver" over him, and he would have to undergo poison-ordeal and other unpleasantness to clear his character. He, however, always keeps a special day in his suhman's honor, and should he be powerful, as a king or big chief, he will keep this day openly. King Kwoffi Karri Kari, whom we fought with in 1874, used to make a big day for his suhman, which was kept in a box covered with gold plates, and he sacrificed a human victim to it every Tuesday, with general festivities and dances in its honour.

I should remark that Sasabonsum is married. His wife, or more properly speaking his female form, is called Shamantin. She is far less malignant than the male form. Her name comes from Srahman—ghost or spirit; the termination "*tin*" is an abbreviation of *sintstin*—tall. She is of immense height, and white; perhaps this idea is derived from the white stem of the silk-cotton trees wherein she invariably abides. Her method of dealing with the solitary wayfarer is no doubt inconvenient to him, but it is kinder than her husband's ways, for she does not kill and eat him, as Sasabonsum does, but merely detains him some months while she teaches him all about the forest: what herbs are good to eat, or to cure disease; where the game come to drink, and what they say to each other, and so forth. I often wish I knew this lady, for the grim, grand African forests are like a great library, in which, so far, I can do little more than look at the pictures, although I am now busily learning the alphabet of their language, so that I may some day read what these pictures mean.

Do not go away with the idea, I beg, that goddesses as a general rule, are better than gods. They are not. There are stories about them which I could—I mean I could not—tell you. There is one belonging also to the Tschwee. She lives at Moree, a village five miles from Cape Coast. She is, as is usual with deities, human in shape and colossal in size, and as is not usual with deities, she is covered with hair from head to foot,—short white hair like a goat. Her abode is on the path to surf-cursed Anamabu near the sea-beach, and her name is Aynfwa; a worshipper of hers has only got to mention the name of a person he wishes dead when passing her abode and Aynfwa does the rest. She is the goddess of all albinos, who are said to be more frequent in occurrence round Moree than elsewhere. Ellis says that in 1886, when he was there, they were 1 percent of the entire population. These albinos are, *ipso facto*, her priests and priestesses, and in old days an albino had only to name anywhere a person Aynfwa wished for, and that person was forthwith killed.

I think I may safely say that every dangerous place in West Africa is regarded as the residence of a god—rocks and whirlpools in the rivers— swamps "no man fit to pass"—and naturally, the surf. Along the Gold Coast, at every place where you have to land through the surf, it fairly swarms with gods. A little experience with the said surf inclines you to

think; as the dabblers in spiritualism say "that there is something in it."
I will back this West Coast surf—"the Calemma," as we call it down South,
against any other malevolent abomination, barring only the English climate. Its ways of dealing with human beings are cunning and deceitful.
In its most ferocious moods it seizes a boat, straightway swamps it, and
feeds its pet sharks with the boat's occupants. If the surf is merely sky-
larking it lets your boat's nose just smell the sand, and then says "Thought
you were all right this time, did you though," and drags the boat back
again under the incoming wave, or catches it under the stern and gaily
throws it upside down over you and yours on the beach. Variety, they say,
is charming. Let those who say it, and those who believe it, just do a
course of surf-work, and I'll warrant they will change their minds.

There is one thing about the surf that I do not understand, and that
is why witches always walk stark naked along the beach by it at night, and
eat sea crabs the while. That such is a confirmed habit of theirs is certain; and they tell me that while doing this the witches emit a bright light,
and also that there is a certain medicine, which, if you have it with you,
you can throw over the witch, and then he, or she, will remain blazing
until morning time, running to and fro, crying out wildly, in front of
the white, breaking, thundering surf wall, and when the dawn comes the
fire burns the witch right up, leaving only a gray ash—and palaver set in
this world and the next for that witch.

A highly-esteemed native minister told me when I was at Cape
Coast last, that a fortnight before, he had been away in the Apollonia
district on mission work. One evening he and a friend were walking
along the beach and the night was dark, so that you could see only the
surf. It is never too dark to see that, it seems to have light in itself. They
saw a flame coming towards them, and after a moment's doubt they knew
it was a witch, and feeling frightened, hid themselves among the bushes
that edge the sandy shore. As they watched, it came straight on and
passed them, and they saw it disappear in the distance. My informant
laughed at himself, and very wisely said, "One has not got to believe
those things here, one has in Apollonia."

To the surf and its spirits the sea-board-dwelling Tschwees bring
women who have had children and widows, both after a period of eight
days from the birth of a child, or the death of a husband.

A widow remains in the house until this period has elapsed, neglecting
her person, eating little food, and sitting on the bare floor in the attitude

of mourning. On the Gold Coast they bury very quickly, as they are always telling you, usually on the day after death, rarely later than the third day, even among the natives; and the spirit, or Srah, of the dead man is supposed to hang about his wives and his house until the ceremony of purification is carried out. This is done, needless to say, with uproar. The relations of each wife go to her house with musical instruments—I mean tom-toms and that sort of thing—and they take a quantity of mint, which grows wild in this country, with them. This mint they burn, some of it in the house, the rest they place upon pans of live coals and carry round the widow as she goes in their midst down to the surf, her relatives singing aloud to the Srah of the departed husband, telling him that now he is dead and has done with the lady he must leave her. This singing serves to warn all the women who are not relations to get out of the way, which of course they always carefully do, because if they were to see the widow their own husbands would die within the year.

When the party has arrived at the shore, they strip every rag off the widow, and throw it into the surf; and a thoughtful female relative having brought a suit of dark blue baft with her for the occasion, the widow is clothed in this and returns homes, where a suitable festival is held, after which she may marry again; but if she were to marry before this ceremony, the Srah of the husband would play the mischief with husband number two or three, and so on, as the case might be.

In the inland Gold Coast districts the widows remain in a state of mourning for several months, and a selection of them, a quantity of slaves, and one or two free men are killed to escort the dead man to Srahmandazi; and as well as these, and in order to provide him with merchandise to keep up his house and state in the under-world, quantities of gold dust, rolls of rich velvets, silks, satins, &c., are thrown into the grave.

Among the dwellers in Cameroon, when you are across the Bantu border-line, velvets, &c., are buried with a big man or woman; but I am told it is only done for the glorification of his living relatives, so that the world may say, "So and so must be rich, look what a lot of trade he threw away at the funeral of his wife," or his father, or his son, as the case may be; but I doubt whether this is the true explanation. If it is, I should recommend my German friends, if they wish to intervene, to introduce the income tax into Cameroon—that would eliminate this custom.

The Tschwis hold that there is a definite earthly existence belonging to each soul of a human kind. Let us say, for example, a soul has a thirty year's bodily existence belonging to it. Well, suppose that soul's body gets killed off at twenty-five, its remaining five years it has to spend, if it is left alone, in knocking about its old haunts, homes, and wives. In this state it is called a Sisa, and is a nuisance. It will cause sickness. It will throw stones. It will pull off roofs, and it will play the very mischief with its wives' subsequent husbands, all because, not having reached its full term of life, it has not learnt its way down the dark and difficult path to Srahmandazi, the entrance to which is across the Volta River to the N.E. This knowledge of the path to Srahmandazi is a thing that grows gradually on a man's immortal soul (the other three souls are not immortal), and naturally not having been allowed to complete his life, his knowledge is imperfect. A man's soul, however, can be taught the way, if necessary, in the funeral "custom" made by his relatives and the priests; but in a case of an incomplete life on earth soul, as a German would say, when it does arrive in the land of Insrah (pl.) it is in a weak and feeble state from the difficulties of its journey, whereas a soul that has lived out its allotted span of life goes straightway off to Srahmandazi as soon as its "custom" or "devil" is made and gives its surviving relatives no further trouble. Still there is great difference of opinion among all the Tschwis and Ga men I have come across on this point, and Ellis likewise remarks on this difference of opinion. Some informants say that a soul that has been sent hence before its time, although it is exhausted by the hardships it has suffered on its journey down, yet recovers health in a month or so; while a soul that has run its allotted span on earth is as feeble as a new-born babe on arriving in Srahmandazi, and takes years to pull round. Other informants say they have no knowledge of these details, and state that all the difference they know of between the souls of men who have been killed and the men who have died, is that the former can always come back, and that really the safest way of disposing of this class of soul is, by suitable spells and incantations, to get it to enter into the body of a new-born baby, where it can live out the remainder of its life.

Before closing these observations on Srahmandazi I will give the best account of that land that I am at present able to. Some day perhaps I may share the fate of the Oxford Professor in *In the Wrong Paradise* and go there myself, but so far my information is second-hand. It is like this world. There are towns and villages, rivers, mountains, bush, plantations, and markets. When the sun rises here is sets in Srahmandazi. It has its pleasures and its pains, not necessarily retributive or rewarding, but dim. All souls in it grow forward or backward into the prime of life and remain there, some informants say; others say that each inhabitant remains there at the same age as he was when he quitted the world above. This latter view is most like the South West one. The former is possibly only an attempt to make Srahmandazi into a heaven in conformation with Christian teaching, which it is not, any more than it is a hell.

I have much curious information regarding its flora and fauna. A great deal of both is seemingly indigenous, and then there are the souls of great human beings, the Asrahmanfw, and the souls of all the human beings, animals, and things sent down with them. The ghosts do not seem to leave off their interest in mundane affairs, for they not only have local palavers, but try palavers left over from their earthly existence; and when there is an outbreak of sickness in a Fantee town or village, and several inhabitants die off, the opinion is often held that there is a big palaver going on down in Srahmandazi and that the spirits are sending up on earth for witnesses, subpoenaing them as it were. Medicine men or priests are called in to find out what particular earthly grievance can be the subject of the ghost palaver, and when they have ascertained this, they take the evidence of every one in the town on this affair, as it were on commission, and transmit the information to the court sitting in Srahmandazi. This prevents the living being incommoded by personal journeys down below, and although the priests have their fee, it is cheaper in the end, because the witnesses' funeral expenses would fall heavier still.

Although far more elaborated and thought out than any other African underworld I have ever come across, the Tschwee Srahmandazi may be taken as a type of all the African underworlds. The Bantu's idea of a future life is a life spent in much such a place. As far as I can make out there is no definite idea of eternity. I have even come across cases in which doubt was thrown on the present existence of the Creating God, but I think this has arisen from attempts having been made to introduce concise conceptions into the African mind, conceptions that are quite foreign to its true nature and which alarm and worry it. You never get the strange idea of the difference between time and eternity—the idea I mean, that they are different things—in the African that one frequently gets in cultured Europeans; and as for the human soul, the African always believes "that still the spirit is whole, and life and death but shadows of the soul."

CHAPTER 16

FETISH (CONCLUDED)

In which the discourse on apparitions is continued,
with some observations on secret societies, both tribal and murder,
and the kindred subject of leopards.

APPARITIONS ARE BY NO MEANS always of human soul origin. All the
Tschwee and the Ewe gods, for example, have the habit of appearing
pretty regularly to their priests, and occasionally to the laity, like
Sasabonsum; but it is only to priests that these appearances are harmless or beneficial. The effect of Sasabonsum's appearance to the layman
I have cited above, and I could give many other examples of the bad
effects of those of other gods, but will only now mention Tando, the
Hater, the chief god of the Northern Tschwee, the Ashantees, &c. He
is terribly malicious, human in shape, and though not quite white, is
decidedly lighter in complexion than the chief god of the Southern
Tschwee, Bobowissi. His hair is lank, and he carries a native sword and
wears a long robe. His well-selected messengers are those awful driver
ants (Inkran) which it is not orthodox to molest in Tando's territories.
He uses as his weapons lightning, tempest, and disease, but the last is
the most favourite one.

There is absolutely no trick too mean or venomous for Tando. For
example, he has a way of appearing near a village he has a grudge against
in the form of a male child, and wanders about crying bitterly, until some

kind-hearted, unsuspecting villager comes and takes him in and feeds him. Then he develops a contagious disease that clears that village out.

This form of appearance and subsequent conduct is, unhappily, not rigidly confined to Tando, but is used by many spirits as a method of collecting arrears in taxes in the way of sacrifices. I have found traces of it among Bantu gods or spirits, and it gives rise to a general hesitation in West Africa to take care of waifs and strays of unexplained origin.

Other things beside gods and human spirits have the habit of becoming incarnate. Once I had to sit waiting a long time at an apparently perfectly clear bush path, because in front of us a spear's ghost used to fly across the path about that time in the afternoon and if any one was struck by it they died. A certain spring I know of is haunted by the ghost of a pitcher. Many ladies when they have gone alone to fill their pitchers in the evening time at this forest spring have noticed a very fine pitcher standing there ready filled, and thinking exchange is no robbery, or at any rate they would risk it if it were, have taken their own pitcher and left the better looking one; but always as soon as they have come within sight of the village huts, the new pitcher has crumbled into dust, and the water in it been spilt on the ground; and the worst of it is, when they have returned to fetch their own discarded pitcher, they find it also shattered into pieces.

There is also another class of apparition, of which I have met with two instances, one among pure Negroes (Okÿon); the other among pure Bantu (Kangwe). I will give the Bantu version of the affair, because at Okÿon the incident had happened a good time before the details were told me, and in the Bantu case they had happened the previous evening. But there was very little difference in the main facts of the case, and it was an important thing because in both cases the underlying idea was sacrificial.

The women who told me was an exceedingly intelligent, shrewd, reliable person. She had been to the factory with some trade, and had got a good price for it, and so was in a good temper on her return home in the evening. She got out of her canoe and leaving her slave boy to bring up the things, walked to her house, which was the ordinary house of a prosperous Igalwa native, having two distinct rooms in it, and a separate cook-house close by in a clean, sandy yard. She trod on some nastiness in the yard, and going into the cook-house found the slave girls round a very small and inefficient fire, trying to cook the evening meal. She blew them up for not having a proper fire; they said the wood was wet, and would not burn. She said they lied, and she would see to them later, and she went into the chamber she used for a sleeping apartment, and trod on something more on the floor in the dark; those good-for-nothing hussies of slaves had not lit her palm-oil lamp, and mentally forming the opinion that they had been out flirting during her absence, and resolving to teach them well the iniquity of such conduct, she sat down on her bed into a lot of messy stuff of a clammy, damp nature. Now this fairly roused her, for she is a notable housewife, who keeps her house and slaves in exceedingly good order. So dismissing from her mind the commercial consideration she had intended to gloat over when she came into her room, she called Ingremina and others in a tone that brought those young ladies on the spot. She asked them how they dared forget to light her lamp; they said they had not, but the lamp in the room must have gone out like the other lamps had, after burning dim and spluttering. They further said they had not been out, but had been sitting round the fire trying to make it burn properly. She duly whacked and pulled the ears of all within reach. I say within reach for she is not very active, weighing, I am sure, upwards of eighteen stone. Then she went back into her room and got out her beautiful English paraffin lamp, which she keeps in a box, and taking it into the cookhouse, picked up a bit of wood from the hissing, spluttering fire, and lit it. When she picked up the wood she noticed that it was covered with the same sticky abomination she had met before that evening, and it smelt of the same faint smell she had noticed as soon as she had reached her house, and by now the whole air seemed oppressive with it.

As soon as the lamp was alight she saw what the stuff was, namely, blood. Blood was everywhere, the rest of the sticks in the fire had it on them, it sizzled at the burning ends, and ran off the other in rills. There were pools of it about her clean, sandy yard. Her own room was reeking, the bed, the stools, the floor; it trickled down the door-post; coagulated on the lintel. She herself was smeared with it from the things she had come in contact with in the dark, and the slaves seemed to have been sitting in pools of it. The things she picked up off the table and shelf left rims of it behind them; there was more in the skillets, and the oil in the open palm-oil lamps had a film of it floating on the oil. Investigation showed that the whole of the rest of her house was in a similar mess. The good lady gave a complete catalogue of the household furniture and its condition, which I need not give here. The slave girls when the light came were terrified at what they saw, and she called in the aristocracy of the village, and asked them their opinion on the blood palaver. They said they could make nothing of it at first, but subsequently formed the opinion that it meant something was going to happen, and suggested with the kind, helpful cheerfulness of relatives and friends, that they should not wonder if it were a prophecy of her own death. This view irritated the already tried lady, and she sent them about their business, and started the slaves on house-cleaning. The blood cleaned up all right when you were about it, but kept on turning up in other places, and in the one you had just cleaned as soon as you left off and went elsewhere; and the morning came and found things in much the same state until "before suntime," say about 10 o'clock, when it faded away.

I cautiously tried to get my stately, touchy dowager duchess to explain how it was that there was such a lot of blood, and how it was it got into the house. She just said "It had to go somewhere," and refused to give rational explanations as *Chambers's Journal* does after telling a good ghost story. I found afterwards that it was quite decided it was a case of "blood come before," and at Okÿon, Miss Slessor told me, in regard to the similar case there, that this was the opinion held regarding the phenomenon. It is always held uncanny in Africa if a person dies without shedding blood. You see, the blood is the life, and if you see it come out, you know, the going of the thing, as it were. If you do not, it is mysterious. At Okÿon, a few days after the blood appeared, a nephew of a person whose house it came into was killed while felling a tree in the forest; a bough struck him and broke his neck, without shedding a drop of blood, and this bore out the theory, for the blood having "to go somewhere" came before. In the Bantu case I did not hear of such a supporting incident happening.

Certain African ideas about blood puzzle me. I was told by a Batanga friend, a resident white trader, that a short time previously a man was convicted of theft by the natives of a village close to him. The hands and feet of the criminal were tied together, and he was flung into the river. He got himself free, and swam to the other bank, and went for bush. He was recaptured, and a stone tied to his neck, and in again he was thrown. The second time he got free and ashore, and was recaptured, and the chief then, most regretfully, ordered that he was to be knocked on the head before being thrown in for a third time. This time palaver set, but the chief knew that he would die himself, by spitting the blood he had spilt, from his own lungs, before the year was out. I inquired about the chief when I passed this place, more than eighteen months after, and learnt from a native that the chief was dead, and that he had died in this way. The objection thus was not to shedding blood in a general way, but to the shedding in the course of judicial execution. There may be some idea of this kind underlying the ingenious and awful ways the Negroes have of killing thieves, by tying them to stakes in the rivers or down on to paths for the driver ants to kill and eat, but this is only conjecture; I have not had a chance yet to work this subject up; and getting reliable information about underlying ideas is very difficult in Africa. The natives will say "Yes" to any mortal thing, if they think you want them to; and the variety of their languages is another great hindrance. Were it not for the prevalence of Kru English or trade English, investigation would be almost impossible; but, fortunately, this quaint language is prevalent, and the natives of different tribes communicate with each other in it, and so round a fire, in the evening, if you listen to the gossip, you can pick up all sorts of strange information, and gain strange and often awful lights on your absent white friends' characters, and your present companions' religion. For example, the other day I had a set of porters composed of four Bassa boys, two Wei Weis, one Dualla, and two Yorubas. None of their languages fitted, so they talked trade English, and pretty lively talk some of it was, but of that anon.

I cannot close this brief notice of native ideas without mentioning the secret societies; but to go fully into this branch of the subject would require volumes, for every tribe has its secret society. The Poorah of Sierra Leone, the Oru of Lagos, the Egbo of Calabar, the Isyogo of the Igalwa, the Ukuku of the Benga, the Okukwe of the M'pongwe, the Ikun of the Bakele, and the Lukuku of the Bachilangi Baluba, are some of the most powerful secret societies on the West African Coast.

These secret societies are not essentially religious, their action is mainly judicial, and their particularly presiding spirit is not a god or devil in our sense of the word. The ritual differs for each in its detail, but there are broad lines of agreement between them. There are societies both for men and for women, but mixed societies for both sexes are rare. Those that I have mentioned above are all male, except the Lukuku, and women are utterly forbidden to participate in the rites or become acquainted with their secrets, for one of the chief duties of these societies is to keep the women in order; and besides it is undoubtedly held that women are bad for certain forms of ju-ju, even when these forms are not directly connected, as far as I can find out, with the secret society. For example, the other day a chief up the Mungo River deliberately destroyed his ju-ju by showing it to his women. It was a great ju-ju, but expensive to keep up, requiring sacrifices of slaves and goats, so what with trade being bad, fall in the price of oil and ivory and so on, he felt he could not afford the ju-ju, and so destroyed its power, so as to prevent its harming him when he neglected it.

The general rule with these secret societies is to admit the young free people at an age of about eight to ten years, the boys entering the male, the girls the female society. Both societies are rigidly kept apart. A man who attempts to penetrate the female mysteries would be as surely killed as a woman who might attempt to investigate the male mysteries; still I came, in 1893, across an amusing case which demonstrates the inextinguishable thirst for knowledge, so long as that knowledge is forbidden, which characterizes our sex.

It was in the district just south of Big Batanga. The male society had been very hard on the ladies for some time, and one day one star-like intellect among the latter told her next-door neighbour , in strict confidence, that she did not believe Ikun was a spirit at all, but only old So-and-so dressed up in leaves. This rank heresy spread rapidly, in strict confidence, among the ladies at large, and they used to assemble together in the house of the foundress of the theory, secretly of course, because husbands down there are hasty with the cutlass and the kassengo, and they talked the matter over. Somehow or other, this came to the ears of the men. Whether the ladies got too emancipated and winked when Ikun was mentioned, or asked how Mr. So-and-so was this morning, in a pointed way, after an Ikun manifestation, I do not know; some people told me this was so, but others, who, I fear, were right, considering the acknowledged slowness of men in putting two and two together, and the treachery of women towards each other, said that a woman had told a man that she had heard some of the other women were going on in this heretical way. Anyhow, the men knew, and were much alarmed; skepticism had spread by now to such an extent that nothing short of burning or drowning all the women could stamp it out and reintroduce the proper sense of awe into the female side of Society, and after a good deal of consideration the men saw, for men are undoubtedly more gifted in foresight than our sex, that it was no particular use reintroducing this awe if there was no female half of Society to be impressed by it. It was a brain-spraining problem for the men all round, for it is clear Society cannot be kept together without some superhuman aid to help to keep the feminine portion of it within bounds.

Grave councils were held, and it was decided that the woman at whose house these treasonable meetings were held should be sent away early one morning on a trading mission to the nearest factory, a job she readily undertook; and while the other women were away in the plantation or at the spring, certain men entered her house secretly and dug a big chamber out in the floor of the hut, and one of them, dressed as Ikun, and provided with refreshments for the day, got into this chamber, and the whole affair was covered over carefully and the floor re-sanded. That afternoon there was a big manifestation of Ikun. He came in the most terrible form, his howls were awful, and he finally went dancing away into the bush as the night came down. The ladies had just taken the common-sense precaution of removing all goats, sheep, fowls, &c., into enclosed premises, for, like all his kind, he seizes and hold any property he may come across in the street, but there was evidently no emotional thrill in the female mind regarding him, and when the leading lady returned home in the evening the other ladies strolled into their leader's hut to hear about what new cotton prints, beads, and things Mr.—- had got at his factory by the last steamer from Europe, and interesting kindred subjects bearing on Mr. —-. When they had threshed these matters out, the conversation turned on to religion, and what fools those men had been making of themselves all the afternoon with their Ikun. No sooner was his name uttered than a venomous howl, terminating in squeals of rage and impatience, came from the ground beneath them. They stared at each other for one second, and then, feeling that something was tearing its way up through the floor, they left for the interior of Africa with one accord. Ikun gave chase as soon as he got free, but what with being half-stifled and a bit cramped in the legs, and much encumbered with his vegetable decorations, the ladies got clear away and no arrests were made—but Society was saved. Skepticism became in the twinkling of an eye a thing of the past; and, although no names were taken, the men observed that certain ladies were particularly anxious, and regardless of expense, in buying immunity from Ikun, and they fancied that these ladies were probably in that hut on that particular evening, but they took no further action against them, save making Ikun particularly expensive. There ought to be a moral to an improving tale of this order, I know, but the only one I can think of just now is that it takes a priest to get round a woman; and I always feel inclined to jump on to the table myself when I think of those poor dear creatures sitting on the floor and feeling that awful thing clapper-clawing its way up right under them.

Tattooing on the West Coast is comparatively rare, and I think I may say never used with decorative intent only. The skin decorations are either paint or cicatrices—in the former case the pattern is not kept always the same by the individual. A peculiar form of it you find in the Rivers, where a pattern is painted on the skin, and then when the paint is dry, a wash is applied which makes the unpainted skin rise up in between the painted pattern. The cicatrices are sometimes tribal marks, but sometimes decorative. They are made by cutting the skin and then placing in the wound the fluff of the silk cotton tree.

The great point of agreement between all these West African secret societies lies in the methods of initiation.

The boy, if he belongs to a tribe that goes in for tattooing, is tattooed, and is handed over to instructors in the societies' secrets and formulæ. He lives, with the other boys of his tribe undergoing initiation, usually under the rule of several instructors, and for the space of one year. He lives always in the forest, and is naked and smeared with clay.

The boys are exercised so as to become inured to hardship; in some districts, they make raids so as to perfect themselves in this useful accomplishment. They always take a new name, and are supposed by the initiation process to become new beings in the magic wood, and on their return to their village at the end of their course, they pretend to have entirely forgotten their life before they entered the wood; but this pretense is not kept up beyond the period of the festivities given to welcome them home. They all learn, to a certain extent, a new language, a secret language only understood by the initiated.

The same removal from home and instruction from initiated members is also observed with the girls. However, in their case, it is not always a forest-grove they are secluded in, sometimes it is done in huts. Among the Grain Coast tribes however, the girls go into a magic wood until they are married. Should they have to leave the wood for any temporary reason, they must smear themselves with white clay. A similar custom holds good in Okÿon, Calabar district, where, should a girl have to leave the fattening-house, she must be covered with white clay. I believe this fattening-house custom in Calabar is not only for fattening up the women to improve their appearance, but an initiatory custom as well, although the main intention is now, undoubtedly, fattening, and the girl is constantly fed with fat-producing foods, such as fou-fou soaked in palm oil. I am told, but I think wrongly, that the white clay with which a Calabar girl is kept covered while in the fattening-house, putting on an extra coating of it should she come outside, is to assist in the fattening process by preventing perspiration.

The duration of the period of seclusion varies somewhat. San Salvador boys are six months in the wood. Cameroon boys are twelve months. In most districts the girls are betrothed in infancy, and they go into the wood or initiatory hut for a few months before marriage. In this case the time seems to vary with the circumstances of the individual; not so with the boys, for whom each tribal society has a duly appointed course terminating at a duly appointed time; but sometimes, as among some of the Yoruba tribes, the boy has to remain under the rule of the presiding elders of the society, painted white, and wearing only a bit of grass cloth, if he wears anything, until he has killed a man. Then he is held to have attained man's estate by having demonstrated his courage and also by having secured for himself the soul of the man he has killed as a spirit slave.

The initiation of boys into a few of the elementary dogmas of the secret society by no means composes the entire work of the society. All of them are judicial, and taken on the whole they do an immense amount of good. The methods are frequently a little quaint. Rushing about the streets disguised under masks and drapery, with an imitation tail swinging behind you, while you lash out at every one you meet with a whip or cutlass, is not a European way of keeping the peace, or per-haps I should say maintaining the dignity of the Law. But discipline must be maintained, and this is the West African way of doing it.

The Egbo of Calabar is a fine type of the secret society. It is exceedingly well developed in its details, not sketchy like Isyogo, nor so red-handed as Poorah. Unfortunately, however, I cannot speak with the same amount of knowledge of Egbo as I could of Poorah.

Egbo has the most grades of initiation, except perhaps Poorah, and it exercises jurisdiction over all classes of crime except witchcraft. Any Effik man who desires to become an influential person in the tribe must buy himself into as high a grade of Egbo as he can afford, and these grades are expensive, £1,500 or £1,000 English being required for the higher steps, I am informed. But it is worth it to a great trader, as an influential Effik necessarily is, for he can call out his own class of Egbo and send it against those of his debtors who may be of lower grades, and as the Egbo methods of delivering its orders to pay up consist in placing Egbo at a man's doorway, and until it removes itself from that doorway the man dare not venture outside his house, it is most successful.

Of course the higher a man is in Egbo rank, the greater his power and security, for lower grades cannot proceed against higher ones. Indeed, when a man meets the paraphernalia of a higher grade of Egbo than that to which he belongs, he has to act as if he were lame, and limp along past it humbly, as if the sight of it had taken all the strength out of him, and, needless to remark, higher grade debtors flip their fingers at lower grade creditors.

After talking so much about the secret society spirits, it may be as well to say what they are. They are, one and all, a kind of a sort of a something that usually (the exception is Ikun) lives in the bush. Last February I was making my way back toward Duke Town—late, as usual; I was just by a town on the Qwa River. As I was hurrying onward I heard a terrific uproar accompanied by drums in the thick bush into which, after a brief interval of open ground, the path turned. I became cautious and alarmed, and hid in some dense bush as the men making the noise approached. I saw it was some ju-ju affair. They had a sort of box which they carried on poles, and their dresses were peculiar, and abnormally ample over the upper part of their body. They were prancing about in an ecstatic way round the box, which had one end open, beating their drums and shouting. They were fairly close to me, but fortunately turned their attention to another bit of undergrowth, or that evening they would have landed another kind of thing to what they were after. The bushes they selected they surrounded and evidently did their best to induce something to come out of them and go into their box arrangement. I was every bit as anxious as they were that they should succeed, and succeed rapidly, for you know there are a nasty lot of snakes and things in general, not to mention driver ants, about the Calabar bush, that do not make it at all pleasant to go sitting about in. However, presently they got this something into their box and rejoiced exceedingly, and departed staggering under the weight. I gave them a

good start, and then made the best of my way home; and all that night
Duke Town howled, and sang, and thumped its tom-toms unceasingly; for I was told Egbo had come into the town. Egbo is very coy, even
for a secret society spirit, and seems to loathe publicity; but when he is
ensconced in this ark he utters sententious observations on the subject
of current politics, and his word is law. The voice that comes out of the
ark is very strange, and unlike a human voice. I heard it shortly after
Egbo had been secured. I expect, from what I saw, that there was some
person in that ark all the time, but I do not know. It is more than I can
do to understand my ju-ju details at present, let alone explain them on
rational lines. I hear that there is a tribe on the slave coast who have
been proved to keep a small child in the drum that is the residence of
their chief spirit, and that when the child grows too large to go in it
is killed, and another one that has in the meantime been trained by
the priests takes the place of the dead one, until it, in its turn, grows
too big and is killed, and so on. I expect this killing of the children
is not sacrificial, but arises entirely from the fact that as ex-kings are
dangerous to the body politic, therefore still more dangerous would
ex-gods be.

Very little is known by outsiders regarding Egbo compared to what
there must be to be known, owing to a want of interest or to a sense of
inability on the part of most white people to make head or tail out of
what seems to them a horrid pagan practice or a farrago of nonsense.

It is still a great power, although its officials in Duke or Creek
Town are no longer allowed to go chopping and whipping promiscuous-
like, because the Consul-General has a prejudice against this sort of
thing, and the Effik is learning that it is nearly as unhealthy to go
against his Consul-General as against his ju-ju. So I do not believe you
will ever get the truth about it in Duke Town, or Creek Town. If you
want to get hold of the underlying idea of these societies you must go
round out-of-the-way corners where the natives are not yet afraid of
being laughed at or punished.

Of the South-West Coast secret societies the Ukuku seems the
most powerful. The Isyogo belonging to those indolent Igalwas, and
M'pongwe is now little more than a play. You pretty frequently come
upon Isyogo dances just round Libreville. You will see stretched across
the street in a cluster of houses, a line from which branches are suspended, making a sort of screen. The women and children keep one

side of this screen, the men dancing on the other side to the peculiar monotonous Isyogo tune. Poorah I have spoken of elsewhere.

I believe that these secret societies are always distinct from the leopard societies. I have pretty nearly enough evidence to prove that it is so in some districts, but not in all. So far my evidence only goes to prove the distinction of the two among the Negroes, not among the Bantu, and in all cases you will find some men belonging to both. Some men, in fact, go in for all the societies in their district, but not all the men; and in all districts, if you look close, you will find several societies apart from the regular youth-initiating one.

These other societies are practically murder societies, and their practices usually include cannibalism, which is not an essential part of the rites of the great tribal societies, Isyogo or Egbo. In the Calabar district I was informed by natives that there was a society of which the last entered member has to provide, for the entertainment of the other members, the body of a relative of his own, and sacrificial cannibalism is always breaking out, or perhaps I should say being discovered, by the white authorities in the Niger Delta. There was the great outburst of it at Brass, in 1895, and the one chronicled in the *Liverpool Mercury* for August 13th, 1895, as occurring at Sierra Leone. This account is worth quoting. It describes the hanging by the Authorities of three murderers, and states the incidents, which took place in the Imperi country behind Free Town.

One of the chief murderers was a man named Jowe, who had formerly been a Sunday-school teacher in Sierra Leone. He pleaded in extenuation of his offense that he had been compelled to join the society. The others said they committed the murders in order to obtain certain parts of the body for ju-ju purposes, the leg, the hand, the heart, &c. The *Mercury* goes on to give the statement of the Reverend Father Bomy of the Roman Catholic Mission. "He said he was at Bromtu, where the St. Joseph Mission has a station, when a man was brought down from the Imperi country in a boat. The poor fellow was in a dreadful state, and was brought to the station for medical treatment. He said he was working on his farm, when he was suddenly pounced upon from behind. A number of sharp instruments were driven into the back of his neck. He presented a fearful sight, having wounds all over his body supposed to have been inflicted by the claws of the leopard, but in reality they were stabs from sharp-pointed knives. The native, who was a powerfully-built man, called out, and his cries attracting the attention of his relations, the leopards made off. The poor fellow died at Bromtu from the injuries. It was only his splendid physique that kept him alive until his arrival at the Mission." The *Mercury* goes on to quote from the *Pall Mall*, and I too go on quoting to show that these things are known and acknowledged to have taken place in a colony like Sierra Leone, which has had unequalled opportunities of becoming christianized for more than one hundred years, and now has more than one hundred and thirty places of Christian worship in it. "Some twenty years ago there was a war between this tribe Taima and the Paramas. The Paramas sent some of their war boys to be ambushed in the intervening country, the Imperi, but the Imperi delivered these war boys to the enemy. In revenge, the Paramas sent the Fetish Boofima into the Imperi country. This Fetish had up to that time been kept active and working by the sacrifice of goats, but the medicine men of the Paramas who introduced it into the Imperi country decreed at the same time that human sacrifices would be required to keep it alive, thereby working their vengeance on the Imperi by leading them to exterminate themselves in sacrifice to the Fetish. The country for years has been terrorized by this secret worship of Boofima and at one time the Imperi started the Tonga dances, at which the medicine men pointed out that supposed worshippers of Boofima—the so-called Human Leopards, because when seizing their victims for sacrifice they covered themselves with leopard skins, and imitating the roars of the leopard, they sprang upon their victim, plunging at the same time two three-pronged forks into each side of the throat. The Government some years ago forbade the Tonga dances, and are now striving to suppress the human leopards. There are also human alligators who, disguised as alligators, swim in the creeks upon the canoes and carry off the crew. Some of them have been brought for trial but no complete case has been made out against them!" In comment upon this account, which is evidently written by some one well versed in the affair, I will only remark that sometimes, instead of the three-pronged forks, there are fixed in the paws of the leopard skin sharp-pointed cutting knives, the skin being made into a sort of glove into which the hand of the human leopard fits. In one skin I saw down south this was most ingeniously done. The knives were shaped like the leopard's claws, curved, sharp-pointed, and with cutting edges underneath, and I am told the American Mendi Mission, which works in the Sierra Leone districts, have got a similar skin in their possession.

The human alligator mentioned, is our old friend the witch crocodile—the spirit of the man in the crocodile. I never myself came across a case of a man in his corporeal body swimming about in a crocodile skin, and I doubt whether any native would chance himself inside a crocodile skin and swim about in the river among the genuine articles for fear of their penetrating his disguise mentally and physically.

In Calabar witch crocodiles are still flourishing. There is an immense old brute that sporting Vice-Consuls periodically go after, which is known to contain the spirit of a Duke Town chief who shall be nameless, because they are getting on at such a pace just round Duke Town that haply I might be had up for libel. When I was in Calabar once, a peculiarly energetic officer had hit that crocodile and the chief was forthwith laid up by a wound in his leg. He said a dog had bit him. They, the chief and the crocodile, are quite well again now, and I will say this in favour of that chief, that nothing on earth would persuade me to believe that he went fooling about in the Calabar River in his corporeal body, either in his own skin or a crocodile's.

The introduction of the Fetish Boofima into the country of the Imperi is an interesting point as it shows that these different tribes have the same big ju-ju. Similarly, Calabar Egbo can go into Okÿon, and will be respected in some of the New Calabar districts, but not at Brass, where the secret society is a distinct cult. Often a neighboring district will send into Calabar, or Brass, where the big ju-ju is, and ask to have one sent up into their district to keep order, but Egbo will occasionally be sent into a district without that district in the least wanting it; but, as in the Imperi case, when it is there it is supreme. But say, for example, you were to send Egbo round from Calabar to Cameroon. Cameroon might be barely civil to it, but would pay it no homage, for Cameroon has got no end of a ju-ju of its own. It can rise up as high as the Peak, 13,760 feet. I never saw the Cameroon ju-ju do this, but I saw it start up from four feet to quite twelve feet in the twinkling of an eye, and I was assured that it was only modest reticence on its part that made it leave the other 13,748 feet out of the performance.

Doctor Nassau seems to think that the tribal society of the Corisco regions is identical with the leopard societies. He has had considerable experience of the workings of the Ukuku, particularly when he was pioneering in the Benito regions, when it came very near killing him. He says the name signifies a departed spirit. "It is a secret society into which all the males are initiated at puberty, whose procedure may not be seen by females, nor its laws disobeyed by any one under pain of death, a penalty which is sometimes commuted to a fine, a heavy fine. Its discussions are uttered as an oracle from any secluded spot by some man appointed for the purpose.

"On trivial occasions any initiated man may personate Ukuku or issue commands for the family. On other occasions, as in Shiku, to raise prices, the society lays its commands on foreign traders."

Some cases of Ukuku proceedings against white traders have come under my own observation. A friend of mine, a trader in the Batanga district, in some way incurred the animosity of the society's local branch. He had, as is usual in the South-West Coast trade several sub-factories in the bush. He found himself boycotted; no native came in to his yard to buy or sell at the store, not even to sell food. He took no notice and awaited developments. One evening when he was sitting on his verandah, smoking and reading, he thought he heard some one singing softly under the house, this, like most European buildings hereabouts, being elevated just above the earth. He was attracted to the song and listened: it was evidently one of the natives singing, not one of his own Kruboys, and so, knowing the language, and having nothing else particular to do, he attended to the affair.

It was the same thing sung softly over and over again, so softly that he could hardly make out the words. But at last, catching his native name among them, he listened more intently than ever, down at a knot-hole in the wooden floor. The song was—"They are going to attack your factory at...tomorrow. They are going to attack your factory at...tomorrow," over and over again, until it ceased; and then he thought he saw something darker than the darkness round it creep across the yard and disappear in the bush. Very early in the morning he, with his Kruboys and some guns, went and established themselves in that threatened factory in force. The Ukuku Society turned up in the evening, and reconnoitered the situation, and finding there was more in it than they had expected, withdrew.

In the course of the next twenty-four hours he succeeded in talking the palaver successfully with them. He never knew who his singing friend was, but suspected it was a man whom he had known to be grateful for some kindness he had done him. Indeed there were, and are, many natives who have cause to be grateful to him, for he is deservedly popular among his local tribes, but the man who sang to him that night deserves much honor, for he did it at a terrific risk.

Sometimes representatives of the Ukuku fraternity from several tribes meet together and discuss intertribal difficulties, thereby avoiding war.

Dr. Nassau distinctly says that the Bantu region leopard society is identical with the Ukuku, and he says that although the leopards are not very numerous here they are very daring, made so by immunity from punishment by man. "The superstition is that on any man who kills a leopard will fall a curse or evil disease, curable only by ruinously expensive process of three weeks' duration under the direction of Ukuku. So the natives allow the greatest depredations and ravages until their sheep, goats, and dogs are swept away, and are roused to self-defence only when a human being becomes the victim of the daring beast. With this superstition is united another similar to the werewolf of Germany, viz., a belief in the power of human metamorphosis into a leopard. A person so metamorphosed is called 'Uvengwa.' At one time in Benito an intense excitement prevailed in the community. Doors and shutters were rattled at the dead of night, marks of leopard claws were scratched on doorposts. Then tracks lay on every path. Women and children in lonely places saw their flitting forms, or in the dusk were knocked down by their spring, or heard their growl in the thickets. It is difficult to decide in many of these reports whether it is a real leopard or only an Uvengwa – to native fears they are practically the same, – we were certain this time the Uvengwa was the thief disguised in leopard's skin, as theft is always heard of about such times."

When I was in Gaboon in September 1895 there was great Uvengwa excitement in a district just across the other side of the estuary, mainly at a village that enjoyed the spacious and resounding name of Rumpochembo, from a celebrated chief, and all these phenomena were rife there. Again, when I was in a village up the Calabar there were fourteen goats and five slaves killed in eight days by leopards, the genuine things, I am sure, in this case; but here, as down South, there was a strong objection to proceed against the leopard, and no action was being taken save making the goat-houses stronger. In Okẏon, when a leopard is killed, its body is treated with great respect and brought into the killer's village. Messages are then sent to the neighboring villages, and they send representatives to the village and the gall-bladder is most carefully removed from the leopard and burnt *coram publico*, each person whipping

their hands down their arms to disavow any guilt in the affair. This burning of the gall, however, is not ju-ju, it is done merely to destroy it, and
to demonstrate to all men that it is destroyed, because it is believed to be
a deadly poison, and if any is found in a man's possession the punishment
is death, unless he is a great chief—a few of these are allowed to keep leopards' gall in their possession. John Bailey tells me that if a great chief
commits a great crime, and is adjudged by a conclave of his fellow chiefs
to die, it is not considered right he should die in a common way, and he
is given leopard's gall. A precisely similar idea regarding the poisonous
quality of crocodiles' gall holds good down South.

The ju-ju parts of the leopard are the whiskers. You cannot get a
skin from a native with them on, and gay, reckless young hunters wear
them stuck in their hair and swagger tremendously while the Elders
shake their heads and keep a keen eye on their subsequent conduct.

I must say the African leopard is an audacious animal, although it
is ungrateful of me to say a word against him, after the way he has let me
off personally, and I will speak of his extreme beauty as compensation
for my ingratitude. I really think, taken as a whole, he is the most lovely
animal I have ever seen; only seeing him, in the one way you can gain a
full idea of his beauty, namely in his native forest, is not an unmixed joy
to a person, like myself, of a nervous disposition. I may remark that my
nervousness regarding the big game of Africa is of a rather peculiar
kind. I can confidently say I am not afraid of any wild animal—until I see
it—and then—well I will yield to nobody in terror; fortunately as I say my
terror is a special variety; fortunately, because no one can manage their
own terror. You can suppress alarm, excitement, fear, fright, and all
those small-fry emotions, but the real terror is as dependent on the
inner make of you as the colour of your eyes, or the shape of your nose;
and when terror ascends its throne in my mind I become preternaturally
artful, and intelligent to an extent utterly foreign to my true nature, and
save, in the case of close quarters with bad big animals, a feeling of rage
against some unknown person that such things as leopards, elephants,
crocodiles, &c., should be allowed out loose in that disgracefully dangerous way, I do not think much about it at the time. Whenever I have
come across an awful animal in the forest and I know it has seen me I
take Jerome's advice, and instead of relying on the power of the human
eye rely upon that of the human leg, and effect a masterly retreat in the
face of the enemy. If I know it has not seen me I sink in my tracks and

keep an eye on it, hoping that it will go away soon. Thus I once came upon a leopard. I had got caught in a tornado in a dense forest. The massive, mighty trees were waving like a wheat-field in an autumn gale in England, and I dare say a field mouse in a wheat-field in a gale would have heard much the same uproar. The tornado shrieked like ten thousand vengeful demons. The great trees creaked and groaned and strained against it and their bush-rope cables groaned and smacked like whips, and ever and anon a thundering crash with snaps like pistol shots told that they and their mighty tree had strained and struggled in vain. The fierce rain came in a roar, tearing to shreds the leaves and blossoms and deluging everything. I was making bad weather of it, and climbing up over a lot of rocks out of a gully bottom where I had been half drowned in a stream, and on getting my head to the level of a block of rock I observed right in front of my eyes, broadside on, maybe a yard off, certainly not more, a big leopard. He was crouching on the ground, with his magnificent head thrown back and his eyes shut. His fore-paws were spread out in front of him and he lashed the ground with his tail, and I grieve to say, in face of that awful danger—I don't mean me, but the tornado—that depraved creature swore, softly, but repeatedly and profoundly. I did not get all these facts up in one glance, for no sooner did I see him than I ducked under the rocks, and remembered thankfully that leopards are said to have no power of smell. But I heard his observation on the weather, and the flip-flap of his tail on the ground. Every now and then I cautiously took a look at him with one eye round a rock-edge, and he remained in the same position. My feelings tell me he remained there twelve months, but my calmer judgment puts the time down at twenty minutes; and at last, on taking another cautious peep, I saw he was gone. At the time I wished I knew exactly where, but I do not care about that detail now, for I saw no more of him. He had moved off in one of those weird lulls which you get in a tornado, when for a few seconds the wild herd of hurrying winds seem to have lost themselves, and wander round crying and wailing like lost souls, until their common rage seizes them again and they rush back to their work of destruction. It was an immense pleasure to have seen the great creature like that. He was so evidently enraged and baffled by the uproar and dazzled by the floods of lightning that swept down into the deepest recesses of the forest, showing at one second every detail of twig, leaf, branch, and stone round you, and then leaving you in a sort of swirling dark until the next flash came; this, and the great conglomerate roar of the wind, rain and thunder, was enough to bewilder any living thing.

I have never hurt a leopard intentionally; I am habitually kind to animals, and besides I do not think it is ladylike to go shooting things with a gun. Twice, however, I have been in collision with them. On one occasion a big leopard had attacked a dog, who, with her family, was occupying a broken-down hut next to mine. The dog was a half-bred boarhound, and a savage brute on her own account. I, being roused by the uproar, rushed out into the feeble moonlight, thinking she was having one of her habitual turns-up with other dogs, and I saw a whirling mass of animal matter within a yard of me. I fired two mushroom-shaped native stools in rapid succession into the brown of it, and the meeting broke up into a leopard and a dog. The leopard crouched, I think to spring on me. I can see it's great, beautiful lambent eyes still, and I seized an earthen water-cooler and flung it straight at them. It was a noble shot; it burst on the leopard's head like a shell and the leopard went for bush one time. Twenty minutes after people began to drop in cautiously and inquire if anything was the matter, and I civilly asked them to go and ask the leopard in the bush, but they firmly refused. We found the dog had got her shoulder slit open as if by a blow from a cutlass, and the leopard had evidently seized the dog by the scruff of her neck, but owing to the loose folds of skin no bones were broken and she got round all right after much ointment from me, which she paid me for with several bites. Do not mistake this for a sporting adventure. I no more thought it was a leopard than it was a lotus when I joined the fight. My other leopard was also after a dog. Leopards always come after dogs, because once upon a time the leopard and the dog were great friends, and the leopard went out one day and left her whelps in charge of the dog, and the dog went out flirting, and a snake came and killed the whelps, so there is ill-feeling to this day between the two. For the benefit of sporting readers whose interest may have been excited by the mention of big game, I may remark that the largest leopard skin I ever measured myself was, tail included, 9 feet 7 inches. It was a dried skin, and every man who saw it said, "It was the largest skin he had ever seen, except one that he had seen somewhere else."

The largest crocodile I ever measured was 22 feet 3 inches, the largest gorilla 5 feet 7 inches. I am assured by the missionaries in Calabar, that there was a python brought into Creek Town in the Rev.

Mr. Godlie's time, that extended the whole length of the Creek Town mission-house verandah and to spare. This python must have been over 40 feet. I have not a shadow of doubt it was. Stay-at-home people will always discredit great measurements, but experienced bushmen do not, and after all, if it amuses the stay-at-homes to do so, by all means let them; they have dull lives of it and it don't hurt you, for you know how exceedingly difficult it is to preserve really big things to bring home, and how, half the time, they fall into the hands of people who would not bother their heads to preserve them in a rotting climate like West Africa.

The largest python skin I ever measured was a damaged one, which was 26 feet. There is an immense one hung in front of a house in San Paul de Loanda which you can go and measure yourself with comparative safety any day, and which is, I think, over 20 feet. I never measured this one. The common run of pythons is 10-15 feet, or rather I should say this is about the sized one you find with painful frequency in your chicken-house.

Of the Lubuku secret society I can speak with no personal knowledge. I had a great deal of curious information regarding it from a Bakele woman, who had her information second-hand, but it bears out what Captain Latrobe Bateman says about it in his most excellent book *The First Ascent of the Kasai* (George Phillip, 1889), and to his account in Note J of the Appendix, I beg to refer the ethnologist. My information also went to show what he calls "a dark inference as to its true nature," a nature not universally common by any means to the African tribal secret society.

In addition to the secret society and the leopard society, there are in the Delta some ju-jus held only by a few great chiefs. The one in Bonny has a complete language to itself, and there is one in Duke Town so powerful that should you desire the death of any person you have only to go and name him before it. "These ju-jus are very swift and sure." I would rather drink than fight with any of them—yes, far.

CHAPTER 17

ASCENT OF THE GREAT PEAK
OF CAMEROONS

*Setting forth how the Voyager is minded to ascend the mountain
called Mungo Mah Lobeh, or the Throne of Thunder,
and in due course reaches Buea, situate thereon.*

AFTER RETURNING FROM CORISCO I remained a few weeks in Gaboon, and then left on the *Niger*, commanded by Captain Davies. My regrets, I should say, arose from leaving the charms and interests of Congo Français, and had nothing whatever to do with taking passage on one of the most comfortable ships of all those which call on the Coast.

The *Niger* was homeward-bound when I joined her, and in due course arrived in Cameroon River, and I was once again under the dominion of Germany. It would be a very interesting thing to compare the various forms of European government in Africa - English, French, German, Portuguese, and Spanish; but to do so with any justice would occupy more space than I have at my disposal, for the subject is extremely intricate. Each of these forms of government have their good points and their bad. Each of them are dealing with bits of Africa differing from each other—in the nature of their inhabitants and their formation, and so on— so I will not enter into any comparison of them here.

From the deck of the *Niger* I found myself again confronted with my great temptation—the magnificent Mungo Mah Lobeh—the Throne of Thunder. Now it is none of my business to go up mountains. There's next to no fish on them in West Africa, and precious little good rank fetish, as the population on them is sparse—the African, like myself, abhorring cool air. Nevertheless, I feel quite sure that no white man has ever looked on the great Peak of Cameroon without a desire arising in his mind to ascend it and know in detail the highest point on the western side of the continent, and indeed one of the highest points in all Africa.

So great is the majesty and charm of this mountain that the temptation of it is as great to me today as it was on the first day I saw it, when I was feeling my way down the West Coast of Africa on the *S.S. Lagos* in 1893, and it revealed itself by good chance from its surf-washed plinth to its skyscraping summit. Certainly it is most striking when you see it first, as I first saw it, after coasting for weeks along the low shores and mangrove-fringed rivers of the *Niger* Delta. Suddenly, right up out of the sea, rises the great mountain to its 13,760 feet, while close at hand, to westward, towers the lovely island mass of Fernando Po to 10,190 feet. But every time you pass it by its beauty grows on you with greater and greater force, though it is never twice the same. Sometimes it is wreathed with indigo-black tornado clouds, sometimes crested with snow, sometimes softly gorgeous with gold, green, and rose-colored vapours tinted by the setting sun, sometimes completely swathed in dense cloud so that you cannot see it at all; but when you once know it is there it is all the same, and you bow down and worship.

There are only two distinct peaks to this glorious thing that geologists brutally call the volcanic intrusive mass of the Cameroon Mountains, viz., Big Cameroon and Little Cameroon. The latter, Mungo Mah Etindeh, has not yet been scaled, although it is only 5,820 feet. One reason for this is doubtless that the few people in fever-stricken, over-worked West Africa who are able to go up mountains, naturally try for the adjacent Big Cameroon; the other reason is that Mungo Mah Etindeh, to which Burton refers as "the awful form of Little Cameroon," is mostly sheer cliff, and is from foot to summit clothed in an almost impenetrable forest. Behind these two mountains of volcanic origin, which cover an area on an isolated base of between 700 and 800 square miles in extent, there are distinctly visible from the coast two chains of mountains, or I should think one chain deflected, the so-called Rumby and Omon ranges. These are no relations of Mungo, being of very different structure and conformation; the geological specimens I have brought from them and from the Cameroons being identified by geologists as respectively schistose grit and vesicular lava.

After spending a few pleasant days in Cameroon River in the society of Frau Plehn, my poor friend Mrs. Duggan having, I regret to say, departed for England on the death of her husband, I went round to Victoria, Ambas Bay, on the *Niger*, and in spite of being advised solemnly by Captain Davies to "chuck it as it was not a picnic," I started to attempt the Peak of Cameroons as follows.

September 20th, 1895.—Left Victoria at 7:30, weather fine. Herr von Lucke, though sadly convinced, by a series of experiments he has been carrying on every since I landed, and I expect before, that you cannot be in three places at one time, is still trying to do so; or more properly speaking he starts an experiment series for four places, man-like, instead of getting ill as I should under the circumstances, and he kindly comes with me as far as the bridge across the lovely cascading Lukole River, and then goes back at about seven miles an hour to look after Victoria and his sick subordinates in detail.

I, with my crew, keep up on the grand new road the Government is making, which when finished is to go from Ambas Bay to Buea, 3,000 feet up on the mountain's side. This road is quite the most magnificent of roads, as regards breadth and general intention, that I have seen anywhere in West Africa, and it runs through a superbly beautiful country. It is, I should say, as broad as Oxford Street; on either side of it are deep drains to carry off the surface waters, with banks of varied beautiful tropical shrubs and ferns, behind which rise, 100 to 200 feet high, walls of grand forest, the column-like tree-stems either hung with flowering, climbing plants and ferns, or showing soft red and soft gray shafts sixty to seventy feet high without an interrupting branch. Behind this again rise the lovely foot hills of Mungo, high up against the sky, colored the most perfect soft dark blue.

The whole scheme of colour is indescribably rich and full in tone. The very earth is a velvety red brown, and the butterflies—which abound—show themselves off in the sunlight, in their canary-coloured, crimson, and peacock-blue liveries, to perfection. After five minutes' experience of the road I envy those butterflies. I do not believe there is a more lovely road in this world, and besides, it's a noble and enterprising thing of a Government to go and make it, considering the climate and the country; but to get any genuine pleasure out of it, it is requisite to hover in a bird- or butterfly-like way, for of all the truly awful things to walk on, that road, when I was on it, was the worst.

Of course this arose from its not being finished, not having its top on in fact: the bit that was finished, and had got its top on, for half a mile beyond the bridge, you could go over in a Bath chair. The rest of it made you fit for one for the rest of your natural life, for it was one mass of broken lava rock, and here and there leviathan tree-stumps that had been partially blown up with gunpowder.

When we near the forest end of the road, it comes on to rain heavily, and I see a little house on the left-hand side, and a European engineer superintending a group of very cheerful natives felling timber. He most kindly invites me to take shelter, saying it cannot rain as heavily as this for long. My men also announce a desire for water, and so I sit down and chat with the engineer under the shelter of his verandah, while the men go to the water-hole, some twenty minutes off.

After learning much about the Congo Free State and other matters, I presently see one of my men sitting right in the middle of the road on a rock, totally unsheltered, and a feeling of shame comes over me in the face of this black man's aquatic courage. Into the rain I go, and off we start. I conscientiously attempt to keep dry, by holding up an umbrella, knowing that though hopeless it is the proper thing to do.

We leave the road about fifty yards above the hut, turning into the unbroken forest on the right-hand side, and following a narrow, slippery, muddy, root-beset bush-path that was a comfort after the road. Presently we come to a lovely mountain torrent flying down over red-brown rocks in white foam; exquisitely lovely, and only a shade damper than the rest of things. Seeing this I solemnly fold up my umbrella and give it to Kefalla. I then take charge of Fate and wade.

This particular stream, too, requires careful wading, the rocks over which it flows being arranged in picturesque, but perilous confusion; however all goes well, and getting to the other side I decide to "chuck it," as Captain Davies would say, as to keeping dry, for the rain comes down heavier than ever.

Now we are evidently dealing with a foot-hillside, but the rain is too thick for one to see two yards in any direction, and we seem to be in a ghost-land forest, for the great palms and red-woods rise up in the mist before us, and fade out in the mist behind, as we pass on. The rocks which edge and strew the path at our feet are covered with exquisite ferns and mosses - all the most delicate shades of green imaginable, and here and there of absolute gold colour, looking as if some ray of sunshine had lingered too long playing on the earth, and had got shut off from heaven by the mist, and so lay nestling among the rocks until it might rejoin the sun.

The path now becomes an absolute torrent, with mud-thickened water, which cascades round one's ankles in a sportive way, and round one's knees in the hollows in the path. On we go, the path underneath the water seems a pretty equal mixture of rock and mud, but they are not evenly distributed. Plantations full of weeds show up on either side of us, and we are evidently now on the top of a foot-hill. I suspect a fine view of the sea could be obtained from here, if you have an atmosphere that is less than 993/4 percent of water. As it is, a white sheet—or more properly speaking, considering its soft, stuffy woolliness, a white blanket—is stretched across the landscape to the south-west, where the sea would show.

We go down-hill now, the water rushing into the back of my shoes for a change. The path is fringed by high, sugar-cane-like grass which hangs across it in a lackadaisical way, swishing you in the face and cutting like a knife whenever you catch its edge, and pouring continually insidious rills of water down one's neck. It does not matter. The whole Atlantic could not get more water on to me than I have already got. Ever and again I stop and wring out some of it from my skirts, for it is weighty. One would not imagine that anything could come down in the way of water thicker than the rain, but it can. When one is on the top of the hills, a cold breeze comes through the mist chilling one to the bone, and bending the heads of the palm trees, sends down from them water by the bucketful with a slap; hitting or missing you as the case may be.

Both myself and my men are by now getting anxious for our "chop," and they tell me, "We look them big hut soon." Soon we do look them big hut, but with faces of undisguised horror, for the big hut consists of a few charred roof-mats, &c., lying on the ground. There has been a fire in that simple savage home. Our path here is cut by one that goes east and west, and after a consultation between my men and the Bakwiri, we take the path going east, down a steep slope between weedy plantations, and shortly on the left shows a steep little hill-side with a long low hut on the top. We go up to it and I find it is the habitation of a Basel Mission black Bible-reader. He comes out and speaks English well, and I tell him I want a house for myself and my men, and he says we had better come in and stay in this one. It is divided into two chambers, one in which the children who attend the mission-school stay, and

wherein there is a fire, and one evidently the abode of the teacher. I
thank the Bible-reader and say that I will pay him for the house, and
I and the men go in streaming, and my teeth chatter with cold as the
breeze chills my saturated garment while I give out the rations of beef,
rum, blankets, and tobacco to the men. Then I clear my apartment out
and attempt to get dry, operations which are interrupted by Kefalla
coming for tobacco to buy firewood off the mission teacher to cook our
food by.

Presently my excellent little cook brings in my food, and in with it
come two mission teacher—our first acquaintance, the one with the
white jacket, and another with a blue. They lounge about and spit in all
directions, and then chiefs commence to arrive with their families complete, and they sidle into the apartment and ostentatiously ogle the
demijohn of rum.

They are, as usual, a nuisance, sitting about on everything. No
sooner have I taken an unclean-looking chief off the wood sofa, than I
observe another one has silently seated himself in the middle of my open
portmanteau. Removing him and shutting it up, I see another one has
settled on the men's beef and rice sack.

It is now about three o'clock and I am still chilled to the bone in
spite of tea. The weather is as bad as ever. The men say that the rest of
the road to Buea is far worse than that which we have so far come along,
and that we should never get there before dark, and "for sure" should
not get there afterwards, because by the time the dark came down we
should be in "bad place too much." Therefore, to their great relief, I say
I will stay at this place—Buana—for the night, and go on in the morning
time up to Buea; and just for the present I think I will wrap myself up in
a blanket and try and get the chill out of me, so I give the chiefs a glass
of rum, plenty of head tobacco, and my best thanks for their kind call,
and then turn them all out. I have not been lying down five minutes on
the plank that serves for a sofa by day and a bed by night, when Charles
comes knocking at the door. He wants tobacco. "Missionary man no fit
to let we have firewood unless we buy em." Give Charles a head and shut
him out again, and drop off to sleep again for a quarter of an hour, then
am aroused by some enterprising sightseers pushing open the window-
shutters; when I look round there are a mass of black heads sticking
through the window-hole. I tell them respectfully that the circus is
closed for repairs, and fasten up the shutters, but sleep is impossible, so

I turn out and go and see what those men of mine are after. They are comfortable enough round their fire, with their clothes suspended on strings in the smoke above them, and I envy them that fire. I then stroll round to see if there is anything to be seen, but the scenery is much like that you would enjoy if you were inside a blanc-mange. So as it is now growing dark I return to my room and light candles, and read Dr. Günther on Fishes. Room becomes full of blacks. Unless you watch the door, you do not see how it is done. You look at a corner one minute and it is empty, and the next time you look that way it is full of rows of white teeth and watching eyes. The two mission teachers come in and make a show of teaching a child to read the Bible. After again clearing out the rank and fashion of Buana, I prepare to try and get a sleep; not an elaborate affair, I assure you, for I only want to wrap myself round in a blanket and lie on that plank, but the rain has got into the blankets and horror! there is no pillow. The mission men have cleared their bed paraphernalia right out. Now you can do without a good many things, but not without a pillow, so hunt round to find something to make one with; find the Bible in English, the Bible in German, and two hymn-books, and a candle-stick. These seem all the small articles in the room—no, there is a parcel behind the books—mission teachers' Sunday trousers—make delightful arrangement of books bound round with trousers and the whole affair wrapped in one of my towels. Never saw till now advantage of Africans having trousers. Civilisation has its points after all. But it is no use trying to get any sleep until those men are quieter. The partition which separates my apartment from theirs is a bamboo and mat affair, straight at the top so leaving under the roof a triangular space above common to both rooms. Also common to both rooms are the smoke of the fire and the conversation. Kefalla is holding forth in a dogmatic way, and some of the others are snoring. There is a new idea in decoration along the separating wall. Mr. Morris might have made something out of it for a dado. It is composed of an arrangement in line of stretched out singlets. Vaseline the revolver. Wish those men would leave off chattering. Kefalla seems to know the worst about most of the people, black and white, down in Ambas Bay, but I do not believe those last two stories. Evidently great jokes in next room now; Kefalla has thrown himself, still talking, in the dark, on to the top of one of the mission teachers. The women of the village outside have been keeping up, this hour and more, a most melancholy coo-ooing. Those foolish creatures are evidently worrying about their husbands who have gone down to market in Ambas Bay, and who, they think, are lost in the bush. I have not a shadow of a doubt that those husbands who are not home by now are safely drunk in town, or reposing on the grand new road the kindly Government have provided for them, either in one of the side drains, or tucked in among the lava rock.

September 21st.—Coo-ooing went on all-night. I was aroused about 9:30 p.m., by uproar in adjacent hut: one husband had returned in a bellicose condition and whacked his wives, and their squarks and squalls, instead of acting as a warning to the other ladies, stimulate the silly things to go on coo-ooing louder and more entreatingly than ever, so that their husbands might come home and whack them too, I suppose, and whenever the unmitigated hardness of my plank rouses me I hear them still coo-ooing.

No watchman is required to wake you in the morning on the top of a Cameroon foot-hill by 5:30, because about 4 a.m.the dank chill that comes before the dawn does so most effectively. One old chief turned up early out of the mist and dashed me a bottle of palm wine; he says he wants to dash me a fowl, but I decline, and accept two eggs, and give him four heads of tobacco.

The whole place is swathed in thick white mist through which my audience arrive. But I am firm with them, and shut up the doors and windows and disregard their bangings on them while I am dressing, or rather redressing. The mission teachers get in with my tea, and sit and smoke and spit while I have my breakfast. Give me cannibal Fans!

It is pouring with rain again now, and we go down the steep hillock to the path we came along yesterday, keep it until we come to where the old path cuts it, and then turn up to the right following the old path's course and leave Buana without a pang of regret. Our road goes N.E. Oh, the mud of it! Not the clearish cascades of yesterday but sticky, slippery mud, intensely sticky, and intensely slippery. The narrow path which is filled by this, is V-shaped underneath from wear, and I soon find the safest way is right through the deepest mud in the middle.

The white mist shuts off all details beyond ten yards in any direction. All we can see, as we first turn up the path, is a patch of kokos of tremendous size on our right. After this comes weedy plantation, and stretches of sword grass hanging across the road. The country is even more unlevel than that we came over yesterday. On we go, patiently doing our mud pulling through the valleys; toiling up a hillside among lumps of rock and stretches of forest, for we are now beyond Buana's plantations; and skirting the summit of the hill only to descend into another valley. Evidently this is a succession of foot-hills of the great mountain and we are not on its true face yet. As we go on they become more and more abrupt in form, the valleys mere narrow ravines. In the wet season (this is only the tornado season) each of these valleys is occupied by a raging torrent from the look of the confused water-worn boulders. Now among the rocks there are only isolated pools, for the weather for a fortnight before I left Victoria had been fairly dry, and this rich porous soil soaks up an immense amount of water. It strikes me as strange that when we are either going up or down the hills, the ground is less muddy than when we are skirting their summits, but it must be because on the inclines the rush of water clears the soil away down to the bed rock. There is an outcrop of clay down by Buana, but though that was slippery, it is nothing to the slipperiness of this fine, soft, red-brown earth that is the soil higher up, and also round Ambas Bay. This gets churned up into a sort of batter where there is enough water lying on it, and, when there is not, an ice slide is an infant to it.

My men and I flounder about; thrice one of them, load and all, goes down with a squidge and a crash into the side grass, and says "damn!" with quite the European accent; as a rule, however, we go on in single file, my shoes giving out a mellifluous squidge, and their naked feet a squish, squash. The men take it very good temperedly, and sing in between accidents; I do not feel much like singing myself, particularly at one awful spot, which was the exception to the rule that ground at acute angles forms the best going. This exception was a long slippery slide down into a ravine with a long, perfectly glassy slope up out of it.

After this we have a stretch of rocky forest, and pass by a widening in the path which I am told is a place where men blow, i.e. rest, and then pass through another a little further on, which is Buea's bush market. Then through an opening in the great war-hedge of Buea, a growing stockade some fifteen feet high, the lower part of it wattled.

At the sides of the path here grow banks of bergamot and balsam, returning good for evil and smiling sweetly as we crush them. Thank goodness we are in forest now, and we seem to have done with the sword-grass. The rocks are covered with moss and ferns, and the mist curling and wandering about among the stems is very lovely.

In our next ravine there is a succession of pools, part of a mountain torrent of greater magnitude evidently than those we have passed, and in these pools there are things swimming. Spend more time catching them, with the assistance of Bum. I do not value Kefalla's advice, ample though it is, as being of any real value in the affair. Bag some water-spiders and two small fish. The heat is less oppressive than yesterday. All yesterday one was being alternately smothered in the valley and chilled on the hill-tops. Today it is more level temperature, about 70°, I fancy.

The soil up here, about 2,500 feet above sea-level, though rock-laden is exceedingly rich, and the higher we go there is more bergamot, native indigo, with its under-leaf dark blue, and lovely coleuses with red markings on their upper leaves, and crimson linings. I, as an ichthyologist, am in the wrong paradise. What a region this would be for a botanist!

The country is gloriously lovely if one could only see it for the rain and mist; but one only gets dim hints of its beauty when some cold draughts of wind come down from the great mountains and seem to push open the mist-veil as with spirit hands, and then in a minute let it fall together again. I do not expect to reach Buea within regulation time, but at 11:30 my men say "we close in," and then, coming along a forested hill and down a ravine, we find ourselves facing a rushing river, wherein a squad of black soldiers are washing clothes, with the assistance of a squad of black ladies, with much uproar and sky-larking. I too think it best to wash here, standing in the river and swishing the mud out of my skirts; and then wading across to the other bank, I wring out my skirts. The ground on the further side of the river is cleared of bush, and only bears a heavy crop of balsam; a few steps onwards bring me in view of a corrugated iron-roofed, plank-sided house, in front of which, towards the great mountain which now towers up into the mist, is a low clearing with a quadrangle of native huts—the barracks.

I receive a most kindly welcome from a fair, grey-eyed German gentleman, only unfortunately I see my efforts to appear before him clean and tidy have been quite unavailing, for he views my appearance with unmixed horror, and suggests an instant hot bath. I decline. Men can be trying! How in the world is any one going to take a bath in the house with no doors, and only very sketchy wooden window-shutters?

The German officer is building the house quickly, as Ollendorff would say, but he has not yet got to such luxuries as doors, and so uses army blankets strung across the doorway; and he has got up temporary wooden shutters to keep the worst of the rain out, and across his own room's window he has a frame covered with greased paper. Thank goodness he has made a table, and a bench, and a washhand-stand out of planks for his spare room, which he kindly places at my disposal; and the Fatherland has evidently stood him an iron bedstead and a mattress for it. But the Fatherland is not spoiling or cosseting this man to an extent that will enervate him in the least.

The mist clears off in the evening about five, and the surrounding scenery is at last visible. Fronting the house there is the cleared quadrangle, facing which on the other three sides are the lines of very dilapidated huts, and behind these the ground rises steeply, the great S.E. face of Mungo Mah Lobeh. It looks awfully steep when you know you have got to go up it. This station at Buea is 3,000 feet above sea-level, which explains the hills we have had to come up. The mountain wall when viewed from Buea is very grand, although it lacks snowcap or glacier, and the highest summits of Mungo are not visible because we are too close under them, but its enormous bulk and its isolation make it highly impressive. The forest runs up it in a great band above Buea, then sends up great tongues into the grass belt above. But what may be above this grass belt I know not yet, for our view ends at the top of the wall of the great S.E. crater. My men say there are devils and gold up beyond, but the German authorities do not support this view. Those Germans are so skeptical. This station is evidently on a ledge, for behind it the ground falls steeply, and you get an uninterrupted panoramic view of the Cameroon estuary and the great stretches of low swamp lands with the Mungo and the Bimbia rivers, and their many creeks and channels, and far away east the strange abrupt forms of the Rumby Mountains. Herr Liebert says you can see Cameroon Government buildings from here, if only the day is clear, though they are some forty miles away. This view of them is, save a missionary of the Basel mission, the only white society available at Buea.

I hear more details about the death of poor Freiheer von Gravenreuth, whose fine monument of a seated lion I saw in the Government House grounds in Cameroons the other day. Bush fighting in these West African forests is dreadfully dangerous work. Hemmed in by bush, in a narrow path along which you must pass slowing in single file, you are a target for all and any natives invisibly hidden in the undergrowth; and the war-hedge of Buea must have made an additional danger and difficulty here for the attacking party. The lieutenant and his small bank of black soldiers had, after a stiff fight, succeeded in forcing the entrance to this, when their ammunition gave out, and they had to fall back. The Bueans, regarding this as their victory, rallied, and a chance shot killed the lieutenant instantly. A further expedition was promptly sent up from Victoria and it wiped the error out of the Buean mind and several Bueans with it. But it was a very necessary expedition. These natives were a constant source of danger to the more peaceful trading tribes, whom they would not permit to traverse their territory. The Bueans have been dealt with mercifully by the Germans, for their big villages, like Sapa, are still standing, and a continual stream of natives come into the barrack-yard, selling produce, or carrying it on down to Victoria markets, in a perfectly content and cheerful way. I met this morning a big burly chief with his insignia of office—great stick. He, I am told, is the chief of Sapa whom Herr von Lucke has called to talk some palaver with down in Victoria.

At last I leave Herr Liebert, because everything I say to him causes him to hop, flying somewhere to show me something, and I am sure it is bad for his foot. I go and see that my men are safely quartered. Kefalla is laying down the law in a most didactic way to the soldiers. Herr Liebert has christened him "the Professor," and I adopt the name for him, but I fear "Windbag" would fit him better.

At 7:30 a heavy tornado comes rolling down upon us. Masses of indigo cloud with livid lightning flashing in the van, roll out from over the wall of the great crater above; then with that malevolence peculiar to the tornado it sees all the soldiers and their wives and children sitting happily in the barrack yard, howling in a minor key and beating their beloved tom-toms, so it comes and sits flump down on them with deluges of water, and sends its lightning running over the ground in livid streams of living death. Oh, they are nice things are tornadoes! I wonder what they will be like when we are up in their home; up atop of that precious wall? I had no idea Mungo was so steep. If I had—well, I am in for it now!

CHAPTER 18

ASCENT OF THE GREAT PEAK
OF CAMEROONS (CONTINUED)

Wherein is recounted how the Voyager sets out from Buea,
and goes up through the forest belt to the top of the S.E. crater of Mungo Mah Lobeh,
with many dilemmas and disasters that befell on the way.

SEPTEMBER 22ND.—WAKE AT 5. Fine morning. Fine view towards Cameroon River. The broad stretch of forest below, and the water-eaten mangrove swamps below that, are all a glorious indigo flushed with rose color from "the death of the night," as Kiva used to call the dawn. No one stirring till six, when people come out of the huts, and stretch themselves and proceed to begin the day, in the African's usual perfunctory, listless way.

My crew are worse than the rest. I go and hunt cook out. He props open one eye, with difficulty, and yawns a yawn that nearly cuts his head in two. I wake him up with a shock, by saying I mean to go on up to-day, and want my chop, and to start one time. He goes off and announces my horrible intention to the others. Kefalla soon arrives upon the scene full of argument, "You no sabe this be Sunday, Ma?" says he in a tone that tells he considers this settles the matter. I "sabe" unconcernedly; Kefalla scratches his head for other argument, but he has opened with his heavy artillery; which being repulsed throws his rear lines into confusion. Bum, the head man, then turns up, sound asleep inside, but quite ready to come. Bum, I find, is always ready to do what he is told, but has no more original ideas in his head than there are in a chair leg. Kefalla, however, by scratching other parts of his anatomy diligently, has now another argument ready, the two Bakwiris are sick with abdominal trouble, that requires rum and rest, and one of the other boys has hot foot.

Herr Liebert now appears upon the scene, and says I can have some of his labourers, who are now more or less idle, because he cannot get about much with his bad foot to direct them, so I give the Bakwiris and the two hot foot cases "books" to take down to Herr von Lucke who will pay them off for me, and seeing that they have each a good day's rations of rice, beef, &c., eliminate them from my party.

In addition to the labourers, I am to have as a guide Sasu, a black sergeant, who went up the Peak with the officers of the *Hyæna*, and I get my breakfast, and then hang about watching my men getting ready very slowly to start. Off we get about 8, and start with all good wishes, and grim prophecies, from Herr Liebert.

Led by Sasu, and accompanied by "To-morrow," a man who has come to Buea from some interior unknown district, and who speaks no known language, and whose business it is to help to cut a way through the bush, we go down the path we came and cross the river again. This river seems to separate the final mass of the mountain from the foot-hills on this side. Immediately after crossing it we turn up into the forest on the right hand side, and "To-morrow" cuts through an over-grown track for about half-an-hour, and then leaves us.

Everything is reeking wet, and we swish through thick undergrowth and then enter a darker forest where the earth is rocky and richly decorated with ferns and moss. For the first time in my life I see tree-ferns growing wild in luxuriant profusion. What glorious creations they are! Then we get out into the middle of a koko plantation. Next to sweet-potatoes, the premier abomination to walk through, give me kokos for good all around tryingness, particularly when they are wet, as, is very much the case now. Getting through these we meet the war hedge again, and after a conscientious struggle with various forms of vegetation in a muddled, tangled state, Sasu says, "No good, path done got stopped up," so we turn and retrace our steps all the way, cross the river, and horrify Herr Liebert by invading his house again. We explain the situation. Grave head-shaking between him and Sasu about the practicability of any other route, because there is no other path. I do not like to say "so much the better," because it would have sounded ungrateful, but I knew from my Ogowé experiences that a forest that looks from afar a

dense black mat is all right underneath, and there is a short path recently
cut by Herr Liebert that goes straight up towards the forest above us. It
had been made to go to a clearing, where ambitious agricultural operations were being inaugurated, when Herr Liebert hurt his foot. Up this
we go, it is semi-vertical while it lasts, and it ends in a scrubby patch that
is to be a plantation; this crossed we are in the *Urwald*, and it is more
exquisite than words can describe, but not good going, particularly at
one spot where a gigantic tree has fallen down across a little rocky ravine,
and has to be crawled under. It occurs to me that this is a highly likely
place for snakes and an absolutely sure find for scorpions, and when we
have passed it three of these latter interesting creatures are observed on
the load of blankets which is fastened to the back of Kefalla. We inform
Kefalla of the fact on the spot. A volcanic eruption of entreaty, advice,
and admonition results, but we still hesitate. However, the gallant cook
tackles them in a sort of tip-cat way with a stick, and we proceed into a
patch of long grass, beyond which there is a reach of amomums. The
winged amomum I see here in Africa for the first time. Horrid slippery
things amomum sticks to walk on, when they are lying on the ground;
and there is a lot of my old enemy the calamus about.

On each side are deep forested dells and ravines, and rocks show up
through the ground in every direction, and things in general are slippery, and I wonder now and again, as I assume with unnecessary violence
a recumbent position, why I came to Africa; but patches of satin-leaved
begonias and clumps of lovely tree-ferns reconcile me to my lot. Cook
does not feel these forest charms, and gives me notice after an hour's
experience of mountain forest-belt work; what cook would not?

As we get higher we have to edge and squeeze every few minutes
through the aërial roots of some tremendous kind of tree, plentiful
hereabouts. One of them we passed through I am sure would have run
any Indian banyan hard for extent of ground covered, if it were measured. In the region where these trees are frequent, the undergrowth is
less dense than it is lower down.

Imagine a vast, seemingly limitless cathedral with its countless
columns covered, nay, composed of the most exquisite dark-green,
large-fronded moss, with here and there a delicate fern embedded in it
as an extra decoration. The white, gauze-like mist comes down from the
upper mountain towards us: creeping, twining round, and streaming
through the moss-covered tree columns—long bands of it reaching

along sinuous, but evenly, for fifty and sixty feet or more, and then ending in a puff like the smoke of a gun. Soon, however, all the mist-streams coalesce and make the atmosphere all their own, wrapping us round in a clammy, chill embrace; it is not that wool-blanket, smothering affair that we were wrapped in down by Buana, but exquisitely delicate. The difference it makes to the beauty of the forest is just the same difference you would get if you put a delicate veil over a pretty woman's face or a sack over her head. In fact, the mist here was exceedingly becoming to the forest's beauty. Now and again growls of thunder roll out from, and quiver in the earth beneath our feet. Mungo is making a big tornado, and is stirring and simmering it softly so as to make it strong. I only hope he will not overdo it, as he does six times in seven, and make it too heavy to get out on to the Atlantic, where all tornadoes ought to go. If he does the thing will go and burst on us in this forest to-night.

The forest now grows less luxuriant though still close—we have left the begonias and the tree-ferns, and are in another zone. The trees now, instead of being clothed in rich, dark-green moss, are heavily festooned with long, greenish-white lichen. It pours with rain.

At last we reach the place where the sergeant says we ought to camp for the night. I have been feeling the time for camping was very ripe for the past hour, and Kefalla openly said as much an hour and a half ago, but he got such scathing things said to him about civilians' legs by the sergeant that I did not air my own opinion.

We are now right at the very edge of the timber belt. My head man and three boys are done to a turn. If I had had a bull behind me or Mr. Fildes in front, I might have done another five or seven miles, but not more.

The rain comes down with extra virulence as soon as we set to work to start the fire and open the loads. I and Peter have great times getting out the military camp-bed from its tight, bolster-like case, while Kefalla gives advice, until, being irritated by the bed's behavior, I blow up Kefalla and send him to chop firewood. However, we get the thing out and put up after cutting a place clear to set it on: owing to the world being on a stiff slant hereabouts, it takes time to make it stand straight. I get four stakes cut, and drive them in at the four corners of the bed, and then stretch over it Herr von Lucke's waterproof ground-sheet, guy the ends out to pegs with string, feel profoundly grateful to both Herr Liebert for the bed and Herr von Lucke for the sheet, and place the baggage under the protection of the German Government's two belongings.

Then I find the boys have not got a fire with all their fuss, and I have to demonstrate to them the lessons I have learnt among the Fans regarding fire-making. We build a fire-house and then all goes well. I notice they do not make a fire Fan fashion, but build it in a circle.

Evidently one of the labourers from Buea, named Xenia, is a good man. Equally evidently some of my other men are only fit to carry sandwich-boards for Day and Martin's blacking. I dine luxuriously off tinned fat pork and hot tea, and then feeling still hungry go on to tinned herring. Excellent thing tinned herring, but I have to hurry because I know I must go up through the edge of the forest on to the grass land, and see how the country is made during the brief period of clearness that almost always comes just before nightfall. So leaving my boys comfortably seated round the fire having their evening chop, I pass up through the heavily lichen-tasseled fringe on the forest-belt into deep jungle grass, and up a steep and slippery mound.

In front the mountain-face rises like a wall from behind a set of hillocks, similar to the one I am at present on. The face of the wall to the right and left has two dark clefts in it. The peak itself is not visible from where I am; it rises behind and beyond the wall. I stay taking compass bearings and look for an easy way up for tomorrow. My men, by now, have missed their "ma" and are yelling for her dismally, and the night comes down with great rapidity for we are in the shadow of the great mountain mass, so I go back into camp. Alas! How vain are often our most energetic efforts to remove our fellow creatures from temptation. I knew a Sunday down among the soldiers would be bad for my men, and so came up here, and now, if you please, these men have been at the rum, because Bum, the head man, has been too done up to do anything but lie in his blanket and feed. Kefalla is laying down the law with great detail and unction. Cook who has been very low in his mind all day, is now weirdly cheerful, and sings incoherently. The other boys, who want to go to sleep, threaten to "burst him" if he "no finish." It's no good—cook carols on, and soon succumbing to the irresistible charm of music, the other men have to join in the choruses. The performance goes on for an hour, growing woollier and woollier in tone, and then dying out in sleep.

I write by the light of an insect-haunted lantern, sitting on the bed, which is tucked in among the trees some twenty yards away from the boys' fire. There is a bird whistling in a deep rich note that I have never heard before.

September 23rd.—Morning gloriously fine. Rout the boys out, and start at seven, with Sasu, Head man, Xenia, Black boy, Kefalla, and Cook.

The great south-east wall of the mountain in front of us is quite unflecked by cloud, and in the forest are thousands of bees. We notice that the tongues of forest go up the mountain in some places a hundred yards or more above the true line of the belt. These tongues of forest get more and more heavily hung with lichen, and the trees thinner and more stunted, towards their ends. I think that these tongues are always in places where the wind does not get full play. All those near our camping place on this south-east face are so. It is evidently not a matter of soil, for there is ample soil on this side above where the trees are, and then again on the western side of the mountain—the side facing the sea— the timber line is far higher up than on this. Nor, again, is it a matter of angle that makes the timber line here so low, for those forests on the Sierra del Cristal were growing luxuriantly over far steeper grades. There is some peculiar local condition just here evidently, or the forest would be up to the bottom of the wall of the crater. I am not unreasonable enough to expect it to grow on that, but its conduct in staying where it does requires explanation.

We clamber up into the long jungle grass region and go on our way across a series of steep-sided, rounded grass hillocks, each of which is separated from the others by dry, rocky watercourses. The effects produced by the seed-ears of the long grass round us are very beautiful; they look a golden brown, and each ear and leaf is gemmed with dewdrops, and those of the grass on the sides of the hillocks at a little distance off show a soft brown-pink.

After half an hour's climb, when we are close at the base of the wall, I observe the men ahead halting, and coming up with them find Monrovia Boy down a hole; a little deep blow-hole, in which, I am informed, water is supposed to be. But Monrovia soon reports "No live."

I now find we have not a drop of water, either with us or in camp, and now this hole has proved dry. There is, says the sergeant, no chance of getting any more water on this side of the mountain, save down at the river at Buea.

This means failure unless tackled, and it is evidently a trick played on me by the boys, who intentionally failed to let me know of this want of water before leaving Buea, where it seems they have all learnt it. I express my opinion of them in four words and send Monrovia boy, who

I know is to be trusted, back to Buea with a scribbled note to Herr Liebert asking him to send me up two demijohns of water. I send cook with him as far as the camp in the forest we have just left with orders to bring up three bottles of soda water I have left there, and to instruct the men there that as soon as the water arrives from Buea they are to bring it on up to the camp I mean to make at the top of the wall.

The men are sulky, and Sasu, Peter, Kefalla, and head man say they will wait and come on as soon as cook brings the soda water, and I go on, and presently see Xenia and Black boy are following me. We get on to the intervening hillocks and commence to ascend the face of the wall.

The angle of this wall is great, and its appearance from below is impressive from its enormous breadth, and its abrupt rise without bend or droop for a good 2,000 feet into the air. It is covered with short, yellowish grass through which the burnt-up, scoriaceous lava rock protrudes in rough masses.

I got on up the wall, which when you are on it is not so perpendicular as it looks from below, my desire being to see what sort of country there was on the top of it, between it and the final peak. Sasu had reported to Herr Liebert that it was a wilderness of rock, in which it would be impossible to fix a tent, and spoke vaguely of caves. Here and there on the way up I come to holes, similar to the one my men had been down for water. I suppose these holes have been caused by gases from an under hot layer of lava bursting up through the upper cool layer. As I get higher, the grass becomes shorter and more sparse, and the rocks more ostentatiously displayed. Here and there among them are sadly tried bushes, bearing a beautiful yellow flower, like a large yellow wild rose, only scentless. It is not a rose at all, I may remark. The ground, where there is any basin made by the rocks, grows a great sedum, with a grand head of whity-pink flower, also a tall herb, with soft downy leaves silver gray in colour, and having a very pleasant aromatic scent, and here and there patches of good honest parsley. Bright blue, flannelly-looking flowers stud the grass in sheltered places and a very pretty large green orchid is plentiful. Above us is a bright blue sky with white cloud rushing hurriedly across it to the N.E. and a fierce sun. When I am about half-way up, I think of those boys, and, wanting rest, sit down by an inviting-looking rock grotto, with a patch of the yellow flowered shrub growing on its top. Inside it grow little ferns and mosses, all damp; but alas! No water pool, and very badly I want water by this time.

Below me a belt of white cloud had now formed, so that I could see neither the foot-hillocks nor the forest, and presently out of this mist came Xenia toiling up carrying my black bag. "Where them Black boy live?" said I. "Black boy say him foot be tire too much," said Xenia, as he threw himself down in the little shade the rock could give. I took a cupful of sour claret out of the bottle in the bag, and told Xenia to come on up as soon as he was rested, and meanwhile to yell to the others down below and tell them to come on. Xenia did, but sadly observed, "softly softly still hurts the snail," and I left him and went on up the mountain.

When I had got to the top of the rock under which I had sheltered from the blazing sun, the mist opened a little, and I saw my men looking like so many little dolls. They were still sitting on the hillock where I had left them. Buea showed from this elevation well. The guard house and the mission house, like little houses in a picture, and the make of the ground on which Buea station stands, came out distinctly as a ledge or terrace, extending for miles N.N.E. and S.S.W. This ledge is a strange-looking piece of country, covered with low bush, out of which rise great, isolated, white-stemmed cotton trees. Below, and beyond this is a denser band of high forest, and again below this stretches the vast mangrove-swamp fringing the estuary of the Cameroons, Mungo, and Bimbia rivers. It is a very noble view, giving one an example of the peculiar beauty one oft-times gets in this West African scenery, namely colossal sweeps of color. The mangrove-swamps looked to-day like a vast damson-coloured carpet threaded with silver where the waterways ran. It reminded me of a scene I saw once near Cabinda, when on climbing to the top of a hill I suddenly found myself looking down on a sheet of violet pink more than a mile long and half a mile wide. This was caused by a climbing plant having taken possession of a valley full of trees, whose tops it had reached and then spread and interlaced itself over them, to burst into profuse glorious laburnum-shaped bunches of flowers.

After taking some careful compass bearings for future use regarding the Rumby and Omon range of mountains, which were clearly visible and which look fascinatingly like my beloved Sierra del Cristal, I turned my face to the wall of Mungo, and continued the ascent. The sun, which was blazing, was reflected back from the rocks in scorching rays. But it was more bearable now, because its heat was tempered by a bitter wind.

The slope becoming steeper, I gradually made my way towards the left until I came to a great land, as neatly walled with rock as if it had been

made with human hands. It runs down the mountain face, nearly vertically in places and at stiff angles always, but it was easier going up this
lane than on the outside rough rock, because the rocks in it had been
smoothed by mountain torrents during thousands of wet seasons, and
the wall protected one from the biting wind, a wind that went through
me, for I had been stewing for nine months and more in tropic and
equatorial swamps.

Up this lane I went to the very top of the mountain wall, and then,
to my surprise, found myself facing a great, hillocky, rock-encumbered
plain, across the other side of which rose the mass of the peak itself, not
as a single cone, but as a wall surmounted by several, three being evidently the highest amount them.

I started along the ridge of my wall, and went to its highest part, that
to the S.W., intending to see what I could of the view towards the sea,
and then to choose a place for camping in for the night.

When I reached the S.W. end, looking westwards I saw the South
Atlantic down below, like a plain of frosted silver. Out of it, barely
twenty miles away, rose Fernando Po to its 10,190 feet with that majestic
grace peculiar to a volcanic island. Immediately below me, some 10,000
feet or so, lay Victoria with the forested foot-hills of Mungo Mah Lobeh
encircling it as a diadem, and Ambas Bay gemmed with rocky islands
lying before it. On my left away S.E. was the glorious stretch of the
Cameroon estuary, with a line of white cloud lying very neatly along the
course of the Cameroon River.

In one of the chasms of the mountain wall that I had come up—in
the one furthest to the north—there was a thunderstorm brewing, seemingly hanging on to, or streaming out of the mountain side, a soft billowy
mass of dense cream-coloured cloud, with flashes of golden lightning
playing about in it with soft growls of thunder. Surely Mungo Mah Lobeh
himself, of all the thousands he annually turns out, never made one
more lovely than this. Soon the white mists rose from the mangrove-
swamp, and grew rose-colour in the light of the setting sun, as they swept
upwards over the now purple high forests. In the heavens, to the north,
there was a rainbow, vivid in colour, one arch of it going behind the
peak, the other sinking into the mist sea below, and this mist sea rose
and rose towards me, turning from pale rose-colour to lavender, and
where the shadow of Mungo lay across it, to a dull leaden gray. It was
soon at my feet, blotting the under-world out, and soon came flowing

over the wall top at its lowest parts, stretching in great spreading rivers over the crater plain, and then these coalescing everything was shut out save the two summits: that of Cameroon close to me, and that of Clarence away on Fernando Po. These two stood out alone, like great island masses made of iron rising from a formless, silken sea.

The space around seemed boundless, and there was in it neither sound nor colour, nor anything with form, save those two terrific things. It was like a vision, and it held me spell-bound, as I stood shivering on the rocks with the white mist round my knees until into my wool-gathering mind came the memory of those anything but sublime men of mine; and I turned and scuttled off along the rocks like an agitated ant left alone in a dead Universe.

I soon found the place where I had come up into the crater plain and went down over the wall, descending with twice the rapidity, but ten times the scratches and grazes, of the ascent.

I picked up the place where I had left Xenia, but no Xenia was there, nor came there any answer to my bush call for him, so on I went down towards the place where, hours ago, I had left the men. The mist was denser down below, but to my joy it was warmer than on the summit of the wind-swept wall.

I had nearly reached the foot of this wall and made my mind up to turn in for the night under a rock, when I heard a melancholy croak away in the mist to the left. I went towards it and found Xenia lost on his own account, and distinctly quaint in manner, and then I recollected that I had been warned Xenia is slightly crazy. Nice situation this: a madman on a mountain in the mist. Xenia, I found, had no longer got my black bag, but in its place a lid of a saucepan and an empty lantern. To put it mildly, this is not the sort of outfit the R.G.S. *Hints to Travelers* would recommend for African exploration. Xenia reported that he gave the bag to the Black boy, who shortly afterwards disappeared, and that he had neither seen him nor any of the others since, and didn't expect to this side of Srahmandazi. In a homicidal state of mind, I made tracks for the missing ones followed by Xenia. I thought mayhap they had grown on to the rocks they had sat upon so long, but presently, just before it became quite dark, we picked up the place we had left them in and found there only an empty soda-water bottle. Xenia poured out a muddled mass of observations to the effect that "they got fright too much about them water palaver."

I did not linger to raise a monument to them, but I said I wished they were in a condition to require one, and we went on over our hillocks with more confidence now that we knew we had stuck well to our unmarked track.

> "The moving Moon went up the sky,
>   And nowhere did abide:
> Softly she was going up,
>   And a star or two beside."

Only she was a young and inefficient moon, and although we were below the thickest of the mist band, it was dark.

Finding our own particular hole in the forest wall was about as easy as finding "one particular rabbit hole in an unknown hay-field in the dark," and the attempt to do so afforded us a great deal of varied exercise. I am obliged to be guarded in my language, because my feelings now are only down to one degree below boiling point. The rain now began to fall, thank goodness, and I drew the thick ears of grass through my parched lips as I stumbled along over the rugged lumps of rock hidden under the now waist-high jungle grass.

Our camp hole was pretty easily distinguishable by daylight, for it was on the left-hand side of one of the forest tongues, the grass land running down like a lane between two tongues here, and just over the entrance three conspicuously high trees showed. But we could not see these "picking-up" points in the darkness, so I had to keep getting Xenia to strike matches, and hold them in his hat while I looked at the compass. Presently we came full tilt up against a belt of trees which I knew from these compass observations was our tongue of forest belt, and I fired a couple of revolver shots into it, whereabouts I judged our camp to be.

This was instantly answered by a yell from human voices in chorus, and towards that yell in a slightly amiable—a very slightly amiable—state of mind I went.

I will draw a veil over the scene, particularly over my observations to those men. They did not attempt to deny their desertion, but they attempted to explain it, each one saying that it was not he but the other boy who "got fright too much."

I closed the palaver promptly with a brief but lurid sketch of my opinion on the situation, and ordered food, for not having a thing save that cup of sour claret since 6:30 a.m., and it being now 11 p.m., I felt sinkings. Then arose another beautiful situation before me. It seems when Cook and Monrovia got back into camp this morning Master Cook was seized with one of those attacks of a desire to manage things that produce such awful results in the African servant, and sent all the beef and rice down to Buea to be cooked, because there was no water here to cook it. Therefore the men have got nothing to eat. I had a few tins of my own food and so gave them some, and they became as happy as kings in a few minutes, listening and shouting over the terrible adventures of Xenia, who is posing as the Hero of the Great Cameroon. I get some soda-water from the two bottles left and some tinned herring, and then write out two notes to Herr Liebert asking him to send me three more demijohns of water, and some beef and rice from the store, promising faithfully to pay for them on my return.

I would not prevent those men of mine from going up that peak above me after their touching conduct to-day. Oh! No; not for worlds, dear things.

CHAPTER 19

The Great Peak of Cameroons
(continued)

Setting forth how the Voyager for a second time reaches the S.E. crater, with some account of the pleasures incidental to camping out in the said crater.

SEPTEMBER 24TH.—LOVELY MORNING, the grey-white mist in the forest makes it like a dream of Fairyland, each moss-grown tree stem heavily gemmed with dewdrops. At 5:30 I stir the boys, for Sasu, the sergeant, says he must go back to his military duties. The men think we are all going back with him as he is our only guide, but I send three of them down with orders to go back to Victoria—two being of the original set I started with. They are surprised and disgusted at being sent home, but they have got "hot food," and something wrong in the usual seat of African internal disturbances, their "tummicks," and I am not thinking of starting a sanatorium for abdominally-afflicted Africans in that crater plain above. Black boy is the other boy returned, I do not want another of his attacks.

They go, and this leaves me in the forest camp with Kefalla, Xenia, and Cook, and we start expecting the water sent for by Monrovia boy yesterday forenoon. There are an abominable lot of bees about; they do not give one a moment's peace, getting beneath the waterproof sheets over the bed. The ground, bestrewn with leaves and dried wood, is a mass of large flies rather like our common house-fly, but both butter-flies and beetles seem scarce; and I confess I do not feel up to hunting much after yesterday's work, and deem it advisable to rest.

My face and particularly my lips are a misery to me, having been blistered all over by yesterday's sun, and last night I inadvertently whipped the skin all off one cheek with the blanket, and it keeps on bleeding, and, horror of horrors, there is no tea until the water comes.

I wish I had got the mountaineering spirit, for then I could say, "I'll never come to this sort of place again, for you can get all you want in the Alps." I have been told this by my mountaineering friends—I have never been there—and that you can go and do all sorts of stupendous things all day, and come back in the evening to *table d'hôte* at an hotel; but as I have not got the mountaineering spirit, I suppose I shall come fooling into some such place as this as soon as I get the next chance.

About 8:30, to our delight, the gallant Monrovia boy comes through the bush with a demijohn of water, and I get my tea, and give the men the only half-pound of rice I have and a tin of meat, and they eat, become merry, and chat over their absent companions in a scornful, scandalous way. Who cares for hotels now? When one is in a delightful place like this, one must work, so off I go to the north into the forest, after giving the rest of the demijohn of water into the Monrovia boy's charge with strict orders it is not to be opened till my return. Quantities of beetles.

A little after two o'clock I return to camp, after having wandered about in the forest and found three very deep holes, down which I heaved rocks and in no case heard a splash. In one I did not hear the rocks strike, owing to a great depth. I hate holes, and especially do I hate these African ones, for I am frequently falling, more or less, into them, and they will be my end.

The other demijohns of water have not arrived yet, and we are getting anxious again because the men's food has not come up, and they have been so exceedingly thirsty that they have drunk most of the water—not, however, since it has been in Monrovia's charge; but at 3:15 another boy comes through the bush with another demijohn of water. We receive him gladly, and ask him about the chop. He knows nothing about it. At 3:45 another boy comes through the bush with another demijohn of water; we receive him kindly; he does not know anything about the chop. At 4:10 another boy comes through the bush with another demijohn of water, and knowing nothing about the chop we are civil to him, and that's all.

A terrific tornado which has been lurking growling about then sits down in the forest and bursts, wrapping us up in a lively kind of fog, with its thunder, lightning, and rain. It was impossible to hear, or make one's self heard at the distance of even a few paces, because of the shrill squeal of the wind, the roar of the thunder, and the rush of the rain on the trees round us. It was not like having a storm burst over you in the least; you felt you were in the middle of its engine-room when it had broken down badly. After half an hour or so the thunder seemed to lift itself of in great forks that flew like flights of spears among the forest trees. The thunder, however, had not settled things amicably with the mountain; it roared its rage at Mungo, and Mungo answered back, quivering with a rage as great, under our feet. One feels here as if one were constantly dropping, unasked and unregarded, among painful and violent discussions between the elemental powers of the Universe. Mungo growls and swears in thunder at the sky, and sulks in white mist all the morning, and then the sky answers back, hurling down lightnings and rivers of water, with total disregard of Mungo's visitors. The way the water rushes down from the mountain wall through the water-courses in the jungle just above, and then at the edge of the forest spreads out into a sheet of water that is an inch deep, and that flies on past us in miniature cascades, trying the while to put out our fire and so on, is—quite interesting. (I exhausted my vocabulary on those boys yesterday.)

As soon as we saw what we were in for, we had thrown dry wood on to the fire, and it blazed just as the rain came down, so with our assistance it fought a good fight with its fellow elements, spitting and hissing like a wild cat. It could have managed the water fairly well, but the wind came, very nearly putting an end to it by carrying away its protecting bough house, which settled on "Professor" Kefalla, who burst out in a lecture on the foolishness of mountaineering and the quantity of devils in this region. Just in the midst of these joys another boy came through the bush with another demijohn of water. We did not receive him even civilly; I burst out laughing, and the boys went off in a roar, and we shouted at him, "Where them chop?" "He live for come," said the boy, and we then gave him a hearty welcome and a tot of rum, and an hour afterwards two more boys appear, one carrying a sack of rice and beef for the men, and the other a box for me from Herr Liebert, containing a luxurious supply of biscuits, candles, tinned meats, and a bottle of wine and one of beer.

We are now all happy, though exceeding damp, and the boys sit round the fire, with their big iron pot full of beef and rice, busy cooking while they talk. Wonderful accounts of our prodigies of valour I hear given by

Xenia, and terrible accounts of what they have lived through from the others, and the men who have brought up the demijohns and the chop recount the last news from Buea. James's wife has run away again.

I have taken possession of two demijohns of water and the rum demijohn, arranging them round the head of my bed. The worst of it is those tiresome bees, as soon as the rain is over, come in hundreds after the rum, and frighten me continually. The worthless wretches get intoxicated on what they can suck from round the cork, and then they stagger about on the ground buzzing malevolently. When the boys have had the chop and a good smoke, we turn to and make up the loads for tomorrow's start up the mountain, and then, after more hot tea, I turn in on my camp bed—listening to the soft sweet murmur of the trees and the pleasant, laughing chatter of the men.

September 25th.—Rolled off the bed twice last night into the bush. The rain has washed the ground away from under its off legs, so that it tilts; and there were quantities of large longicorn beetles about during the night—the sort with spiny backs; they keep on getting themselves hitched on to my blankets and when I wanted civilly to remove them they made a horrid fizzing noise and showed fight—cocking their horns in a defiant way. I awake finally about 5 a.m. soaked through to the skin. The waterproof sheet has had a label sewn to it, so is not waterproof, and it has been raining softly but amply for hours.

About seven we are off again, with Xenia, Head man, cook, Monrovia boy and a labourer from Buea—the water carriers have gone home after having had their morning chop.

We make for the face of the wall by a route to the left of that I took on Monday, and when we are clambering up it, some 600 feet above the hillocks, swish comes a terrific rain-storm at us accompanied by a squealing, bitter cold wind. We can hear the roar of the rain on the forest below, and hoping to get above it we keep on; hoping, however, is vain. The dense mist that comes with it prevents our seeing more than two yards in front, and we get too far to the left. I am behind the band today, severely bringing up the rear, and about one o'clock I hear shouts from the vanguard and when I get up to them I find them sitting on the edge of one of the clefts or scars in the mountain face.

I do not know how these quarry-like chasms have been formed. They both look alike from below—the mountain wall comes down vertically into them—and the bottom of this one slopes forward, so that if we had had the misfortune when a little lower down to have gone a little further to the left, we should have got on to the bottom of it, and should have found ourselves walled in on three sides, and had to retrace our steps; as it is we have just struck its right-hand edge. And fortunately, the mist, thick as it is, has not been sufficiently thick to lead the men to walk over it; for had they done so they would have got killed, as the cliff arches in under so that we look straight into the bottom of the scar some 200 or 300 feet below, when there is a split in the mist. The sides and bottom are made of, and strewn with, white, moss-grown masses of volcanic cinder rock, and sparsely shrubbed with gnarled trees which have evidently been under fire—one of my boys tells me from the burning of this face of the mountain by "the Major from Calabar" during the previous dry season.

We keep on up a steep grass-covered slope, and finally reach the top of the wall. The immense old crater floor before us is today the site of a seething storm, and the peak itself quite invisible. My boys are quite demoralized by the cold. I find most of them have sold the blankets I gave them out at Buana; and those who have not sold them have left them behind at Buea, from laziness perhaps, but more possibly from a confidence in their powers to prevent us getting so far.

I believe if I had collapsed too—the cold tempted me to do so as nothing else can—they would have lain down and died in the cold sleety rain.

I sight a clump of gnarled sparsely-foliaged trees bedraped heavily with lichen, rowing in a hollow among the rocks; thither I urge the men for shelter and they go like storm-bewildered sheep. My bones are shaking in my skin and my teeth in my head, for after the experience I had had of the heat here on Monday I dared not clothe myself heavily.

The men stand helpless under the trees, and I hastily take the load of blankets Herr Liebert lent us off a boy's back and undo it, throwing one blanket round each man, and opening my umbrella and spreading it over the other blankets. Then I give them a tot of rum apiece, as they sit huddled in their blankets, and tear up a lot of the brittle, rotten wood from the trees and shrubs, getting horrid thorns into my hands the while, and set to work getting a fire with it and the driest of the moss from beneath the rocks. By the aid of it and Xenia, who soon revived, and a carefully scraped up candle and a box of matches, the fire soon blazes, Xenia holding a blanket to shelter it, while I, with a cutlass, chop stakes to fix the blankets on, so as to make a fire tent.

The other boys now revive, and I hustle them about to make more fires, no easy work in the drenching rain, but work that has got to be done. We soon get three well alight, and then I clutch a blanket—a wringing wet blanket, but a comfort—and wrapping myself round in it, issue orders for wood to be gathered and stored round each fire to dry, and then stand over Cook while he makes the men's already cooked chop hot over our first fire, when this is done getting him to make me tea, or as it more truly should be called, soup, for it contains bits of rice and beef, and the general taste of the affair is wood smoke.

Kefalla by this time is in lecturing form again, so my mind is relieved about him, although he says, "Oh ma! It be cold, cold too much. Too much cold kill we black man, all same for one as too much sun kill you white man. Oh, ma...," &c. I tell him they have only got themselves to blame; if they had come up with me on Monday we should have been hot enough, and missed this storm of rain.

When the boys have had their chop, and are curling themselves up comfortably round their now blazing fires Xenia must needs start a theory that there is a better place than this to camp in; he saw it when he was with an unsuccessful expedition that got as far as this. Kefalla is fool enough to go off with him to find this place; but they soon return, chilled through again, and unsuccessful in their quest. I gather that they have been to find caves. I wish they had found caves, for I am not thinking of taking out a patent for our present camp site.

The bitter wind and swishing rain keep on. We are to a certain extent sheltered from the former, but the latter is of that insinuating sort that nothing but a granite wall would keep off.

Just at sundown, however, as is usual in this country, the rain ceases for a while, and I take this opportunity to get out my seaman's jersey. When I have fought my way into it, I turn to survey our position, and find I have been carrying on my battle on the brink of an abysmal hole whose mouth is concealed among the rocks and scraggly shrubs just above our camp. I heave rocks down it, as we in Fanland would offer rocks to an Ombwiri, and hear them go "knickity-knock, like a pebble in Carisbrook well." I think I detect a far away splash, but it was an awesome way down. This mountain seems set with these man-traps, and "some day some gentleman's nigger" will get killed down one.

The mist has now cleared away from the peak, but lies all over the lower world, and I take bearings of the three highest cones or peaks carefully.

Then I go away over the rocky ground southwards, and as I stand looking round, the mist sea below is cleft in twain for a few minutes by some
fierce down-draught of wind from the peak, and I get a strange, clear,
sudden view right down to Ambas Bay. It is just like looking down from
one world into another. I think how Odin hung and looked down into
Nifelheim, and then of how hot, how deliciously hot, it was away down
there, and then the mist closes over it. I shiver and go back to camp, for
night is coming on, and I know my men will require intellectual support
in the matter of procuring firewood.

The men are now quite happy; over each fire they have made a tent
with four sticks with a blanket on, a blanket that is too wet to burn,
though I have to make them brace the blankets to windward for fear of
their scorching.

The wood from the shrubs here is of an aromatic and a resinous
nature, which sounds nice, but it isn't; for the volumes of smoke it gives
off when burning are suffocating, and the boys, who sit almost on the
fire, are every few moments scrambling to their feet and going apart to
cough out smoke, like so many novices in training for the profession of
fire-eaters. However, they soon find that if they roll themselves in their
blankets, and lie on the ground to windward they escape most of the
smoke. They have divided up into three parties: Kefalla and Xenia, who
have stuck up a great friendship, take the lower, the most exposed fire.
Head man, Cook, and Monrovia boy have the upper fire, and the
labourer has the middle one—he being an outcast for medical reasons.
They are all steaming away and smoking comfortably.

I form the noble resolution to keep awake, and rouse up any gentleman who may catch on fire during the night, and see to wood being
put on the fires, so elaborately settle myself on my wooden chop-box,
wherein I have got all the lucifers which are not in the soap-box. Owing
to there not being a piece of ground the size of a sixpenny piece level in
this place, the arrangement of my box camp takes time, but at last it is
done to my complete satisfaction, close to a tree trunk, and I think, as I
wrap myself up in my two wet blankets and lean against my tree, what a
good thing it is to know how to make one's self comfortable in a place
like this. This tree stem is perfection, just the right angle to be restful to
one's back, and one can rely all the time on Nature hereabouts not to let
one get thoroughly effete from luxurious comfort, so I lazily watch and
listen to Xenia and Kefalla at their fire hard by.

They begin talking to each other on their different tribal societies; Kefalla is a Vey, Xenia a Liberian, so in the interests of Science I give them two heads of tobacco to stimulate their conversation. They receive them with tragic grief, having no pipe, so in the interests of Science I undo my blankets and give them two out of my portmanteau; then do myself up again and pretend to be asleep. I am rewarded by getting some interesting details, and form the opinion that both these worthies, in their pursuit of their particular ju-jus have come into contact with white prejudices, and are now fugitives from religious persecution. I also observe they have both their own ideas of happiness. Kefalla holds it lies in a warm shirt. Xenia that it abides in warm trousers; and every half-hour the former takes his shirt off, and holds it in the fire smoke, and then puts it hastily on; and Xenia, who is the one and only trouser wearer in our band, spends fifty per cent of the night on one leg struggling to get the other in or out of these garments, when they are either coming off to be warmed, or going on after warming.

There seem but few insects here. I have only got two moths tonight—one pretty one with white wings with little red spots on, like an old-fashioned petticoat such as an early Victorian-age lady would have worn—the other a sweet thing in silver.

(Later, i.e., 2:15 a.m.) I have been asleep against that abominable vegetable of a tree. It had its trunk covered with a soft cushion of moss, and pretended to be a comfort—a right angle to lean against, and a softly padded protection to the spine from wind, and all that sort of thing; whereas the whole mortal time it was nothing in this wretched world but a water pipe, to conduct an extra supply of water down my back. The water has simply streamed down it, and formed a nice little pool in a rocky hollow where I keep my feet, and I am chilled to the innermost bone, so have to scramble up and drag my box to the side of Kefalla and Xenia's fire, feeling sure I have contracted a fatal chill this time. I scrape the ashes out of the fire into a heap, and put my sodden boots into them, and they hiss merrily, and I resolve not to go to sleep again. 5 a.m.—Have been to sleep twice, and have fallen off my box bodily into the fire in my wet blankets, and should for sure have put it out like a bucket of cold water had not Xenia and Kefalla been roused up by the smother I occasioned and rescued me—or the fire. It is not raining now, but it is bitter cold and cook is getting my tea. I give the boys a lot of hot tea with a big handful of sugar in, and they then get their own food hot.

CHAPTER 20

THE GREAT PEAK OF CAMEROONS
(CONCLUDED)

Setting forth how the Voyager attains the summit of Mungo Mah Lobeh,
and descends therefrom to Victoria, to which is added some remarks on the natural
history of the West Coast porter, and the native methods of making fire.

SEPTEMBER 26TH.—THE WEATHER IS UNDECIDED AND SO AM I, for I feel
doubtful about going on in this weather, but I do not like to give up the
peak after going through so much for it. The boys being dry and warm
with the fires have forgotten their troubles. However, I settle in my mind
to keep on, and ask for volunteers to come with me, and Bum, the head
man, and Xenia announce their willingness. I put two tins of meat and
a bottle of Herr Liebert's beer into the little wooden box, and insist on
both men taking a blanket apiece, much to their disgust, and before six
o'clock we are off over the crater plain. It is a broken bit of country with
rock mounds sparsely overgrown with tufts of grass, and here and there
are patches of boggy land, not real bog, but damp places where grow little
clumps of rushes, and here and there among the rocks sorely-afflicted
shrubs of broom, and the yellow-flowered shrub I have mentioned
before, and quantities of very sticky heather, feeling when you catch hold
of it as if it had been covered with syrup. One might fancy the entire race
of shrubs was dying out; for one you see partially alive there are twenty
skeletons which fall to pieces as you brush past them.

It is downhill the first part of the way, that is to say, the trend of the
land is downhill, for be it down or up, the details of it are rugged

mounds and masses of burnt-out lava rock. It is evil going, but perhaps not quite so evil as the lower hillocks of the great wall where the rocks are hidden beneath long slippery grass. We wind our way in between the mounds, or clamber over them, or scramble along their sides impartially. The general level is then flat, and then comes a rise towards the peak wall, so we steer N.N.E. until we strike the face of the peak, and then commence a stiff rough climb.

We keep as straight as we can, but get driven at an angle by the strange ribs of rock which come straight down. These are most tiresome to deal with, getting worse the higher we go, and so rotten and weather-eaten are they that they crumble into dust and fragments under our feet. Head man gets half a dozen falls, and when we are about three parts of the way up Xenia gives in. The cold and the climbing are too much for him, so I make him wrap himself up in his blanket, which he is glad enough of now, and shelter in a depression under one of the many rock ridges, and head man and I go on. When we are some 600 feet higher the iron-grey mist comes curling and waving round the rocks above us, like some savage monster defending them from intruders, and I again debate whether I was justified in risking the men, for it is a risk for them at this low temperature, with the evil weather I know, and they do not know, is coming on. But still we have food and blankets with us enough for them, and the camp in the plain below they can reach all right, if the worst comes to the worst; and for myself—well—that's my own affair, and no one will be a ha'porth the worse if I am dead in an hour. So I hitch myself on to the rocks, and take bearings, particularly bearings of Xenia's position, who, I should say, has got a tin of meat and a flask of rum with him, and then turn and face the threatening mist. It rises and falls, and sends out arm-like streams towards us, and then Bum, the head man, decides to fail for the third time to reach the peak, and I leave him wrapped in his blanket with the bag of provisions, and go on alone into the wild, grey, shifting, whirling mist above, and soon find myself at the head of a rock ridge in a narrowish depression, walled by massive black walls which show fitfully but firmly through the mist.

I can see three distinctly high cones before me, and then the mist, finding it cannot drive me back easily, proceeds to desperate methods, and lashes out with a burst of bitter wind, and a sheet of blinding, stinging rain. I make my way up through it towards a peak which I soon see through a tear in the mist is not the highest, so I angle off and go up the one to the left, and after a desperate flight reach the cairn—only, alas! to find a hurricane raging and a fog in full possession, and not a ten yards' view to be had in any direction. Near the cairn on the ground are several bottles, some of which the energetic German officers, I suppose, had emptied in honour of their achievement, an achievement I bow down before, for their pluck and strength had taken them here in a shorter time by far than mine. I do not meddle with anything, save to take a few specimens and to put a few more rocks on the cairn, and to put in among them my card, merely as a civility to Mungo, a civility his Majesty will soon turn into pulp. Not that it matters—what is done is done.

The weather grows worse every minute, and no sign of any clearing shows in the indigo sky or the wind-reft mist. The rain lashes so fiercely I cannot turn my face to it and breathe, the wind is all I can do to stand up against.

Verily I am no mountaineer, for there is in me no exultation, but only a deep disgust because the weather has robbed me of my main object in coming here, namely to get a good view and an idea of the way the unexplored mountain range behind Calabar trends. I took my chance and it failed, so there's nothing to complain about.

Comforting myself with these reflections, I start down to find Bum, and do so neatly, and then together we scramble down carefully among the rotten black rocks, intent on finding Xenia. The scene is very grand. At one minute we can see nothing save the black rocks and cinders under foot; the next the wind-torn mist separates now in one direction, now in another, showing us always the same wild scene of great black cliffs, rising in jagged peaks and walls around and above us. I think this walled cauldron we had just left is really the highest crater on Mungo.

We soon become anxious about Xenia, for this is a fearfully easy place to lose a man in such weather, but just as we get below the thickest part of the pall of mist, I observe a doll-sized figure, standing on one leg taking on or off its trousers—our lost Xenia, beyond a shadow of a doubt, and we go down direct to him.

When we reach him we halt, and I give the two men one of the tins of meat, and take another and the bottle of beer myself, and then make a hasty sketch of the great crater plain below us. At the further edge of the plain a great white cloud is coming up from below, which argues badly for our trip down the great wall to the forest camp, which I am anxious to reach before nightfall after our experience of the accommodation afforded by our camp in the crater plain last night.

While I am sitting waiting for the men to finish their meal, I feel a chill at my back, as if some cold thing had settled there, and turning round, see the mist from the summit above coming in a wall down towards us. These mists up here, as far as my experience goes, are always preceded by a strange breath of ice-cold air—not necessarily a wind.

Bum then draws my attention to a strange funnel-shaped thing coming down from the clouds to the north. A big waterspout, I presume: it seems to be moving rapidly N.E., and I profoundly hope it will hold that course, for we have quite as much as we can manage with the ordinary rain-water supply on this mountain, without having waterspouts to deal with.

We start off down the mountain as rapidly as we can. Xenia is very done up, and Head man comes perilously near breaking his neck by frequent falls among the rocks; my unlucky boots are cut through and through by the latter. When we get down towards the big crater plain, it is a race between us and the pursuing mist as to who shall reach the camp first, and the mist wins, but we have just time to make out the camp's exact position before it closes round us, so we reach it without any real difficulty. When we get there, about one o'clock, I find the men have kept the fires alight and Cook is asleep before one of them with another conflagration smoldering in his hair. I get him to make me tea, while the others pack up as quickly as possible, and by two we are all off on our way down to the forest camp.

The boys are nervous in their way of going down over the mountain wall. The misadventures of Cook alone would fill volumes. Monrovia boy is out and away the best man at this work. Just as we reach the high jungle grass, down comes the rain and up comes the mist, and we have the worst time we have had during our whole trip, in our endeavours to find the hole in the forest that leads to our old camp.

Unfortunately, I must needs go in for acrobatic performances on the top of one of the highest, rockiest hillocks. Poising myself on one leg I take a rapid slide sideways, ending in a very showy leap backwards which lands me on the top of the lantern I am carrying today, among miscellaneous rocks. There being fifteen feet or so of jungle grass above me, all the dash and beauty of my performance are as much thrown away as I am, for my boys are too busy on their own accounts in the mist to miss me.

After resting some little time as I fell, and making and unmaking the idea in my mind that I am killed, I get up, clamber elaborately to the top of the next hillock, and shout for the boys, and "Ma," "ma," comes back from my flock from various points out of the fog. I find Bum and Monrovia boy, and learn that during my absence Xenia, who always fancies himself as a path-finder, has taken the lead, and gone off somewhere with the rest. We shout and the others answer, and we join them, and it soon becomes evident to the meanest intelligence that Xenia had better have spent his time attending to those things of his instead of going in for guiding, for we are now right off the track we made through the grass on our up journey, and we proceed to have a cheerful hour or so in the wet jungle, ploughing hither and thither, trying to find our way.

At last we pick up the top of a tongue of forest that we all feel is ours, but we—that is to say, Xenia and I, for the others go like lambs to the slaughter wherever they are led—disagree as to the path. He wants to go down one side of the tongue, I to go down the other, and I have my way, and we wade along, skirting the bushes that fringe it, trying to find our hole. I owe I soon begin to feel shaky about having been right in the affair, but soon Xenia, who is leading, shouts he has got it, and we limp in, our feet sore with rugged rocks, and everything we have on, or in the loads, wringing wet, save the matches, which providentially I had put into my soap-box.

Anything more dismal than the look of that desired camp when we reach it, I never saw. Pools of water everywhere. The fire-house a limp ruin, the camp bed I have been thinking fondly of for the past hour a water cistern. I tilt the water out of it, and say a few words to it regarding its hide-bound idiocy in obeying its military instructions to be water-proof; and then, while the others are putting up the fire-house, Head man and I get out the hidden demijohn of rum, and the beef and rice, and I serve out a tot of rum each to the boys, who are shivering dread-fully, waiting for Cook to get the fire. He soon does this, and then I have my hot tea and the men their hot food, for now we have returned to the luxury of two cooking pots.

Their education in bush is evidently progressing, for they make themselves a big screen with boughs and spare blankets, between the wind and the fire-house, and I get Xenia to cut some branches, and place them on the top of my waterproof sheet shelter, and we are fairly comfortable again, and the boys quite merry and very well satisfied with themselves.

Unfortunately the subject of their nightly debating society is human conduct, a subject ever fraught with dangerous elements of differences of opinion. They are busy discussing, with their mouths full of rice and beef, the conduct of an absent friend, who it seems is generally regarded by them as a spendthrift. "He gets plenty money, but he no have none no time." "He go frow it away on woman, and drink." "He no buy clothes." This last is evidently a very heavy accusation, but Kefalla says, "What can a man buy with money better than them thing he like best?"

There is a very peculiar look on the rotten wood on the ground round here; tonight it has patches and flecks of iridescence like one sees on herrings or mackerel that have been kept too long. The appearance of this strange eerie light in among the bush is very weird and charming. I have seen it before in dark forests at night, but never so much of it.

September 27th.—Fine morning. It's a blessing my Pappenheimers have not recognized what this means for the afternoon. We take things very leisurely. I know it's no good hurrying, we are dead sure of getting a ducking before we reach Buea anyhow, so we may as well enjoy ourselves while we can.

I ask my boys how they would "make fire suppose no matches live." Not one of them thinks it possible to do so, "it pass man to do them thing suppose he no got live stick or matches." They are coast boys, all of them, and therefore used to luxury, but it is really remarkable how widely diffused matches are inland, and how very dependent on them these natives are. When I have been away in districts where they have not penetrated, it is exceedingly rarely that the making of fire has to be resorted to. I think I may say that in most African villages it has not had to be done for years and years, because when a woman's fire has gone out, owing to her having been out at work all day, she just runs into some neighbor's hut where there is a fire burning, and gives compliments, and picks up a burning stick from the fire and runs home. From this comes the compliment, equivalent to our "Oh ! don't go away yet," of "You come to fetch fire." This will be said to you all the way from Sierra Leone to Loanda, as far as I know, if you have been making yourself agreeable in an African home, even if the process may have extended over a day or so. The hunters, like the Fans, have to make fire, and do it now with a flint and steel; but in districts where their tutor in this method—the flint-lock gun—is not available, they will do it with two sticks, not always like the American Indians' fire-sticks. One stick is placed horizontally on the ground and the other twirled rapidly between the palms of the hands, but sometimes two bits of palm stick are worked in a hole in a bigger bit of wood, the hole stuffed round with the pith of a tree or with silk cotton fluff, and the two sticks rotated vigorously. Again, on one occasion I saw a Bakele woman make fire by means of a slip of raffia palm drawn very rapidly, to and fro, across a notch in another piece of raffia wood. In most domesticated tribes, like the Effiks or the Igalwa, if they are going out to their plantation, they will enclose a live stick in a hollow piece of a certain sort of wood, which has a lining of its interior pith left in it, and they will carry this "fire box" with them. Or if they are going on a long canoe journey, there is always the fire in the bow of the canoe put into a calabash full of sand, or failing that, into a bed of clay with a sand rim round it.

By 10 o'clock we are off down to Buea. At 10:15 it pours as it can here; by 10:17 we are all in our normal condition of bedraggled saturation, and plodding down carefully and cheerfully among the rocks and roots of the forest, following the path we have beaten and cut for ourselves on our way up. It is dangerously slippery, particularly that part of it though the amomums, and stumps of the cut amomums are very likely to spike your legs badly—and, my friend, never, never, step on one of the amomum stems lying straight in front of you, particularly when they are soaking wet. Ice slides are nothing to them, and when you fall, as you inevitably must, because all the things you grab hold of are either rotten, or as brittle as Salviati glass-ware vases, you hurt yourself in no end of places, on those aforesaid cut amomum stumps. I am speaking from sad experiences of my own, amplified by observations on the experiences of my men.

The path, when we get down again into the tree-fern region, is inches deep in mud and water, and several places where we have a drop of five feet or so over lumps of rock are worse work going down than we found them going up, especially when we have to drop down on to amomum stems. One abominable place, a V-shaped hollow, mud-lined, and with an immense tree right across it—a tree one of our tornadoes has thrown down since we passed—bothers the men badly, as they slip and scramble down, and then crawl under the tree and slip and scramble up with their loads. I say nothing about myself. I just take a flying slide of twenty feet or so and shoot flump under the tree on my back, and then deliberate whether it is worth while getting up again to go on with such a world; but vanity forbids my dying like a dog in a ditch, and I scramble up, rejoining the others where they are standing on a cross-path: our path going S.E. by E., the other S.S.W. Two men have already gone down the S.W. one, which I feel sure is the upper end of the path Sasu had led us to and wasted time on our first day's march; the middle regions of which were, as we had found from its lower end, impassable with vegetation. So after futile attempts to call the other two back, we go on down the S.E. one, and get shortly into a plantation of giant kokos mid-leg deep in most excellent fine mould—the sort of stuff you pay 6s. a load for in England to start a conservatory bed with. Upon my word, the quantities of things there are left loose in Africa, that ought to be kept in menageries and greenhouses and not let go wild about the country, are enough to try a Saint.

We then pass through a clump of those lovely great treeferns. The way their young fronds come up with a graceful curl, like the top of a bishop's staff, is a poem; but being at present fractious, I will observe that they are covered with horrid spines, as most young vegetables are in Africa. But talking about spines, I should remark that nothing save that precious climbing palm—I never like to say what I feel about climbing palms, because one once saved my life—equals the strong bush rope which abounds here. It is covered with short, strong, curved thorns. It creeps along concealed by decorative vegetation, and you get your legs twined in it, and of course injured. It festoons itself from tree to tree, and when your mind is set on other things, catches you under the chin, and gives you the appearance of having made a determined but ineffectual attempt to cut your throat with a saw. It whisks your hat off and grabs your clothes, and commits other iniquities too numerous to catalogue here. Years and years that bush rope will wait for a man's blood, and when he comes within reach it will have it.

We are well down now among the tree-stems grown over with rich soft green moss and delicate filmy-ferns. I should think that for a botanist these south-eastern slopes of Mungo Mah Lobeh would be the happiest hunting grounds in all West Africa.

The vegetation here is at the point of its supreme luxuriance, owing to the richness of the soil; the leaves of trees and plants I recognize as having seen elsewhere are here far larger, and the undergrowth particularly is more rich and varied, far and away. Ferns seem to find here a veritable paradise. Everything, in fact, is growing at its best.

We come to another fallen tree over another hole; this tree we recognize as an old acquaintance near Buea, and I feel disgusted, for I had
put on a clean blouse, and washed my hands in a tea-cupful of water in
a cooking pot before leaving the forest camp, so as to look presentable
on reaching Buea, and not give Herr Liebert the same trouble he had to
recognize the white from the black members of the party that he said he
had with the members of the first expedition to the peak; and all I have
got to show for my exertion that is clean or anything like dry is one cuff
over which I have been carrying a shawl.

We double round a corner by the stockade of the station's plantation, and are at the top of the mud glissade—the new Government path,
I should say—that leads down into the barrack-yard.

Our arrival brings Herr Liebert promptly on the scene, as kindly
helpful and energetic as ever, and again anxious for me to have a bath.
The men bring our saturated loads into my room, and after giving them
their food and plenty of tobacco, I get my hot tea and change into the
clothes I had left behind at Buea, and feeling once more fit for polite
society, go out and find his Imperial and Royal Majesty's representative
making a door, tightening the boards up with wedges in a very artful and
professional way. We discourse on things in general and the mountain
in particular. The great southeast face is now showing clear before us,
the clearness that usually comes before nightfall. It looks again a vast
wall, and I wish I were going up it again tomorrow. When "the Calabar
major" set it on fire in the dry season it must have been a noble sight.

The north-eastern edge of the slope of the mountain seems to me
unbroken up to the peak. The great crater we went and camped in must
be a very early one in the history of the mountain, and out of it the present summit seems to have been thrown up. From the sea face, the
western, I am told the slope is continuous on the whole, although
there are several craters on that side; seventy craters all told are so far
known on Mungo.

The last recorded eruption was in 1852, when signs of volcanic activity were observed by a captain who was passing at sea. The lava from this
eruption must have gone down the western side, for I have come across
no fresh lava beds in my wanderings on the other face. Herr Liebert has
no confidence in the mountain whatsoever, and announces his intention
of leaving Buea with the army on the first symptom of renewed volcanic
activity. I attempt to discourage him from this energetic plan, pointing

out to him the beauty of that Roman soldier at Pompeii who was found, centuries after that eruption, still at his post; and if he regards that as merely mechanical virtue, why not pursue the plan of the elder Pliny? Herr Liebert planes away at his door, and says it's not in his orders to make scientific observations on volcanoes in a state of eruption. When it is he'll do so—until it is, he most decidedly will not. He adds Pliny was an admiral and sailors are always as curious as cats.

Buea seems a sporting place for weather even without volcanic eruptions, during the whole tornado season (there are two a year), over-charged tornadoes burst in the barrack yard. From the 14th of June till the 27th of August you never see the sun, because of the terrific and continuous wet season downpour. At the beginning and end of this cheerful period occurs a month's tornado season, and the rest of the year is dry, hot by day and cold by night.

They are talking of making Buea into a sanatorium for the fever-stricken. I do not fancy somehow that it's a suitable place for a man who has got all the skin off his nerves with fever and quinine, and is very liable to chill; but all Governments on the Coast, English, German, or French, are stark mad on the subject of sanatoriums in high places, though the experience they have had of them has clearly pointed out that they are valueless in West Africa, and a man's one chance is to get out to sea on a ship that will take him outside the three-mile-deep fever-belt of the coast.

Herr Liebert gives me some interesting details about the first establishment of the station here and a bother he had with the planta-tions. Only a short time ago the soldiers brought him in some black wood spikes, which they had found with their feet, set into the path leading to the station's koko plantations, to the end of laming the men. On further investigation there were also found pits, carefully concealed with sticks and leaves, and the bottoms lined with bad thorns, also with malicious intent. The local Bakwiri chiefs were called in and asked to explain these phenomena existing in a country where peace had been concluded, and the chiefs said it was quite a mistake, those things had not been put there to kill soldiers, but only to attract their attention, to kill and injure their own fellow-tribesmen who had been stealing from plantations latterly. That's the West African's way entirely all along the Coast; the "child-like" native will turn out and shoot you with a gun to attract your attention to the fact that a tribe you never heard of has been and stolen one of his ladies, whom you never saw. It's the sweet infant's way of "rousing up popular opinion," but I do not admire or approve of it. If I am to be shot for a crime, for goodness sake let me commit the crime first.

September 28th.—Down to Victoria in one day, having no desire to renew and amplify my acquaintance with the mission station at Buana. It poured torrentially all the day through. The old chief at Buana was very nice today when we were coming through his territory. He came out to meet us with some of his wives. Both men and women among these Bakwiri are tattooed, and also painted, on the body, face and arms, but as far as I have seen not on the legs. The patterns are handsome, and more elaborate than any such that I have seen. One man who came with the party had two figures of men tattooed on the region where his waist-coat should have been. I gave the chief some tobacco though he never begged for anything. He accepted it thankfully, and handing it to his wives preceded us on our path for about a mile and a half and then having reached the end of his district, we shook hands and parted.

After all the rain we have had, the road was of course worse than ever, and as we were going through the forest towards the war hedge, I noticed a strange sound, a dull roar which made the light friable earth quiver under our feet, and I remembered with alarm the accounts Herr Liebert has given me of the strange ways of rivers on this mountain; how by Buea, about 200 metres below where you cross it, the river goes bodily down a hole. How there is a waterfall on the south face of the mountain that falls right into another hole, and is never seen again, any more than the Buea River is. How there are in certain places underground rivers, which though never seen can be heard roaring, and felt in the quivering earth under foot in the wet season, and so on. So I judged our present roar arose from some such phenomenon, and with feminine nervous-ness began to fear that the rotten water-logged earth we were on might give way, and engulf the whole of us, and we should never be seen again. But when we got down into our next ravine, the one where I got the fish and water-spiders on our way up, things explained themselves. The bed of this ravine was occupied by a raging torrent of great beauty, but alarming appearance to a person desirous of getting across to the other side of it. On our right hand was a waterfall of tons of water thirty feet high or so. The brown water wreathed with foam dashed down into the swirling pool we faced, and at the other edge of the pool, striking a ridge of higher rock, it flew up in a lovely flange some twelve feet or so high, before making another and a deeper spring to form a second waterfall. My men shouted to me above the roar that it was "a bad place." They never give me half the credit I deserve for seeing danger, and they said, "Water all go for hole down there, we fit to go too suppose we fall." "Don't fall," I yelled which was the only good advice I could think of to give them just then.

Each small load had to be carried across by two men along a submerged ridge in the pool, where the water was only breast high. I had all I could do to get through it, though assisted by my invaluable Bakwiri staff. But no harm befell. Indeed we were all the better for it, or at all events cleaner. We met five torrents that had to be waded during the day; none so bad as the first but all superbly beautiful.

When we turned our faces westwards just above the wood we had to pass through before getting into the great road, the view of Victoria, among its hills, and fronted by its bay, was divinely lovely and glorious with colour. I left the boys here, as they wanted to rest, and to hunt up water, &c., among the little cluster of huts that are here on the right-hand side of the path, and I went on alone down through the wood, and out on to the road, where I found my friend, the Alsatian engineer, still flourishing and busy with his cheery gang of wood-cutters. I made a brief halt here, getting some soda water. I was not anxious to reach Victoria before nightfall, but yet to reach it before dinner, and while I was chatting, my boys came through the wood and the engineer most kindly gave them a tot of brandy apiece, to which I owe their arrival in Victoria. I left them again resting, fearing I had overdone my arrangements for arriving just after nightfall and went on down that road which was more terrible than ever now to my bruised, weary feet, but even more lovely than ever in the dying light of the crimson sunset, with all its dark shadows among the trees begemmed with countless fire-flies— and so safe into Victoria—sneaking up the Government House hill by the private path through to Botanical Gardens.

Idabea, the steward, turned up, and I asked him to let me have some tea and bread and butter, for I was dreadfully hungry. He rushed off, and I heard tremendous operations going on in the room above. In a few seconds water poured freely down through the dining room ceiling. It was bath palaver again. The excellent Idabea evidently thought it was severely wanted, more wanted than such vanities as tea. Fortunately,

Herr von Lucke was away down in town, looking after duty as usual, so I was tidy before he returned to dinner. When he returned he had the satisfaction a prophet should feel. I had got half-drowned, and I had got an awful cold, the most awful cold in the head of modern times, I believe, but he was not artistically exultant over my afflictions.

My men having all reported themselves safe I went to my comfortable rooms, but could not turn in, so fascinating was the warmth and beauty down here; and as I sat on the verandah overlooking Victoria and the sea, in the dim soft light of the stars, with the fire-flies round me, and the lights of Victoria away below, and heard the soft rush of the Lukola River, and the sound of the sea-surf on the rocks, and the tom-tomming and singing of the natives, all matching and mingling together, "Why did I come to Africa?" thought I. Why! who would not come to its twin brother Hell itself for all the beauty and the charm of it!

National Geographic
Adventure Classics

The Oregon Trail
Francis Parkman

The Worst Journey in the World
Apsley Cherry-Garrard

The Exploration of the Colorado River and Its Canyons
John Wesley Powell

The Journals of Lewis and Clark
Meriwether Lewis and William Clark

Scrambles Amongst the Alps
Edward Whymper